ADVANCE TO BARBARISM

THE DEVELOPMENT OF TOTAL WARFARE FROM SARAJEVO TO HIROSHIMA

F.J.P. VEALE

OSTARA PUBLICATIONS

Advance to Barbarism

The Development of Total Warfare From Serajevo to Hiroshima

by F.J.P. Veale

First published 1953

This edition 2013

Ostara Publications

ISBN 978-1-300-97612-7

SHEFFIELD LIBRARIES & ARCHIVES	
213326322	
Bertrams	
355	£16.99

Contents

Foreword by The Very Rev. William Ralph Inge 1

Foreword by The Rt. Hon. Lord Hankey 4

Author's Introduction 6

Chapter 1 — Primeval Simplicity 30

Chapter 2 — Organized Warfare 45

Chapter 3 — Europe's Civil Wars 64

Chapter 4 — Civilized Warfare (The First Phase) 82

Chapter 5 — Civilized Warfare (The Second Phase) 106

Chapter 6 — The Splendid Decision 155

Chapter 7 — The Nuremberg Trials 201

Chapter 8 — The Last Phase 260

Postscript 339

Bibliography 344

Footnotes 347

Index 361

To

PROFESSOR HARRY ELMER BARNES

A TIRELESS EXPOSER OF HISTORICAL MYTHS

FOREWORD

By The Very Rev. William Ralph Inge, Dean of St. Paul's[1]

An early version of this book was first published in England in 1948. A second revised and greatly enlarged version appeared in the United States in 1953. This version was then translated into German and published in Hamburg in 1954; and a second edition was published in Wiesbaden in 1962. The present edition is a major revision of the earlier versions.

I am glad that a new edition of *Advance to Barbarism* is called for. In this book, first published in England in 1948 under the *nom de plume* "A. Jurist", the author, Mr. F. J. P. Veale, said, and said very well, what needed to be said by someone, and, we may add, what in 1948 in most countries nobody would have been allowed to say.

I disliked the Nuremberg Trials for three reasons: First, trials of the vanquished by the victors are never satisfactory and are generally unfair. Secondly, the execution of the political and military leaders of a beaten side by the victors sets a most dangerous precedent. The Germans were certainly guilty of "crimes against humanity"; but war is not a humane business and it would always be possible for the victors in any way to find enough examples of atrocities to justify vindictive punishments. After the next war, if there is one, trials and hangings will follow as a matter of course. We may go further. One of the indictments of the German leaders was not that they waged war inhumanly, but that they made war aggressively. They did; they desired large annexations of territory in the East. But have we not heard of other nations who have acquired extensive empires without consulting the wishes of the inhabitants? Thirdly, one of the judges—Russia—ought certainly to have been in the dock and not on the bench.

The main object of *Advance to Barbarism* is to call attention to the terrible retrogression of civilized humanity towards the worst cruelties of barbarism. The so-called Wars of Religion were sometimes savage, but in the eighteenth century it was possible to talk of civilized warfare, in which certain humane conventions were observed. Gibbon notices this advance in decent behaviour with complacency. A writer in the eighteenth century might reasonably speak of war as a relic of barbarism which might soon be abolished altogether. The Napoleonic Wars, except the guerilla fighting in Spain, were not fertile in atrocities; the decadence came later.

I comforted myself at one time by thinking that these horrors were confined to three nations, Germany, Spain and Russia. Nothing can be said to extenuate the excesses practised by the Germans. The only fair questions were, who were the culprits? and who ought to be the judges? It is not usual to hang officers for obeying cruel orders. The citizens in a police state in abdicating their rights as men have ceased to admit the duty of obeying conscience. As for Spain, it is high time to resume friendly relations with a noble people. But it must be admitted that there is a strain of cruelty in the Spanish character. In the country of the Inquisition and the bull-ring, civil war was not likely to be gentle. In speaking of Russia, one cannot do better than quote what Amiel, whose perspicacity is never at fault, wrote as early as 1856: "The harsh gifts of late have left their stamp on the race of the Muscovites. A certain sombre obstinacy, a sort of primitive ferocity, a background of savage harshness, which under the sway of circumstances might become implacable and even ruthless, a coldly indomitable force that would rather wreck the world than yield, the indestructible instinct of the barbarian horde still persisting in a half-civilized nation.... What terrible masters would the Russians be if ever they should spread the might of their rule over the southern countries! A polar despotism, a tyranny such as the world has not yet known, silent as the darkness, keen as ice, unfeeling as bronze, a slavery without compensation or relief."

Perhaps in times to come, not so far distant, it may not be so readily forgotten that this was the enemy against whom the Germans fought.

But are there only three culprits, two of whom may plead some excuse? What of the destruction of Hiroshima by the Americans, of Dresden by the British, when the war was practically over? It is not pleasant to think of these things. We must not speak too positively of retrogression. There was another

Foreword — William Ralph Inge

side to European humanity before the insanity of nationalism. In dealing with "inferior races" the record was not good. The Irish have not forgotten the Tudors and Oliver Cromwell. Or listen to this horrible extract from the *Daily Journal* of March 1737: "They write from Antigua that they continued executing the Negroes concerned in the plot to murder all the inhabitants of the island: sixty-nine had been executed, of whom five had been broken on the wheel, six were hung upon gibbets and starved to death, of whom one lived nine nights and eight days and fifty-eight were chained to stakes and burnt." Or think of the tortures inflicted on the assailant of Louis XV, which were gleefully witnessed by at least one English gentleman. Our ancestors were not all saints.

Some of us hope that now that war has been divested of all romance and chivalry, it may soon go the way of cannibalism and human sacrifice. It is a matter of life or death for civilization.

W. R. INGE
26th March 1951.

FOREWORD

By The Rt. Hon. Lord Hankey, P.C., G.C.B., G.C.M.G., G.C.V.O.[2]

In the Introduction of my book, *Politics: Trials and Errors*, published in 1950, I wrote, "I am indebted for inspiration and suggestion to *Advance to Barbarism* by F. J. P. Veale who wrote as "A. Jurist"; it displays great knowledge of the military art and profound research into the historical aspects of all that relates to War Crime Trials."

Advance to Barbarism was first published in England in 1948. It was a noteworthy little book because it dealt for the first time with such then recent innovations as the indiscriminate bombing of civilian populations and the trial of prisoners of war by their captors as symptoms of a world-wide development which had begun in 1914.

At the time of its publication this point of view was considered so wilfully perverse that no British newspaper with a national circulation would review this book.

Fortunately, however, this book did not pass unnoticed. Among those who praised it was the Very Rev. William Ralph Inge, formerly Dean of St. Paul's, who later contributed a Foreword to the revised and greatly enlarged Edition which was published in the United States in 1953. This American edition was translated into Spanish and published in Spain under the title "El Crimen de Nuremberg" in 1954, and later in the same year into German and published in Germany under the title "Der Barbarei entgegen".

Since the publication of the first edition in 1948 many new facts have come to light and public opinion has changed.

Few now maintain that an accuser is a fit person to act as judge of his own charges, in fact many now remember that they were always opposed to the Nuremberg Trials, although they omitted to make public their opinion at the time.

Foreword — Lord Hankey

The publication of *The Strategic Air Offensive against Germany, 1939-45* by H.M. Stationery Office in September 1961 confirmed officially with a wealth of detail the view expressed in this book concerning the character of the air attack on Germany during the Second World War.

I recommend this new edition to the reader.

HANKEY, 7th February 1962

AUTHOR'S INTRODUCTION

Tardily professional historians have at last begun to realise that the events of the first half of the 20th century have presented them with a problem of unique difficulty.

From the first it was apparent that 1914 was certain to be a memorable date in history because in that year began a war in which a vast number would be doomed to die violent deaths and which would certainly lead to sweeping changes to the map of Europe if only for the worse. For a decade historians limited themselves to investigating the origins of this struggle which they explained to their own satisfaction by attributing it to the chance that Germany was ruled by an emperor who was obsessed by an insane ambition to conquer the world. From patriotic motives, at first to assist the war effort and later to justify the dictated terms of peace, professional historians, many of them men of great eminence and learning, laboured to confirm and endorse the Wicked Kaiser Myth. Once however this had been exposed as an impudent propaganda fiction, they failed to find any generally acceptable explanation for the blind homicidal frenzy which seized the nations of Europe during the period, 1914-1918, and ultimately they became resigned to leaving the problem for solution to the psychologists and psychiatrists. Thus the First World War came to be regarded as a bizarre episode of history, mainly of significance as a grim warning to posterity of the consequences of allowing greed and pugnacity to overcome reason.

The conclusion that the great struggle which broke out in Europe in 1914 resulted from a pathological wave of hysteria which afflicted the most advanced nations of mankind in that year is now held up for admiration as the most remarkable achievement of modern historical research. But this diagnosis was first put forward over thirty years ago by Field-Marshal Lord Allenby who bluntly declared, "The Great War was a lengthy period of general

Author's Introduction

insanity."[3] The view that the beginning of this struggle in 1914 and still more that its continuation after 1916 were essentially the result of an irrational and compulsive urge was accepted as self-evident and undeniable throughout the thirty-nine weekly televised programmes entitled 'The Great War' broadcast by the B.B.C. in 1965.

Not until after 1939 when another world war broke out, rendered inevitable by the terms of peace imposed on the vanquished after the First World War, was it realised how profound were the effects which the latter struggle had had on the character, outlook and ethics of the average Western civilized man. Since the times when the Dark Ages had gradually evolved into the Middle Ages, the story of civilization in Europe had been one of slow but steady upward progress. The advance of civilization apart from occasional fluctuations remained continuous until the beginning of the 20th century, by which time it had come to be regarded as an established law of nature that progress was an automatic process of unending duration.

As the late Dean Inge observed, belief in Progress became a kind of religion with most educated men. Apart from the steady accumulation of scientific knowledge, arbitrary violence had gradually become controlled by the rule of law, manners had become milder and in warfare primitive savagery had become modified by the tacit adoption at the end of the 17th century of an unwritten code of restrictions and restraints which later codified at the conventions of Geneva and the Hague, became known as the Rules of Civilized Warfare. The fundamental principle of this code was that hostilities should be restricted to the armed and uniformed forces of the combatants, from which followed the corollary that civilians must be left entirely outside the scope of military operations. It was widely believed that war, being an essentially barbarous method of settling international disputes, was bound ultimately to die out. With seemingly full justification the outlook at the beginning of the 20th century was one of unclouded optimism.

As early as 1770, by which time the horrors of the Thirty Years War had become generally forgotten, the Comte de Guibert could express the already prevailing complacency by writing: —

"Today the whole of Europe is civilized. Wars have become less cruel. Save in combat no blood is shed; prisoners are

Advance to Barbarism

respected; towns are no more destroyed; the countryside is no more ravaged; conquered peoples are only obliged to pay some sort of contributions which are often less than the taxes they pay to their own sovereign."

In the 19th century this happy state of affairs was taken for granted: no one dreamed that it would shortly come to an abrupt end. To us it seems fantastically unreal, now that prisoners of war are faced with the prospect of being subjected to war-crimes trials at the pleasure of their captors, or of being sent to work indefinitely as slave labour; towns with their inhabitants are obliterated by terror bombing; conquered peoples are uprooted from their homelands and mass-deported abroad; and the property of the vanquished is either appropriated as a matter of course by the victors or systematically destroyed.

The war which broke out in Europe in 1914 seemed at first indistinguishable from the civil wars which previously had periodically devastated that continent. During the struggle, however, quite unforeseen by any one, civilization began a retrograde movement without a parallel in history. While the struggle lasted this retrograde movement was not generally perceived but after the wave of optimism generated by the creation of the League of Nations had faded, the realization dawned that somehow the times had become out of joint. Working below the surface a profound psychological change had been taking place. Many of the men then living in obscurity who in the next decade were to rise to power and fame—for example Yagoda, Stalin's chief of the G.P.U. during the Great Purge, Heinrich Himmler, the S.S. leader, and Adolf Eichmann—might have been reincarnations of men who had flourished in the times of the Merovingian Kings. Even the outlook of so irreproachable a character as Air Marshal Sir Hugh Trenchard with his then novel recipe for victory—"bomb the enemy civilian population until they surrender"—was nearer akin to that of an Iroquois war chief than to that of a professional European soldier of the 19th century.[4]

Hardly perceptible for twenty-one years, when hostilities were resumed in 1939 the reversion to primitive practices in warfare soon became headlong until at last all pretence of complying with the Rules of Civilized Warfare was abandoned and both sides tacitly adopted the principle that any act was justifiable if it held out even a remote hope that it might stave off the frightful

Author's Introduction

consequences of defeat. An explanation is clearly needed to account for the fact that governments composed of educated men, reared in the 19th century and brought up to accept as a matter of course the standards of conduct then accepted by everyone, should have so quickly and easily overcome their natural repugnance and adopted and carried out such enormities as the systematic extermination of a defenceless minority on account of its racial Origin, the mass-deportation of enemy populations numbering millions, and the deliberate slaughter of enemy civilians by terror bombing in order to generate among the survivors a disposition to surrender unconditionally.

It was many years after hostilities had ceased in 1945 before historians realized that this problem existed. In Germany the thinking powers of historians were for long paralysed by the ruthless brainwashing to which they with the rest of their countrymen were subjected in 1945 to force them to accept the propaganda fictions of the victors. In Britain and the United States historians were so preoccupied investigating the crimes against humanity committed by the vanquished that they overlooked the background of concentrated terror bombing against which these crimes had been committed. They failed to realize that genocide and terror bombing were not isolated phenomena but symptoms of the same retrograde movement which had mysteriously overtaken Western civilization.

It is commonly assumed that genocide and terror bombing were accepted respectively by the governments of Germany and Britain without protest or opposition from those they ruled who, it is assumed, were as completely subject to the spirit of the times as their rulers. The facts as now disclosed do not support either assumption but the subject remains uninvestigated.

Taking first the case of Germany, a strict censorship enforced by drastic penalties controlled the publication of news and the expression of opinion. It is impossible to determine the number of those who expressed opposition to the regime as any who so ventured came to an untimely end. One cannot protest effectively in secret and to protest publicly was equivalent to suicide. It is doubtful also whether any specific information was available concerning what was taking place behind barbed wire in the concentration camps, most of which were in remote occupied territory, inaccessible to civilians. It has been contended that it would have been impossible to put to death millions of persons without some facts about it becoming generally known. Estimates of the number of victims vary from ten millions to less than a quarter of a million, and the larger the estimate accepted the stronger this contention becomes.

It will always be a subject for regret that the victorious Allies did not put the question beyond dispute by appointing in 1945 a commission composed of impartial judges selected from neutral countries to investigate the facts. The findings of such a body would have been accepted by posterity as final. The Allies however deliberately rejected this obvious course.

The findings of the Nuremberg Tribunal are of course worthless: a court which convicted Admiral Dönitz against whom the prosecution had failed to produce even the shadow of a *prima facie* case was clearly incapable of disposing even of the simplest problem. After the kidnapping of Adolf Eichmann in 1961 another opportunity arose to dispose of this question by an enquiry by an impartial tribunal. Once again this course was emphatically rejected, a fact which in itself is highly significant. It remains therefore impossible to say with confidence whether the German people consented without protest to the departures from civilized standards, by its rulers during the Second World War.

Recently indeed several books have appeared disclosing that throughout the war there was an active underground resistance movement in Germany. Those who participated however seem to have been mainly political rivals of Hitler, jealous of his rise to power and intent on bringing about the downfall of his regime so as to be able to replace it by a regime of their own. His crimes against humanity do not seem to have greatly concerned them.

The situation in Britain was very different. There was no official prohibition on expressions of opinion as such, but persons who ventured to express opinions which the authorities deemed might hamper the war effort were put in prison without a trial or even without a specific complaint against them. With regard to the bombing of the enemy civilian population, everyone knew that civilians in Germany were being slaughtered wholesale but it was believed that this was an unavoidable by-product of an air offensive against military objectives. The comforting reflection was accepted that the German civilian population could at any moment bring its sufferings to an end by surrendering unconditionally.

Author's Introduction

It would not indeed be correct to say that what was officially termed "the strategic bombing offensive" was carried out to the last day of the war without opposition, protest or misgivings. Questions were asked in Parliament as to the character of this air offensive which were fully reported in the Press with the answers given. Certainly it cannot be said that the Ministers of the Crown upon whom fell the duty of answering these questions, resorted to evasion or equivocation.

In accordance with the British tradition they kept a stiff upper lip and gave clear and emphatic replies, without any signs of embarrassment such as might have been expected from them having regard to the fact that as recently as March 1942 Mr. Churchill's War Cabinet had accepted the plan laid before it by Professor Lindemann by which 'top priority' as an objective for air attack was in future to be given to "working-class houses in densely populated residential areas."

This decision of the War Cabinet was kept a closely guarded secret from the British public for nearly twenty years until it was unobtrusively revealed in 1961 in a little book entitled *Science and Government* by the physicist and novelist, Sir Charles Snow, in which occurred the following oft-quoted passage which was immediately translated and published in every language in the world:

"Early in 1942 Professor Lindemann, by this time Lord Cherwell and a member of the Cabinet, laid a cabinet paper before the Cabinet on the strategic bombing of Germany. It described in quantitative terms the effect on Germany of a British bombing offensive in the next eighteen months (approximately March 1943–September 1943). The paper laid down a strategic policy. The bombing must be directed essentially against German working-class houses. Middle-class houses have too much space round them and so are bound to waste bombs; factories and "military objectives" had long since been forgotten, except in official bulletins, since they were much too difficult to find and hit. The paper claimed that — given a total concentration of effort on the production and use of aircraft — it would be possible, in all the larger towns of Germany (that is, those with more than 50,000 inhabitants), to destroy 50 per cent of all houses." (Pages 47-48).

Terror bombing as proposed in the Lindemann Plan was a novelty in warfare rendered possible by the conquest of the air during the first two decades of the 20th century. Genocide, on the other hand, was only the revival of an ancient practice, once probably worldwide, which had long been abandoned in Europe and which barely survived, in company with cannibalism, among the savages of Africa. It has never seriously been contended by anyone that either genocide or terror bombing were in accordance with the moral standards accepted at the time by all civilized peoples.

We know however that the members of the British War Cabinet who accepted the Lindemann Plan fully realized its enormity because concurrently with its acceptance it was decided that on no account must any inkling of its terms reach the public. The following extracts from the parliamentary reports of Hansard are set out verbatim here immediately after the passage quoted above, not to suggest that British politicians are exceptionally mendacious — politicians whatever their nationality have never been renowned for veracity — but to establish that those responsible for the acceptance of the Lindemann Plan were conscious of a feeling of guilt. They instructed those entrusted with the task of answering questions on the subject to give emphatic and unambiguous denials designed to stifle all further enquiries, as the following passages from Hansard show. Some or indeed most of them may have replied in the innocence of their hearts without personal knowledge of the truth but credulously believing what they were told by their departments.

On the 11th March, 1943 (a year after the acceptance of the Lindemann Plan) in the House of Commons, Mr. Montague, a Labour Member, having expressed the hope that our air raids on Germany were still being concentrated, as he believed they were, on military and industrial objectives, Captain Harold Balfour, Under-Secretary for Air, replied that he could give the House "an assurance that our objectives in bombing the enemy were industries, transport and war potential. There is no change in our policy. We were not bombing women and children wantonly for the sake of so doing. It is not for us to turn back. If innocent people, women and children suffer in the execution of our policy in Germany the remedy lies with the German men and women themselves." (Hansard, 12 March 1943.)

On the 30th March, 1943, in reply to the Labour Member, Richard Stokes, the Secretary for Air, Sir Archibald Sinclair,

Author's Introduction

replied blandly that, "The targets of Bomber Command are always military but night-bombing of military objectives necessarily involves bombing the area in which these are situated." (Hansard, 31 March, 1943.)

On the 9th February, 1944, in the House of Lords, Dr. Bell, the Bishop of Chichester, in a memorable speech demanded a statement of the Government's policy "in regard to the bombing of enemy towns with special reference to the effect of such bombing on civilian life." Viscount Cranbourne, Secretary of State for Dominion Affairs, replied for the Government that he was "very ready to give an assurance that the aim of our intensive attacks on German cities was to hamper and, if possible, to bring to a standstill enemy war production and not aimlessly to sprinkle bombs with the object of spreading damage among the enemy population. *The R.A.F. had never indulged in purely terror raids.*" (Hansard, 10 February, 1944.)

The last and most illuminating debate on the subject of terror bombing took place in the House of Commons on the 6th March, 1945, only three weeks after the ghastly mass air raid on Dresden on the 13th February, 1945.

This debate was initiated by the irrepressible Richard Stokes who demanded to be told the truth concerning an authorised report, issued regarding this raid by the Associated Press Correspondent from Supreme Allied Headquarters in Paris which gloatingly described "this unprecedented assault in daylight on the refugee-crowded capital, fleeing from the Russian tide in the East," and declared it showed that "the long-awaited decision had been taken to adopt deliberate terror-bombing of German populated centres as a ruthless expedient to hasten Hitler's doom."

Mr. Stokes began by reading this report which he reminded the House had been widely published in America and had been broadcast by Paris Radio. In Britain on the morning of the 17th February it had been released by the Censor but in the evening of that day it had been suppressed from publication, presumably as a result of the indignant protests which it had aroused. Mr. Stokes insisted on being told, "Is terror bombing now part of our policy? Why is it that the people of this country who are supposed to be responsible for what is going on, the only people who may not know what is being done in their name? On the other hand, if terror bombing be not part of our policy, why was this statement put out at all? I think we shall live to rue the day we did this, and that it (the air raid on Dresden) will stand for all time as a blot on our escutcheon."

Here a private member, Rear-Admiral Sir Murray Sueter, interposed with the fatuous observation that "all targets are very carefully planned by the Bombing Committee. The Committee go into each target which is of military importance, necessitating the carrying out of this bombing."

Commander Brabner, Joint Under-Secretary for Air, then spoke on behalf of the Government. "May I conclude on a note of denial," he observed apologetically. "The report which has just been read stated that the Allied Commanders had adopted a policy of terror bombing.

This is absolutely not so. This has now been denied by Supreme Allied Headquarters and I should like to have an opportunity of denying it here. We are not wasting our bombers or time on purely terror tactics. Our job is to destroy the enemy. It does not do the Hon. Member justice to come to this House and try to suggest that there are a lot of Air Marshals or pilots or anyone else sitting in a room trying to think of how many German women and children they can kill. We are concentrating on war targets, and we intend to remain concentrated on them until Germany gives up."

Quite unabashed by this expression of official disapproval, Mr. Stokes asked two supplementary questions, "If the report issued with the authority of Allied Headquarters in Paris was untrue, why when protest was made against it was this not stated at once, and why was it said at first that it was impossible to suppress a report approved by Allied Headquarters stating its official policy, although in fact it was immediately afterwards suppressed?"

Sir Archibald Sinclair, the Secretary for Air, had pointedly left the House when Mr. Stokes began to read this report so imprudently approved by Supreme Headquarters in Paris. No doubt by this time he knew the contents of this compromising production by heart. Realising that Commander Brabner's rambling evasions of the questions put to him, instead of disposing of them, would be more likely to arouse curiosity as to the truth and so lead to further enquiries, he decided to dispose of the

Author's Introduction

subject finally himself. "This report," be declared, "is certainly not true. The Hon. Member can take that from me. How it was handled, what newspapers published it, and whether publication was authorised, are matters which the Hon. Member had better discuss with the Ministry of Information." (Hansard, March 7th, 1945.)

In passing it may be noted that this denial was in a sense true. No decision, long-awaited, had just been reached to adopt deliberate terror bombing of German main centres of population. The decision to do this had been reached three years before when in March 1942 the Lindemann Plan was accepted by the British War Cabinet. Ever since then it had been ruthlessly carried into effect: the Dresden massacre was merely the culmination of this policy.

Referring to the above quoted report issued from Allied Headquarters, the subject of the above debate, David Irving in his book, *The Destruction of Dresden*,[4] published in 1963, observes complacently, "What might be termed the 'mask' of the Allied Bomber commands for one extraordinary moment appears to have slipped." It was however only a brief moment. "The debate on the 6th March, 1945," he writes proudly, "was the last wartime debate on Bomber Command's policy: the British Government was able to preserve its secret from the day when the first area raid had been launched on Mannheim, the 16th December, 1940, right up to the end of the war."

The apparent indifference of the British public to the adoption of terror bombing as a method of waging war may be explained by the fact that the emphatic denials of the Ministers of the Crown were almost universally accepted as true. Officially this problem did not exist, hence the public apathy which certainly contrasts strangely with the frenzied moral indignation professed in Britain and elsewhere in 1966 when the Americans began to bomb communist troop concentrations, oil depots and ammunition dumps in Vietnam on the ground that bombs which missed their mark might endanger civilian life. The distinction between these cases is that the outcry in 1966 was perhaps more an expression of anti-American feeling than of a humanitarian regard for human life. In 1945 the death of German civilians troubled few people in Britain simply because the victims were Germans. Be this as it may, the worldwide outcry of 1966 certainly tends to support the view that Winston Churchill and his colleagues were justified in fearing in 1942 that if the terms of the Lindemann Plan were made known to the public, an outcry, similar to that which arose in 1966, was to be expected.

Long afterwards in 1961 H.M. Stationery Office described in four volumes with a wealth of horrifying details the terror bombing offensive against Germany carried out from March 1942 to May 1945 in accordance with the Lindemann Plan.[5]

Immediately after hostilities had ceased in 1945, various aspects of the Second World War began to be subjected in print to unqualified condemnation. With regard to terror bombing, the eminent military critic, Captain Liddell Hart, in a little book entitled *The Evolution of Warfare*,[6] published in 1946, declared that victory had been achieved "through practising the most uncivilized means of warfare that the world had known since the Mongol devastations." Adverse criticism was at first mainly directed to the adoption of the novel system of 'war-crimes trials' as a method of disposing of enemy prisoners of war. Widely reported with gusto in the Press these so-called trials were soon in progress all over Europe and in the Far East. With regard to them therefore no question arises, as in the cases of genocide and terror bombing, whether an innocent public was kept in ignorance of what was happening. It cannot be denied that this particular reversion to barbarism was accepted by the public with astonishingly few misgivings.

Nevertheless there were occasional faint and disregarded protests. A booklet written by the present author twenty years ago provides the core of this book. Much of it is reproduced here in the same words in which it was written except that what was then put forward as daring and, in the opinion of most people, perverse speculation, is here stated as undeniable and long established fact. This booklet was published in 1948 under the pseudonym 'A. Jurist', under the title *Advance to Barbarism*.[7] The word "Advance" was chosen in preference to "Retreat" or "Reversion" in deference to the belief, then still widely held, that progress was an unending and automatic process, from its essential nature advancing ever upwards. It was the first book which attempted to deal with the retrograde movement into which civilization entered in 1914, of which terror bombing, genocide and war-crimes trials were the principal symptoms, as a single phenomenon. From the lack of

Author's Introduction

authoritative information available, much of this booklet consisted of speculations. In 1948 no one had ever heard of the Lindemann Plan, or for that matter of Lindemann himself except as a professor of physics who was known to be an adviser of Mr. Churchill on scientific subjects. Terror bombing was not a recognised term since officially it had never taken place. The term used in this booklet was "indiscriminate bombing" which means of course something quite different: terror bombing was not indiscriminate, being directed, as we now know, against working-class houses. With regard to war-crimes trials, the present author briefly pointed out the objections to trials in which the accusers of a prisoner of war acted as judges of their own charges, objections which were as obvious in 1948 as they are now.

This little book is cited here as an example of a small group of books published within a few years of the end of hostilities in 1945 which prove that the main features of the retrograde movement which had begun in 1914 were not accepted entirely without opposition or comment as is so generally believed. Probably numerous similar books were written at the same time which failed to find publishers bold enough to defy the rigid taboo then in force on all mention of the subjects with which they dealt.

Outstanding among the few books fortunate enough to find publishers immediately after the War was a little book entitled *Epitaph on Nuremberg*, by the influential man of letters, Montgomery Belgion, in which for the first time were examined the flimsy arguments put forward to justify the trial at Nuremberg of the captured leaders of the vanquished side.[8] To this day this book, published in 1946, remains one of the most outspoken and boldest examinations of the nature of the Nuremberg Trials. After a brief but lucid outline of the circumstances leading up to the decision at the Yalta Conference to adopt an entirely novel method of disposing of captured enemy leaders, and a careful analysis of the legal principles involved, the author found himself driven to the conclusion that the Nuremberg Trials were not inspired by any overwhelming passion for justice and by a righteous determination that crime should not escape punishment. In essence, he pointed out, a trial is a means by which an existing law is enforced, and that at Nuremberg there was no existing law to enforce. The Tribunal merely invented the law as it proceeded and adjudicated accordingly. "The hands may have been the hands of Justice," Mr. Montgomery Belgion wrote, "but the voice was Propaganda's voice." In short, the purpose of the trials was purely political. "The giving of a delusive appearance that Germany had caused the War," he declared, "was an act of high policy which the Tribunal was entrusted to perform when it was given the job of passing sentence on most of the accused." (Page 86.)

It had soon been recognised, he pointed out, that "Article 231 of the Treaty of Versailles which declared Germany solely guilty for the First World War had neither moral weight nor judicial validity," and so the victors of the Second World War decided to hold trials of the vanquished that would, they hoped, conclusively establish for all time Germany's guilt. "That", he submitted, "was the real object of the Nuremberg Trial; it was a gigantic 'put up show', a gigantic piece of propaganda." (Page 88.) "The Trial was decked out to look like an authentic judicial process: the victors showed a really astonishing contempt for justice and truth and a really pathetic faith in sophistry." (Page 74.)

The conclusions of the author of this little book are remarkable if only because it was published three years before these conclusions were confirmed beyond any possible doubt by the publication in 1949 by the U.S. State Department of the short hand transcript of the deliberations held in London in 1945 to make arrangements for the so-called trials in Nuremberg during which General Nikitchenko, who later acted as one of the two Russian judges on the Tribunal, clearly disclosed the real nature of the trials.

"We are dealing here," General Nikitchenko declared, "with the chief war criminals who have *already* been convicted and whose conviction has *already* been announced at both the Moscow and Yalta Conferences by the heads of State.... The fact that the Nazi leaders are criminals has already been established. The task of the Tribunal is only to determine the measure of guilt of each particular person and to mete out the necessary punishment."[9]

The publication of such books as *Epitaph on Nuremberg* and *Advance to Barbarism* within a few years of the end of hostilities proves conclusively that the reversion to barbarism which began in 1914 and reached its culmination in 1946 was not accepted entirely without at least some opposition or protest as is so commonly believed. It must be admitted however that such books at the time exercised no perceptible influence on public

Author's Introduction

opinion. So far as war-crimes trials were concerned the man in the street naturally preferred to rely on such weighty authorities as Professor Arthur Goodhart, Professor of Jurisprudence at Oxford University, who emphatically pronounced that war-crimes trials were an admirable innovation which would facilitate the speedy administration of justice, and Lord Justice Wright, one of the greatest English lawyers of his generation, who declared that so long as accused persons did in fact receive justice, it was immaterial that the court which tried them was composed of their accusers.

It is indeed hard to account for the equanimity with which the vast majority of lawyers accepted this view.[10] For thousands of years in all civilized countries the principle has been accepted that criminal prosecutions and civil actions could only be decided by the decision of a strictly impartial court. "The very essence of a fair trial is a third-party judgement," as Victor Gollancz pointed out in 1961 with regard to the trial of Adolf Eichmann by Jewish judges.[11] For lawyers to dispute this was no less astonishing than if a conference of eminent surgeons unanimously passed a resolution that no example could be found of anyone having benefited by a surgical operation, or as if a synod of leading Christian ecclesiastics approved a declaration that prayer could never be anything but a waste of time.

Had the Council of Nicaea, for example, passed such a resolution, historians of the Christian Church would have been set a difficult task reconciling this resolution with Christian thought and practice both before and since. Future historians of the development of jurisprudence will have similar difficulty in explaining how it came about that the Nuremberg Trials were approved by so many leading jurists from the most highly civilized countries in the world.

With regard to terror bombing which ranks with genocide and war-crimes trials as one of the three culminating features of the retrograde movement of civilization which began imperceptibly in 1914, it must be admitted that this innovation was accepted by public opinion without opposition or misgivings. The reason was that officially terror bombing was merely a figment of the imagination of the mendacious Dr. Goebbels. As previously stated, on the 7th February, 1944, two years after the Lindemann Plan had been put into operation, Viscount Cranborne solemnly declared,

"The R.A.F. has never indulged in purely terror raids." Also the British public first heard of this infamous plan when its adoption by Mr. Churchill's War Cabinet in March 1942 was casually disclosed in the paragraph quoted above from the little booklet entitled *Science and Government*, by Sir Charles Snow, published in 1961.[12] Some six months afterwards voluminous details of the air offensive launched in accordance with this plan were published by H.M. Stationery Office in the four massive volumes referred to above. Nothing also was generally known to distinguish the mass air raid on Dresden as the crowning atrocity of this campaign. When the character of this air raid was disclosed in a book written with official approval and assistance in 1963, it was presented and widely accepted as an original discovery by an enterprising and industrious author.

With the wealth of information now available, it is hard to realise how little was known in the years immediately following the end of the Second World War of the nature of that struggle. Such booklets as *Epitaph on Nuremberg* and *Advance to Barbarism* mentioned above, whatever merits or shortcomings they may have possessed, at least demonstrated the possibility of making bricks without straw. They also expressed in print the misgivings and suspicions felt by many at the time, hitherto only expressed in Parliament by such upholders of earlier standards of conduct as Dr. Bell, the Bishop of Chichester, and Richard Stokes, M.P.

The British authorities, while the "strategic air offensive" was going on, were under no delusions as to what would be the reaction of a wide section of the public if its true nature was allowed to become known. Thus, in a minute dated the 28th February, 1943, Sir Archibald Sinclair explained to Sir Charles Portal, Chief of the Air Staff, that it was necessary to stifle all public discussion on the subject because if the truth had been disclosed in response to the enquiries being made by influential political and religious leaders, their inevitable condemnation would impair the morale of the bomber crews and consequently their bombing efficiency.

For nearly two decades it remained possible to do little more than speculate concerning the so-called Allied strategic air offensive against Germany. The particulars given in *Advance to Barbarism* were derived from the disclosures made in a little book entitled *Bombing Vindicated*[13] by J. M. Spaight, Principal

Assistant Secretary of the Air Ministry, published in 1944, perhaps the most illuminating book written during the Second World War, as confirmed by Air Marshal Harris's book, *Bomber Offensive*,[14] published in 1947.

It is not in the least remarkable that Hitler and his adherants were able to keep hidden from their countrymen the crimes against humanity being committed in Germany: anyone who ventured to protest at what was taking place faced death or being sent to a concentration camp which not seldom amounted to the same fate. When the war came to an end and the victims of the Nazi regime were released, a flood of information poured forth concerning the iniquities of the vanquished: nothing however was revealed concerning the conduct of the victors which remained as shrouded as ever by a cloak of silence. It may seem strange that it was considered necessary to maintain this cloak of silence for so long after victory had been won when the Government was in a position to say like Lady Macbeth, "What is done cannot be undone." It is even stranger that it was found possible to do so after the emergency war legislation designed to suppress all expression of opinion deemed likely to hamper the successful conduct of the war had been allowed to lapse. In contemporary Russia or Spain this would have been an easy matter as in these countries functioned an official censor whose duty it was to censor the publication of all books and newspapers. But in Britain no censor had existed since the times of the Stuart kings. After 1945 everyone in Britain enjoyed the right once again to express any opinion they liked which was not libellous, seditious, blasphemous or obscene.

Nevertheless it was found possible to keep the truth from leaking out concerning terror bombing for upwards of two decades, although no legal machinery existed to control public expressions of opinion.

In no other country in the world would this have been possible. The British however are politically the most advanced people in the world, with unique powers of self-discipline when it is made to appear to them that national interests are at stake. These powers had first fully bloomed in 1936 when all the European and American newspapers were freely discussing an alleged association between King Edward VIII and a Mrs. Wallis Simpson. Yet for many months the entire British Press, as if edited by one man, preserved an unbroken silence. Naturally there was verbal speculation and gossip in Britain but only those who read the Press knew any details, and as those British newspapers that specialised in scandalmongering remained silent with regard to *l'affaire Simpson* most people discounted as mere rumours what the foreign Press was saying. Few realized in Britain that a grave constitutional crisis was threatening which was causing the Government the gravest anxiety.

It was not until after the abdication that it became known how the Prime Minister, Mr. Stanley Baldwin, had dealt with the matter. Fortunately the leading national newspapers had recently fallen under the control of a few wealthy men, the so-called Press Barons of Fleet Street. Mr. Baldwin approached them personally, explained the situation frankly and appealed to them not to report *l'affaire Simpson* in the newspapers controlled by them and to bring pressure to bear on the smaller newspapers to ignore the subject until he had had time to ascertain the King's intentions and to decide what had best be done. He stressed that the Crown was the link which bound together the British Empire and if this link was weakened, the unity of the Empire would be in peril.

Mr. Baldwin did not appeal in vain. The British Press remained silent. It was not until he had consulted at length with the Prime Ministers of the Dominions that he gave the signal to his stooge, the Bishop of Bradford, to give public expression to the heartfelt misgivings felt by the latter concerning the King's mode of life and in particular the erring monarch's resolve not to follow the example of his grandfather, Edward VII, when involved in an affaire de coeur, but to marry the lady in question. The taboo of silence was lifted. Edward VIII abdicated and retired into exile. Before the bulk of the British public had realised the gravity of the situation, this unique episode of British history was over with a minimum of excitement, scandal and recrimination.

In 1945 the Baldwin technique was adopted to prevent facts from being disclosed concerning two outstanding features of the war which had just been brought to a victorious conclusion. A taboo of silence was imposed on editors and publishers similar to that imposed so successfully nine years before in regard to *l'affaire Simpson*. In some ways this taboo was even more remarkable than the earlier taboo because no national interests seemed to be involved and yet it was found possible to maintain it, practically unbroken, for upwards of two decades.

Author's Introduction

An explanation still remains to be found why in 1945 the British authorities should have considered it necessary or even desirable to impose a taboo of silence on all mention of terror bombing and war-crimes trials.

Except that they were both, like genocide, symptoms of a world-wide tendency to revert to primitive practices in warfare, they were otherwise quite unconnected. They became linked entirely by a chance circumstance. The conception of terror bombing can be traced back to as early as the 1920s when Air Marshal Trenchard recommended the construction of large, long-range bombers designed for attacks on the civilian population of an enemy. The conception of war-crimes trials had originated as recently as November 1943, from an unconsidered suggestion by Mr. Winston Churchill at an alcoholic orgy held to celebrate the conclusion of the Teheran Conference. Without seemingly premeditation, the communist dictator, Stalin, proposed that when victory was achieved 50,000 German officers and technicians should be massacred. This proposal could not be dismissed as merely a result of drinking numerous toasts in vodka because everyone present knew that as recently as the spring of 1940 Stalin had carried out such a massacre of 15,000 Polish officers in the Katyn Forest where their bodies were subsequently found. President Roosevelt made the suggestion the subject for one of his tasteless jokes but Mr. Churchill indignantly declared that "the British public will never stand for mass-murder!" adding, probably as an afterthought, "No one, Nazi, or no, shall be dealt with summarily without a legal trial."

An open breach between these ill-assorted allies was ultimately averted by a makeshift compromise. In deference to the strange susceptibilities of his British guest, Stalin agreed to forego his massacre and consented to "a legal trial" taking place before the prisoners were put to death. Later this compromise was formally confirmed at the conferences held in Moscow and in Yalta.

It was not until after the unconditional surrender of Germany in 1945 that the difficulties of carrying out in practice this novel idea became apparent. At the Yalta Conference it had been agreed that a score of the most prominent political and military leaders of the vanquished should be selected, labelled 'war-criminals' and subjected to a trial before a court composed of British, American, French and Russian judges. According to the Russian judge, General Nikitchenko, the only duty of the court would be to rubberstamp the decision of the politicians at the Yalta Conference that the prisoners were guilty. All seemed plain sailing. This view of the matter was naturally acceptable to Russian judges as being in accordance with communist theory and practice, but many were doubtful if Western judges could be found who would be equally accommodating. This difficulty was eventually surmounted by agreeing that the facts upon which the charges were based should be laid before the court in the usual way for adjudication, each judge being left free to reach his own conclusions on the facts placed before him.

This solution however immediately aroused widespread consternation. Most of the victorious Powers had skeletons in their national cupboards and were determined that no evidence should be produced to the court which would reveal these skeletons. To meet these objections, it became necessary to sift the evidence carefully beforehand. In addition, the court was directed, as it saw fit, to exclude any evidence submitted by the defence as irrelevant, by which was meant any evidence which would not support a conviction.

Britain had a particularly gruesome skeleton in her cupboard in the shape of her terror bombing campaign. In popular estimation in 1945 the most obvious of Hitler's crimes was his initiation of what was then known as indiscriminate bombing, that is to say, bombing unrestricted to military objectives. Nevertheless, to the general astonishment, no charge relating to German bombing was preferred against any of Hitler's surviving colleagues. "To have done so," Mr. Justice Jackson, the chief American prosecutor at Nuremberg, later declared frankly, "would have been to invite recriminations which would not have been useful at the trial."

In short in 1945 the British Government found itself in a painful dilemma. A verdict based on carefully selected facts would not accomplish the purpose the trial was intended to serve, namely, to act as a substitute for Article 231 of the Treaty of Versailles by establishing Germany's war-guilt for all time. As the trial proceeded it would soon become clear to all that it was a mere bizarre farce, to use the description applied to it by the Oxford historian, Dr. Alan Taylor, twenty years afterwards.

Author's Introduction

Yet although it had become clear that the trial would serve no useful purpose of any kind, it was impossible for the British Government to refuse to take part because the proposal that a trial of the vanquished leaders should take place after victory had come in the first place on behalf of Britain from Mr. Churchill himself.

To preserve their secret the British authorities realized that it would not be sufficient to provide that evidence of British terror bombing should be excluded from consideration by the court at Nuremberg if concurrently the fact that terror bombing had taken place was allowed to become common knowledge as a result of free discussion in Britain of the subject. The court might then be tempted to take judicial notice thereof and enquire further, with the result the veracity of H.M. Ministers would ultimately be called in question.

It was therefore decided to impose a stringent taboo on all discussion of terror bombing. But it was realised that if free discussion were permitted of the nature of the Nuremberg trials and the other similar war-crimes trials then going on, the question was bound to be asked why had it been considered necessary to sift the evidence before it was laid before the court, thereby rendering worthless any verdict it might give, and why no charge of having initiated indiscriminate bombing had been included in the indictments. It was soon realised that too many people knew the answer to the latter question and if free discussion on the subject was permitted the truth would soon leak out. A similar taboo to that on discussion on terror bombing was therefore imposed on discussion of war-crimes trials.

Scores of memoirs, books and articles have made familiar to all every detail of the Abdication: the taboo of silence imposed by Mr. Baldwin is remembered with unstinted admiration by foreigners as an outstanding example of British self-discipline in a national crisis.

This taboo of 1936 remained in force for only a few months and was limited to newspaper editors. The taboo imposed in 1945 extended not only to editors but to authors, reviewers and historians: it remained in force for upwards of sixteen years. Only persons personally affected by this taboo realised that it existed: when in 1961 it was lifted surprise was expressed that no one until then had heard of the Lindemann Plan. Except for Air Marshal Harris, terror bombing found few defenders.

Although the British public seemed outwardly indifferent to this belated revelation, it may be that the vehement outcry in Britain when the American air force began to bomb military objectives in Vietnam in 1966 was a retarded expression of the horror subconsciously felt in 1961.

Those upon whom fell the task of enforcing the taboo of 1945 were no respecters of persons. They suppressed not only would-be authors striving to express their views for the first time in print but authors of long established repute and men of international fame. For example, the memorable book *Politics: Trials and Errors*[15] by the late Lord Hankey was accorded 'the silent treatment' because it revealed the truth concerning the invasion of Norway in 1940 and denounced the conviction as a war-criminal of the former Japanese ambassador to London, Shigemitsu. Fortunately Lord Hankey's appeal for rectification of this glaring miscarriage of justice won the support of General MacArthur and Shigemitsu was shortly released. Of all the books published in the post-war period, this book alone can be said to have definitely influenced the course of events.

Another distinguished victim of the taboo was Dean Inge, from 1911 to 1933 Dean of St. Paul's. Not only was he the author of many learned works on philosophy and mysticism but he was also one of the most gifted journalists of his time. Among contemporary writers he had no rival in expressing a point of view lucidly, adequately and in the fewest possible words: his epigrammatic sayings, terse, stimulating and uncompromising, were quoted in the Press throughout the world. Editors competed eagerly for his articles: he commanded the highest rates of pay in journalism. Although a tireless critic of the shallow optimism, muddled thinking and the catchwords of democracy accepted by all but a few in the years after the First World War, the possibility that his articles needed censorship had never before 1945 occurred to anyone.

Naturally great was the Dean's surprise and indignation when after the Second World War he found that his articles when they appeared in print had been drastically revised. His protests were vain. Fortunately a copy of the booklet by the present author entitled *Advance to Barbarism* published in 1948 came into his hands and he wrote at once, "In this book you have well said what it was high time was said by someone." His efforts to review the

Author's Introduction

book were politely rejected. "I had intended to write a book on similar lines to yours," he remarked to the present author, "but at my age (he was then in his eighties) I cannot undertake the labour of finding a bold enough publisher." Another effort to give public expression to his views on the Nuremberg Trials was again foiled by a watchful editor. "I hardly recognised my article when I saw it in print. It had been shamefully mutilated," he lamented. "All mention of your book had been carefully omitted. My protests to the editor of the *Evening Standard* were politely evaded."

Finding himself deprived of the right of free speech in his own country, the Dean at once complied with a request that he should contribute a preface to a revised and greatly lengthened edition of *Advance to Barbarism* which was awaiting publication in the United States. Within three days he supplied an admirable preface of some nine hundred words in his own handwriting. Thus supported, the American edition appeared in 1953 and aroused wide attention in the United States, receiving no less than thirty-nine favourable reviews. Its appearance was ignored in Britain except by *Encounter*, a publication, subsidised with foreign money by an organization labelled grandiloquently the Congress for Cultural Freedom, which denounced it hotly, presumably on the ground that a breach of the taboo was detrimental to 'cultural freedom'.[16]

An amusing sequel to Dean Inge's vain efforts to defy the taboo occurred after his death in February 1954 when a valiant attempt was made to clear his memory of the stigma of having held opinions conflicting with the convictions of those considered right-thinking people. A certain Rev. C. Magraw wrote at once to *The Times* to say that although the Dean might at time have expressed regrettable doubts concerning the legal validity of war-crimes trials, yet his final conclusion was these doubts were baseless. "In the summer of 1947," he wrote, "the Dean told me that he had changed his mind and he considered the Nuremberg Trials scrupulously fair."

A brief correspondence in *The Times*, initiated by the present author, followed, but was ended abruptly on the 9th March, 1954 by a letter from Mr. W. C. Inge, the Dean's son, who pointed out that whatever his father may have said to the Rev. Magraw in a casual conversation in 1947, his final and considered views had been clearly set in the preface which he had contributed to *Advance to Barbarism* in 1953. Mr. Inge added that he himself had often discussed the subject of war-crimes trials with his father who, while considering that the Nuremberg Trials had been fairly conducted, "never changed his opinion that they set a dangerous precedent and that the necessity for justice appearing to be done had been vitiated by the presence of the Russians on the Nuremberg Tribunal."

One of the essential characteristics of a taboo is that even when innocently infringed an irrational feeling of guilt is engendered not only in the mind of the culprit but also in the minds of his relations and friends. Even as late as 1960 this feeling of guilty shame persisted with regard to the Dean's unorthodox views which, it was felt, he had only been saved from expressing by watchful editors. When in that year his friend and former pupil, Canon Adam Fox, published what purported to be a complete biography of Dean Inge,[17] with the aid and approval of the Dean's family, he not only avoided all mention of the Dean's views on the Second World War and its aftermath but pointedly excluded from reference in the voluminous bibliography in his book mention of the preface which the Dean had contributed to the American edition of *Advance to Barbarism*. This omission could hardly have been accidental as this preface was the last production of the Dean's pen.

When in the following year the true nature of what was then still known as "the strategic bombing offensive" was casually revealed by Sir Charles Snow in his little book, *Science and Government*, no attempt was made to maintain the taboo of silence on the subject. The exact contents of the Lindemann Plan came as a surprise to everyone who had not had access to official sources of information. No one was deeply disturbed to learn of a decision of the British Government so long before as 1942. As the war had been won, it did not seem to matter very much how it had been won. It is perhaps significant that less concern was expressed that terror bombing should have been formally adopted than that H.M. Ministers should have lied to conceal this guilty secret. Long before 1961 all inclination to discuss war-crimes trials had disappeared, and now it was felt that the question of terror bombing was also an unpleasant subject about which the less said the better.

In short, the taboos imposed in 1945 triumphantly fulfilled their essential purpose which was to gain time until the British public could regard terror bombing and war-crimes trials dispassionately as happenings of long past history which were best forgotten.

Both taboos were based on the principle so well expressed by the lines of the Victorian poet, Coventry Patmore, in his poem *Magna est Veritas*:

"When all its work is done the lie shall rot;
The truth is great, and shall prevail,
When none cares whether it prevails or not."

Chapter I – Primeval Simplicity

Once the theory of evolution had during the 19th century become generally accepted, a belief in human progress, automatic and ceaseless, naturally followed. The record of the rocks seemed conclusive: in the lowest and most ancient strata were to be found fossils of simple and primitive forms of life and above them the fossils of ever increasing complexity, culminating in the evolution of man. The story of life on this planet was a story of steady improvement, of better adaptations of each species to its environment. The most fitted survived.

The survival of the fittest became popularly interpreted as the survival of the strongest. As applied to mankind this was held to mean that the strongest races survived, their superiority being demonstrated by success in war. Naturally this view found favour among the leading nations of Europe who since the days of Marathon had repeatedly on the battlefield proved their military superiority to the oriental and coloured peoples. Down to 1914 White Supremacy by this or any other test seemed indisputable. Warfare was accepted as a characteristic of human life consistent with the irrevocable laws of nature. As the British economist Walter Bagehot (1826-77) wrote in his *Physics and Politics*, "war is the most showy fact in human history." It was generally assumed that war was as old as mankind, expressing a fundamental human instinct. In his *International Law* the famous jurist Sir Henry Maine refers casually to "the universal belligerency of primitive man," and adds clearly without fear of contradiction, "It is not peace which is natural and primitive but war."

Since the war of 1914-18, the so-called War to end War, the truth of this assumption has been widely disputed, in particular by the psychologist, Havelock Ellis. The life of early man in the remote past, he argued, can best be determined from the mode of life of the most primitive of modern races living at the present day. "When

Chapter I — Primeval Simplicity

Australia was first visited by Europeans," he pointed out, "war in the sense of a whole tribe taking the field against another tribe had no existence among the Australian aborigines."[18] Undeniably for thousands of years the aborigines of Australia lived in conditions of contented and peaceful stagnation. Some indeed find it hard to believe that this exceptional state of affairs provides an example of conditions probably widely prevailing elsewhere in the world. They regard the case of the aborigines of Australia as evidence that when no struggle for survival has to be fought, no progress takes place. In Europe, Asia and Africa, man had to contend with dangerous beasts of prey, thereby developing daring and courage, qualities for which he found an outlet later in warfare with his fellow man. Notoriously the descendents of the original inhabitants of Australia lack ambition, enterprise and initiative, qualities necessary in a struggle for survival, qualities which some maintain are generated and stimulated by warfare.

The contrary view that war is an unmitigated evil of comparatively recent origin is well expressed by Dr. R. L. Worrall in his *Footsteps of Warfare* who contends that, until mankind began to settle in communities depending on agriculture for support, warfare was unknown. "In those days of savagery," he writes, "men and women lacked every feature of modern life including all the savageries of civilization. Only with the passing of the Stone Age and of primitive communism did there come the supreme savagery of war."[19] He pictures the sparse population of the hunting period wandering freely through country abounding with game of every kind and dismisses as baseless the view that clashes must have occurred between the various groups of hunters since no subject for conflict would exist in such conditions. There is, he points out, an entire lack of evidence of warfare in primitive times, although he admits that had warfare occurred it is difficult to imagine what evidence of it could have survived so vast a length of time.

From time to time in certain areas, no doubt, such idyllic conditions may have persisted for long periods and we are at liberty to imagine that during these periods man may have come dimly to resemble the Noble Savage of Rousseau. Thus, on the Australian continent, for tens of thousands of years mankind lived undisturbed by intrusive neighbours and probably by any major changes of climate. In such static conditions, occasions for

Advance to Barbarism

warfare would seldom if ever arise: the Australian aborigines were certainly peaceful if not noble savages, and so they remained until modern times. On the other hand in Europe, Central Asia, and in North Africa, major changes of climate occurred during the Pleistocene Period with great frequency according to geological standards. At one period Europe enjoyed a temperate climate as far north as Lapland; southern Europe was tropical. Later began a succession of ice ages separated by mild periods lasting thousands of years. During the ice ages the climate of all Europe north of the Alps may be compared to that of Greenland at the present day. How did the hunting communities of northern Europe, during the oncoming of a glacial period, deal with the communities already occupying the lands to which they gradually withdrew as their own hunting grounds became less and less habitable? They had been accustomed, no doubt, to act summarily when, for example, they found a desirable cave already occupied by cave bears or wolves. Can it be doubted that in comparable circumstances they dealt with human obstructors by similar methods? And can it be doubted that the original inhabitants of these more habitable lands took up the natural attitude that changes of climate were no concern of theirs and that these intruders ought to have been content to die resignedly and quietly of hunger and cold in their own home lands without disturbing their neighbours? Surely, points of view so different and so irreconcilable could have only one outcome. One party had been doomed by nature to perish and each frankly preferred this fate should be suffered by the other.

Probably every major change of climate in the Stone Ages resulted in a series of minor wars—minor because in each only a few hundred individuals or less would be involved, but other wise presenting the essential characteristics of a modern war. It is a popular delusion that man in prehistoric times was a stupid, half-animal creature altogether different from modern man. Some types of man as long ago as 30,000 years—the Cro-Magnon man who inhabited southern France in the Aurignacian Epoch—had a brain of equal or even of greater capacity to that of the average modern European. (The average cubic capacity of a Cro-Magnon skull was 1590 c.c.: that of a modern European is 1480 c.c.) From this we can deduce that, as modern European brains have proved capable of grasping the fact that it is less trouble to dismantle and remove to one's own country a factory belonging to a conquered

Chapter I — Primeval Simplicity

people than to build a factory for one's self, it should not have been beyond a Cro-Magnon brain to have grasped the fact that it was less laborious to appropriate the stone axe of a vanquished enemy than to chip out a new one. By the same argument, this much vaunted achievement of modern reasoning should not even have been beyond modern man's cousins in the Stone Age, the celebrated Neanderthal species of the human race which, in spite of a shambling gait, great beetling ape-like eyebrow ridges and massive chinless jaws, possessed a capacious brain of a far from simple type. In fact, certain specimens of Neanderthal man possessed brains above the average in size—the skull found at La Chapelle had a capacity of over 1600 c.c., at least 120 c.c. above the modern average, according to Sir Arthur Keith.[20] We are justified in believing, therefore, that the La Chapelle man, in spite of his unprepossessing simian appearance, would have been fully capable of grasping all the motives for a modern war, of conducting warfare in entirely the contemporary spirit, so far as his limited resources permitted, and of dealing with a defeated enemy in accordance with the same principles and with precisely the same objects in view as were applied to a defeated enemy in that Year of Grace, 1945.

One fact relating to Neanderthal man, established beyond question but otherwise inexplicable, makes it possible to say that the first major European war took place during the Old Stone Age at a date which experts have estimated to have been approximately between thirty and fifty thousand years ago. For tens of thousands of years preceding this approximate date Neanderthal man was in occupation of a vast area stretching from Gibraltar in the West to Palestine in the East and extending southward from the great ice fields which then covered the northern half of Europe. Having been in undisturbed possession of this area for an enormous length of time, Neanderthal man disappeared, apparently rather suddenly. In strata of a later date his remains are no longer found; thereafter are found only traces of men of the same type as now occupy Europe.

What brought about the extinction of Neanderthal man will probably always remain a matter of speculation. All that is known for certain is that above a certain level all traces of his culture—known as the Mousterian—abruptly disappear and are replaced by traces of a distinct culture known as the Aurignacian.

It is, of course, possible that Neanderthal man died out through some unknown natural cause so that his vacated hunting grounds were peaceably occupied by his successors, the men of the Aurignacian Epoch. Dismissing this vague possibility, Sir Arthur Keith writes: "Those who observe the fate of the aborigines of Australia and Tasmania will have no difficulty in accounting for the disappearance of *Homo Neanderthalensis*."[21]

It is hard to believe, however, that the Neanderthals passively allowed themselves to be dispossessed of their means of subsistence. Through hundreds of centuries they had successfully adapted themselves to a most rigorous climate and had succeeded in the struggle for survival in competition with some of the most formidable carnivores that have ever existed — sabre-tooth tigers, lions, and cave bears. To quote Sir Arthur Keith again: "Neanderthal man's skill as a flint-artist shows that his abilities were not of a low order.

He had fire at his command, he buried his dead, he had a distinct and highly evolved form of culture." He was a fearless and skilful hunter of big game. He was confronted by no such superiority in weapons as that which made it impossible for the aborigines of Australia to resist the firearms of the European invaders. The conclusion reached by Professor Henry Fairfield Osborn in his *Men of the Old Stone Age* is that the Aurignacian invaders "competed for a time with the Neanderthals before they dispossessed them of their principal stations and drove them out of the country or killed them in battle."[22]

There is, thus, good ground for believing that the Mousterian Period ended as a consequence of a struggle which conforms with the definition of warfare accepted by Havelock Ellis — "War is an organised attack of one community on another." The outcome of this struggle was ultimately the complete extermination of that distinct species of the human race, Neanderthal man. Regarding this grim outcome Professor Osborn observes:

"In the racial replacements of savage as well as of historic peoples the men are often killed and the women spared and taken into the families of the warriors, but no evidence has thus far been found that even the Neanderthal women were spared or allowed to remain in the country, because in none of the burials of Aurignacian times is there any evidence of the crossing or admixture of the Aurignacian peoples with the Neanderthals."[23]

Chapter I — Primeval Simplicity

There is no need for us to explain the fate which overcame the Neanderthals by stressing the superior intelligence of their conquerors or by attributing to the latter the possession of more effective weapons. It seems probable that Neanderthal man lived in small, isolated communities, each community quite unconcerned with the fate and perhaps unaware of the existence of other Neanderthal communities. Each community no doubt defended itself desperately — to quote Professor Osborn — "with wooden weapons and with stone-headed dart and spear," probably each such isolated struggle was finally decided by weight of numbers.

If the conclusions of the authorities quoted above be accepted, it becomes possible to say with confidence that there took place in Europe in the Old Stone Age, according to the experts more than thirty thousand years ago, a decisive struggle between the representatives of two distinct branches of the human race, the Neanderthals and a tribe or tribes of men similar in all physical respects to modern man. Such a struggle would certainly merit the title of the First Great European War since its results were infinitely more momentous than the results of any of the tribal and civil wars which have occurred since in Europe — including any of the celebrated European wars of modern times.

It is probable also that some of those features of contemporary warfare which are popularly regarded as unprecedented innovations were a normal feature of warfare in the most remote times. What is now regarded as the old distinction between uniformed combatant forces and the civilian population is, judged on the scale of time by which man's history on this planet is recorded, an innovation of yesterday — a matter of a mere couple of centuries. In prehistoric warfare, every member of the whole hunting community would be equally involved with no more regard to age or sex than in warfare to-day. In the event of defeat, all would suffer the same fate.

Often, no doubt, during hostilities the women and children left behind in a settlement were in greater danger than the able-bodied males of the community away on a hunting expedition to collect food. It would surely not have been beyond brains with 120 c.c. greater capacity than the modern average to realize the tactical, material, and psychological benefits which would result from a sudden and devastating raid on "the enemy's main centres of population."

Even a recent innovation regarded as especially without any kind of precedent may not have been lacking in the earliest warfare. In the Stone Age men lived by hunting the herds of wild horses, deer, and wild cattle then living in profusion on the great Eurasian plains which were also the prey of various carnivorous animals, such as the sabre-tooth tiger and the cave bear. No doubt, these dangerous animals were bitterly hated as rivals for the available supplies of food, and feared owing to their taste for human flesh when occasion offered. Opportunities for reprisals would from time to time have occurred. We can only deduce the nature of these reprisals from what occurs at the present day in primitive lands. In parts of Indo-China, for example, the chief enemy is the tiger whose depredations are, as a rule, endured with resignation by the natives. Occasionally, however, a tiger blunders into a trap or is found overcome by old age, accident, or disease. A formal act of retribution is then staged in which the whole village community, men, women, and children, takes an enthusiastic part. The victim is first reduced to complete helplessness by being deprived of food and is then mocked, baited to frenzy, terrified by fireworks, and finally finished off in a slow and painful manner amid general rejoicings. The same custom prevails in far-off Tibet, where the chief enemy is the wolf. The Swedish traveller, Sven Hedin, tells us that, when the herdsmen manage to catch one of the wolves who live by preying on their flocks, they first blind the victim and then beat it to death with their knouts.

By analogy we can safely assume that the men of the Stone Age acted in the same way when chance placed at their mercy so dangerous and hated a rival as the cave bear. Upon one individual animal would be inflicted a kind of symbolic punishment for all the offences committed by the whole species to which it belonged. And, if the men of the Stone Age were accustomed to deal with animal enemies in this way, is it not probable that, on occasion, they dealt with particularly feared and hated human enemies in the same way? It follows that, if the above reasoning is justified, the practice of mock-trials recently introduced solemnly as an epoch-making innovation is nothing but a revival of a practice so long abandoned by civilized peoples that its origin in the remote past has become forgotten.

Although, as has been repeatedly demonstrated of late, a mock-trial can be carried out more or less in the form of a judicial

Chapter I — Primeval Simplicity

trial, the origin and purpose of a mock-trial is entirely distinct from the origin and purpose of a judicial trial. The former, an act of symbolic vengeance in which the victim suffers for the misdoings of his species or nation, dates from remote antiquity, from the dawn period of humanity when the shadowy border line between the subhuman and the human had barely been passed. The judicial trial is obviously of much later origin, originating at the time when human communities had begun to adopt customs and taboos and the necessity arose of deciding whether these had been infringed. The person condemned at a judicial trial suffers not as a symbol but for personal acts of which he has personally been found guilty.

It is assumed that the reader is sufficiently familiar with the details of the Nuremberg proceedings of 1945-1946, so that there is no need to point out how closely primitive precedents were unconsciously followed in them. The underlying spirit will be further examined later in these pages. One indication of this spirit may, however, be given here. The announcement was actually made in the British Press that three British housewives were to be selected and sent to Nuremberg at public expense to attend these proceedings as representatives of the British housewives who had endured the Blitz.

Incredible as it now appears, the likelihood of some such arrangement being adopted was at the time widely discussed in responsible and influential circles. A variation of the idea, specifically reported not as a vague possibility under consideration but as a serious arrangement being actively carried into effect, will be found in the *Daily Mail* of November 29, 1945, under front page headlines, "Blitz Housewife to Face Goering & Co." Beneath is printed a report from "our special correspondent in Nuremberg, Rhona Churchill," which begins, "'Mrs. Jones,' typical British housewife, who has stood in the fish-queue, been through the Blitz, and had her whole domestic life turned upside down by the war, is to be invited to come to Nuremberg and see in court the men who caused her troubles."

Rhona Churchill cites as her authority for this announcement, Major Peter Casson, whom she describes as an "officer in charge of V.I.P.s" (Very Important People). This military gentleman, she states, assured her that plans already existed to carry into effect this proposal, and that he himself "was

Advance to Barbarism

asking Lord Justice Lawrence's Marshal to make the necessary arrangements, because technically 'Mrs. Jones' will come here as a guest of the British judges."

Unfortunately, it is not known what was the reaction of Lord Justice Lawrence when he was informed by his Marshal that the V.I.P. Officer had appointed him to act the part of host to the fish-queueing "Mrs. Jones". We can but hazard the guess that it was both dignified and vigorous. Until definite information on this point comes to hand, Rhona Churchill's message will remain incomplete. Nevertheless, as it stands, this message is of unique interest to historians and anthropologists, although clearly neither Rhona Churchill nor Peter Casson had the least comprehension of its significance. That there could exist any reasonable objection to such a proposal evidently occurred to neither of them although the sapient Major expressed fears that red-tape might cause some delay. As "Mrs. Jones" would "travel here as a V.I.P., possibly by air, live in a V.I.P. hotel, and use one of the V.I.P. gallery seats," Major Casson had no doubt that there would be keen competition for the post, but he added, "We are hoping there will be no wire-pulling and the woman who comes here will really be a typical housewife." He gathered that the Home Office would make the selection and that the housewife selected would be accompanied not by two female companions but by an A.R.P. warden and "a rank and file soldier who had won the V.C." He concluded by telling Rhona Churchill that he understood that Lord Justice Lawrence had sent Mr. Winston Churchill a cordial invitation to come to Nuremberg, not as a member of "Mrs. Jones'" troop but as his personal guest. A close personal friend had reported, however, that the Prime Minister was hesitating to accept "for fear that he might give a false impression of gloating over his defeated enemies."

It will be observed that both Rhona Churchill and the democratically-minded Major Casson assumed as a matter of common knowledge that "Goering & Co." were, in fact, the men who had caused "Mrs. Jones'" troubles. Yet, only eighteen months before, an authoritative book had been published by a former Principal Secretary of the British Air Ministry, Mr. J. M. Spaight, C.B., C.B.E., for the express purpose of establishing the fact that the origin of the Blitz could be traced to a brain wave which came to British military experts as long before as 1936. Mr. Spaight made it clear that "Mrs. Jones" and everyone else who experienced the Blitz had endured it not as helpless and passive victims but as a result of "a splendid decision" to make them endure it which the British experts themselves had come to. This most remarkable book, *Bombing Vindicated*,[24] will be examined in detail later in these pages: it is only necessary here to note that its conclusions were accepted by all informed persons without question at the time of its publication in April, 1944. In fact, no attempt has been made since by anyone to contradict or refute its claims. The British public gladly accepted Mr. Spaight's contentions as a well-deserved compliment, but at the same time remained as firmly convinced as ever that "Goering & Co." were entirely responsible for the Blitz.

To social psychologists, also, Rhona Churchill's message to the *Daily Mail* is of the greatest interest because it provides a classic example of that system of thought which George Orwell has analysed in his startling book, *Nineteen Eighty-four*,[25] under the name, *doublethink*, the system which turns to practical account the philosophical proposition that truth is what best serves the interest of the community.

Now, clearly, in 1945 it was in the interests of the community that the belief should be maintained that the Blitz had been endured as a result of a splendid decision to endure it by the British public. It was desirable that "Mrs. Jones" should remain convinced that she had voluntarily elected to undergo this ordeal as a result of her intellectual conviction that only by undergoing it could Right and Justice triumph. Therefore, Mr. Spaight's facts were true and his contentions justified. But, at the same time, for the purposes of the trial at Nuremberg, it was desirable—and therefore true—that "Mrs. Jones" should be an entirely helpless victim. Not only was "Mrs. Jones" a symbol: "Goering & Co." were also symbols. They symbolized, of course, evil overcome. The trial at Nuremberg was not what James Whistler would have called an "Arrangement in Grey." It was an arrangement in black and white, jet Black and dazzling White. The Blitz was undeniably an evil.

For the purposes of the trial no limitations of the evil symbolized by "Goering & Co." could be admitted. It was, therefore, necessary—and, therefore, true—to maintain that "Goering & Co." were responsible for the Blitz, or as Rhona Churchill puts it, "they had caused 'Mrs. Jones' troubles."

Advance to Barbarism

Acceptance of the plans disclosed by Major Casson to Rhona Churchill would thus have imposed on the British public the task of believing simultaneously two contradictory and utterly irreconcilable assertions. This, in itself, however, would have been no obstacle to their acceptance since, during the war years, the British public had been carefully trained in *doublethink* as an essential part of the war effort. The gallant Major himself only apprehended difficulty from official red-tape in arranging details. Nevertheless, after that first triumphant announcement of these plans in the *Daily Mail*, nothing further was heard of them. No alternative plans were put forward by anyone. For a reason or reasons unknown, discussion of the matter ceased and the whole subject as quickly forgotten.

Although abruptly cut short and consigned to oblivion, this episode provides an invaluable starting point for inquiry. The mere fact that it was possible without causing general astonishment to announce the existence of plans to carry out such a purpose, indicates that the British public in 1945 was in a frame of mind which it is impossible to describe as judicial in any accepted sense of the word. But the underlying idea is so entirely in accord with primitive tradition that the possibility is at once suggested that it might have been inspired by what Dr. Jung would call a dim racial memory. Among primitive peoples of the present day and, by inference, among those of the remote past, an essential feature of the symbolic act of retribution was the formal mocking of the victim. Whether a modern tiger, a prehistoric cave bear, or a captive human enemy, the preliminary part of the ceremony consists of reminding the captive of his past power and strength, contrasted with his present helplessness, and followed by a description of the torments which he must shortly endure. It seems also to have been a general practice to leave this part of the ceremony to the women of the community, probably with the idea that this would add to the humiliation of the victim.

A ceremony of this kind, carried out in accordance with prehistoric ritual is clearly indicated in the story of the downfall of King Agag in the first Book of Samuel. In a few terse, vivid sentences we are told how the gallant Saul defeated and captured Agag but spared his life contrary to ancient tradition and to the outspoken annoyance of the prophet Samuel, who strongly disapproved of what has now come to be called "pampering".

Chapter I — Primeval Simplicity

By threats of revolution, Saul is reduced to admitting that he had sinned in not acting in accordance with traditional ferocity and, to prevent any possibility of the captive escaping death by what we should call a "wangle", Samuel undertook the role of judge-executioner himself, and "hewed Agag in pieces before the Lord in Gilgal"—clearly the form of execution called by the Chinese "death by a thousand and one cuts." Before this gruesome work was commenced, however, the fallen King of Amalek is recorded as observing to the prophet, "Surely the bitterness of death is past."

As it stands in the text this observation is utterly incomprehensible. Brought forth suddenly from honorable captivity as a prisoner of war to find himself arbitrarily condemned to a horrible and lingering death by a self-appointed judge-executioner, this is surely the last comment one would expect the unfortunate monarch to make to the bloodthirsty old prophet awaiting him, knife in hand.

If, however, we assume that the ancient ritual had been strictly followed—as a matter of course, and therefore not worth recording—the significance of Agag's remark becomes clear. For some hours previously, Agag would have stood tied to a stake surrounded by the daughters of Zion screaming insults, enlarging on his shortcomings, and describing with a wealth of oriental imagery the details of the treatment which he would shortly endure at the hands of the prophet. Even if this ordeal had only been a matter of hours—and not twelve months—it is easy to understand how Agag could have reached the state of mind of exclaiming to Samuel, "I realize what you are going to do with me, but for pity's sake begin it at once without any further waiting!"

Passing through space and time from Gilgal, in 1079 B.C., to Nuremberg, in A.D. 1945, it is interesting to speculate why ancient practice was not followed in this respect at Nuremberg. Perhaps it was feared that the presence of three housewives performing the symbolic act of gloating would prove embarrassing to the eminent members of the English Bar, who had been prevailed upon to take part in the proceedings on the assurance that these would partake strictly of a judicial character? Or perhaps the problem of deciding what exactly should be the role of these three females proved insoluble—should their participation be limited to one ladylike stare directed at each of the captives, or should certain sounds and

Advance to Barbarism

gestures, strictly in accordance with the most ancient tradition, be barred because these had become associated in the modern mind with the music hall? A suitable attire for the ceremony would also not have been easy to find—traditional attire might have suggested fancy dress or a Hawaiian chorus, while umbrellas and handbags would have been an obvious anachronism for participants in so ancient a ceremonial. Most probably, however, the idea was abandoned owing to the stage managers despairing of being able to find three females who, however carefully selected and trained, could be trusted to act the role decided upon in such unfamiliar surroundings. Women of whatever class would to-day find it difficult to assume to order the manners of their remote ancestresses and in which ever way their deportment failed—whether it was too theatrical or too wooden—the result would introduce an atmosphere of farce or even of burlesque which, beyond all else, it was desired to avoid so far as it was possible.

To summarize the conclusions which we may arrive at with regard to warfare in prehistoric times, we may say that, in essentials, it in no way differed markedly from warfare to-day. It will be found that neither in causes, conduct, nor results do fundamental distinctions exist.

With regard to causes, in prehistoric times warfare probably usually arose as a result of a change of climatic conditions causing a shifting of population from an area which had become uninhabitable to another already populated. In modern times, one of the commonest causes of war is an over-populated country seeking to find by violence an outlet for its surplus population.

With regard to conduct, the spirit in which warfare was conducted in prehistoric times was probably exactly similar to that in which warfare has come to be conducted during the last three decades.

In both, the main characteristics are directness, simplicity, and an entire lack of artificial restraints. In both, the only rule is to damage the enemy in any way physically possible. Above all, in neither will any trace be found of that perhaps arbitrary distinction between combatants and non-combatants, that is to say between the enemy's armed forces and the enemy's women and children. In both, democratic principles are followed: no privilege of immunity is granted to anyone—however weak and defenceless.

Chapter I — Primeval Simplicity

With regard to results, certain distinctions appear, but these cannot be termed fundamental. In prehistoric times, wars were wars of extermination: one killed all the enemies one could and took away or destroyed all enemy property upon which one could lay one's hands. In present-day warfare, to date at any rate, only distinguished enemy leaders are done to death, although it must not be forgotten that, in 1945, many quite minor German political leaders and officials were summarily murdered. The fact remains, however, that the bulk of the enemy population is not at present deliberately exterminated. Still, much the same result however is achieved when an industrial population is dealt with by dismantling and removing the factories on which it depends for subsistence, by cutting imports, forbidding exports, and leaving the population to starve. The consequence of this procedure will be realized if one can imagine the fate of the inhabitants of Birmingham or Coventry if all their factories were dismantled, and the essential machinery removed to some foreign land. Prehistoric warfare created a desert and called it peace — *solitudinem faciunt, pacem appellant* — warfare to-day creates a slum and calls that peace.

If the Second World War be taken as an example of contemporary warfare, the consequences to the vanquished are not merely the unintentional result of wholesale plundering inspired by simple greed and carried out regardless of the subsequent fate of the victims such as so frequently followed victorious wars in classical and mediaeval times. What the victors in 1945 intended should be the fate the vanquished was clearly set out in the infamous Morgenthau Plan, formulated by Henry Morgenthau, the Secretary of the U.S. Treasury, under the influence and guidance of a fellow Jew, Harry Dexter White (alias Weit), Assistant Secretary to the Treasury, and later unmasked as a Communist spy. This plan was accepted by President Roosevelt and the British Prime Minister, Winston Churchill, at the Quebec Conference on the 15th September, 1944.

Under this plan Germany was to be transformed into a pastoral country by the simple process of blowing up the mines and demolishing the factories. With regard to the existing population, numbering some seventy millions, mostly relying on industry for support, reliance was placed on starvation reducing their number to a level which could be supported by agricultural and pastoral pursuits.[26]

It was only owing to an unforeseen change in the political situation which began soon after the conclusion of hostilities, that the Morgenthau Plan was not carried out in its entirety. Still extensive sabotage operations, as distinct from systematic looting, were undertaken, for details of which the reader is referred to Freda Utley's memorable book, *Kostspielige Rache* (Hamburg, 1950, Nölke Verlag). An enormous amount of wanton destruction was systematically carried out and this campaign was only reluctantly abandoned when the "Cold War" broke out between the United States and the Soviet Union. The memory of this campaign of planned destruction has been obscured by the "Wirtschaftswunder" which to the amazement of everyone began in Western Germany some ten years after the conclusion of hostilities and brought unprecedented prosperity and wealth to a land which so shortly before had consisted mainly of ruins and slums. This astonishing outcome of defeat was of course in no way connected with the intentions of the victors, so dearly propounded by them at the Quebec Conference in September 1944. It was in fact in every way the exact opposite to what Morgenthau and his sinister satellite Harry Dexter White, alias Weit, had so carefully planned and intrigued to bring about.

In summation it may be said that prehistoric and contemporary warfare share the same essential characteristics. The main distinction between them is that in prehistoric warfare all prisoners are killed as a matter of course, while in contemporary warfare only the leaders are done to death. The employment of captive enemies for forced labour for the benefit of their captors and of course mass-deportations are characteristics of present-day warfare which have been adopted from warfare as it developed after mankind had formed settled communities, a development which will be considered in the next chapter.

Chapter 2 — Organized Warfare

Wars in prehistoric times were unplanned, unrelated, and probably rare happenings. They might be what we should term wars of aggression, but they were certainly not wars of planned aggression.

A community living somewhere in northern Europe, let us say on the shores of the Baltic, would find their hunting grounds becoming less and less able to support them owing to the gradual advance of icefields from Scandinavia. In desperation, they would trek southward in search of less rigorous conditions and would find such in, say, some river valley in southern France. The inhabitants of this valley would resent this trespass on their hunting grounds. A clash — quite unintended by both sides — would result. One side would be wiped out or scattered, and for the victors life would proceed as peaceably as of yore.

All this was changed when mankind began to practise agriculture and to form settled communities. In the first place, this permitted a great increase in the density of populations. Secondly, it led for the first time to the accumulation in one spot of stores of food and desirable articles, such as weapons, tools, pottery and jewellery — that is to say, wealth, or to use military nomenclature, loot.

From this early period at the dawn of history, wars of conquest must be dated. The hunters, and, after the domestication of animals, herdsmen and shepherds of the surrounding country, were inevitably filled with covetousness when they visited those early agricultural settlements in the valleys of the Nile and Euphrates.

It is no accident that the composer of the Ten Commandments included covetousness among those sins under the particular displeasure of the Almighty. Perhaps, as he wrote, he had just seen in the eyes of some half-savage visitors to his native city the feelings which they could not disguise when they contrasted the wealth and comfort which they saw around them with their own poverty and precarious mode of life.

From the earliest times, the settled agricultural communities along the Nile and Euphrates were subjected to periodic raids and invasions by the savage tribes inhabiting the desert or mountain hinterland. These alternated with preventive wars undertaken in self-protection by the agricultural communities. The news would come in that the tribes were planning another attack and, to forestall this attack, a punitive expedition would be sent forth.

Thus, as early as the times before the first dynasty in Egypt, and in the days of the Sumerian Kings of Southern Mesopotamia, two of the commonest varieties of warfare had arisen—the war of conquest undertaken to acquire the property of others, and the preventative war designed to frustrate an expected attack. These two varieties of warfare together form one of the two main divisions into which warfare may be divided, namely primary warfare, that is warfare between combatants at different stages of civilization. Most of the really important wars of history have been primary wars.

The second of these two main divisions of warfare may be labelled secondary warfare. Secondary wars are wars between combatants at the same or approximately the same stage of civilization. In this division are included all civil wars and, in fact, all the wars in this division are in essence only civil wars. Although often extremely protracted and sanguinary, their results are generally far less important than those of primary wars.

The question of primary and secondary wars will be dealt with in more detail later in this book. It is only necessary here to make clear the distinction between them since they are often confused. From the standpoint of world history, the political and cultural results of a war between states at different levels of civilization are always important, even though the bloodshed may be small. In wars between states having similar or identical civilizations, the institutional changes are often unimportant although the loss of life may be very great.

It is a curious fact that, although the civilized inhabitants of the Nile Valley lived under the constant menace of primary warfare in the shape of devastating invasions by the savage tribes of Syria, Nubia and the Libyan desert, they seemed to have indulged with enthusiasm in secondary warfare, that is to say, in minor wars between the various principalities into which Egypt, in pre-dynastic times, was divided. What an attack by savage nomadic tribes upon a civilized agricultural community could entail, we can ascertain from the glowing description of such an attack contained in the Book of Joshua. There we read that the Hebrews, when they invaded the land of Canaan slew "both man and woman, young and old, and ox and sheep and ass with the sword ... the young man and the virgin, the suckling also and the man with grey hairs."

In view of this ghastly performance in which the holy men of Israel evidently took great pride, it is certainly remarkable that the prophet Samuel should have had the effrontery to chide King Agag because "his sword had made women childless." One cannot help wondering why it did not occur to the King of Amalek to make the obvious retort. It may be in fact that he did so retort, but the Hebrew scribe in attendance did not think his words worthy of record. Alternatively, it must be remembered that Samuel had appointed himself judge-executioner and, therefore, it is likely that, in his role of judge, he ruled any defence or objection by the prisoner as *per se* irrelevant. We are required to assume that Samuel throughout acted on inspiration from On High which, if the case, satisfactorily explains how he managed to grasp the most novel discovery of recent international jurisprudence, namely, that the most assured method of securing a conviction is to permit the accuser also to act the part of judge.

Returning to the times when civilization first dawned in Egypt, we find evidence in plenty of primary wars in the shape of periodic invasions by various barbarous peoples alternating with preventive wars, leading to punitive expeditions penetrating far into Sinai, Nubia, and, even Syria. At the same time, secondary wars were frequent in the shape of civil wars between the native Egyptians.

The inhabitants of the lower Euphrates Valley were even more exposed to attack by barbarous neighbours than their contemporaries living in the Valley of the Nile. Precisely the same conditions existed there, however. Invasions were sometimes victoriously repulsed and at other times they led to massacres, devastation and the enslavement of the survivors. Invariably, however, the victorious nomads ended by adopting the civilization of the vanquished, so that in a few generations life proceeded very

Advance to Barbarism

much as before. Energetic rulers waged preventative wars and led punitive expeditions far into the mountains of Elam and Armenia and even into the plains of Syria. The ancient inhabitants of the Euphrates Valley were more warlike than the inhabitants of the Valley of the Nile and frequent civil wars occurred between the leading city states, Ur, Kish, Akkad, Lagash, Umma and Eridu.

One of the earliest records of those distant times which have survived is the famous Stele of the Vultures, now in the Louvre, dating from about 2700 B.C. On it King Eannatum of Lagash commemorates his defeat of the men of the neighbouring city of Umma. He proudly claims to have killed 3,500 of them and the stele takes its name from one of its panels portraying vultures partaking of the bodies of the slain. King Eannatum shows himself to have been a civilized opponent. The citizens of Umma were granted an honourable negotiated peace by which they ceded to Lagash certain fields lying between the two cities, the new frontier being marked by a newly dug ditch, safeguarded, no doubt, for all time by the invocation of the curses of the gods upon the head of anyone who should presume to vary this settlement by unilateral action. From the terms of peace it is clear that no demand for unconditional surrender was made; the gentlemanly Eannatum would no doubt have considered this bad form as between neighbours. A mock-trial of the leaders of the citizens of Umma apparently did not appeal to him: probably he would have found it an embarrassing farce. Eannatum was satisfied with the annexation of some fields, and the payment of an indemnity in grain by annual instalments. Realizing that the prosperity of his subjects was dependent on the prosperity of their neighbours, he did not insist that a valuable market for the goods of Lagash should either be destroyed or turned into a slum. Altogether, warfare in those remote times in Mesopotamia seems to have attained much the same stage of reason and restraint as warfare between civilized European Powers during the nineteenth century.

Such moderation would, of course, only have been practised in secondary wars; in wars that is to say between states of similar culture such as Lagash and Umma. It would not have been practised in primary warfare, even by so enlightened a monarch as King Eannatum, against the mountaineers of Elam or the nomads of Arabia. But, with regard even to primary warfare, an entirely new and potent factor was beginning to make its influence felt as a consequence of the introduction of agriculture and the establishment of settled communities.

To a hunting community, a prisoner of war is merely an extra mouth to feed. He is an encumbrance to be retained, if at all, only long enough to provide diversion by torturing him to death. Generally, prisoners taken in battle would be disposed of summarily with a stone club.[27]

But as soon as a state of civilization had been reached in which there were fields to be tilled, walls, temples, palaces and tombs to be built, and mines to be worked, a prisoner of war ceased to be merely an extra mouth to feed, and came to possess a definite economic value as a slave.

Professor M. R. Davie expresses the opinion that "the mitigation of war received its greatest impetus from the institution of slavery which put an end to slaughter and alleviated torture in order not to impair the efficiency of the captive as a worker."[28]

The direct, and still more the indirect, consequences of this innovation were far reaching. Portable loot ceased to be the only glittering prize, or, in fact, the chief of the glittering prizes, offered by a successful war. Punitive expeditions undertaken by civilized communities against barbarous neighbours ceased to be arduous and costly measures only to be undertaken to frustrate an attack, but became profitable slave collecting expeditions. In wars of conquest between civilized states, frequently the proceeds of the sale of prisoners of war was the most satisfactory feature of victory in the eyes of the victors. This was always the case in preventative wars, waged by civilized states to safeguard their frontiers — such, for example, as the wars of the Romans in Gaul and Germany.

An equally important consequence of the introduction of slavery was that it relieved a section of the community from the necessity of taking part in any form of manual labour. Thus arose, for the first time in the history of mankind, a leisured class not dependent on its own exertions for maintenance and with little to do except when called upon to take part in war. Since slaves performed manual labour, there gradually became implanted in this class the idea there was something degrading about taking part in any form of labour. In short, to work was equivalent to sinking to the level of a slave. The only form of work which a member of the leisured class could undertake without loss of dignity was work connected with warfare, since from such work slaves were naturally debarred. Once implanted, this idea continued to flourish unchallenged in influential circles in most countries down to 1918.

The establishment of a leisured class, the members of which could only justify their existence even to themselves by taking part in or preparing for war, gradually introduced an entirely new variety of warfare. Hitherto, wars had been waged as a means to an end — for example, to find additional territory for a surplus population, to collect loot, whether portable property or slaves, to extort tribute from a weaker neighbour, or to forestall an expected attack. But, from the rise of a leisured class onward there will be found numerous examples of wars in which such objects play quite a secondary role. These considerations served merely as excuses for war. Such wars, for want of a better term, may be labelled *wars for glory*.

Wars for glory are the natural expression of the need of a ruling military caste, cut off by an oppressive sense of its own dignity from taking part in activities open to civilians, to find an outlet for its energies. Brought up to regard military exploits as alone worthy of admiration, only in warfare can the members of such a caste prove themselves worthy of their ancestors and of the traditions of the service which is their sole pride. Only on the battlefield can they escape boredom and find fulfilment. In days when warfare was conducted in accordance with rules which controlled and kept within limits the destruction and suffering inseparable from warfare, this attitude of mind enjoyed considerable respect.

To regard warfare as a means of self-expression was formerly considered picturesque and romantic, whereas now it appears only grotesque or exasperating. It depended, of course, on the unquestioned belief that success in a war demonstrated the superior courage and general manliness of the victors, where as now, as Captain Liddell Hart has well pointed out, it merely demonstrates that the victors possess greater resources or superior technical equipment.[29] During the last decade, the idea of making war for honour or glory has become completely obsolete and may soon become incomprehensible. Perhaps it was always more readily associated with Don Quixote than with St. George. Still there may be something to be said for the obsolete view which

Chapter 2 — Organized Warfare

esteems fighting in order to prove oneself worthy of a tradition of which one is justly proud. It is certainly a higher motive than inducing others to fight so that by their fighting one can obtain possession of an oil field or eliminate a trade rival.

In the earliest times, no dominant military caste seems to have arisen in Mesopotamia. On one panel of the Stele of the Vultures above-mentioned, King Eannatum had himself portrayed at the head of a phalanx of heavy infantry armed with large square shields and copper-tipped spears. To fight in this formation would have required some peacetime training and leadership by officers who had studied the art of war.

Judged by their own accounts of their achievements, there was no lack in those days of able generals. Eannatum tells us that he waged successful wars from Elam in the East to Ur in the West. A later monarch, the famous Sargon of Akkad (2360-2305 B.C.), boasts that he conquered "all lands from the rising to the setting of the sun." One of the latter's successors, Naram-Sin (2280-2242 B.C.), considered his conquests entitled him to adopt the title of "King of the Four Quarters of the World." When Babylon rose to supremacy in Mesopotamia, a widespread Empire was consolidated by the famous Hammurabi (1728-1676 B.C.) and his successors.

But the inhabitants of lower Mesopotamia, whether of Sumerian or Semitic stock, were not primarily a military people. Their main concerns were agriculture and trade. To find a state created by and existing for successful warfare, we must pass over some nine hundred years which followed the reign of King Hammurabi, and come to the beginning of the ninth century B.C., when the Kings of Assyria had established themselves as the most powerful rulers in Western Asia.

The Empire of Assyria demands consideration in some detail as the outstanding example of a state which existed mainly by warfare for warfare. Other nations which have excelled in warfare have excelled also in other activities. The Romans were not only soldiers but statesmen, law makers and builders. The Normans produced great rulers, builders and ecclesiastics. The Germans of modern times have excelled in science, music and literature. But the Assyrians were interested in and were solely pre-eminent in warfare. Many of their rulers were, indeed, indefatigable builders of huge palaces, but they used the vast wall spaces chiefly for

Advance to Barbarism

bas-reliefs which depicted their glorious military achievements. Assyrian artists reached very high levels of achievement, but their work was usually limited to portraying battle and hunting scenes. Apart from the art of war and the science of imperial administration the Assyrians adopted almost entirely the civilization of their neighbours and kinsmen, especially the Babylonians, though they did make noteworthy contributions to sculpture and to literature, particularly in the compilation of the royal annals.[30]

Like Prussia in the seventeenth century, the greatness of Assyria can be traced to her original natural weakness. Of all the German states, Prussia had the longest and most exposed frontiers: to put a stop to repeated invasions by predatory neighbours, the Great Elector established a strong army, the victories of which laid the foundations of a great military tradition. In the same way, Assyria, in part a wide plain lying between the upper Euphrates and the upper Tigris, was exposed to attack by the mountain tribes of Kurdistan and Armenia to the East and North, to invasions by the powerful princes of Syria to the West, and to tribute-collecting expeditions by the kings of Babylon to the South.

For centuries, invasions and raids had been patiently endured, but at length there arose less patient rulers who began to lead more and more frequently punitive expeditions against the most troublesome of Assyria's enemies, the fierce mountain tribes of Armenia. In these petty wars in most difficult country, a standing army of veteran troops was gradually established which lay ready to hand when a ruler should arise capable of realizing the possibilities which the possession of such a weapon offered. It was perhaps inevitable that this army, originally created for defence, would sooner or later be employed for aggrandizement.

As a consequence of this employment, the fact has been long overlooked that Assyria performed a real service to the civilized nations of the Middle East by providing a barrier between them and the wild nomadic tribes of Central Asia. In recognition of this service, Professor A. T. Olmstead has preferred to call the Assyrians the "shepherd dogs of Mesopotamian civilization" rather than the "wolves" they have been called by earlier historians. From their contemporaries, however, the Assyrians received no such recognition. They were regarded with unqualified fear and hatred. Not until after three centuries of security from external foes, when the Sythian hordes broke through the Assyrian barrier and carried

Chapter 2 — Organized Warfare

fire and sword throughout the Middle East, was the fact realized that there could exist an even greater evil than subjection to the Assyrian yoke.

Perhaps the nearest parallel to the role of Assyria in the affairs of the ancient Middle East is the role of Prussia in the affairs of modern Europe. Relying on the possession of a splendid army originally created as the price of survival, the rulers of Prussia earned for their country general unpopularity and ill-will, not only among foreigners but among their German fellow countrymen, by their high-handed and aggressive dealings. As a consequence, few in Germany now care to remember that German unity was first achieved by Prussian efficiency, self-sacrifice and discipline; few in Western Europe yet realize the fact that only so long as the army created by the Prussian Kings existed could the possibility of attack and subjugation by enemies from the East be safely disregarded.

For many centuries the history of Assyria seems to have been that of a minor oriental state. At times, she rose to power under able rulers — such as Tiglath Pileser I (1120-1100 B.C.) — and then under feeble rulers sank into obscurity again.

The military potentialities of the Assyrian veterans were fully realized by Asshurnazirpal who ascended the throne of Nineveh in 883 B.C. He began by chastising in eight consecutive campaigns the mountaineers of the North with unprecedented severity. He then turned his attention westward and reached the Mediterranean where the rich Phoenician cities of Tyre and Sidon purchased safety by a payment of "gold, silver, tin and copper, woollen and linen garments and much strong timber from Lebanon." His successor, Shalmaneser, extended his dominions from Syria to the Persian Gulf, and for nearly three centuries we find an unbroken record of conquests which carried the arms of Assyria over the entire Middle East as far as the banks of the Nile.

Probably, no other state in world history can compare with Assyria as the incarnation of implacable, untiring, efficient militarism. In a later age, in the Greek state of Sparta, all the comforts and amenities of life were sacrificed for the benefit of military efficiency, but the Spartans made no contributions worth mentioning to the art of war. A Spartan army was only a large commando force composed of highly trained athletes fighting on foot and equipped like other Greek soldiers of the time. On the other hand, no other people until the twentieth century so revolutionized the technique and methods of warfare as did the Assyrians. An Assyrian army was composed of specialists in every branch of warfare. There were regiments of heavy infantry armed with shields and spears, regiments of archers and slingers, a chariot corps, and light cavalry. There was a corps of sappers skilled in undermining the walls of a town and in working the various types of movable battering rams and siege towers, some with six wheels and some with four. There was a pontoon section able to throw a bridge across a river or to supply bladders upon which, when inflated, the infantry was trained to cross a stream by swimming. There was a transport section with camels to carry baggage and even field kitchens for use during campaigns. Last, but not least, there were execution squads, expert in disposing of prisoners of war in a score of ingenious and painful ways.

When the records of the Assyrian warrior kings were first discovered and deciphered in the mid-nineteenth century, our worthy Victorian forefathers were filled with uncomprehending horror when they read the awesome details of atrocities so proudly described therein. In their eyes, Asshurnazirpal and his successors on the throne of Assyria appeared as sadistic monsters, the subjects of a pathological obsession. But we, more fortunately placed to understand their mental processes, can see that they might have given a plausible explanation of their conduct. One reason why the Assyrians so horrified readers of their history a century ago was that less was then known about the military excesses and massacres of their predecessors and contemporaries

When the atomic bomb was dropped on Hiroshima in 1945, whereby a civilian population of some 70,000 was wiped out, it was explained that this act in fact saved the lives of many soldiers, who would otherwise have been sacrificed in costly landings on the Japanese mainland. Justification along the same lines can be urged with regard to the British terror bombing campaign waged against Germany from after the adoption of the Lindemann Plan in March 1942 until the end of hostilities in May 1945, with the exception only of the bombing of Dresden in February, 1945, which took place after victory had become certain and the war had ceased to be a military operation. Could not King Asshurnazirpal have said in reply to his critics: "When I impaled, blinded, flayed alive, burned and otherwise tortured to death my prisoners, the terror of my glorious name spread through the surrounding lands. As a result, valuable human life was saved. Thereafter, when I desired to capture a city, my gallant troops had no longer to storm it, suffering cruel losses; since the inhabitants came forth straightway to kiss the dust at my feet. Thereby the precious lives of my brave soldiers were spared."

That there is some substance in this argument cannot be denied. It fails, however, to account for the fact that Asshurnazirpal and other monarchs preferred bas-reliefs portraying these horrors to most other decorations for the walls of their palaces. Evidently, therefore, they must have taken pleasure in being reminded of them. It is upon this predilection that the charge of sadism can be based, and not upon their method of dealing with prisoners of war in itself, which was only the traditional method inherited from their prehistoric forefathers, carried out by the Assyrians on a larger scale and in a more spectacular manner. Many peoples, it is true, have dealt with captive enemies in accordance with this venerable tradition both in ancient and modern times. The reputation of the Red Indians of North America is particularly black in this respect, although some have contended that they only adopted such practices, along with warlike and predatory habits, from the European settlers. This charitable view is, however, at variance with the evidence of Samuel de Champlain, one of the earliest French pioneers in Canada, who professes to have been horrified by the treatment meted out to some Iroquois prisoners by the Huron allies of the French after a skirmish in which, thanks to the firearms of Champlain and his men, the Hurons were successful. It speaks volumes for the skill and ingenuity of untutored savages that they should have been able to shock a Christian European of the sixteenth century.

Until restrained by more civilized or at any rate more powerful neighbours professing different and perhaps more artificial standards of conduct, most savage peoples have observed the ancient traditional practice in their dealing with enemies taken captive in war. Among some peoples an interesting variation of traditional practice is met with. The actual work of disposing of prisoners is handed over to the women, the men merely acting as spectators. The authorities differ as to whether this custom was due in the first place to masculine indolence, to the longer persistence of malice in the female mind, or to recognition of the superior

Advance to Barbarism

dexterity of the feminine hand in achieving artistic results.[31] At all events it is certain that prisoners in the hands of the Apaches of Arizona, of many nomad tribes of Arabia and the Sahara, or of the Druses of Syria have never had much occasion for thankfulness that their captors had adopted this strange custom.[32]

There is no trace that any such custom existed among the Assyrians. We have no evidence that a woman ever secured admission to the military execution squads. There seem to have been in the Assyrian army no regiments of lady warriors such as were a dread feature of the army of old Dahomey, the powerful West African state founded in the early 18th century. In the latter native African kingdom, which in some respects bore a crude resemblance to Assyria, there existed a crack corps of virgin warriors, whose virginity, it may be added, was safeguarded by the infliction of a horrible death in the case of moral lapses. Dahomey also provided a novel variation with regard to the treatment of prisoners of war. The Assyrians, as we have seen, executed enemy leaders publicly in various ingenious ways and enslaved the survivors. The negro kings of Dahomey trained their schoolboy subjects in the use of weapons and accustomed them to the sight of bloodshed by handing prisoners of war over to them for execution.

Original variation from accepted practice did not appeal to the Assyrians. Strictly practical and conservative in outlook, they believed that the activities of women should be limited to bearing future warriors, to solacing the leave of warriors at home from the various fronts, and to taking part with due enthusiasm in the annual "V Day" rejoicings. Executions of prisoners of war, they considered, should be carried out with proper pomp and ceremony without regard to utilitarian considerations unfitting to the solemnity of the occasion. Another item which does credit to the Assyrians is that their victory massacres were restricted mainly to males. There was little of the indiscriminate massacring of women and children—even young babies—which was so common among many ancient oriental peoples.

The collection of trophies has, in all ages, exercised a singular fascination over the military mind. After the war of 1870, every public square in Germany had its display of weapons captured at Wörth, Sedan or Metz; similarly, after 1918, every town and village in Great Britain had pieces of artillery prominently displayed as mementoes of the "War-to-end-war"—from which disfigurements they were, by the irony of fate, only rescued by another war following shortly which made it necessary to melt down these mementoes for munitions.

As one might expect, the Assyrians had a passion for trophies, a passion no doubt inherited from their prehistoric forefathers. Bulky chattels such as cannon not being available, savages are limited to a twofold choice. Most savages, peoples as widely separated as the Maoris of New Zealand, the Indians of northern Mexico and the Negroes of Dahomey, have selected the human skull as the memento or symbol of victory. The weapons of a primitive enemy may be stolen or reproduced, but an enemy's skull is conclusive proof of his defeat. While warfare remained on a small scale, skulls of deceased enemies served only for display: individual heroes erected them on poles before their front doors. But when slaughter on a more extensive scale began, more elaborate collections became possible. In popular belief the credit has been given to the medieval Tartar Conqueror, Tamerlane, for originating the idea of erecting pyramids composed of the skulls of fallen enemies. But, more than two thousand years before the days of Tamerlane, we find the Assyrians proudly erecting pyramids of skulls. Thus King Tiglath Pileser records that while campaigning "by the shores of the Upper Sea" (probably the Black Sea), he captured a city and "piled high the heads of the inhabitants before the gates thereof." The only credit for originality which can justly be given to Tamerlane is that he erected pyramids of skulls of outstanding size—or at least such was the firm opinion of his contemporaries.

As an alternative to collecting heads, some savage peoples have preferred to collect the private parts of their enemies. In modern times this predilection has been displayed by the Sumalis and Gallas of Northern Africa, certain tribes of Arabia and Syria, and the Kaffirs of South Africa, not forgetting, of course, our gallant allies in the last war, the Abyssinians. The immoderate gratification of this taste after their great victory of Adowa over the Italians in 1896 aroused such intense horror throughout Italy that some forty years later it greatly facilitated Benito Mussolini's efforts to rouse his countrymen to undertake the reconquest of Abyssinia. Tastes vary in this as in so many other matters, and for reasons unknown the Assyrians seem to have limited themselves to skull collecting.

Advance to Barbarism

The Assyrians would have had nothing to learn from the most up-to-date technique with regard to despoiling a vanquished country and to insuring that it should be open to attack for the future. A Reparations Commission and a Disarmament Commission both military and industrial, must have functioned as permanent state departments. One of the most interesting of the bas-reliefs now in the British Museum shows in the background the walls of a captured city being demolished with pick and spade by Assyrian sappers lest they should become a menace to Assyrian security. In the foreground is shown a procession of soldiers in military formation marching along a path by the bank of a stream, each man carrying some article of plunder. Contrasted with this unit, clearly acting under the orders of the Reparations Commission, is a straggling line also composed of soldiers laden with plunder, but in this case, scampering along through a wood. The small size of the figures and their hurried unobtrusive progress screened by trees, obviously symbolizes the appropriation of the goods of the vanquished by individual plunderers, doubtful of the full approval of the authorities, but relying upon the repeated official exhortations not to pamper the vanquished. The whole, masterly in composition and execution, must be regarded as the earliest example of the recruiting poster.

With regard to warfare in all its varied aspects, the Assyrians maintained a rigid sense of proportion; they never permitted one aspect to become so exaggerated as to distort the whole. A religious people, they never sacked a city nor executed an enemy war criminal without piously associating God with the deed and, in all circumstances, they acted strictly in accordance with traditional religious practice; on the other hand, they never allowed their warlike activities to become subservient to religion like the Aztecs of Mexico whose wars were fought mainly for the purpose of making prisoners for use as human sacrifices in honour of their god, Huitzilopochtli. The Assyrians felt a proper pride in collecting military trophies and carefully recorded the erection of any pyramid of skulls of outstanding size but they never, like the Dyaks of Borneo, permitted warfare to degenerate into simple head-hunting. No doubt, the Assyrians derived keen satisfaction from the gruesome rites of their "V Days", but such remained to them merely an enjoyable ceremony fitly marking the end of a campaign. A very different attitude this, for example, from the

Chapter 2 — Organized Warfare

attitude of the Iroquois of North America to whom a campaign was but an irksome, if necessary, preliminary to the customary orgy round the torture stake. To the Assyrians, religion, the collecting instinct, and even the gratification of sadistic impulses remained subsidiary emotions, adorning warfare but in no way essential to its conduct. To them, as in the opinion of Nietzsche, a good war was its own justification.

No practice of the Assyrians can be of greater interest to the present generation than their method of dealing with the survivors of a vanquished population by mass-deportation. Whether the Assyrians originated this practice is not known with certainty, but they certainly adopted it as a routine procedure and carried it out on a scale unprecedented until the present day.

In defence of the Assyrians, it is only fair to point out that there are fundamental differences between the mass-deportations carried out by them and those of recent times. In the first place, the intent in the two cases was quite different. The purpose of the Assyrian rulers was to create a homogeneous population and, to this end, it was their custom to transfer the surviving population of a recently conquered country to some distant part of the empire, at the same time filling their vacant places with the inhabitants of another conquered district intermingled with voluntary settlers from Assyria itself, so as to provide the new population with a loyal core. Such shiftings of population can better be termed mass-transfers. They are obviously totally different from recent mass-deportations which served the simple twofold purpose of wreaking vengeance on the outlying members of a vanquished race by robbing them of all they possessed.

Again, the methods adopted in the two cases are totally different. The evidence of the Assyrian bas-reliefs indicates that the people forcibly transferred from one country to another were allowed to take with them to their new homes their portable property and cattle. Brutality may not have been lacking, but it would not have had official approval since the intention was that the peoples transferred and their descendants should ultimately become loyal subjects and supporters of the King of Assyria. There can be no real comparison between this procedure, drastic though it may have been, and the contemporary practice of collecting droves of defenceless persons, men, women, and children, to the number of several millions, against whom no personal charge

Advance to Barbarism

of any kind is made (any so charged would now be summarily murdered), selected merely because their native language is the same as that of the inhabitants of the state over the border which happens to have been defeated in a war, robbing them of all they possess, and then dumping them in a strange country already overcrowded and short of food, there to live or die as fate might decree. Here in our day the motive of mass-deportations is mainly greed, combined with a desire for revenge on the vanquished state, if only, as it were, by proxy.

A further point may be urged in extenuation of the Assyrians. The latter were generally, dealing with semi-nomadic peoples, or peoples who had only recently acquired by conquest the lands from which they were forcibly deported. The injustice and suffering involved must, in consequence, have been far less than in such mass-deportations as those recently carried out by the Czechs and Poles in the case of the inhabitants of Pomerania, Silesia, and the Sudetenland, who were expelled from lands which their ancestors had occupied for many centuries. Probably the mass transfers of the Assyrians generally amounted to little more than the rounding up of the primitive agriculturists, herdsmen, and shepherds of a thinly-populated country and transferring them to a distant but equally desirable country made vacant for their reception. There is no real comparison between this and the expulsion, for example, of the population of Silesia, a population whose right consisted of undisturbed possession since the days when Plantagenet Kings ruled England and the greater part of France, when Moscow was the capital of a small principality paying tribute to the Tartar Khans, and only Red Indians wandered where New York was long after to be built. The three million despoiled victims of the Sudetenland could claim an even longer possessory title since their ancestors were in occupation of this corner of Bohemia before the first Anglo-Saxon pirates landed in England and long before the rest of Bohemia was occupied by the Czechs.

For three centuries, the Assyrian shadow lay like a dark cloud over all Western Asia. Striking first in one direction and then in another, their armies, splendidly organised and equipped, never found an enemy able to resist them in the open field when the odds were anything like equal. In turn, they overthrew the famous chariotry of Syria, the heavy infantry of Babylonia, and the archers of Egypt. Widespread revolts were crushed and powerful alliances shattered. In 645 B.C., King Asshurbanipal, after a victorious campaign in which the powerful state of Elam was crushed and systematically devastated, celebrated a triumph of particular splendour. Three captive kings walked in chains behind his chariot. It must have seemed on that proud "V Day" that the Assyrian Empire might well endure for ever.

Within less than forty years of that day the Assyrian Empire was blotted out so completely that it soon became nothing but a hazy memory kept alive only by mention in the Jewish scriptures and stray references preserved in the writings of later Greek authors. It was not until the mid-nineteenth century when the records of the Assyrian Kings were discovered and deciphered, that their achievements became more than legendary.

The comparison has often been made between the Assyrian Empire and the Second Reich founded by Bismarck. Such comparisons may not be odious, but they are often difficult to establish. Any such comparison is hardly reconcilable with the fact that the Reich, after its foundation in 1871, preserved unbroken peace with its neighbours until 1914, a period of forty-three years period during which these neighbours all under took aggressive wars, Great Britain in Egypt and South Africa, France in Tunis and Indo-China, Russia in the Balkans against Turkey and in Manchuria against Japan, the United States against Spain, and even Italy against Turkey in Tripoli. On the other hand, in its swift and dramatic downfall at least, the Assyrian Empire certainly offers some scope for comparison with the Third Reich established by Adolf Hitler.

When, in 645 B.C., King Ashhurbanipal celebrated the last great "V Day" of Assyrian arms, the military strength of the Empire, seemingly unshakable, was spread out over a vast area from the Nile to the mountains of modern Persia. Suddenly, without warning, there issued from the far and unknown North one of those great hordes of nomads such as in historic times the plains of Eurasia have periodically sent forth. This horde of nomads, known to their victims as Sythians, was no less formidable than the similar hordes of Huns, Magyars, Mongols, Tartars, and Turks destined to follow them. They swept in an irresistible flood over the entire Middle East as far as the borders of Egypt. Resistance in the field was overwhelmed by weight of numbers: only strongly

Advance to Barbarism

fortified cities escaped devastation and pillage. Then, after a decade of blood and rapine, the Sythians withdrew as suddenly and mysteriously as they had appeared.

All the states of Western Asia suffered from this visitation, but the Assyrian Empire, the largest and most complex political structure of the time, was shaken to its foundations. It was not the practice of the Assyrian High Command to record disasters and we have no details of the fate of the Assyrian armies which tried to withstand in battle the rush of the wild horsemen of the steppes. Only the great cities were safe behind their walls: the countryside was devastated. Immediately the wave of barbarians had withdrawn laden with plunder to their northern homes, the peoples of the Middle East joined together to end the Assyrian menace for ever.

The United Nations of the 7th century B.C. were united only in their hatred of the Assyrians. We may be sure that the shattered remnants of the Assyrian army resisted to the last and, when the odds against them were not too fantastic, continued to win splendid but profitless victories. Finally, however, only the capital, Nineveh, held out behind the vast and scientifically planned fortifications erected by King Sennacherib. After a long siege, the Medes broke into the doomed city in August, 612 B.C., and the last Assyrian King in despair heaped up his treasures in one vast funeral pile and perished in the blaze with his wives, chief officers of state, and the surviving generals of his army.

We may not feel surprised, perhaps, that, having thus triumphed, the United Nations immediately turned upon each other. The Medes attacked the Lydians, and the Egyptians came into conflict with the Babylonians. The latter, under Nebuchadnezzar, defeated the Egyptians and established a short-lived empire which faithfully reproduced all the characteristic features of Assyrian rule—wars of conquest, mass deportations, massacres and mutilations, as the Second Book of Kings bears eloquent witness. Within a few decades, the Babylonians had been conquered by the Medes, who, in their turn, were overthrown by the Persians under Cyrus, who established an empire of unprecedented extent which realized in essentials the aims towards which the later Assyrian Kings had been striving.

Thus was swiftly and utterly blotted out the great Assyrian Empire, leaving to our Victorian forefathers a memory

Chapter 2 — Organized Warfare

which to them seemed to symbolize bestial force, cold-blooded ferocity, and ruthlessness systematized. We, however, with our wider experience of such matters, should be ready to grant to the Assyrians the credit of having expressed warfare in terms which, for simplicity and purity, have never been surpassed. In their wars may be found all the essentials of warfare without a trace of scruples or restraints. The rules and restrictions by which warfare later became entangled and cramped would have seemed to the generals of King Asshurbanipal just as artificial and vexatious as they now seem to an air marshal of to-day.

It is not only because the Assyrians were a people chiefly interested in war, but because they were so rigidly orthodox and conventional in their attitude to, and dealings with, anything connected with war which makes a study of them almost sufficient in itself for a student of warfare. Until the present generation, the course of wars in modern times has been influenced by many extraneous influences, moral, ethical and religious. The Assyrians acknowledged the existence of little except military considerations. If they were extreme, it was only because they carried to its furthest limits conventional military practice. One feels that, if one knew all there was to know about the Assyrians, there would remain nothing essential to learn about the nature of warfare.

Chapter 3 — Europe's Civil Wars

As pointed out in the last chapter, the first great step towards the amelioration of the cruelties and crudities of primitive warfare arose from the institution of slavery which bestowed on prisoners taken in war an economic value to their captors as slaves. What produced the next important step forward in this direction?

The answer seems obvious. Suppose a stranger to this planet were first asked to peruse the Sermon on the Mount and was then informed that a religion professing to be based on its teaching was within three centuries accepted as a state religion by the most civilized section of mankind. Would not this stranger immediately decide that the effect of this must have been completely to transform the conduct of war if not, as between Christians at any rate, to abolish war altogether?

A priori this is certainly what might reasonably be expected. Still, as we all know, after nearly two thousand years, Christianity has not abolished war, neither has Christianity to any very marked extent, even as between Christians, transformed it. To what extent and at what date it began to exercise an ameliorating influence is a matter of dispute. It is also a matter of dispute to what extent it was a case of cause and effect that its acceptance by the rulers and peoples of the Roman Empire and the decline and fall of the Roman Empire were concurrent events. Be this as it may, the dissolution of the Roman Empire was followed by the so-called Dark Ages, during which period warfare was conducted with the most primitive savagery, although Christianity was professed in the various barbarian kingdoms into which Western Europe became divided.

If it be complained that the bloody doings of the Frankish and Gothic kings cannot fairly be taken as representative of Christian conduct, in general, or of warfare, in particular, we can

Chapter 3 — Europe's Civil Wars

turn to the Byzantine Empirewhere a Christianized variety of Roman civilization survived down to the close of the Middle Ages. The result, it is to be feared, will be disappointing. The Byzantine emperors conducted their wars strictly in accordance with ancient oriental tradition and, in spite of the fact that most of them were devout Christians, little distinction can be detected except by the eye of faith between their methods and those of the warrior kings of Assyriaa thousand years before. The principal claim to fame of one of the most successful rulers of the Byzantine Empire, Basil the Bulgar-Slayer, is that he made it a practice in his campaigns with the Bulgarians to put out the eyes of his prisoners, on one occasion to the number of 15,000.

It is also an unfortunate fact, impossible to deny, that those European wars which have been waged with special ferocity have been those waged in the name of religion. As an early example, the famous Albigensian Crusade of 1209, inspired and directed by one of the greatest of the Popes, Innocent III, to root out heresy in southern France, may be cited.

A contemporary estimate puts the total number of those who perished at 500,000. Exact statistics are lacking, however, since the Crusaders, immersed in their pious labours, had probably little more idea of the number of persons whom they had done to death than have the crew of a modern bombing unit returning from an operational flight over a densely populated residential area. At Béziers, the entire population, to the number of some 20,000, men, women and children were slaughtered "by reason of God's wrath wondrously kindled against it." After the capture of Minerve, in place of the usual massacre, 140 leading heretics were burnt together in one huge bonfire.

The Thirty Years War (1618-1648) supplies a late example of warfare between Christians. Reliable, if incomplete, statistics are available in this instance, and it is generally agreed that, as a result of this protracted struggle, one-third of the population of Central Europe perished. It has been calculated the population of Bohemia was reduced from three millions to 800,000. At the beginning of the war, the important city of Augsburghad 70,000 inhabitants and at the end only 18,000.

For more than a generation after the war, one-third of the arable land in North Germany remained uncultivated. Such appalling massacres as that of Magdeburg in 1631[31] will bear

Advance to Barbarism

comparison with similar happenings in ancient or modern times. In brief, the preference expressed by the Emperor Ferdinand to rule over a desert rather than a country filled with heretics, was very substantially realized. The evidence of sixteen centuries thus clearly demonstrates that, whatever consequences might have been expected in theory, the acceptance of Christianity had no perceptible practical influence in mitigating the barbarous conduct of war. On the other hand it is a fact that what, for want of a better term, is called *"civilized warfare"* originated in Europe, and Christianity is, and for many centuries has been, the religion of Europeans.

It cannot be too strongly stressed that what is called "civilized warfare" is a European product and has never been practised outside Europe or in countries not under European influence. In the East, warfare continued to be conducted precisely as the Assyrians conducted their wars. When Nadir Shah invaded India, in 1739, he acted exactly as Asshurbanipal acted when he invaded Elam. When the Turks set about repressing the revolt of the Greeks in 1821, or the revolt of the Bulgarians in 1876, they applied exactly the same methods as the Persians of Darius' time would have applied in the same circumstances.

Civilized warfare may, therefore, be defined as warfare conducted in accordance with certain rules and restrictions subject to which the nations of Europe became accustomed to wage their wars with each other. When they had achieved military predominance, they also insisted that these rules and restrictions should be observed by non-European States in wars with Europeans.

It certainly requires explanation why the peoples of Europe, alone among the peoples of the earth, should gradually have evolved a code of conduct governing the waging of warfare, a code of conduct which, most ancient and many modern authorities agree, is totally contrary to the whole spirit of war. Why could not they have been content to wage war in the good old simple way, as their forefathers had waged it, and with which so many great military peoples of other Continents have remained content?

To answer this question regard must be had to the unique political development of Europe. The following is a simple statement of facts, many of which have never been wholly or even partly explained.

Chapter 3 — Europe's Civil Wars

At the time of the birth of Christ, there existed on the largest continuous land surface of the globe (divided by geographers into the continents of Europe, Asia and Africa) three main centres of settled population, living independently of each other, each of which had recently crystallized into an empire. The first, known as the Roman Empire, centred round that unique geographical feature known as the Mediterranean Sea and comprised some hundred million inhabitants. The second great centre of population was centred in the valleys of the Indus and the Ganges in Northern India. No statistics have survived from which the number of its inhabitants can be estimated, but this area is very large and has always been extremely fertile, so it may be safely assumed that its population was comparable to that of the Roman Empire and to that of the third great centre of population situated far away to the East in the valley of the Yellow River in Northern China, which, as statistics show, even at that early date, numbered not less than sixty millions.

The political development of these three main centres of population was curiously different. In India, the Empire known as the Mauryan Empire, established in the third century B.C., and reaching its zenith under the famous Buddhist Emperor, Asoka (264 to 228 B.C.), soon dissolved into a number of conflicting fragments. It had no successor for some eighteen hundred years when the Mogul Empire was founded by the Mongol conqueror, Barbar. This empire also dissolved within a century, leaving India the prey of invaders from Europe, of whom the English, after a hard struggle with the French, ultimately achieved supremacy.

In China, on the other hand, the Han Dynasty (202 B.C. to A.D. 220), after flourishing for four hundred years, broke up approximately at the same time as the contemporary Roman Empire. After a period of civil war and anarchy, it was succeeded by the T'ang Dynasty, which flourished for three hundred years. From the earliest times to the present day, Chinese history has consisted of a succession of long periods of strong central government, separated by relatively short periods of disunity and internal disorder. In 1933, Adolf Hitler's slogan—"Ein Volk, ein Reich, ein Führer"—came as a novel and stirring appeal to the peoples of Central Europe. To the Chinese, from the beginning of their long history, the proposition "One people, one empire, one emperor" seemed self-evident, although they frankly recognised

Advance to Barbarism

that incursions by barbarians or the shortcomings of an individual emperor might now and then bring about an unwelcome but temporary interlude of disorder. As a consequence, in China, unity has been regarded as a normal and natural condition, subject only to temporary periodic lapses into anarchy, whereas, in India, long and bitter experience has accustomed the people to look upon anarchy as normal.

Thus, when Indian unity was re-established by the Mogul emperors it was regarded as a unique achievement, Indian unity under the Buddhist Emperors having passed away so long before that it had become merely a dim memory of the learned. In a nutshell, the settled populations of both India and China early crystallized into strong centralized empires: but, whereas, in the case of China, the state thus formed has survived apart from temporary eclipses to the present day, in India, this crystallization had but a brief existence and amorphous political conditions have prevailed, except for relatively short periods.

In Europe political development took a third and entirely different course. As in India and China and at approximately the same time, Europe (or that part of it bordering on the Mediterranean) crystallized into a strong centralized state. Like the Mauryan Empire in India and the Han Empire in China, the Roman Empire declined and broke up. But unlike the Han Empire, the Roman Empire was never restored. Its downfall was final. And, unlike the case of India, amorphous political conditions did not continue indefinitely. The peoples of Europe soon began to crystallize into small independent states, each generally (but not always) based on a more or less clearly defined geographical area. This local crystallization is the distinctive characteristic of the political development of Europe. Europeans have for so long been accustomed to this local crystallization that they find it hard to realize what an extraordinary development it is. In India, until the establishment of British supremacy, civil wars went on without cessation, but they were haphazard and disconnected happenings.

One local ruler or another, abler or more ambitious than his neighbours, would establish his authority over an area of greater or lesser extent, and his successors would maintain the state so formed for several generations. When, however, they were ultimately overcome, the subjects of this state had never come to regard this area as their "motherland". Amid general

Chapter 3 — Europe's Civil Wars

indifference, it would become divided up or merged in another equally arbitrarily formed area, and its exact boundaries would soon be forgotten. Men fought for the love of fighting, from personal ambition, for loot, or from loyalty to a certain leader, family or clan, but never for the glory or aggrandizement of a geographical area personified as a distinct entity such as Britannia, La France, or Germania. Even such a well-marked geographical area as the Punjab, "the Land of the Five Rivers," never developed "a national consciousness."

Similarly, in China, the world has never been troubled by the conflicting territorial ambitions of Sze-chwan and Kweichow, the rights and wrongs of brave little Honan, or the integrity of the frontiers of Shan-tung. No foreign prime minister has ever been moved to acclaim Honan as "sublime in the jaws of peril" and no disinterested foreign ecclesiastic has ever been inspired to pray, even for the briefest period, for Hu-peh as "a beacon of religious freedom."

In Europe, on the other hand, such states, with as little geographical justification as Portugal and Holland, have arisen and survived with practically unchanged frontiers for centuries. In Switzerland, three distinct races, speaking three distinct languages, have long come to consider themselves "a nation," while, more remarkable still, the artificial union, so late as 1830, of the Flemings, speaking a dialect of Dutch, and the French-speaking Walloons, has blossomed forth into the national consciousness of Belgium.

It is agreed that the Walloon-Fleming compound, under the name of Belgians, "joined the European family of Nations" in 1850. There is no agreement, however, as to precisely what is a nation in the special sense it has come to mean in Europe. "Nationalism," admits Sir John Marriott, "is a singularly elusive term." He proceeds to define it as "the sentiment which binds together a body of people who have certain things in common and not infrequently induces antagonism between one body of persons so connected and another." This antagonism, often violent and always quite irrational, is generally its most outstanding characteristic. Professor Alfred E. Zimmern insists that it is always "related to a definite home country." But this "home country" need have no natural boundaries, he admits, and may indeed be inhabited by foreigners.

Advance to Barbarism

Although enjoying in essentials the same civilization and professing the same religion, the peoples of Europe have gradually lost their sense of unity inherited from the days of the Roman Empire. This sense of unity, so strong in China, has been replaced by "national consciousness" linked with geographical areas. Once national consciousness had developed in England, France, and elsewhere, civil wars ceased to be haphazard and disconnected happenings. Defeats had to be avenged while victories inspired ambitions to achieve even greater victories. In this way, whatever its result might be, each war paved the way to the next.

Unlike their contemporaries in India and China, the inhabitants of Europe were able to indulge in civil wars with each other with relative impunity. In China, any weakening of the central government through internal disorder was inevitably followed by invasion by the wild nomadic peoples ever waiting beyond the Great Wall for an opportunity to attack. In India, the penalty for continual civil war was a succession of invasions through the Himalayan Passes by the warlike peoples of Central Asia, each of which resulted in orgies of slaughter and rapine. It was not until 1945, however, that the inhabitants of Europe paid the natural penalty for civil war. Only three times after the downfall of the Roman Empire had Europe been menaced by primary warfare on a grand scale. Each time, the danger was averted, not so much through the efforts of Europeans themselves as by good fortune.

The first occasion was at the close of the Dark Ages, when Europe was threatened by invasion and conquest by the Saracens. Spain was conquered and France invaded, but the Saracens were repulsed at Poitiers by Charles Martel, and, more as a result of dissensions among the Saracens themselves than as a consequence of this setback, the danger passed.

The second occasion was in the middle of the thirteenth century, at the very time when European medieval civilization had reached its peak. This time, the danger came from the formidable military machine that the great Mongol conqueror, Genghis Khan, had recently created out of the wild horsemen of the Steppes and with which he had overthrown, in turn, the great Empires of China and Persia. After his death, his grandson, Batu, set forth in 1237 with a great army, mainly composed of mounted archers, but supported by a corps of Chinese engineers, equipped with portable catapults for hurling not only great stones but masses

Chapter 3 — Europe's Civil Wars

of flaming naphtha, material for creating artificial smoke screens, and probably, gunpowder for use in mines in siege work. Against this highly-organized barbarian host, the peoples of Europe could put in the field only feudal armies, individually brave but totally without discipline. In addition, they were, as usual, divided amongst themselves by a dozen petty civil wars, and, in particular, by the long-drawn-out conflict between the Holy Roman Emperor and the Pope which had just reached a climax.

The great campaign of 1241-1242 is of particular interest at the present time since it was fought over precisely the same area as the recent campaign of 1944-1945 between the *Wehrmacht* and the Red Army, was aimed at the same objectives, and came to rest approximately on a line along which now runs the so-called "Iron Curtain" that marks the present boundary between Europe and Asia. It provides also a classic example of primary warfare, the issue at stake being whether the extremely complex Christian medieval civilisation should be replaced by the simple nomadic culture of an Asiatic khanate. Upon the one side were the clansmen of High Asia, wonderful horsemen and splendid archers but otherwise illiterate barbarians, and upon the other the civilization that had already produced such men as Hildebrand and Innocent III, Frederick II and St. Louis, Dante and St. Francis of Assisi, and from which the civilization of the Modern World was destined to evolve.

The Mongol plan of campaign was Napoleonic in conception, design and execution. First, the powerful Russian principalities were crushed in one great battle and Kiev was razed to the ground. Then, the chivalry of Germany and Poland under the Duke of Silesia, including a strong contingent of the famous Teutonic Knights under their Grand Master himself, was annihilated at Liegnitz, chiefly through the scientific use of an artificial smoke screen throwing the Christian chivalry into confusion. Breslau, which held out so heroically seven hundred years later against the Red Army, was taken and sacked. Next, another wing of the Mongol host overthrew a great crusading army with a backbone of veteran Knights Templars under the King of Hungary near Tokay on the Sayo River. Like the Teutonic Knights, the Knights Templars, mostly French, perished to a man on the field, but in vain. Buda was stormed and sacked. City after city was captured and their inhabitants methodically massacred.

Advance to Barbarism

Advanced units of the invaders had reached Neustadt on the Danube and had penetrated to the Adriatic within a day's march of Venice, when the death of the Great Khan in far off Karakoram on the edge of the Gobi Desert caused the recall of the Mongol armies. Thus was European civilization saved from destruction before the gravity of the peril had become generally known. "There can be no doubt," writes Harold Lamb, "that the Mongols could have destroyed the Emperor Frederick and his armies and the French chivalry led by the hapless St. Louis might have fared no better. The European monarchs had proved themselves incapable of acting together. The Europeans had shown themselves helpless before the manoeuvring of the Mongol cavalry divisions directed by a strategist like Subotai.[32]

It was indeed a fortunate miracle for the peoples of Europe, that the death of the Great Khan caused the recall of the conquering Mongol army which, in the space of two years, had not merely defeated but annihilated three great European armies and had overrun nearly all Europe east of the line now marked by the Iron Curtain.

It is noteworthy and, perhaps, significant that the foreign policy of the medieval Mongols aimed at surrounding their dominions with a zone of devastated and depopulated territory, broken up into helpless satellite states, an aim which has become the most prominent feature of the foreign policy of their successors, the Union of Soviet Socialist Republics. With this end always in view, the Mongols dealt with conquered populations in accordance with an unwavering procedure. When a city was taken, whether it was situated on the shores of the Yellow Sea or on the banks of the Oder, the inhabitants were brought forth, tied together with ropes, and were then divided into three groups, the men in one group, the women in another, and the children in a third. Skilled craftsmen and attractive women were then carefully selected for dispatch to Central Asia, there, if they survived the frightful journey, to labour as slaves or serve as concubines. Lastly, the remainder were forced to kneel with outstretched necks in rows down which the Mongol soldiers proceeded, expeditiously slicing off with their long sabres the bent heads which were then gathered in neat pyramids, not in a spirit of vainglory, but to facilitate the work of the scribes whose duty it was to supply the Great Khan with accurate statistics of the carnage.

Chapter 3 — Europe's Civil Wars

It was this procedure, methodical, deliberate, and businesslike, rather than the scale on which the Mongol massacres were carried out, which filled contemporary Christians with speechless horror. In medieval Christian Europe, wholesale homicide on an unlimited scale was considered justifiable, in fact meritorious, if religious issues were involved—witness the Albigensian Crusade above mentioned. Wholesale homicide was also considered excusable, if committed on the lower orders by a high-spirited prince in a temporary fit of irritation—witness the sack of Limoges by the Black Prince, later to be mentioned. In other words, pious zeal was held to justify anything, including every variety of gratuitous cruelty, in which to do them justice, the Mongols seem rarely to have indulged. Brutal actions, *prima facie* crimes, were also held to be pardonable lapses in Christian Europe, if committed by persons of gentle birth in a frenzy of blind emotion, or as Field Marshal Montgomery would express it, when "seeing red." But the coldblooded slaughterings of these terrible pagans from High Asia were beyond the comprehension of the medieval Christian. He could no more understand such passionless wickedness than he could withstand the disciplined sweep of those slit-eyed Oriental horsemen in their armour of lacquered leather, shooting with their deadly bows. Good fortune and not his own exertions saved him, but not until all Europe between the Volga and the Oder had been devastated with ruthless efficiency.

Not until seven centuries had elapsed was their fatal passion for civil war again to bring the European peoples so close to the brink of irreparable disaster. In the sixteenth and seventeenth centuries, Europe was menaced by the Ottoman Turks, since their conquest of the Byzantine Empire, in 1453, firmly established at Constantinople. The Turks succeeded in conquering the whole of the Balkans, Greece and Hungary, and twice besieged Vienna. The peoples of Europe were as hopelessly divided against each other as ever; at moments of particular peril, the Sultans generally found the Kings of France happy to render them assistance and support so that the Emperor might be distracted from French aggression on the Rhine. The Turks possessed a formidable army—thanks to the help of Christian renegades, their artillery was the best in the world at the time—but the resources of the Turkish Empire were never adequate for the task of conquering Europe, although with

Advance to Barbarism

but a slight variation of fortune the area overrun and devastated by their armies might have been very much greater. In fact, it probably would have been but for the strategic ability and courage of John Sobieski, King of Poland, who turned back the Turkish army at the gates of Vienna in 1683.

From one point of view, it is perhaps a pity that the Sultans' armies failed to penetrate deeper into Europe. The appearance of a corps of janissaries at Magdeburg in 1631 might have served, as nothing else would have done, to bring the frenzied and fratricidal Catholics and Protestants to their senses.

Apart from these unrelated and isolated examples of primary warfare most of the wars which have been waged in Europe since the Dark Ages must be classified as secondary wars. Under this general heading must be grouped the innumerable petty local wars such as that in the fifteenth century in the West of England between Lord Bonville and the Earl of Devon, or that in the North of England between the Percies and the Nevilles, and such a great civil war as that of the Roses; the struggles of the Guelphs and Ghibellines in Italy, and the various civil wars of religion from the Albigensian Crusade to the Thirty Years War. In the same group must be included such so-called nationalist wars as the Hundred Years War (according to Professor Trevelyan "the first European war that can be called National") which arose from the resolve of the half-French Kings of England to assert their claim to the throne of France. Except for the numbers engaged, the amount of bloodshed, and the extent of the devastation and suffering caused, there is no real distinction between this long-drawn-out feud between Edward III and his successors with their cousins, the Kings of France, and the local broils of the Nevilles and the Percies. Both, for example, are utterly distinct from the wars of the kings of Castile, undertaken to drive the Moors out of Spain, or the ceaseless campaigns of the Teutonic Knights to defend the Eastern frontiers of Christendom from the Slavonic heathen.

After the Thirty Years War ended in 1648, religion ceased in Europe to be a reason—one is tempted to write a pretext—for civil war. In many respects, this great struggle is remarkable, apart from the special barbarity with which it was waged by both sides. Long before its outbreak in 1618, it was widely felt that a great political explosion was imminent. It began inconspicuously in Bohemia, so inconspicuously that it was not at first realized that the expected upheaval had at last begun. Once started, the original issues were quickly forgotten. In the history books, the Thirty Years War is labelled a war of religion, a war between the Roman Catholics and the Protestants. Yet, the so-called Protestant cause derived its main inspiration and support from the leading Catholic Power, France, then ruled by that great Prince of the Catholic Church, Cardinal Richelieu; throughout, the two chief Catholic potentates in Europe, the Pope and the Emperor, were at bitter enmity and most of the fighting was done by godless mercenaries drawn from every country in Europe. The result achieved, after thirty years' fighting, during which some fifteen million people perished by violence, starvation or disease, was an agreement that the belief of each individual concerning the eternal truths upon which his or her salvation depended should be decided by the predilections or whims of the prince whose subject he or she should happen to be — a very commonsensical practical solution, but one difficult to justify by any system of theology. The best that can be said for the Thirty Years War is that is ended more or less in a *status quo* settlement, so that Europe was spared the orgy of revenge which would have inevitably followed a complete triumph by either side.

Far more important than the actual terms of settlement was the fact that this futile and murderous struggle brought about the tacit conclusion that, thenceforth, religious differences must never again serve as a reason for civil war. This conclusion did not, indeed, prevent civil wars continuing to break out, but it profoundly altered their character. In the Thirty Years War had finally perished that sense of European unity, inherited from the days of the Roman Empire, which had persisted throughout the Middle Ages. Europe had by now become permanently broken up into a number of more or less self-contained national territorial entities, sovereign and irresponsible. The old practice of electing a ruler from the supposedly ablest members of a governing family had died out: even the imperial crown of the Holy Roman Empire had become, in fact if not in theory, subject to the lien of the House of Hapsburg. The various crowns of Europe passed by heredity and with them the right to rule various territories, the title to many of these being subject to dispute. Since no court or means of arbitration existed to settle such disputes, the only means of

Advance to Barbarism

settlement was by war. By a curious reasoning process, it was universally agreed that the prince who went to war and won had established his hereditary right while the prince who proved not strong enough to retain the territory in question thereby lost his right to inherit it. Thus, when the Prussian Army proved stronger than the Austrian Army, Frederick the Great was held to have established his right to Silesia; when the British Fleet proved stronger than the French Fleet, Britain's claims to Cape Breton or St. Vincent were considered to have been placed on a proper legal footing.

Although "national consciousness" was developing gradually all over Europe, in general the inhabitants of disputed territories still took but a languid interest as to which prince had inherited or achieved by conquest the right to govern them. Thus, the German population of Alsace soon settled down contentedly under Louis XIV, and the inhabitants of Silesia seemed to have raised no objection to transferring their allegiance from the House of Hapsburg to the House of Hohenzollern.

A ruler who disturbed the peace of Europe by asserting by force of arms some real or imaginary claim incurred thereby no general odium. Shakespeare expresses the public attitude very clearly when he makes Hamlet soliloquize concerning the war started by the Norwegian prince "to gain a little patch of ground" from Poland not worth five ducats a year. Far from condemning Fortinbras as a public nuisance, a warmonger, a Kriegshetzer, Hamlet meditates complacently that he is:

"A delicate and tender prince
Whose spirit, with divine ambition puff'd,
Makes mouths at the invisible event,
Exposing what is mortal and unsure
To all that fortune, death and danger dare,
Even for an egg-shell."

Until very recently, a unique importance was attached to the civil wars of Europe. It was agreed that even those European civil wars, the causes of which were more than usually inadequate and that most signally failed to achieve lasting results of any kind, were nevertheless momentous and glorious in a way no wars between Asiatic peoples or between American states could possibly be. At the end of each, everyone was certain that its glorious memory would go down the ages undimmed to eternity — and, in fact, the

Chapter 3 — Europe's Civil Wars

glorious memory of each endured undimmed until the outbreak of the next. Looking back, it is now possible to realize these civil wars of Europe were important for only two reasons. Firstly, they led naturally and inevitably to the present plight of Europe. Secondly, during the last two centuries of their course, they gave rise to an entirely novel method of warfare which has come to be known as "civilized warfare."

Now that disaster, to a greater or lesser extent, has overtaken all the peoples of Europe, there is no longer any interest in the details of these civil wars. So naturally did each follow its predecessor that they hardly merit individual study. Probably a new nomenclature will ultimately be adopted to indicate their essential unity. From the Dark Ages down to the end of the Thirty Years War in 1648, civil war in Europe was continuous, local wars and private feuds never ceasing and large scale political explosions, such as the Hundred Years War and the Hussite War, taking place from time to time. After 1648, minor warfare gradually ceased, but a series of general upheavals began, each separated from the other by several decades of uneasy tranquillity.

First came the series of wars waged to frustrate the ambition of Louis XIV to dominate Europe. These may be grouped together as European Civil War No. 1. There followed the War of the Austrian Succession — European Civil War No. 2. The Seven Years War may be labelled as European Civil War No. 3, and the War of 1775-83, in which Great Britain survived an attack by a European coalition but lost her American Colonies, European Civil War No. 4. The Revolutionary and Napoleonic Wars were European Civil Wars Nos. 5a and 5b, respectively. The Crimean War, although it did not involve all Europe, may be counted as European Civil War No. 6, because it had the important result of bringing to an end the military supremacy which the Czars had achieved in 1815. The group of wars between 1864 and 1871, which established the German Empire as the leading European Military Power, may be labelled European Civil War No. 7. If the Balkan Wars of 1877 and 1912 be dismissed as minor European conflicts with Asia, represented by the decadent Turkish Empire, Europe may be said to have enjoyed peace for the unprecedented spell of 43 years after the establishment of the German Empire in 1871.

The adoption by historians of a nomenclature such as this would be no startling innovation. It would express what was once the universally recognized distinction between primary warfare, that is to say, warfare between rival civilizations, and warfare between peoples sharing a common civilization, that is to say, in essence, civil warfare. Throughout the Middle Ages, the essential unity of Christendom was acknowledged without question. The feuds of the Hohenstaufen, Valois, Plantagenet, and other princely houses were never seen out of proportion: they aroused interest and excitement which, however, rarely prevented a feudal army from disbanding when the fixed period of military service due from each vassal to his lord had expired. Such conflicts were internal affairs, never to be confused in importance with the primary duty of defending the borders of Europe from the attacks of the enemies of Christendom.

At the present time, it appears to many to be a minor outcome of the 1939-1945 War that the old university city of Königsberg, the former capital of East Prussia, and the birthplace and home of that great European thinker Immanuel Kant, should have become the submarine base and arsenal of Kaliningrad. But, to his contemporaries, the most creditable episode in the life of Henry of Bolingbroke, afterwards King Henry IV of England, was the term he served in 1390 as a volunteer with the Teutonic Knights defending East Prussia from the Lithuanian and Polish heathen.[33] At best, warfare between Christians was considered a regrettable happening, attributed by theologians to man's fallen nature. Such warfare the Popes and Church Councils did their best to discourage, restrict and humanize.

Regulations, seldom observed it is true, were laid down from time to time for the conduct of the civil wars of Christendom. Thus, in 1139, the Lateran Council denounced the newly-invented crossbow as a weapon "hateful to God and unfit for Christians." But this prohibition only extended to the killing of fellow Christians. The Council expressly permitted the use of the crossbow for the killing of infidels, a meritorious work in which even weapons "hateful to God" were permissible.

Faint traces of this outlook are perceptible even at the present day and account for the fact that the hanging of Field Marshal Keitel appears to be a more regrettable event than the hanging of General Yamashita, and the bombing of the refugees at Dresden more repugnant than the dropping of the atomic bomb on Hiroshima.

Chapter 3 — Europe's Civil Wars

Popularly, and even officially, the war of 1914-1918 has come to be known as the First World War. This is a plain misnomer. It began as a European civil war in no essential way different from any of its predecessors. On the one side were the peoples of Central Europe and on the other side the chief Atlantic Powers, Great Britain and France, allied to the Russian Empire. It remained a civil war although two non-European Powers joined in: the Japanese Empire at the beginning in order to seize the opportunity to acquire without resistance the German overseas possessions in the Pacific, and the United States at the end mainly for the purpose of safeguarding the huge loans which she had made to Great Britain and France to buy munitions. The participation of Japan remained throughout strictly limited, while as soon as the interests of the Wall Street financiers had been secured by victory, the American public turned violently against all intervention in European affairs, disowned President Wilson and all his works, and insisted on the passing of neutrality legislation expressly designed to prevent the United States from again being drawn into another European civil war.

The so-called First World War should, therefore, be classified as European Civil War No. 8. The war which broke out in 1939, after a precarious interval of twenty-one years, was really only a continuation of the struggle which it was believed had ended on the 11th of November, 1918. It is submitted, therefore, that the war 1914-1918 should be labelled European Civil War No. 8a, and the war 1939-1940 European Civil War No. 8b.[34]

It is the war 1940-1945 which really merits the title of the First World War since during it, for the first time in history, continents came into conflict rather than mere countries. On the one side were arrayed the British Empire, North America and the great Eurasian Power, first established in the Middle Ages by the Mongol Conqueror, Genghis Khan, and recently re-established by Lenin under the name of the Union of Soviet Socialist Republics. On the other side was arrayed the greater part of Europe led by the Third Reich, joined, in 1941, by the Japanese Empire.

The war of 1940-1945 was not conducted in accordance with the code of warfare subject to which for the preceding two centuries Europeans had been accustomed to wage war upon each other. Neither the Americans nor the Eurasians of the Soviet Union had any regard for what Europeans of past generations

Advance to Barbarism

had been pleased to consider permissible in warfare. Throughout, they fought in accordance with their own views on this subject. Further, when the end at last came, there was no select gathering of European statesmen such as had met together after every European civil war to decide with dignity and decorum the form the latest peace settlement should take in accordance with (in Europe) long recognized principles. For the first time in history, the peoples of Europe found themselves saved the trouble of coming to decisions concerning their own affairs since everything of importance had already been decided for them in Washington and Moscow.

This book is not concerned with the woes of the present generation of Europeans. The existing situation is merely the natural consequence of reckless indulgence in civil war. The penalty came near to being claimed when the Saracens overran Spain and invaded France in the eighth century. The danger was yet more acute in the thirteenth century, when the Mongols conquered all Europe up to a line now marked by the "Iron Curtain." Finally, during the sixteenth and seventeenth centuries, the Turkish Sultans were a serious menace to European civilization; their armies twice penetrated to Vienna and their fleets commanded the Mediterranean. All these dangers passed away, but in 1939 Nemesis was heedlessly mocked once too often.

The civil wars of Europe are of interest here because, during their final phase, there was gradually established a code subject to which it was tacitly agreed Christian neighbours should wage war upon each other. The code won general acceptance in Europe about the beginning of the eighteenth century — that is to say, little more than two hundred years before 1939, the date of the outbreak of Europe's latest and possibly last civil war.

The fundamental principle of this code was that hostilities between civilized peoples must be limited to the armed forces actually engaged. In other words, it drew a distinction between combatants and non-combatants by laying down that the sole business of the combatants is to fight each other and, consequently, that non-combatants must be excluded from the scope of military operations.

The credit for formulating the code based on this fundamental principle cannot be attributed to any one statesman or political thinker or, in fact, to any one nation in particular. With surprising rapidity, we find that it had become tacitly accepted by the nations of Western and Central Europe in the conduct of their wars with each other around the beginning of the eighteenth century. Warfare conducted according to this code became known as "civilized warfare." Its acceptance never extended beyond Europe or countries not under European influence, but for two hundred years it was acknowledged by all the European States. In the main it was complied with and, when infringed, was paid the tribute of indignant denials. After holding sway for two centuries, it was repudiated more swiftly and more mysteriously than it had been accepted.

Here, then, are two facts requiring explanation. How was it that the European nations so quickly and easily at last came to a belated decision to accept a code limiting the brutalities of warfare, after having for so many centuries practised warfare in its most primitive and unrestrained shape? And how was it that the European nations, after having practised warfare in accordance with this code for two hundred years and having scorned all peoples who refused to acknowledge it as self-confessed barbarians, reverted, in the space of a decade, without apparent hesitation or misgiving, to what was, in the opinion of Captain Liddell Hart "the most uncivilized method of warfare the world has known since the Mongol devastations."[35]

Chapter 4 — Civilized Warfare (The First Phase)

As above remarked, the introduction of Christianity and its acceptance by the peoples of Europe did not have that immediate influence on the conduct of war which, theoretically, one would expect. It was not, indeed, until the rise of chivalry many centuries after the peoples of Europe had become Christian that any amelioration in the conduct of war became perceptible.

The origins of chivalry may be traced back to those dark times when Europe was being ravaged by various barbarian invaders after the collapse of the Roman military system. Originally, the orthodox attitude of the devout Christian to the horrors taking place around him was to withdraw from the world and pray, since it was agreed the Last Day was near at hand and Christ himself has forbidden resistance to evil. When, however, it appeared that the Last Day was being unaccountably delayed, while prayer seemed to have surprisingly little influence on the doings of the Huns, Magyars, Saracens, and Vikings who were devastating Europe, the idea naturally dawned of opposing the onslaught of these invaders which was inspired only by a love of fighting or a desire for loot by a resistance inspired by an unselfish resolve to defend the suffering Christian faithful. There thus gradually arose the ideal of the Christian Warrior. Naturally and logically, the duty to defend weak and helpless Christians from infidel oppressors gradually became extended to include a duty to defend the weak and helpless generally from oppression. "Chivalry had two outstanding marks," says Professor R. B. Mowat, "two things that were as its essence: it was Christian and it was military."

Chivalry, as it ultimately developed, became a collective term embracing a code of conduct, manners, and etiquette, a system of ethics and a distinctive "Weltanschauung" (philosophy

Chapter 4 — Civilized Warfare (The First Phase)

of life) as the Germans call it. For our purpose, its principal importance is that, when the code of chivalry was adopted as the code of the military caste in all the European states, it provided a common bond between them. Whatever his nationality, the European knight professed the code of the Christian warrior. With his reputation as such to maintain, a European knight could not afford to use the capture of a prisoner of the same class as himself as an opportunity to indulge his resentment against a helpless enemy either in the manner of an Assyrian King, by flaying or impalement, or, in the present-day manner, by a mock-trial followed by hanging. Sadism could no longer freely masquerade as moral indignation, as in the brave days of Samuel the Prophet: a prisoner whatever his nationality, so long as he was a member of the European ruling class, had to be treated when a prisoner with honour and courtesy.

From nursery days, everyone is familiar with Froissart's account of the capture of King John of France by the Black Prince at Poitiers, in 1356. To-day, the story seems so wildly incredible that it reads more like a fairy story for children than an event of sober history. Having described with characteristic gusto the details of the fighting, Froissart tells us the Black Prince made inquiries of those about him, asking whether anything was known of the fate of the King of France, and was informed that he must either be slain or captured "since he had maintained his place in the forefront of the battle."

The Prince, therefore, sent the Earl of Warwick and Lord Cobham to discover the truth, and at last they found the King of France surrounded by a crowd of warriors angrily disputing which one had actually captured him. "The two barons, dismounting, advanced to the royal prisoner with reverence and conducted him in a peaceable manner to the Prince of Wales." Thus brought to the Prince, the latter "made a low obeisance to him and ordered wine and spices to be brought which, as a mark of his great affection, he presented to the King himself."

After being treated with every honour and consideration, the King was brought in due course to England where "mounted on a white horse richly caparisoned he rode through the streets of London with the Prince of Wales on a little black payfrey by his side. The Palace of the Savoy was first appropriated to his use; but soon after his arrival he was moved to Windsor Castle, where he was treated with the greatest possible attention and hunting, hawking, and other amusements were provided for him."

One can well imagine how King Asshurbanipal would have piously evoked, "Asshur, Belit and Ishtar, the great gods, my lords" at such sinful weakness. An Iroquois war chief would have deplored in picturesque language the folly of letting slip such an opportunity for time-honoured recreation at the torture-stake, while a modern editor would certainly declaim volcanically in headline English: "Black Prince Goes Soft: War-Criminal Escapes Trial."

Such criticisms, however, inflict a grave injustice on the memory of the Black Prince who can be taken in all respects as fairly representing the chivalrous ideal. To another member of the European military caste, he was ever a model of unfailing generosity and courtesy. But he was never soft: those not of gentle blood could expect little indulgence at his hands. When he lost his temper, which he did not infrequently, the consequences were terrible. In 1370, for example, after he had worked his will in a fit of temper on Limoges, the unfortunate city must have looked as if "strong formations of our Bomber Command" had recently visited it.

To summarize, it can be said that the general acceptance of the ideals of chivalry had considerable influence on the conduct of warfare in the Middle Ages, although this influence was generally restricted in practice to dealings of the ruling classes with each other. At the least, it made impossible such demonstrations of primitive crudity as that, for example, of Sapor I, King of Persia, who having taken prisoner the gallant but thick-headed Roman Emperor, Valerian, used his unfortunate captive as a portable footstool to assist him in mounting his horse. Chivalry, as a code of behaviour and courtesy, survived the Middle Ages and even persisted during the Wars of Religion, as witness Velasquez's famous picture "The Surrender at Breda."[36]

Some may, perhaps, be unable to repress a cynical doubt whether any human being ever succeeded in appearing quite as gracious and courtly as Velasquez has represented the Spanish Commander-in-Chief, Ambrose Spinola, as appearing on that celebrated occasion in 1625. Spinola was a fervent patriot and a devout Catholic, and, in his eyes, the Dutch Governor of Breda and his officers were obstinate heretics and national enemies.

Chapter 4 — Civilized Warfare (The First Phase)

At this moment of triumph, which was to prove to be the final episode of a ferocious war that had lasted an entire generation and had been waged with almost unparalleled brutality by both sides, could Spinola have really greeted his defeated enemies with such amiability and courtly grace?

The point is quite without significance. Admittedly, Velasquez was not an eye-witness: he painted the scene twenty years later on instructions. Very possibly, he idealized the bearing of Spinola. What is significant is that this picture proves how the Spanish Government preferred that this triumph of Spanish arms should be remembered by posterity. Clearly, neither Spinola nor the Spanish Government were obsessed with dread lest their memory should be stained by the charge of having pampered a defeated enemy. Velasquez's picture proves conclusively how Spinola liked to imagine he appeared on this memorable occasion. It may not portray exactly what occurred, but it certainly portrays what contemporary opinion considered should have occurred. In the same way, some of the happenings proudly described in the Press and on the radio at the downfall of the Third Reich in 1945 may not have occurred exactly as described, or may have been offset to some extent by individual acts of courtesy and chivalry, report of which was deliberately suppressed. Here again, these descriptions have a significance quite independent of their veracity or accuracy; they prove what the British and American leaders of opinion and their publics desired to believe was taking place.

Unfortunately it has become increasingly difficult as the years pass by to adopt the charitable view that most of the accounts of the ill-treatment of prisoners of war by their captors in 1945 described at the time with gusto, were baseless fictions by self-slanderers. Alas, numerous photographs exist which make the truth clear beyond dispute that the victors at the end of the Second World War, far from striving to win with grace like Ambrose Spinola, if they did not consciously model their behaviour on the Persian monarch, Sapor I, seem often to have regarded victory as an opportunity to force their captives to act with them a sort of burlesque, a variation of the children's game "Robbers and Cops". One of the most frequently reproduced of these photographs shows a British soldier strutting along behind an elderly man in a great coat walking with bowed head, at whose back this warrior is pointing a sub-machine gun, presumably loaded. From the captions attached we learn that this photograph shows Field Marshal von Blaskowitz, the German C-in-C in Holland, after his surrender at Appeldoorn, being marched to captivity — a captivity which was to last until the Field Marshal in despair took his own life shortly afterwards in a French prison.[37]

It can hardly be denied that the effect of Velasquez's masterpiece would have been marred if he had shown the Governor of Breda being prodded into Spinola's presence by a Spanish soldier with a halbert: likewise the well-known picture of Lord Nelson at the battle of Cape St. Vincent receiving the swords of the captain and officers of the *San Josef*, would not have been improved if the artist had had the bad taste to portray one of Nelson's tars brandishing a cutlass over the heads of the vanquished Spaniards.

Chivalry may be described as the product of Christian idealism. Or it may be described as the product of belated common sense. What has become known as "civilized warfare" arose quite independently. At long last the fact dawned on the human understanding that it would be for the benefit of all in the long run if vindictive passions were restrained and if warfare could be conducted according to tacit rules, so that the sufferings, loss and damage inevitable in warfare might be reduced so far as possible. At times no doubt the stronger side in a war might feel aggrieved at having to overcome the weaker side by slow and costly methods, because an obviously swift and easy method had been debarred as uncivilized: at times a victor might feel frustrated of the full enjoyment of victory by being precluded from dealing with complete freedom with a prostrate enemy. But it was realized that such acts of self-restraint contributed to the establishment of a general security shared by all, since no European state was so supremely strong that its people could feel indifferent to the possibilities which a change of fortune or a shift of the balance of power might bring about.

Civilized warfare, as waged in Europe for some two hundred years down to the present generation, cannot be dated earlier than the beginning of the eighteenth century, but a somewhat similar form of warfare had arisen in Italy in the fifteenth century and flourished for a short time. In one of his essays Macaulay describes at length how this came about. In brief, the rich burghers and merchants of medieval Italy were too busy

Chapter 4 — Civilized Warfare (The First Phase)

making money and enjoying life to undertake the hardships and dangers of soldiering themselves. So they adopted the practice of hiring mercenaries to do their fighting for them, and, being thrifty, business-like folk, they dismissed these mercenaries immediately after their services could be safely dispensed with. Wars were, therefore, fought by armies hired for each campaign. Writing in the security of Victorian England, Macaulay pours scorn on the result. "War," he says, "completely changed its character. It became left to the conduct of men who neither loved whom they defended nor hated those whom they opposed. Every man came into the field impressed with the knowledge that, in a few days, he might be taking the pay of the power against which he was then employed. The strongest interest and the strongest feelings concurred to mitigate the hostility of those who had lately been brothers in arms and who might soon be brethren in arms once more. Their common profession was a bond of union. Hence it was that operations, languid and indecisive beyond any recorded in history, marches and countermarches, bloodless capitulations and equally bloodless combats make up the military history of Italy for nearly two centuries."

To the reflective reader to-day, this result seems wholly excellent. For the first time, soldiering became a reasonable and comparatively harmless profession.[38] The generals of that period manoeuvred against each other, often with consummate skill, but when one had won the advantage, his opponent generally either retreated or surrendered. It was a recognized rule that a town could only be sacked if it offered resistance: immunity could always be purchased by paying a ransom fixed according to its importance. As a natural consequence, no town ever resisted, it being obvious that a government too weak to defend its citizens had forfeited their allegiance. Civilians had little to fear from the dangers of war which were the concern only of professional soldiers. The latter, however, continued to run considerable risks since, although deaths by weapons of war were happily rare, yet complete ignorance of the rudiments of camp sanitation often brought disaster. An army which was compelled to remain stationary for any length of time ran the risk of being decimated by plague.

This relatively satisfactory state of military affairs was brought to an abrupt end by the invasion of Italy by Charles VIII

Advance to Barbarism

of France, in 1494. Thereafter, Italy became the prey of armies of foreign invaders, French, Germans, Swiss, and Spaniards, who recognized no rules of warfare of any kind. Thereafter, a succession of wars raged throughout the Peninsula, waged with the most primitive ferocity and resulting in enormous loss of life and causing irreparable damage.

For roughly two hundred years (1500 to 1700) unrestricted civil wars continued to rage throughout Europe, on occasion attaining new levels of barbarity and ferocity, as during the revolt of the Netherlands against Philip of Spain or during the Thirty Years War in Germany. The evolution of civilized warfare was roughly concurrent with the long reign of Louis XIV of France; at least, no traces of it can be detected at the beginning of his reign in 1643, and it appears fully established at his death in 1715. No credit for this development, however, can be attributed to Louis personally. On the contrary, one of the most deliberate and least excusable barbarities in European history was perpetrated by his armies as late as 1689 when the Palatinate was systematically devastated in order to create an *Odlandsgürtel* (waste-land-zone) along the French frontier. "Brûlez bien le Palatinat" ("Burn the Palatinate thoroughly"), ordered his Minister of War, Louvois, and, from the old imperial city of Spryer on the upper Rhine as far north as the Moselle, a thickly populated area 100 miles long and 50 miles wide was first pillaged and then laid waste with fire and sword.

But already a great and mysterious change had come over public opinion: a new spirit was abroad. Forty years before, any of the generals of the Thirty Years War would have carried out the work of devastation according to orders as lightheartedly as a modern air marshal but, in 1689, the French general ordered to loot and destroy Heidelberg reported to Louvois, "I must represent to His Majesty the bad effect which such a desolation may make upon the world in respect of his glory and reputation."

Condemnation of the devastation of the Palatinate was, indeed, general and the indignation it aroused contributed not a little to the ultimate frustration of Louis' ambition to dominate Europe with his armies. Yet, strange to say, it was largely the domination achieved by France over European civilization — in art, literature, dress, manners and thought — which indirectly brought about the acceptance of new standards in warfare.

Chapter 4 — Civilized Warfare (The First Phase)

Fundamentally, this development probably originated as a reaction to the Thirty Years War, popularly regarded as a war of religion. It was as if men said, "We have seen the consequences of religious enthusiasm: to fanatical zeal we owe the massacres of Magdeburg and Drogheda and Central Europe being depopulated by a third. It is trying to be saints which has led us to commit all these horrors. Let us, as an alternative, now strive to be gentlemen!"

Having experienced in the seventeenth century the consequences of religious ardour and unreflective credulity, mankind in the eighteenth century inclined naturally towards restraint, moderation, and doubt. The eighteenth century styled itself the Age of Reason. Poise, balance, and urbanity were the qualities most admired. The new code of polite manners forbade a gentleman from becoming unduly excited about anything. Even in religion, extreme fervour was condemned: "enthusiasm" became a term of reproach as John Wesley was later to discover.[39] Muddled thinking was despised: clarity was preferred to profundity. A limitless capacity to believe without a reason and to hate without a cause was not then, as at present, prized as an essential quality of the good citizen. Above all things, a gentleman was required to maintain his sense of proportion. From this, it followed naturally that wars ceased to be waged for vague undefined objects in a frenzy of emotion, regardless of whether the suffering and loss occasioned were grotesquely out of proportion to any benefit that could possibly result. The wars of the eighteenth century were fought for limited objects—for example, a border province or a colonial possession—and they were fought with limited means, that is to say, the means employed to wage them were limited in accordance with a for long unwritten but generally recognized code. Warfare conducted in accordance with this code has come to be known as *civilized warfare*.

As stated in the last chapter, this code was based on one simple principle, namely that warfare should be the concern only of the armed combatants engaged. From this follows the corollary that non-combatants should be left entirely outside the scope of military operations.

From the acceptance of this principle, all later developments followed naturally and logically. If non-combatants must be treated as outside the scope of military operations, it necessarily followed that an enemy civilian did not forfeit his rights as a human being merely because the armed forces of his country were unable to defend him. So long as he took no part in the hostilities, he became entitled to claim from the enemy combatant forces protection for his life and property. If he suffered as a consequence of hostilities, it must be only indirectly owing to regrettable and unavoidable mischance—for example, as when the inhabitants of a town are killed by missiles fired to compel its garrison to surrender. The sufferings of civilians must never be made a means by which the course of hostilities can be influenced—for example, when, in accordance with the common practice of barbarous warfare, a country is deliberately laid waste to induce its rulers to surrender.

Other and important developments following from the acceptance of the above principle are, first, that a combatant who surrenders, by so doing ceases to be a combatant and re-acquires the status of a non-combatant, subject only to a liability to be detained by his captors during the continuance of hostilities. Secondly, a combatant who has become incapacitated through wounds or disease ceases to be a combatant and acquires certain privileges—privileges which were accorded by civilized states long before they were formulated and formally recognized at the Geneva Convention.

In regard to prisoners of war, in 1785, in a treaty between the United States and Prussia, the principle was first expressed and formally confirmed that a prisoner of war should be treated by his captors as a person under military discipline transferred by his capture from the command of his own countrymen to the command of his captors. This treaty expressly provided that the captor should treat prisoners of war as troops transferred to his command. It follows from the acceptance of this principle that (to quote Article 27 of the Brussels Declaration of 1865 which formally confirmed what had long been the established practice): "A prisoner of war shall be subject to the rules and regulations in force in the captor's army."

Article 45 of the Geneva Convention re-affirms the principle in practically the same words. "Rules and regulations" includes, of course, all regulations in force in the captor's army relating to trials by court-martial. In short, a captor is bound in all cases to give a prisoner of war a fair trial, the definition of "a fair trial" being what the captor himself considers a fair trial for his own personnel.

Chapter 4 — Civilized Warfare (The First Phase)

In passing, it may be noted that this principle was the principle which, beyond all others, was most flagrantly violated by the war-crimes trials which began in 1945.

Obviously, the principle that non-combatants must be left outside the scope of operations was capable of different interpretations. Admittedly, a commander was justified in refusing to permit the presence of civilians to impede his operations against the enemy armed forces; consequently, a town could be bombarded regardless of the safety of the inhabitants in order to prepare an attack upon its garrison. On the other hand, it was admittedly barbarous to bombard a town outside the theatre of war, in the hope that the suffering of the inhabitants would affect the morale of the enemy combatant forces. In every case, the test was what was the real intention behind the act in question. Inevitably, occasions arose when genuine differences of opinion could exist. But the code was safeguarded by the knowledge that violation, even if profitable at the moment, would bring ultimate retribution and the weakening of the general security enjoyed by all.

So long as the civil wars of Europe remained the private business of Europeans, evasions of the code supported by pettifogging pretexts were rare. Repeatedly, the question arose whether future security should be sacrificed to immediate advantage. What triumphed on each occasion was not sentimental humanitarianism, as an ancient Assyrian war lord or a present-day air marshal would contend, but farsighted realism. It was not until 1940 that this question was answered with an emphatic affirmative.

The inhabitants of Great Britain have long been convinced that not the least of the many virtues which raise them above their neighbours on the European mainland is an inborn devotion to "playing the game." Waging war by terrorizing the enemy civilian population is equivalent to hitting below the belt in boxing. It is, therefore, remarkable that the only persistent refusal to comply with the new code of civilized warfare should have come from the British Admiralty. Long after civilized methods had been accepted in land warfare, in sea warfare the British insisted upon using their naval superiority to bring pressure on an enemy by bombarding coastal towns. Beginning with Dieppe, virtually destroyed in 1694 by a ruthless bombardment, few French ports

Advance to Barbarism

escaped attack by British fleets during the next hundred years, although no large scale invasion in any case followed. In the war of 1812-1814, the coasts of America were similarly ravaged and several important towns, notably Washington and Baltimore, burned by landing parties, the openly expressed intention being to instil into the American people "a will to peace." Again, in the Crimean War, British fleets in pursuance of the same policy bombarded Russian ports not only on the Black Sea, as ancillary to the military operations going on round Sevastopol, but on the Baltic and White Seas.

The official justification for these acts, which in land warfare would have been regarded as incontestably barbarous, was that Great Britain, lacking the military resources to fight on land great continental states like France or Russia, could only carry on a war by coastal raids. Britain's war aims were strictly limited and, once the enemy had been sufficiently inconvenienced, a frame of mind was created which resulted in a peace being negotiated on reasonable terms.

The underlying reason, however, for the refusal of Great Britain to conform with the code of civilized warfare adopted on the Continent was that, so long as the British Navy commanded the sea, the British people had no reason to fear a reversion of warfare to the methods of primitive times. If defeated in a war, a continental people faced the prospect of being dealt with in accordance with the standards then prevailing. To a continental people, therefore, it was a matter of vital concern whether these standards were civilized or barbarous. The people of Britain on the other hand, enjoyed the comforting knowledge that, so long as the British Navy ruled the waves, defeat at the worst would only mean a withdrawal for the time being from the Continent. In fact, until the conquest of the air, Great Britain could hardly be regarded politically as a part of Europe; as a consequence of her sea supremacy, she enjoyed the position of a sixth continent. So happily situated, there was lacking any urgent reason to sacrifice the convenience of the moment to ensure security.

Few episodes in the life of Queen Victoria are better known than the story of how she cut short Mr. Balfour when he was describing to her the dismay caused by the initial reverses sustained by British arms at the commencement of the South African War. "Please understand," said the Queen, "there is no one

Chapter 4 — Civilized Warfare (The First Phase)

depressed in this house. We are not interested in the possibilities of defeat: they do not exist."

The story is generally quoted as an example of the indomitable spirit of the old lady, or as an example of British tenacity in adversity, or as an example of British arrogance. But the Queen was being neither brave, boastful, nor arrogant. She was merely reminding the cabinet minister of a plain political fact which had existed from the time Great Britain had achieved naval supremacy. Until the time, some fifteen years later, when mankind won final mastery of the air, the possibilities of defeat for Great Britain, in the sense these possibilities existed for every other European state, simply did not exist.

Other European nations less happily situated resolutely resisted the temptation to revert to primitive methods of war, a temptation at times almost irresistible. For example, in the long and doubtful struggle, known as the Seven Years War, a swift and easy triumph was offered by such a reversion. On the one side in this war was Prussia, a small state exposed to attack from every direction across its straggling artificial frontiers. On the other side, were ranged the three great military powers, France, Austria and Russia. In accordance with the accepted principle of civilized warfare that hostilities must be directed solely against the combatant forces of the enemy, the armies of the Allies crossed the Prussian frontier and, relying on great numerical superiority, offered battle in turn to the Prussian army moving swiftly from one threatened point to another. Taking advantage of interior lines and the fact that his enemies neglected to act together, Frederick the Great managed to achieve a succession of brilliant victories and wonderful recoveries until, after seven years, war-weariness at last put an end to the unequal struggle.

From the start, however, it must have been obvious to the able leaders of the Allied armies, the Austrian Generals Daun and Loudon and the Russian General Soltikov, that Frederick the Great could be easily overcome without a single major battle with the Prussian army. The Allies were possessed of numerous and highly trained forces of light cavalry. All that was necessary to bring about Frederick's speedy downfall was to pour across the open and exposed frontiers of Prussia small units of Hungarian hussars and Russian cossacks with instructions to destroy everything which could be destroyed by means of a torch or a charge of gunpowder.

Advance to Barbarism

The Prussian army would have been helpless in the face of such tactics, designed to turn Prussia into a desert. Without supplies of food and material for the manufacture of munitions and the whole country overrun, except for the ground actually occupied by the Prussian army, no other course would have been open to Frederick but submission within the space not of seven years but of seven months.

The advantages of such tactics were as apparent in 1756 as they were to be in 1940. The drawbacks were equally apparent. On both occasions, the question was whether a swift and easy triumph would be too dearly purchased at the price of creating a precedent which, once created, would inevitably be followed in later wars with the result that mankind would live again under the shadow of a possible outbreak of primitive warfare, with all the horrors this entails.

In 1756, when the memories of the Thirty Years War and devastation of the Palatinate were still comparatively fresh, it was decided this price was too great. In 1940, after civil war in Europe had been conducted by civilized methods for over two hundred years, the contrary decision was arrived at. When, in the fullness of time, the penalty of this latter decision can be assessed from experience, it will be possible to express an opinion whether greater wisdom and foresight was displayed in 1940 than in 1756.

In the Middle Ages, the code of chivalry had been readily accepted throughout Europe because the ruling classes in all countries accepted the teaching of the Catholic Church and acknowledged the spiritual supremacy of the Pope. Except politically, Europe was a single unit, subject to the same movements and developments. In the same way, in the eighteenth century the new code governing the conduct of warfare was readily accepted because the ruling classes in the leading European countries had become linked by a similar outlook — by similar tastes, manners and standards — originating at the Court of Louis XIV. Edward Gibbon, the historian, thus speaks of "universal politeness" radiating from France. No other European nation could attempt to challenge the leadership of the French — the Germans at the time were backward, disunited, and impoverished as a consequence of the Thirty Years War, the English were insular in outlook and divided against each other by political and religious differences, the Spaniards were hidebound and decadent, the Italians degenerate, and the

Chapter 4 — Civilized Warfare (The First Phase)

Russians barbarous. Although the French political dominion over Europe was brief—the French fleet was virtually destroyed at Cape La Hogue and the French army suffered a series of crushing disasters, being driven headlong out of Germany at Blenheim, out of Italy at Turin, and out of the Netherlands at Ramilles—the ruling classes of Europe continued to model themselves in all but military matters on French standards of taste and conduct. A member of the European ruling class, whatever his nationality, prided himself first and foremost on possessing the outlook and manners of a European gentleman—which in practice meant the outlook and manners of a French gentleman. As such, he acknowledged an obligation to treat those whom he regarded as his social equals, irrespective of their nationality, as gentlemen and expected to be so treated by them in return. In Germany, and still more in Russia, members of the ruling class felt themselves far more closely bound to the ruling classes of the other European countries than to their own countrymen who were their social inferiors. Frederick the Great, for example, prided himself far more on his capacity to write French verses and on the fact that he was welcomed on an equal footing in intellectual circles in Paris than for his military achievements. The fact that one of the most brilliant of these—his victory at Rossbach—was won over a French army in no way disturbed on either side the friendship which existed between himself and a number of leading French poets, philosophers, mathematicians and scientists. Macaulay speaks disparagingly of Frederick's contemporary Horace Walpole as "the most Frenchified Englishman of the 18th century," and complains that even his literary style was "deeply tainted with Gallisms." The interest which Walpole took in "the fashions and scandals of Versailles" particularly arouses Macaulay's indignation. In all this, however, Walpole was only characteristic of his time. His social equals in Germany habitually spoke French, using German only to give directions to underlings. In Russia, a veneer of French culture completely separated the ruling class from the bulk of the population.

From this it naturally followed that the officers of the various European armies, when they came in contact, should treat each other with elaborate courtesies in accordance with the manners of the time. A capitulation, especially, was an occasion for an exchange of courtesies. Thus, as early as 1708, when the citadel

Advance to Barbarism

of Lille was surrendered by Marshal Bouffiers after a terrible and costly siege, not only was the French army permitted to withdraw with the honours of war, but the gallant Marshal, before being allowed to return to France, was entertained at a dinner given in his honour by his conquerors, the Duke of Marlborough and Prince Eugene. Already, therefore, a stage had been reached in the conduct of civil warfare in Europe as far removed, on the one hand, from King Sapor mounting his horse from the back of a captive emperor as, on the other hand, from Field Marshal Keitel being handed over to a hangman and then buried, rather shamefacedly, in a nameless grave. A sense of unity, irrespective of nationality, created by a common pride in the profession of arms, made exhibitions of barbarous primitive emotion unthinkable. Far from seizing an opportunity to inflict vengeance for a defeat, it became a point of honour to pay generous recognition to the courage and skill of an enemy in adversity.

Frederick the Great's plan of campaign in 1762 was completely disarranged by the unexpectedly obstinate resistance of the minor fortress of Schweidnitz, due to the skill of a French engineer named Gribeauval serving in the Austrian army who, we are told, "understood countermining like no other." The siege cost the Prussians the lives of 3,000 men and occasioned Frederick himself the greatest personal hardship. But when the fortress at last surrendered, Frederick's first act was to invite Gribeauval to dinner in order to compliment him on the superiority which he had shown to the Prussian engineers.

"No terms are too good for you!" was Admiral Keith's reply, in 1800, when Marshal Massena at last indicated his willingness to surrender Genoa after having held the city against over whelming odds until complete exhaustion of his supplies made further resistance impossible. It seems to have occurred to no one that this defence, which largely contributed to the final outcome of the campaign, deserved personal retribution. Marshal Davout, indeed, in 1814, was threatened with a trial after his surrender of Hamburg for having "rendered the name of French man odious" by his brutal treatment of the inhabitants during the siege. This threat, however — which was never seriously pressed — came from his own countrymen and political enemies, the French Royalists. Had this trial taken place, the court would, of course, have been French. Whatever may have been his deserts and in

Chapter 4 — Civilized Warfare (The First Phase)

spite, no doubt, of the views of the inhabitants of Hamburg, Davout received nothing but courtesy from his foreign enemies.

The story is well known of how, at the opening of the battle of Fontenoy in 1745, the French officers greeted their advancing enemies with the polite invitation, "Gentlemen of the English Guards, fire first!" In the same strain is the story of how Captain Savage of the *Hercules*, at the battle of the Iles des Saintes, stood upon his quarter deck, solemnly raising his cocked hat as each French ship drew abreast to deliver her broadside. These stories and many similar may be fictions, but at least they prove what public opinion at home desired to believe took place on the battlefield. Even if acts of courtesy took place in war to-day, the report of them would be suppressed for fear of outraging public opinion.

Perhaps the most significant of these stories is that of James Wolfe, afterwards the conqueror of Canada. When serving as a Major in the army of the Duke of Cumberland in 1746, Wolfe was ordered at the battle of Culloden by his superior officer, none other than the commander-in-chief himself, to pistol a wounded Highlander on the ground. He could refrain only at the peril of his military career to which he was wholeheartedly devoted. Wolfe, nonetheless, indignantly refused, with the remark that he was a soldier and not an executioner!

Some may suspect this story originated as a piece of Jacobite propaganda, but it was at once widely accepted and repeated, not as a tribute to the invincible repugnance rightly felt by His Royal Highness, the Duke of Cumberland, for (as we should say) pampering the enemy, but as demonstrating how firmly James Wolfe maintained his high standard of professional honour. It is hard to believe that the sentiments which animated James Wolfe and most of his European contemporaries in 1746 could have died out entirely by 1940. At the latter date, of course, the spiritual descendants of the Duke of Cumberland abounded in all the belligerent armies and, in particular, in the air forces. It would be interesting to learn whether they were often embarrassed by the scruples of the spiritual descendants of James Wolfe? If so, by what means were such scruples, so prejudicial to good order and discipline, overcome? In the Mongol invasion of 1241, enormities were perpetrated by barbarous nomads of High Asia, and in the Thirty Years War by godless mercenaries; in the War of 1940-

Advance to Barbarism

1945, enormities were frequently committed by young gentlemen of sheltered upbringing and blameless character. That incidents prejudicial to good order and discipline of the kind associated with the name of James Wolfe have now become seemingly so rare speaks volumes for the efforts of the emotional engineers working behind the scenes. The attitude towards James Wolfe's conduct held by his contemporaries contrasts strangely with the present-day view that it merely indicates that his reactions had not been scientifically conditioned by effective propaganda before he set forth for the campaign.

The obedience demanded from a professional soldier in the eighteenth and nineteenth centuries was by no means unqualified, so far as officers were concerned. The respective roles of the soldier and the politician were then clearly distinguished. The definition of war as "an extension of policy by force" later formulated by Clausewitz, had already won general acceptance, and policy was admittedly the sole concern of the politicians. A gentleman who had accepted a commission in the army or navy was, consequently, held in honour bound to take part in any war upon which the executive government might decide to embark. He could not pick and choose: the rights and wrongs of a war were not his concern. As Macaulay put it, "A man who belongs to the army only in time of peace — who appears at reviews in Hyde Park, escorts his Sovereign with the utmost valour and fidelity to and from the House of Lords and retires as soon as he thinks it likely that he may be ordered on an expedition — is justly thought to have disgraced himself." James Wolfe, of course, no more concerned himself with the ethics of the various campaigns in which he took part than did in our own day Lord Roberts, when he planned and directed in 1900 the operations to bring about the subjugation of the Boer Republics, or did Admiral Raeder, when he planned and directed the occupation of Norway in 1940. It was without the least sense of personal guilt that Sir Charles Napier reported cheerfully to his government in 1843 the successful conclusion of a war of naked, unashamed aggression against the Ameers of Scinde with the single word "Peccavi" — "I have Scinde."[40]

On the other hand, the manner of conducting a war, whether just or unjust, was recognized to be the sole concern of the professional soldiers conducting it. A soldier did not feel himself bound to commit promiscuous homicide as and when directed —

Chapter 4 — Civilized Warfare (The First Phase)

like a modern blockbuster or underworld gunman. So long as warfare in Europe continued to be warfare between Europeans, it was conducted in accordance with a recognized code, in the interpretation of which no civilian interference was tolerated.

How jealously the exclusive right to interpret this code was guarded may be illustrated by one episode from the career of General Charles George Gordon. In 1863, he had been lent to the Chinese Imperial Government to direct the repression of the Tai-Ping Rebellion and, having captured Soo-chow, had accepted the surrender of a number of rebel leaders.

To his horror, these were promptly beheaded by the Chinese civil authorities. It is recorded that General Gordon, beside himself with rage, went in search of the mandarin whom he considered responsible, revolver in hand, declaring that his own professional honour and reputation had been indelibly stained by the execution of his prisoners of war.

It need hardly be remarked that latitude to exercise private judgment was only conceded to officers. Among the rank and file what may, for convenience, be labelled the Light Brigade spirit, prevailed. The attitude of the gallant Six Hundred which so aroused Lord Tennyson's admiration arose from the fact that the least disposition to ask the reason why was discouraged by tricing the would-be inquirer to the triangle and flogging him into insensibility. The same spirit prevailed in the ranks of all the European armies and was the product of the same simple but effective treatment.

Of more practical importance than the code of good manners which it imposed on the combatants was the security given to civilian life and property by the introduction of civilized methods of warfare. Not only was the massacre of civilians no longer left to the judgment of individual commanders, but pillage, a recognized practice in the seventeenth century, was gradually replaced by requisitions for which payment was made. "The Austrian armies," writes Captain Liddell Hart, "were particularly restrained, even to the point of handicapping their own operations by extreme scrupulousness in abstaining from any demands on the civilian population."[41]

In the Prussian Army, the regulations against looting were so strict that, after the disaster at Jena in 1806, it is recorded that the retreating Prussians endured without fires the bitter cold of an

October night in central Europe rather than seize civilian stores of wood which lay to hand but for which they were unable to pay.

Civilized warfare reached its furthest extension during the last half of the eighteenth century. The principles and practice of civilized warfare were worked out by a number of writers during this period and, in particular, by the Swiss jurist, Emeric de Vattel, in 1758, in his famous work *The Law of Nations, or the Principles of Natural Law as Applied to the Administration of National Affairs and of Sovereigns*. At the time he wrote, much of what he said must have seemed platitudinous to a degree, but to us it has come to appear grimly prophetic.

Not only does Vattel point out that, if barbarous methods of warfare are adopted, the enemy will do likewise, so that the only ultimate result will be to add to the horrors of war; not only does he argue that "harsh, disgraceful and unendurable peace terms" will only be fulfilled as long as the defeated enemy lacks the means to repudiate them; Vattel actually condemns the use by rulers at war of "offensive expressions indicating sentiments of hatred, animosity and bitterness" since such expressions must ultimately stand in the way of a settlement on reasonable terms.

At a first glance, this would appear a condemnation of the whole system of modern war propaganda. But, of course, Vattel had no means of conceiving even dimly one of those imposing collections of fabrications and calumnies which it has now become the first business of nations at war to concoct and broadcast concerning each other. Probably, he merely had in mind one of those witty but ill-advised jibes which Frederick of Prussia was in the habit of circulating against his brother monarchs, and which, later, he so often had cause to regret as being unnecessary impediments in the way of negotiations for a new understanding.

Vattel would have been astonished to learn how exasperating a later generation of Europeans would find his book. In justice to him, it should be said that from his style it is clear that he was under no illusion that he was propounding anything original or profound. When his contemporary, Hogarth, drew the "Idle and Industrious Apprentices" series, he did not imagine that they illustrated a new discovery that thrift and diligence (aided by marriage to the only daughter of one's employer) are more likely to lead to prosperity than indolence and improvidence! In the same way, Vattel realized that he was only stating what everyone

Chapter 4 — Civilized Warfare (The First Phase)

who troubled to think about the subject knew as well as himself. His modest ambition, when he took his pen in hand, was to set forth a number of recognized truisms more clearly and concisely than they had ever been set forth by anyone else previously.

It is only when read in the light of the developments which the future held in store, that Vattel's book seems so ominously prophetic. But in no passage is there indicated any apprehension of such developments. On the contrary, the great progress which had been made towards establishing a code of civilized warfare not only filled him with complacency, but clearly inspired in him the hope that this progress would lead finally to the abolition of civil warfare in Europe altogether.

Civil warfare being the prized prerogative of the European kings, it would have been dangerous for most of Vattel's contemporaries to have expressed the opinion that warfare in any form was barbarous. But as a Swiss subject, Vattel was able to deal with the question frankly. He is prepared to admit that war may at times serve the useful purpose of settling disputes between nations. Nevertheless, he points out that war can only serve this purpose if, in the first place, it be conducted by methods which do not leave behind a legacy of hatred and bitterness, and, in the second place, if the victors be not so carried away by their success as to impose by violence harsh and unreasonable terms, since this inevitably prepares the way for another war.

Vattel's complacency may be found exasperating by many readers to-day, but it cannot be said to have been unjustified by the circumstances of the time when he wrote. The progress made by European civilization during the preceding hundred years had been truly amazing. Already, the times of the Thirty Years War seemed remote when soldier and bandit were practically synonyms and every civilian knew that good fortune alone protected him from being overtaken by horrors and indignities of every imaginable kind.

The fate of Magdeburg might have been the fate of any European city in 1631. True, civil warfare still continued to burst forth at intervals in Europe, but, like the practice of duelling, it had become so circumscribed by rules that its worst consequences were eliminated or reduced to a minimum. The possibility that civil warfare might entail the penalty of invasion and conquest by a non-European power seemed to have passed away for ever. The

Advance to Barbarism

Turkish Empire now only gave cause for alarm lest its dissolution might disturb the European balance of power; the formerly semi-Asiatic state of Muscovy appeared successfully to have adopted European civilization — the court of Catherine the Great was to all outward appearances a reproduction of Versailles; the recent exploits of the English and French in India seemed to indicate that a wise Providence had ordained a special law of nature by which the smallest number of European troops was superior to an Oriental army however numerous; and across the Atlantic, there seemed no reason to doubt that the European colonists in America would always follow submissively European precept and example in all things — did not such men as George Washington and Benjamin Franklin comply in all respects with the highest European standards in conduct and outlook?

To such an eminently reasonable representative of the Age of Reason as Emeric de Vattel, it would barely have occurred as a conceivable possibility that the inhabitants of Europe, having once adopted the standards of civilized warfare, would ever again revert to the standards of the Thirty Years War which permitted any enormity to civilian life and property while still maintaining a sort of rough code of professional etiquette between the opposing leaders. A reversion to the even more barbarous standards of a far more remote time, when the primary objective of warfare was to attack the enemy civilian population and when captured enemy generals would be slaughtered as such by their captors, would have seemed to him utterly inconceivable.

When Vattel wrote, the nations of Europe had achieved such pre-eminent military supremacy that non-European nations seemed only to count in world affairs as subjects for exploitation by Europeans. The occasions when European civilization was threatened with destruction by invaders from Central Asia, who had penetrated unchecked to the Oder and the Adriatic, were so far past as to have become unreal and mythical. Russia, Europeanized by Peter the Great, had been accepted as a member of the European family of nations, and had spread her sway across Asia to the Pacific Ocean. In the latter half of the eighteenth century, the most perverse pessimist could not have foreseen that the Europeanized Russia of Peter was doomed to vanish utterly and to be replaced by the long dissolved Eurasian Empire founded by Genghis Khan, resurrected in a new but even more formidable shape, not only

Chapter 4 — *Civilized Warfare (The First Phase)*

non-European in origin, outlook and organization, but avowedly hostile to traditional European civilization.

No such nightmares disturbed reasonable men in the Age of Reason. The rising tide of complacency in that happy period reached its high-watermark in the passage written in 1770 by the Comte de Guibert quoted in the introduction to this book.

"Save in combat," declares the Comte proudly, "no blood is shed: prisoners are respected." In short, a temporary midway position had been reached between Gilgal and its Prophet sharpening his knife, on the one hand, and Nuremberg with its collection of foreign hangmen, on the other.

"Towns are no more destroyed," continues the Comte, "the countryside is no more ravaged." Again, the contrast is striking between, on the one hand, Magdeburg in 1631, with Tilly's soldiers rushing through the streets, hacking down men, women and children in a frenzy of slaughter, and, on the other hand, Dresden, that night in 1945, when an enemy air fleet arrived over the city "at the timely moment" when it was crowded with refugee women and children.

"Conquered peoples," concludes the Comte, "are only obliged to pay some sort of contributions which are often less than the taxes which they pay to their own sovereign."

For countless generations, the civilian population of Europe had patiently borne the consequences when "some delicate and tender prince whose spirit with divine ambition puff'd" decided to battle with some equally delicate and tender prince across the frontier, occasionally at the risk of his own skin, but invariably of theirs. For the first time, the result of such wars could be awaited with indifference.

The actual fighting would be done by long-service professional soldiers recruited from the dregs of the population — the scum of the earth as the Duke of Wellington frankly described them — guaranteed from acting otherwise than as machines by a ferocious discipline enforced by repeated flogging, led by officers who under no circumstances would forget they were gentlemen first and officers afterwards.

If one's prince managed to win, one could applaud his glorious triumph loyally, even if one derived no benefit therefrom. If he lost, there was no occasion for despair. Even a change of rulers would make little practical difference to the average citizen, who

Advance to Barbarism

generally transferred his allegiance in such circumstances without perceptible emotional disturbance.

If the Age of Reason did not endure long enough to bring about the abolition of civil warfare in Europe, it at least bestowed for a few decades upon the civilian population of Europe a very passable substitute for peace.

We have now described the manner in which warfare lost much of its barbarism and took on civilized traits. In the following chapters will be traced the steps by which it degenerated into the brutalities of the Second World War in which the imagined atrocities alleged by hate-propaganda during the First World War were enacted in grim fact. Three main steps in this process may be noted, each following naturally from the one preceding it.

This political chain reaction was set in motion by the French Revolution. Deprived of the services of the professional army officered by aristocrats of the Monarchy, the revolutionary government had recourse to a *levée en masse* of the population. The people of the countries overrun by the French armies, after their own professional armies had been shattered, achieved liberation by means of similar armies of conscripted civilians. The European wars waged between 1792 and 1815 were the first of the Peoples' Wars, so called because they were fought between peoples in arms and not as hitherto by professional armies maintained in peacetime by the rulers to enforce their wishes.

At first appeals to simple patriotism proved sufficient to inspire conscripted civilians with military ardour. Later the discovery was made that conscripted civilians fought better if they had been induced to hate the enemy against whom they were fighting. So gradually was evolved and perfected the modern science of emotional engineering, the purpose of which is to convince the average citizen that the citizens of the state against which it has been decided to wage war were monsters of depravity, barbarous, perfidious and cruel, with whom any thought of peace was impossible, to overcome whom no personal sacrifice would be too great.

Inevitably warfare conducted in an artificially inspired frenzy of fear and hatred changed its character. Thus began the period of so-called Total War to use the term adopted to describe hostilities waged regardless of the Rules of Civilized Warfare. Naturally the average civilian serving as a soldier, knowing

Chapter 4 — Civilized Warfare (The First Phase)

nothing and caring less of military traditions, and having been taught that it was his patriotic duty to believe that the enemy was committing atrocities of every description, felt himself free to act as he had been assured the enemy was acting. Hate propaganda always lays the greatest stress on the contention that the enemy is solely responsible for the outbreak of hostilities in order to generate in the mind of every individual soldier a personal grievance against the enemy for having wantonly forced him to leave home and endure the hardships and dangers of a campaign.

The act which may be cited as marking the end of the age of civilized warfare and the beginning of the age of Total War was the acceptance of the Lindemann Plan on the 30th March 1942.

The last stage of the chain reaction was the adoption of war-crimes trials as a method of disposing of captured leaders of the vanquished side which inevitably must make the future conduct of warfare more ruthless than ever. Now that every general knows that in the event of defeat he will assuredly be done to death by the victors if he falls into their hands, he can hardly be expected to hesitate to order the commission of any enormity which seems to him to offer some hope of staving off defeat.

In the next chapter will be considered the characteristics of Peoples' Wars, the first stage of the chain reaction which initiated the gradual rebarbarization of warfare.

Chapter 5 — Civilized Warfare (The Second Phase)

With the outbreak of the French Revolution civil warfare in Europe entered upon a new phase.

The epoch of Kings' Wars ended that happy interlude when wars were undertaken by kings against kings with small professional armies for objects which their subjects were neither expected to approve nor to understand. Then began the epoch of Peoples' Wars, that is to say wars which, if rarely undertaken from any genuine regard for the peoples' benefit, were waged by an increasingly large proportion of the adult male population.

The introduction of Peoples' Wars produced two marked changes in the character of warfare: 1. the appearance of huge hastily collected armies, raised by conscription, thus making wars much more savage and lethal; and 2. the rise of the science of propaganda or "emotional engineering" needed to induce these conscripted armies to fight with enthusiasm and with the hearty support of the populace at home.

The best treatment of the first phase or result of this change is presented by the eminent American expert on warfare, Mr. Hoffman Nickerson, in his book, *The Armed Horde*.[42] The loss of life, even as early as the wars of the French Revolution and Napoleon, vastly exceeded those of any previous wars, at least so far as those killed on the field of battle are concerned. Only 5,000 English had been killed during the whole year 1704, during which the decisive battle of Blenheim had been fought. By the time of Dumouriez and Napoleon, wars had become mass-murder on the battlefield. Napoleon was especially prodigal of men in battle. He lost about 40,000 in the Battle of Borodino alone. Moreover, disease in these mass-armies, with little provision for sanitation and medical treatment, killed even more than gunfire. While, at first, the rules

Chapter 5 — Civilized Warfare (The Second Phase)

of civilized warfare were continued in Peoples' Wars, there is no doubt that this new type of war contributed greatly to the increase of unrestrained savagery and mortality in warfare. One reason for the increase of ferocity was the necessary parallel development of propaganda.

Kings' Wars were fought by small armies of professional soldiers obeying orders: Peoples' Wars were fought by huge armies of conscripted civilians who, in order to fight with enthusiasm, had to be led to imagine that they knew for what they were fighting. The production, quickly and effectively, of a war psychosis thus became an imperative necessity. To meet this need the modern science of *emotional engineering*, as Aldous Huxley has labelled it, was gradually evolved.

In the Kings' Wars of the eighteenth century, the man in the street was not required to fight and he was preserved from suffering therein more than a minimum of loss and inconvenience. There was no occasion, therefore, to trouble him with explanations of the reasons for such wars. In the Peoples' Wars, which began in 1792 and have lasted to the present day, the man in the street was compelled to do the fighting and it became, therefore, no longer impudent presumption on his part to inquire the reason. As a consequence, it became necessary to work out a technique by which plausible reasons could be found on short notice to meet any contingency, or, as an alternative, a technique by which a condition of public hysteria could be created in which any reason would be accepted as plausible.

Thus was evolved the science of emotional engineering. To wage war, it had become necessary to generate hatred. Fear begets hatred. If the reasoning powers of the man in the street could be paralysed by a sufficiently vivid portrayal of a real or imaginary danger, not only would his natural but inconvenient curiosity as to his rulers' doings be stifled but he would fight the better in a state of blind hatred. It soon became recognized that neither professional military pride nor an intelligent conviction of the justice of a cause was sufficient inspiration. Every man must "see red," as Field Marshal Montgomery frankly told his troops before they landed on the Normandy beaches on "D-Day." Carnot's *levée en masse*, in 1793, and the Dresden holocaust of 1945 are linked together by a series of developments, each following naturally and logically from the other.

Advance to Barbarism

During the Revolutionary and Napoleonic wars (1792-1815) the standards of European civil warfare suffered a marked decline. The citizen soldiers of the new French Republic who invaded the Rhinelands, Belgium, and Italy were inspired by official proclamations about the prospect of riches as well as glory: in exchange for the blessings of liberty, the armies of France shamelessly plundered the countries which they overran. On the other hand, it must be admitted that a wide gulf exists between the looting of churches and art galleries, as during Napoleon's campaign in Italy, in 1796, and the systematic dismantling of factories, leaving a highly skilled industrial population dependent on them to starve in accordance with the Potsdam Agreement of a century and a half later. Stealing pictures and statues for the adornment of the victors' art galleries is one thing, but the stealing of essential machinery in order to impoverish the vanquished is quite another.[43]

After the restoration of order and discipline under the Napoleonic Empire, a marked return set in towards the high standards of the eighteenth century. Lapses, however, were not infrequent. Thus, in 1806, after the victory of Jena, the city of Lübeck was pillaged by the pursuing French troops; in 1808, Cordova was ruthlessly sacked by Dupont's army. On the other side, the most outstanding lapse was the celebrated sack of Badajoz in 1812, described with shame by an eye-witness, Sir William Napier.

But from the perspective of nearly 150 years, something can be said in extenuation of the orgy of robbery, rape, and murder with which Wellington's troops sullied the laurels they had won in one of the most heroic and costly assaults in the annals of the British Army. The outrages were limited to the rank and file, were committed in hot blood by troops who had just sustained terrific losses, and stern repression swiftly followed. It is absurd to compare this comparatively isolated incident with either the habitual pillage and homicide in which European armies had been wont to indulge during the Thirty Years War, or with the systematic and wholesale plundering of Germany after the Second World War which in extent and thoroughness stands without a parallel in history since it included in every part of Germany the official looting of public property and the equipment of factories in accordance with the Morganthau Plan and the appropriation

Chapter 5 — Civilized Warfare (The Second Phase)

of portable private property of every description by individual members of the occupying forces: in the eastern provinces the inhabitants who escaped with their lives considered themselves fortunate, everything they possessed being appropriated with the express approval of the Potsdam Conference.[44]

In Napoleonic times, the nearest parallel to such doings is to be found in the campaigns of the French armies in Spain. Even in these, however, depredations seem to have been generally limited to churches and monasteries; civilians, except in exceptional circumstances, were rarely molested. The primitive theory that, on defeat, all the property of the vanquished is vested automatically in the victors had not yet been re-affirmed.

What is most important about any war is the peace which it brings about. From this point of view, the wars of 1792-1815 maintained the highest standards. The moderation of the victors in 1815 appears to modern eyes simply superhuman. In accordance with Vattel's argument that only a peace based on reason and justice could be lasting, France was neither penalised nor humiliated. Not only was no French territory annexed, but France was left in possession of the German territory on the left bank of the Rhine which had been conquered by Louis XIV. No restrictions were imposed on the French army or navy, and the indemnity demanded was paid without difficulty within a decade.

The shooting of Marshal Ney after Waterloo is considered by many as a blot on the memory of the Duke of Wellington, and it has even been suggested that it will even bear some comparison with the doing to death of various enemy commanders in 1946. This suggestion is, of course, too absurd to consider, but in justice to the Duke of Wellington it should be remembered that Marshal Ney was shot by the Bourbon Government after a conviction by a French Court on a charge of treason against Louis XVIII — of which he was undeniably guilty. The most that can justly be said against the Duke of Wellington is that he did not bestir himself — as much as his admirers could with — to save a gallant opponent from the spite of his political enemies by interfering with the course of French justice.[45]

Throughout the nineteenth century civil wars in Europe continued to be waged in accordance with the rules of civilized warfare without any noteworthy lapses. European Civil War No. 6, otherwise known as the Crimean War, may be taken as representative of European warfare during this period in its least harmful aspect. Characteristically, at its commencement, there was general bewilderment as to the aims for which it was to be fought: once fairly started, however, this difficulty was quickly remedied by declaring that "the continuance of the war was essential to the vindication of the national honour." In the peace treaty which concluded it, there is not a single reference to the question of the Holy Places in Palestine, the ostensible cause of the war.

On the other hand, during its course each side had abundant opportunity to display the greatest courage and self-sacrifice: in fact, one episode, the Charge of the Light Brigade, has become symbolic of unreasoning heroism. The scope of the hostilities was strictly limited, damage to civilian life and property was negligible, and the casualties among the combatants, amounting to about a quarter of a million lives, was well below the average. No noteworthy or enduring political results were achieved and, consequently, European civilization as a whole sustained no serious setback.

No legacy of bitterness was left behind: the terms of peace, if read carefully, merely indicate that Russia had had the worst of the fighting. In the Crimea itself, "a spirit of amity and relief prevailed when a salute of 101 guns denoted the end of the war. Reviews and races took the place of battles, the troops of the allies and the Russians mingled in friendly intercourse — or at least in the common delight of cheerful inebriation."[46]

It must, however, be again stressed that the rules governing civil warfare in Europe were held to have little or no application to warfare between Europeans and non-Europeans outside Europe. Thus, Canton was savagely bombarded by a British fleet in 1841: the famous Summer Palace in Peking was deliberately sacked and burned by a Franco-British army in 1860; and, in 1863, the Japanese city of Kagoshima was ruthlessly destroyed by a fleet under Admiral Kuper as the readiest means of extorting trade concessions from the Japanese. In the Indian Mutiny, all restraints were quickly forgotten in a blaze of moral indignation and racial hatred. Colonel Neill hanged his prisoners wholesale; John Lawrence ceremoniously blew his captives from the mouths of cannons; and John Nicholson, while practising both methods of disposal on the widest scale, was so oppressed by their inadequacy that he urged "the flaying alive, impalement or burning" of the

Chapter 5 — Civilized Warfare (The Second Phase)

mutineers and quoted the Old Testament copiously in support of inflicting on them "the most excruciating tortures."[47]

In passing, it should be noted that there was abundant precedent for the doing to death of a number of distinguished Japanese prisoners of war after the overthrow of the Japanese Empire with the aid of the atom bomb in 1945. The mock-trial in 329 B.C. of Bessos the Persian governor, who attempted to maintain the Persian resistance to the Macedonian invaders, affords perhaps the earliest precedent. Having undergone various tortures as a preconviction punishment, Bessos was condemned to a formal trial, Alexander the Great himself assuming the role of prosecutor. After delivering an eloquent speech demanding conviction, Alexander then assumed the role of judge, convicted the unfortunate Oriental and sentenced him to death by torture.[48] Throughout the ages which have passed since the days of Bessos down to the present day, Europeans have always in practice refused to admit that any rules which might exist governing European civil wars had any application to Asiatics. The hanging, therefore, of a number of Japanese generals and admirals in 1946, was not so revolutionary a departure from recognized practice as was the doing to death, during the same year, of professional European soldiers at Nuremberg.

In Asia, methods of warfare have remained completely unchanged throughout the ages. In Africa, the native races have remained entirely uninfluenced by European rules and conventions, as the French from experience in Algeria, the British in the Sudan, and the Italians in Abyssinia, can eloquently testify. Only in South Africa, in the wars between the Dutch settlers and the British Empire, have European traditions in the main been followed although Captain Liddell Hart considers that the plan adopted by Lord Kitchener, in 1900, "of laying waste the countryside, burning the Boers' farms and removing the women and children to concentration camps in which some 25,000 died may be regarded as the inauguration of total warfare."[49] Reluctantly granting this and admitting that similar charges could have been brought against Lord Roberts and Lord Kitchener for their treatment of the Boer partisans as those brought forty-five years later against Field Marshal Kesselring for his treatment of Italian irregulars and banditti, it must be conceded that the peace terms imposed on the Boers at Vereeniging complied in most respects

Advance to Barbarism

with the requirements laid down by Emeric de Vattel in 1758 for a just and, therefore, lasting settlement. The subsequent careers of General Botha and General Smuts may be cited as conclusive proof of the wisdom of the great Swiss jurist's contentions.

In spite also of virulent hate propaganda, quite in the modern style, which raged in the British Press against the Boers, and in the Press of the rest of the world against Great Britain, the struggle itself was conducted on the whole in accordance with European traditions. In fact, some of the episodes of this war have come to appear well nigh unbelievable. Thus when on March 6, 1902, Lord Methuen was defeated and captured at Tweebosch, his captor, De la Rey, at once sent him in the charge of his chief medical officer to the nearest British post since, owing to lack of medical supplies, he was unable to provide the attention which the British general's wound seemed to need. However useful Lord Methuen might have been to the Boers as a hostage, the health of a prisoner of war was too sacred to imperil by retaining him in captivity. The idea of making this capture an opportunity to avenge the deaths of Scheepers, Lotter, and other Boer partisan leaders, recently executed by the British, does not seem even to have occurred to De la Rey's ingenuous mind.

In America, methods of warfare have varied roughly in accordance with the extent of European influence. In South America, with its large Indian and half-caste population, this influence has been weakest and, as a consequence, warfare has been little influenced by restraints. Thus, in the great war waged in 1865 against Paraguay by the Argentine, Uruguay, and Brazil, no pretence was long maintained of distinguishing between combatants and the civil population—the essential characteristic of civilized warfare as it had evolved in Europe—with the result that, after five years of desperate conflict, two-thirds of the inhabitants of Paraguay had perished.

In North America, European influence had always been predominant and one would therefore expect to find warfare conducted there more or less in accordance with European standards. The facts, however, do not confirm this reasonable expectation. Thus, the crowning episode of the war of 1812-14 between Britain and the United States was when a British column of some 4,000 men was landed in Chesapeake Bay, marched inland to Washington and there burnt the Capitol, the White House and various other public buildings.[50] It is difficult to reconcile this exploit with the European code, or many similar British raids on the American coasts and the American raids across the Canadian border, in all of which the destruction of enemy property was the sole aim. Compare, for example, General Haddick's raid on Berlin during the Seven Years War when the Austrians carefully refrained from all violence to persons and property and withdrew after collecting a ransom from the City Council so moderate that Frederick was able to reimburse it at once out of his own private funds.

Inasmuch as the settlers in the English colonies in America and who later became citizens of the United States had experienced little contact with European civilized warfare as it had developed during the 18th century, but had undergone long experience of primary warfare against the American Indians, it is not strange that the first serious departure from the European code by a people of European descent should have taken place in the United States.

Most of the wars in which the white settlers in North America had been involved before 1861 were with the Red Indians and these may be cited as classic examples on a small scale of harsh and rudimentary primary warfare. No unqualified interludes were provided by the wars waged by the British and French settlers in America with each other as colonial militia fighting loyally in the service of the King of England and the King of France respectively, alongside the professional troops of these monarchs. Neither side scrupled to enlist the Red Indians who continued as auxiliaries of their European allies to wage war in the manner of their remote ancestors. Lapses into barbaric practices were consequently frequent. The only true exception to be found is the War of Independence which was conducted in accordance with European standards. The Mexican War of 1845 was a brief and relatively trivial conflict between the United States and a people on a much lower mechanical and military level. Thus the inhabitants of the United States at the middle of the 19th century had had no experience nor any tradition of a major war conducted according to the European code which required that hostilities be limited to the military forces and that non-combatants and private property be respected. But they had a long background of experience and tradition of primary warfare in a most savage form.

Advance to Barbarism

Hence, it is not surprising that the first great historic break with European practice should have taken place in the sanguinary American Civil War (or "The War Between the States", as the Southerners still prefer to designate it). The military precedents in the United States were nearly all in the pattern of primary warfare. Even President Lincoln himself had fought briefly in his youth against the Red Indians and he exerted a dominant influence on Northern military policy and strategy.

It was the Northern or Federal armies which produced this historic reversion to primary or total warfare. The North had endured much more bellicose contact with the Red Indians and was much less influenced by Europe than the South. The latter was culturally a European colony until after the Civil War, Southern children were educated in Europe, and the Southern aristocracy travelled widely in Europe. Southern professional soldiers were very familiar with European military ideals. General Robert E. Lee, the military leader of the South, was the perfect example of Southern military chivalry in complete accord with the European ideals of civilized warfare. It is for this reason that Professor T. Harry Williams accurately calls Lee "the last of the great old-fashioned generals." His "old-fashioned" trait was his fidelity to the European code of civilized warfare. While General John H. Morgan and other Southern raiders reverted to primary warfare in their attacks on the countryside, Lee was generally able to keep the Southern strategy in harmony with the European code.

There has been a traditional habit of saddling the responsibility for the Northern departure from civilized warfare on General William Tecumseh Sherman who conducted the famous march through Georgia from Atlanta to the sea, and continued it along the Atlantic seaboard. This is quite unjust. Sherman only executed the most dramatic and devastating example of the strategy which was laid down by President Lincoln himself and was followed faithfully by General Ulysses S. Grant as commander-in-chief of the Northern armies. That Lincoln determined the basic lines of Northern military strategy has been well established in such books as Collin R. Ballard's *The Military Genius of Abraham Lincoln* and T. Harry Williams' *Lincoln and His Generals*. Grant only efficiently applied Lincoln's military policy in the field. Professor Williams calls Grant "the first of the great moderns." He goes on to say that the "modernity of Grant's

Chapter 5 — Civilized Warfare (The Second Phase)

mind was most apparent in his grasp of the concept that war was becoming total and that the destruction of the enemy's economic resources was as effective and legitimate a form of warfare as the destruction of his armies." Hence, it is apparent that Sherman was only carrying out effectively the military policy which Lincoln and Grant had adopted. The exploit upon which his fame rests opened a new epoch in modern warfare.

In the Spring of 1864, General Sherman was in command of the Tennessee sector far from the northern theatre of war in Virginia. Unexpectedly taking the offensive, he pushed forward and captured Atlanta, one of the most important industrial centres of the South upon which the Confederates greatly relied for supplies of all kinds.

According to the accepted rules of civilized warfare in this exposed position two simple alternatives lay before him, either to retreat to his base before he was cut off or to prepare to withstand a siege in Atlanta. Sherman, however, saw no reason why he should be fettered by rules which it had pleased the European nations to adopt in their wars with each other. His first act was to expel the inhabitants of Atlanta from their homes. His second was systematically to destroy the factories and mills of the city so that they could never again serve the enemy. His third was to abandon the devastated city and to push on to the Atlantic coast across Georgia, laying waste the country as he went. "Until we can repopulate Georgia, it is useless to occupy it," he wrote to headquarters. "I can make this march and make Georgia howl!"

Some of the richest lands of the South were devastated. Having captured and looted Savannah, Sherman turned northwards along the Atlantic coast to Charleston. He made no secret of his intentions: "I sincerely believe," he wrote General Halleck in Washington, "the whole United States would rejoice to have my army turned loose on South Carolina, to devastate that state in the manner we have done in Georgia." To which Halleck replied with admiring approval and the expression of a hope that "should you capture Charleston, by some accident the place may be destroyed." To this, Sherman responded with charming simplicity that the division assigned to occupy Charleston had a reputation "of doing their work pretty well." "The truth is," he added, "the whole army is burning with insatiable desire to wreak vengeance upon South Carolina."

Advance to Barbarism

To do him justice, Sherman was no simple-minded barbarian carried away by the heat of the moment; nor was he vindictive against a people who practised Negro slavery. Before the Civil War he had criticized the extremists on both sides of the slavery question. On the eve of the War he wrote his brother that: "I recoil from a war when the Negro is the only question." Sherman was capable of formulating his principles and defending them on logical grounds. With regard to the destruction of Atlanta he wrote to General Halleck, "if the people raise a howl against my barbarity and cruelty, I will answer war is war. If the enemy wants peace, they and their relatives must stop the war." In answer to the protest of the Mayor of Atlanta, Sherman said: "You cannot qualify war in harsher terms than I will. War is cruelty, and you cannot refine it."

The crisp argument that war is war, which Sherman propounds with the pride of a discoverer, as justification for the destruction of Atlanta, is of extreme antiquity. On the Assyrian bas-reliefs the complaint often occurs, made more in sorrow than in anger, that the inhabitants of this or that city had "hardened their hearts" when threatened by an Assyrian army. Peace could so easily have been purchased by prompt surrender followed by payment of tribute consisting of all they possessed. Instead, it is recorded sorrowfully, they decided to resist and naturally suffered the consequences. The following passage from King Asshurbanipal's annals illustrates what these consequences normally were: "The wells of drinking water I dried up: for a journey of a month and twenty-five days the districts of Elam I laid waste: destruction, servitude and drought I poured over them. The passage of men, the treading of oxen and sheep and the springing up of good trees I burnt off the fields."

In short, probably quite as justifiably as General Sherman, King Asshurbanipal could claim that his warriors had a reputation for doing their work pretty well.

But the discovery which Sherman may have regarded as original in 1864, was of immemorial antiquity even in the days of King Asshurbanipal. The procedure which he advocated is neatly set forth in the Book of Deuteronomy. The ancient Hebrews invading Canaan were directed "when they came nigh to a city to fight against it, to proclaim peace unto it." (Ch. 20. v. 10.) If the offer of peace were accepted, the inhabitants were to be made slaves but

Chapter 5 — Civilized Warfare (The Second Phase)

not otherwise maltreated. But if they were so presumptuous as to refuse peace and "to make war on thee" (i.e., defend themselves), "thou shalt smite the males thereof with the edge of the sword but the women and little ones and the cattle and all that is in the city even all the spoil thereof, thou shalt take unto thyself."

Here is set out concisely the exact purport of Sir Arthur Harris' verbose broadcast to the German people on July 28, 1942, except, of course, the gallant Air Marshal naturally refrained from informing his hearers that slavery would be the price of accepting his offer of peace, while, as a herald of unrestricted bombing, he could not, like the ancient Hebrews of the 12th century B.C., profess any intention to discriminate between the adult male population and "the women and little ones."[51]

Though the Northern military policy of Lincoln, Grant and Sherman marked the first great example of the reversion to primary or total warfare and set a precedent for the "Splendid Decision" of the British on May 11, 1940, it provided no precedent or example for the liquidation of conquered enemy leaders by massacre, mock-trials, or war-crimes trials which followed the Second World War. In this respect, Lincoln and Grant followed faithfully in the chivalrous European tradition, a procedure best exemplified by Grant's treatment of Lee after the Southern forces had surrendered at Appomattox.

The story of Grant's famous meeting with Lee to discuss the terms upon which the Southern Army would surrender reads today like a fairytale fit to be placed alongside Froissart's story of the capture of the French King by the Black Prince at Poitiers. The terms were expressly framed to provide for the termination of hostilities with as little humiliation for the vanquished as possible. In brief, they stipulated that the Southern Army should simply disband and each man return to his home, the officers giving their parole for themselves and their men and retaining their side arms and horses. Characteristically, Lee requested only that all ranks be permitted to retain their horses and, equally characteristically, Grant made this concession without haggling. Later, when the politicians at Washington began to scream wildly against the "pampering" of a defeated enemy and to demand that Lee should be tried for treason, Grant pointed out that the Southern Army had surrendered on definite terms and that, so long as these terms were observed, Lee could not be tried for treason. "Good faith as

Advance to Barbarism

well as true policy dictate that we should observe the conditions of the convention," Grant wrote scathingly to those who demanded a legalized lynching of Southern military leaders.

The Federal methods of total warfare and the arguments which were used to justify them aroused curiously little interest at the time in Europe. Naturally, supercilious eyebrows were raised in professional circles in Aldershot, Potsdam, and Longchamps. But, after all, they reasoned, what better could be expected of colonials led by militia officers whose only training had been wars with Red Indians. Von Moltke dismissed the American Civil War as "a colossal conflict between two armed mobs chasing each other around in a wilderness." No lesson was to be learnt by European professional soldiers from such disorderly proceedings, least of all the hoary truth that one way of winning a war was to terrorize the enemy civilian population. In the fullness of time, this hoary truth was to be impressed upon Europeans, not by observing a distant campaign between armed mobs on the far side of the Atlantic, but by personal experience.

Fortunately for their peace of mind, no vision of the future was vouchsafed to the military panjandrums of Europe. To them, the possibility would have seemed grotesque that within a few decades the descendants of the "armed mobs" fighting under Grant and Lee in Virginia should have the presumption to intervene decisively in a European civil war. Even if Eisenhower's men could hardly be dismissed, like their ancestors, as an armed mob, yet, by European professional standards of the 1860's, they would have been classed less as soldiers than as specialists in the use of various new mass-produced instruments for taking human life. Their whole outlook on warfare—which was precisely that of General Sherman—would have been considered in the 1860's as the exact opposite of all that was meant by the word soldierly.

General Sherman's views on war were shared and applied by his dashing colleague, General Philip H. Sheridan, one of whose claims to fame was his merciless devastation of the Shenandoah Valley in the campaign of 1864. In 1870, General Sheridan visited Europe and, as the guest of German Headquarters, was a favoured eye-witness of the memorable campaign in France in that year—for the night after the battle of Gravelotte he shared the bare boards of an abandoned house within range of the forts round Metz with Count Bismarck and the Grand Duke of Mecklenburg, and he

Chapter 5 — Civilized Warfare (The Second Phase)

was one of the distinguished gathering on the Hill of Cheveuge which witnessed General Reille hand to King Wilhelm the letter from Napoleon III announcing the surrender of the French Army encircled in Sedan. The fighting capacity of the German troops and the skill of their leaders filled General Sheridan with boundless admiration but their lack of enterprise in allowing themselves to be cramped and hampered by the rules of civilized warfare then prevailing in Europe, aroused his contemptuous amusement. Having by a swift and unbroken series of victories destroyed or captured the bulk of the French regular forces, the Germans were experiencing great difficulty in defending the communications of their armies blockading Paris from the raids of irregulars working behind the German lines and from the attacks of the new French armies being gathered in the provinces for the relief of the capital. "You know how to hit an enemy as no other army does," Sheridan remarked to Bismarck, "but you have not learnt how to annihilate him. *One must see more smoke of burning villages, otherwise you will not finish off the French."*

Bismarck did not, of course, need to have it pointed out to him that France could be quickly brought to her knees by sending forth punitive expeditions to lay waste the countryside. To sully the glory of their victories over the French armies by a barbarous campaign against the French civilian population did not appeal to the German leaders. The smoke of burning villages seemed to Europeans of that generation more in keeping with fighting Red Indians in the Wild West than with orderly warfare between civilized European nations. In spite of Sheridan's doubts, they remained confident that the war could be won by civilized methods of warfare in accordance with European traditions. This confidence proved fully justified. The war was at length crowned by a victorious but negotiated peace and Europe enjoyed a respite from civil war which lasted for forty-three years.

An interesting sidelight on the thought and manners of those ethically inconceivably remote days of the Franco-Prussian War is given by a long out-of-print and forgotten book, *Im Grossen Hauptquartier 1870-71,* which recently came by chance into the present writer's possession. Published in 1910 as filial tribute by the author's daughter, this book consists of the collected articles contributed to a long defunct Berlin paper by its special war correspondent, Hermann Salingré.

Advance to Barbarism

From a literary point of view little merit can be claimed for these articles. In them Salingré shows himself to have been a simple-minded man, unassuming, diffident, and prosaic. No one can be imagined further removed than he from that flamboyant militarism which characterized so conspicuously many of the next generation of Germans and French. While rejoicing naively in the succession of German victories, he neither glorifies nor idealizes a soldier's life. On the contrary, he dwells continually on the deprivations of the men compelled by the call of duty to leave their homes in Germany to undertake a few months campaigning in France. In fact, his lamentations over the cruel fate of the troops, prevented by the unexpectedly prolonged resistance of Paris from rejoining their dear ones for Christmas, strikes a modern reader as little short of comic in their extravagance. Accepting without question or argument that his country was entirely in the fight, he expresses no bitterness against the French, presumably, in his view, entirely in the wrong. The sight of damaged property merely fills him with thankfulness to God that his country had been spared the horrors of war. While repeating all the stock chestnuts of war reporting of the kind which no doubt delighted Assyrian readers in cuneiform characters and certainly delighted the British public in 1945 – for example, that while the enemy was tenacious in fighting at long range, he could not withstand attack at close quarters with the bayonet – he regales his readers with no enemy atrocity stories.

The supreme moment of Salingré's experiences was after the surrender of Sedan when he was privileged to witness from a distance of twenty paces the meeting of the Emperor Napoleon III with Count Bismarck at Donchery. His reflections on this epoch-making occasion were as ever platitudinous, but he describes vividly enough the sight of this "once so powerful man" waiting patiently, seated on a peasant's chair outside the cottage of a Belgian weaver named Fournaise, the arrival of his conqueror. He naively comments that he found the Emperor's appearance very different from what he had been led to expect by the German comic papers. His natural jubilation, he tells us, was quickly replaced by "a sad, heartrending impression" at so complete a downfall. Upon the Emperor happening to glance in his direction he felt that one could not "tread so unfortunate a man deeper in the mud" – "I respectfully removed my hat and

Chapter 5 — Civilized Warfare (The Second Phase)

experienced a thrill of satisfaction when I saw that the Emperor had noted my greeting and thanked me."[52]

Salingré was an entirely conventional and commonplace individual. He was not only a typical German but a typical journalist of his generation. Herein lies the whole significance of this incident. In no circumstances would his natural diffidence have allowed him either to rise far above or sink much below the accepted standards of his time. Even if one can imagine a present-day war correspondent being moved to such an act, it is impossible to imagine him reporting it and still less his editor accepting and printing it. One trembles to think of the fate of anyone who had committed such an act of courtesy to Field Marshal Keitel during the proceedings at Nuremberg! Whether he would have been instantly committed for contempt of court turns, of course, on the knotty legal point whether it is possible to commit contempt of court to a court sitting without jurisdiction. Probably one of the non-European jailors posted menacingly at the back of each prisoner would have settled the matter summarily by a blow with his club. At the least, immediate expulsion from occupied territory would have resulted, followed by instant dismissal on the culprit's return to Fleet Street.

Judged by what is the only valid test, the battle of Sedan must be assigned a unique position among European battles. War is not a sporting event in which victory is an end in itself: it can only be justified as a means by which an equitable and lasting peace is achieved. A century before, the Swiss jurist, Emeric de Vattel, had convincingly argued that only an equitable peace could be lasting and that an equitable peace must conform to certain specified principles. Although it contravened several of the most vital of these principles, the peace which followed Moltke's triumph at Sedan endured for no less than forty-three years. Relieved from the waste and destruction of civil war for a period longer than any in the history of Europe, civilization throughout Europe made enormous strides between 1871 and 1914. Within a few decades of its close, this period began to appear in public memory as a remote and semi-mythical epoch of universal contentment and security, of unbroken tranquillity and prosperity. Prosperity, in fact, seemed to flow naturally from peace. Never before had the rich been so rich and never before had there been such opportunities to enjoy riches. With only colonial wars and few social services

Advance to Barbarism

to be paid for, taxation was incredibly light. As wealth increased, the standard of living rose: new discoveries and improvements brought comforts and luxuries within the reach of ever widening circles of the population. In most European countries, measures of social reform improved to a greater or less extent the lot of those who depended on their daily earnings. A belief in inevitable and unending progress became universal: there was a general feeling of security. It appeared incredible that European supremacy would ever be challenged: the rest of the world seemed created by a kindly Providence for exploitation by one or other of the European Powers. There was the best reason for thinking this happy state of affairs would continue indefinitely, since it was utterly impossible to conceive any issue arising between the European Powers important enough to tempt any sane statesman to run the risk of a general disaster by plunging Europe into another civil war.

It rarely happens that even the victors in a modern war derive any lasting benefit from their victory, and any examples of mankind in general benefiting from warfare are rare indeed. The fact that the peoples of Europe benefited by the German victory over France in 1870 was assuredly not due to any strain of altruism in the German character, still less that it was one of the aims of Bismarck's policy to confer benefits on mankind. Bismarck's altruism was a by-product of his realism and his nationalism. Fundamentally, his aims were as selfish as those of any later statesman. But his selfishness was intelligent selfishness. He was no lover of peace in the abstract: he had no more moral scruples against resorting to war, if policy required it, than had Franklin D. Roosevelt. Down to 1870, his aims could only be achieved by war, while, thereafter, his aims could only be achieved by peace. Having saved the German people by three victorious wars from that condition of disunity and political impotence which for centuries had made their country a battle field for their neighbours, Bismarck realized that a long period of peace was essential for recovery and development. If Germany's neighbours began to fight each other, Germany was certain to become involved. Therefore, he devoted himself, from the downfall of France in 1870 to his dismissal by the young Kaiser Wilhelm in 1890, to making Europe safe for Germany. This he achieved by negotiating a series of defensive alliances and treaties designed to preserve the peace of Europe. As Esme Cecil Wingfield-Stratford puts it:

Chapter 5 — Civilized Warfare (The Second Phase)

"Bismarck had gone about his task of establishing German unity with a skill and finesse never surpassed, if ever equalled, in the records of diplomacy. So far as the world could be made safe for peace and for Germany he made it so. He was no philanthropist. He had no scruples, and no ideals beyond that of a simple loyalty to his country. He was never more sincere than when he described Germany as a saturated Power. Now that all was German from the Vosges to the Vistula, he had no sentimental dreams of expansion, even in the colonial field."[53]

One of the indirect consequences which followed from Bismarck's peace policy was that Europe became for nearly half a century little short of an Utopia for its ruling classes, and particularly for its royalties. The kings and princes of Europe whose grandfathers had lived in dread of the guillotine and whose grandsons were mostly destined to die violent deaths or become forgotten exiles, enjoyed unparalleled security, prestige and esteem. In public, they were regarded with awe and reverence when they went forth to attend each other's weddings and funerals, to review their own or each other's troops and navies, or to pay state visits on each other. In private, there was frequent bickering among them and occasionally antipathies such as that between Queen Victoria's eldest son, Edward, Prince of Wales, and her grandson, the young German Kaiser, but, publicly, the most cordial sentiments were always expressed. The European royal families were all more or less nearly related by blood or marriage to each other and to that strong-minded old lady who resided in Windsor Castle and who exercised over them a matriarchal influence which few ventured to defy.

Happy were kings in those days and happy the subjects whom kings delighted to honour. It might well be thought that the ruling classes in the leading European states, for whom the various royalties acted as leaders or figureheads, would at least refrain from conduct which would endanger this, for them, ideal state of affairs. Had only the ruling classes of Germany, Austria, and Russia held together in mutual self-protection, the established order might have continued indefinitely. The Haves had nothing to fear from an uprising of the Have-nots: a dozen Lenins could have achieved nothing more than the stirring up of local disturbances, easily suppressed. So long as peace was preserved, the Haves were secure. The Haves in all the states of Europe were thus linked by one paramount interest, the preservation of peace. As all effective political power was vested in the Haves, it is hard to imagine how peace could have rested on a securer foundation.

In fact, however, the peace of Europe rested on nothing more substantial than the political life of one old man. So long as Bismarck remained Chancellor, the German Empire served as a mighty makeweight for a stable equilibrium. Once he had gone, his successors were free to join with zest in that time-honoured game of European diplomacy which in the past had always been the prelude to the outbreak of European civil warfare. The other great Powers joined with equal zest in the game. In the circumstances then existing, this was not a difficult game in which to take part.

Europe was covered by a network of alliances, treaties, secret agreements, guarantees, ententes, and understandings and there was ready to hand a profusion of unsatisfied claims, concessions, spheres of influence, grievances, and prescriptive rights. It was an easy matter, therefore, to find, for example, an ambiguous clause in a treaty and then, having secretly purchased in advance the support of neighbouring Powers by promises of concessions, to put forward a claim, based on a novel interpretation of this clause, against some other Power, either a weaker Power or a Power distracted at the moment by some similar activity. If the diplomatist in charge played his cards so well that this other Power felt compelled to give way, he was held to have scored a diplomatic triumph and his grateful sovereign would reward him with titles and honours. On the other hand, if he played his cards so badly that the other Power felt itself strong enough to reject his claim, his country was held to have received a diplomatic rebuff. In that case, he would probably be dismissed, and his successor would be entrusted with the task of vindicating the national dignity, it being an inflexible rule of the game that the losing side must take immediate steps to avenge a diplomatic rebuff, a rule which ensured that the game went on *ad infinitum*.

Seen in retrospect, the issues at stake in the periodic crises which distracted Europe after Bismarck's dismissal seem indescribably trivial. For example, the outstanding diplomatic triumph of the epoch 1870-1914 was when Austria, in 1908, succeeded, by a masterpiece of sharp practice, in scoring off against Russia by formally annexing the former Turkish province of Bosnia, a province she had administered with the consent of

Chapter 5 — Civilized Warfare (The Second Phase)

all the Powers, entirely as she saw fit, for upwards of thirty years. This achievement, from which Austria derived no practical benefit and from which no one suffered any material harm, imperilled the whole structure of capitalist civilization in Europe and proved to be an important step towards the final catastrophe six years later.

The behaviour of the ruling caste in Europe during the first years of the twentieth century can only be compared with that of the inhabitants of a beautiful and comfortable house who persist in descending into the basement in which a store of gun powder is kept for the purpose of letting off fireworks. The fact could not be disguised that there was an acute danger of war every time a crisis occurred. It was, indeed, one of the inflexible rules of the diplomatic game that if the parties involved in a crisis muddled themselves into a position so that neither side could withdraw "with honour" there was no alternative open to them but to go to war. Reliance seems to have been placed on the assumption that when another war came it would be a strictly limited war similar to those of the eighteenth century — after the generals had fought a few battles, the diplomatists would again resume control and negotiate a settlement by which existing treaties would be varied slightly in favour of the side which on the whole had had the best of the fighting. No one seems to have realized that conditions had changed markedly since the eighteenth century or suspected that new and potent forces would be released on the outbreak of war.

The power of one of these new forces, namely the power of the Press, should at least have been foreseen, since in peace time it had already developed a disastrous influence over international relations. By the rules of the diplomatic game, double-dealing and sharp-practice were permissible within certain ill-defined limits. If these limits were exceeded, a formal "sharp note of protest" was sent to the offending party. Such notes, couched in stereotyped diplomatic language, gave no offence. It was a recognized move in the game to profess indignation on occasion at the doings of the other side. But to the Press these protests possessed news value: they served as a means of arousing public interest, and, if well handled, of increasing sales. The offending Power was, therefore, roundly denounced for trickery and perfidy, and, needless to say, its Press retorted in the same strain. The language employed, although moderate compared with the language now habitually employed by the Press on such occasions, served to accustom the publics of the various European countries to regard certain groups of foreigners as gallant allies and certain groups of foreigners as treacherous enemies. Wingfield-Stratford puts the matter in a nutshell where he writes:

"A disease was infecting the whole of civilization, causing the international temperature to rise to a fever heat, with danger of ultimate collapse. The whole system by which the world was governed was hopelessly, fatally, out of date. With civilization becoming every year more international, with the world drawing together into a single economic unit, the last resort of human wisdom was to set up an uncontrolled anarchy of nations and nationalisms, and to employ all the resources of science to make that anarchy more deadly. Hatred was now engendered by scientific mass-suggestion, commerce was choked by scientific tariffs, "backward peoples" were bled white by scientific exploitation, and the ultimately inevitable suicide of war would be rendered scientifically complete. Even the best that Bismarck could do, by the diplomatic finesse of which he was master, was to maintain an unstable equilibrium, and the worst that Wilhelm II could do, by an almost incredible series of diplomatic blunders, was to hasten the catastrophe that was bound to come sooner or later, and would be worse later than sooner."[54]

Outwardly, in 1914, no great change had taken place in the structure of civilization during the respite of forty-three years which followed Sedan. This is the best apology which can be made for the men who so lightheartedly embarked on war in that memorable year. At the outset of the First World War, all the belligerents were actuated by strictly limited objects and all probably quite honestly intended to achieve them by limited means. The Allies were paying a quite undeserved compliment to his intelligence when they attributed to Kaiser Wilhelm vast Machiavellian schemes of world conquest; comparable was the intricate plot to encircle Germany which the Germans attributed to their enemies. All parties blundered helplessly into war with minds singularly innocent of ideas, good or bad. All, to a greater or lesser extent, had been striking attitudes in shining armour until a situation had arisen in which hallowed tradition and national honour could only be preserved by war.

No other explanation is tenable on the facts except on the assumption that a sudden wave of insanity swept the governments

Chapter 5 — Civilized Warfare (The Second Phase)

of Europe. Mr. Wingfield-Stratford's final conclusion indeed seems to be that the utter irresponsibility of the European ruling classes in the decade preceding 1914 was tinged by actual madness. Writing in 1933 he declares:

"I am aware that a plain, unvarnished account of the years immediately preceding the War reads rather like the chronicle of a vast lunatic asylum.... If a number of prosperous gentlemen were to start cutting each others' throats, and wrecking all the luxurious furniture of their common abode, we might fairly assume that when, ten minutes before, they had sat politely glaring at each other and fingering their knives, they were not quite right in the head."[55]

After the passage of another thirty years it is hardly possible to say more with any confidence than that we shall fully understand the root causes of the First World War when we know exactly why the Gadarene Swine rushed down a steep place into the sea. St. Mark tells us that the whole herd perished and so in that case this was the end of the matter. But if any members of the herd had been swimmers and so had escaped drowning, we may be sure that an acrimonious controversy would have started among the survivors as to which particular pig was mainly responsible for leading that fatal headlong rush down the steep place into the sea.

In 1914, life on this planet had become exceedingly pleasant for the ruling classes. For those who already had much, more was being given abundantly, the amenities of life were being constantly increased, and absolute security was assured, providing only that the ruling classes would refrain from suicidal civil war. Conquest from without was out of the question — even Kaiser Wilhelm knew in his heart that he was talking melodramatic nonsense when he made the flesh of his contemporaries creep by warnings of the Yellow Peril. Revolution from within could easily have been repressed — even in Czarist Russia only a disastrous foreign war could seriously imperil the security of the established order.

The two main immediate causes of the First World War — the Russian desire for the Straits leading out of the Black Sea and the French desire for the return of Alsace Lorraine — could surely have been handled by diplomacy. Britain and Sir Edward Grey were the main obstacles to awarding Russia the Straits, and Germany was willing to discuss the extension of considerable autonomy to Alsace-Lorraine. From all conceivable external dangers the established order was, indeed, absolutely secure. Danger came from within. As early as 1900, certain symptoms might have been detected by acute observers which suggested that, in the next European civil war, the belligerents might not be disinclined to hearken to tempting counsel of the kind that General Sheridan had offered Bismarck in 1870. A new spirit was abroad or, perhaps to put it more correctly, an old spirit dating from the times of King Sennacherib was showing signs of reviving. One of the earliest spokesmen of the new age which lay ahead was the young German emperor, Wilhelm II, whose true spiritual home, it can now be seen, was not, as he imagined, at the Round Table of King Arthur in the remote past, but at the Yalta Conference half a century later.

By most of his contemporaries Wilhelm was regarded as an ill-balanced neurotic, obsessed with his own perfections and the unqualified wickedness of anyone who opposed him. As a consequence, his most outrageous assertions caused nothing more than embarrassment at home and amusement abroad. Even his appeal to his troops embarking at Bremerhaven to take part in the Boxer Campaign that they should emulate the doings of King Attila and his Huns, aroused no general apprehensions as to what the future might hold in store. It was felt that such sentiments could at any rate have no possible application to warfare between European nations. Had not the existing standards of European civilization endured for two centuries and survived even so severe a test as the Napoleonic Wars? When another test came, everyone, including Queen Victoria's grandson, could be trusted to act like gentlemen.[56]

Another symptom which might have given ground for reflection came from across the Atlantic where President Theodore Roosevelt was carrying out his "policy of the big stick" with characteristic vigour. Although by many, including his fellow-countryman, Henry James, the President might be dismissed as "a mere monstrous embodiment of unprecedented resounding noise", the small states of Latin America found it perilous not to treat him seriously. When Colombia failed to come to terms with him in regard to the building of a canal across the Isthmus of Panama, a mysterious revolution immediately broke out in the canal zone, the Colombian Government was peremptorily

Chapter 5 — Civilized Warfare (The Second Phase)

forbidden to send troops to restore order and a treaty providing for the building of the canal on terms most favourable to the United States was promptly concluded with the newly-established provisional government of Panama. No more workmanlike job can be attributed to Hitler or Stalin. It is significant that Theodore Roosevelt's brusque rejection of the German demands at the time of the Venezuelan crisis of 1902 won for him the lasting respect and admiration of Kaiser Wilhelm. Although unlike in many ways, the two men were linked by a fellow-feeling arising from the lack of appreciative understanding which they both found in their contemporaries.

Perhaps, however, the dawning spirit of the days which were to come most clearly revealed itself in Admiral Lord Fisher who, with the possible exception of Lord Haldane, was probably the ablest of the men who surrounded King Edward VII. Speaking to the journalist, W. T. Stead, in 1900, Admiral Fisher declared:

"I am not for war, I am for peace. If you rub it in, both at home and abroad, that you are ready for instant war with every unit of your strength in the front line, and intend to be first in, and hit your enemy in the belly, and kick him when he is down, and boil your prisoners in oil if you take any, and torture his women and children, then people will keep clear of you."

Of course, no one in 1900 was prepared to believe that any civilized man could really hold such an opinion, still less that within half a century this opinion would become a commonplace. For this reason only, the expression of such sentiments did the speaker no harm professionally or socially: they were dismissed as mere examples of quarterdeck humour. The Admiral's favourite maxim, "Hit first, hit hard and hit anywhere" was considered rather stirring but without any particular significance. Writing, in 1912, to Lord Esher, Lord Fisher defended his views by insisting that "It's quite silly not to make war damnable to the whole mass of your enemy's population. When war comes, might is right, and the Admiralty will know what to do."

It not, of course, known at the time that Admiral Fisher had no hesitation it urging that his views should be carried into practice. When it became clear that the naval building programme commenced by Admiral Tirpitz was becoming a menace to British naval supremacy, Admiral Fisher begged for permission to end summarily the armament race by taking his battleships over to

Advance to Barbarism

Kiel and sinking the German High Seas Fleet in harbour. This proposed operation he picturesquely termed "Copenhagening the lot" — a reference to the British attack on Denmark in 1807, an episode which might have provided the framers of the London Agreement of 1945 with a classic example of an aggressive war. It well illustrates how dominant the nineteenth century code still remained that Edward VII was neither shocked nor angry at the Admiral's proposal but merely dismissed it with a brief, "Fisher, you're mad!"

In retrospect however it is hard to accept King Edward's view that the opinions Admiral Fisher expressed were intended by him merely to startle and shock his hearers. In the Age of Security, talk of "boiling your enemies in oil and torturing his women and children" seemed like the stories to amuse children which adults tell them about man-eating ogres and fire-breathing dragons. Admiral Fisher died in 1920 leaving a memory unsullied by any of the atrocities which he professed to justify in theory. As an alternative to King Edward's view that this was merely flamboyant talk not to be taken seriously, it may be suggested that Admiral Fisher during the First World War may have restrained his natural instincts by an enormous exercise of will power. It should however be pointed out that whatever his natural instincts may have been, they were circumscribed by the fact that the weapons of war in his time were relatively limited in range and in destructive power. It is perhaps fortunate for his reputation and for the enemies of his country that he did not have at his command a fleet of long-range bombers, still less the means to despatch a salvo of rockets armed with atomic war-heads. His remarks to W. T. Stead in 1900 quoted above would have served Professor Lindemann admirably for use as a sort of preamble to the infamous plan which he laid before the British Cabinet in 1942, a preamble which would certainly have appealed to the literary-minded Prime Minister, Winston Churchill.

Admiral Fisher expressed in words the spirit of the times to come: his contemporary, Field Marshal Lord Kitchener, the perfect example of the Strong Silent Man idealised by the poet Rudyard Kipling, said little but expressed that spirit by deeds. Although it was his strange fate to be selected in 1914 to serve as the figurehead for a crusade against Imperialism and Militarism, Lord Kitchener's whole life was devoted to extending and

Chapter 5 — Civilized Warfare (The Second Phase)

strengthening the British Empire by warfare and he earned a well-deserved reputation of being a ruthless soldier. His conquest of the Sudan in 1898 made him the idol of the British public. The campaign began with his victory of Atbara after which he made a triumphal march through the town of Berber (to quote his most recent and not unsympathetic biographer, Sir Charles Magnus), "Kitchener rode in front on a white horse while behind him the defeated Dervish general, Emir Mahmoud, dragging chains riveted to his ankles and wearing a halter round his neck, was made to walk and sometimes to run by his guards who lashed him with whips when he stumbled."[57] When Kitchener soon after captured Khartoum, he had the Tomb of the Madhi blown up and the body of the Madhi thrown into the Nile. The Madhi's skull he retained as a trophy and was only dissuaded from having it exhibited in the museum of the College of Surgeons in London by the strongly expressed disapproval of Queen Victoria herself.

Such exploits were indeed rather a reversion to the military practices of the ancient Assyrians than a foretaste of the military practices of the times to come. But the proposal which Kitchener put forward in 1901 to solve the problem of the Dutch-speaking majority in South Africa was identical with the proposal which Stalin was to put forward at Yalta in 1945 to solve the problem of the German inhabitants of Silesia and Pomerania. His policy of farm-burning and concentration camps having failed to break the objection of the Boers to their country being annexed by the British Empire, Kitchener proposed that the whole Boer population should be deported from South Africa and settled in various remote parts of the world such as Sumatra, Borneo, the Fiji Islands and Madagascar, their property being confiscated without compensation. He attributed the rejection of this plan by the British Government to that sentimental weakness so characteristic, in his opinion, of all civilians. There can be no doubt that if he had been given permission, Kitchener would have carried out his plan ruthlessly and efficiently.

Lord Kitchener was a professional soldier. He acted always in what he considered were the interests of the British Empire without troubling himself to find explanations or excuses, a task he left to the politicians whom, like all civilians, he heartily despised. He was contemptuously indifferent to public opinion. Only subconsciously was he influenced by the spirit of the age.

Advance to Barbarism

His contemporary, Admiral Fisher, on the other hand, understood exactly the spirit of the age and expressed openly what so many at the time were thinking but were ashamed to admit.

In one respect only may Admiral Fisher be regarded as old-fashioned in his outlook. Although he foresaw the principles upon which the wars of the future would be fought, he had no conception of the enormous power which would come to be wielded by scientific propaganda. He never realized that, to achieve victory under contemporary conditions, a well selected and maintained moral pose was not less indispensable than the skilful use of unfettered violence. Thus, when in 1917, Germany adopted unrestricted submarine warfare, Lord Fisher had no patience with the frantic outcry which followed. Being from the German point of view a necessary step towards winning the war, no other justification seemed to him to be needed by the German Government, and he flatly declined to join in the chorus of denunciation. As his proposal "to Copenhagen the lot", proves, Lord Fisher had no scruples about starting a war which he considered desirable. There is no reason to think that moral or humanitarian scruples would have restrained him during a war from applying his maxim: "Hit first, hit hard and hit anywhere." On the other hand, after a war had been won it is hard to believe that he would have countenanced a brother admiral being hypocritically condemned to life imprisonment for doing just what he himself would not have hesitated to have done.

The decisive role destined to be played by propaganda in warfare was, however, a development which no one, not even Lord Fisher, could reasonably be expected to have foreseen. Once hostilities had started, two factors left out of account by everyone operated to bring about a quite unexpected result. In the first place, after a respite of forty-three years Europeans had become unaccustomed to war; consequently, the sufferings and loss inseparable from war, even when waged in accordance with the strictest rules, aroused quite genuine horror. In the second place, there had long been growing unnoticed the power of the popular Press to which the gory details of any war, however petty, served as a welcome change from accounts of crimes, accidents, and earthquakes. A major war was an opportunity for sensational embellishment not to be missed. Reacting each upon the other, these factors created a frame of mind which was quickly turned to

Chapter 5 — Civilized Warfare (The Second Phase)

account by the belligerent governments — and in particular by the British Government — at first seriously embarrassed by the problem of supplying the man-in-the-street with a plausible explanation of what the war was about. The answer to this problem lay ready to hand: "The enemy is committing atrocities: to commit atrocities is uncivilized: we are fighting the enemy: therefore we are fighting to save civilization!"

But when hostilities first commenced in August 1914 there was no need for any of the belligerent governments involved to seek for any such far-fetched explanation of the reasons for which the war was being fought.

In Germany, most people from the Kaiser downwards welcomed the war as an opportunity to prove that they had inherited the martial virtues displayed by their ancestors at Leipzig and Sedan: in France, the war was regarded as a heaven-sent opportunity to resume the war of 1870 and with the aid of powerful allies to regain Alsace-Lorraine: in the Austro-Hungarian Empire the outstanding characteristic of the Edwardian Age, frivolity, was more strongly marked than anywhere else in Europe, the ruling classes still lived mentally in the eighteenth century when periodic outbreaks of warfare were regarded as unavoidable incidents of normal political life: the aged Emperor and his advisers resignedly took their part in the war of 1914, probably without much hope that the outcome would be any more successful than that of any of the other wars of his long reign, but without apprehension that the outcome would in this case lead to complete disaster.

In Russia, hostility to Germany was widespread among the illiterate masses for no other reason than that so many members of the hated bureaucracy were of German extraction. That this hostility was also strong in court circles is certainly hard to explain since the Romanovs had generally chosen their consorts from one or other of the German princely families, and there was much German blood also in the Russian aristocracy. It happened, however, that Czar Alexander III had departed from the usual practice by marrying Princess Dagmar of Denmark, a sister of Princess Alexandra who had married the Prince of Wales, afterwards King Edward VII. For both these beautiful, but feather-brained women, history had remained stationary since 1864. The family feud between the Danish royal family and the House of Hohenzollern generated in that year through the incorporation

Advance to Barbarism

of Schleswig-Holstein with Prussia remained for them the central event of European politics. The antipathy of Edward VII for his German relations constantly fanned into flame by the prejudices of his frivolous wife was a minor factor in bringing about the situation which culminated in the First World War. Her sister as the Empress Marie of Russia, contributed her minor part in the same direction, first by the influence she exercised over her husband; Alexander III, and later over her son, Nicholas II.

In Great Britain there was at first little difficulty in obtaining acceptance of the explanation that British treaty obligations to Belgium compelled her to enter the war in defence of Belgian neutrality. To the British man-in-the-street the role of Knight-errant going to the rescue of a small nation attacked by a ruthless aggressor seemed both honourable and profitable. It was honourable because Britain was entering the war in fulfilment of her plighted word: it promised to be profitable because while Germany was vainly striving to halt the irresistible advance of "the Russian steam-roller" (the popular name at the time for the Czar's countless hordes), her colonial possessions scattered throughout the world would lie exposed to easy occupation by Great Britain with her unchallengeable command of the sea. To a generation brought up on the poems of Rudyard Kipling, this was indeed a stirring prospect: "Wider still and wider should the bounds of the British Empire be set!" To the great industrialists of Britain the war offered a chance to eliminate (for many years at any rate) a dangerous trade rival. But the most spontaneous and wholehearted of all in their enthusiasm for the war were the clergy of the Church of England. Ever since the middle years of the nineteenth century when the dogmas and beliefs of Christianity had been challenged by Science, the influence of organised religion had been rapidly declining. From the moment war was declared, the pulpits of the country became in effect recruiting platforms. In the forefront of the drive to attract volunteers for the victorious march to Berlin was the boyishly romantic Arthur Foley Winnington-Ingram, Bishop of London, the idol of the most exclusive society drawing-rooms, who declared: "This is the greatest fight ever made for the Christian Religion: the choice lies between the Nailed Hands and the Mailed Fist." For his services to recruiting, the Bishop received a special letter of thanks from the War Office. It was perhaps a little unfortunate that a similar letter of thanks for his ardent recruiting

Chapter 5 — Civilized Warfare (The Second Phase)

activities was also sent to Horatio Bottomley, a notorious company promoter, who after the war received a well-deserved sentence of penal servitude for swindling ex-servicemen of their savings.

The Knight-errant explanation of the nature of the war had the great merit of simplicity and it did not conflict too glaringly with the known facts. For the first six months it served excellently to explain the participation of Britain in the struggle. But by the Spring of 1915 it had become inadequate. By that time expectations of a swift and spectacular triumph had everywhere been disappointed. The German advance had been held on the Marne, the French had failed to conquer Alsace, the picked troops of the Czar had received a crushing defeat at Tannenberg and the Austrians had suffered disaster at Lemberg and in Serbia. To many, peace by agreement began to seem attractive. The appeals of the Pope for the opening of peace negotiations at last began to find hearers. What was referred to in Britain as the danger of a separate peace began to cast a shadow over many minds besides those of Horatio Bottomley and Arthur Foley Winnington-Ingram.

It thus became no longer a question of putting forward a plausible explanation of why Britain had entered the war. It became urgently necessary to explain why Britain should refuse to consider making peace. The possibility had to be faced that the Germans would become so disheartened by lack of success that they would offer to evacuate Belgium and pay full compensation for all the damage which they had done. If Britain was fighting merely as a Knight-errant in defence of "brave little Belgium", how could she reject such an offer? If the wrongs of Belgium were rectified, what reason could she have to continue to fight?

Although trivial in comparison with the wholesale slaughter which was to follow, the British casualties during the first six months of the struggle had far exceeded those in any war since the Crimean Campaign. Was all this shedding of precious blood, it was indignantly asked, to lead merely to a restoration of the old faulty political system which had led to disaster in the previous August. Of course, thanks to the labours of a group of professional historians who had fabricated "the Wicked Kaiser Myth", no one doubted entire responsibility for this disaster rested upon one supremely evil man but the enforced abdication of Wilhelm II seemed an inadequate result for a national effort on so gigantic a scale. Only by breaking completely with the past and by creating an entirely new social order which would endure for all time, could justification be found for this terrible sacrifice of life and expenditure of wealth. To achieve this aim, the war must be continued regardless of losses, without a thought of compromise.

Assertions by well-meaning clerics that the war was a struggle between Good and Evil were based on religious conceptions which had become meaningless to the average man-in-the-street. The problem was solved by dealing with it from an entirely different angle of approach: —

Belgium was indisputably a little country; the British Empire, allied to the Russian Empire, was fighting for Belgium and also for Serbia; another little country. Therefore, the British and Russian Empires were fighting for the liberty of little countries. Now, all over the world were little countries which did not enjoy liberty. Their inhabitants were clearly as much entitled to liberty as the Belgians and Serbs. There were, for example, those parts of Poland so fortunate as to have escaped annexation by Russia by being annexed by Prussia or by Austria. The inhabitants of these parts of Poland were entitled to be liberated from their Prussian and Austrian rulers. Similarly the Czech majority in Bohemia must be liberated from the oppression of the Hapsburg Emperors and given the right to oppress the German and Slovak minorities in that province. As Turkey had allied herself to Germany her Arab subjects had clearly become eligible for liberation. In all the German colonial possessions in Africa and the Far East were various tribes of savages who must be deemed to be yearning for liberation from German rule. Justice demanded that their claims should not be overlooked, particularly as all of them would need a long period of education to render them fit for freedom during which time their self-appointed tutors would be in a position to exploit the labours of the expelled German colonizers. A Knight-errant could not of course demand payment for his services but there could be no objection if his altruism should turn out to be profitable to him. Similarly, if a crippling indemnity was extorted from Germany when victory was achieved, this should not be regarded as an expression of greed but merely as a wise precautionary measure designed to prevent Germany again becoming strong enough to endanger her peace-loving neighbours.

In this way finally emerged the political dogma that every people in the world was entitled as of right to self-government.

Chapter 5 — Civilized Warfare (The Second Phase)

In default of any other available definition, self-government was defined as the rule of the majority in each self-governing country. The Kaiser had been violently denounced as an autocrat and gradually the Allies found themselves committed to upholding, in words at least, the cause of democracy. Autocracy was held to be responsible for bringing about the war and all its attendant evils and it was natural, therefore, to attribute to democracy all the virtues which autocracy was held so obviously to lack.

The view generally accepted by historians is that during the early part of the First World War there took place a complete transformation of outlook unparalleled in the previous history of mankind. Democracy in one form or another was accepted as the only proper form of government and militarism and aggression were condemned in any form. It was agreed that it was plainly contrary to justice that Germans or Turks should rule over any other peoples and from this a general principle could be deduced which might be possible of extension with proper safeguards until in theory at any rate it had general application.

There is no reason for surprise that this transformation of outlook took place without articulate opposition in France where any novel political views, however absurd or repugnant, were acceptable providing acceptance would facilitate the recovery of Alsace-Lorraine. Similarly in Russia, to the ruling class any theoretical views were acceptable provided they would help the Czar to carry out far-reaching annexations and in particular to occupy Constantinople and to establish a great naval base on the shores of the Mediterranean. But it is truly astonishing that in Great Britain this transformation of outlook took place so swiftly without the least apparent opposition. Down to the outbreak of war on the 4th August, 1914, the favourite boast of the British public had been that Britain ruled an empire over which the sun never set: no one doubted that "the lesser breeds without the law," as Kipling called them, had been created by Providence to be ruled by Britons. The ready acceptance of democracy as the only defensible form of government was equally remarkable. In Great Britain had long flourished a caste system only less elaborate and irrational than that which flourished among the contemporary Hindus. Society was divided and subdivided into innumerable classes, each regarding the one above it with awe and envy and despising heartily the one below it. Yet the proposition was

Advance to Barbarism

accepted without demur that to spread democracy throughout the world was a cause for which a man ought to be willing gladly to lay down his life. There was no opposition, or at least no articulate opposition, when Lloyd George finally proclaimed that in essence Great Britain was fighting to make the world safe for democracy. With regard to the somewhat earlier claim that the war was being fought to ensure the liberty of small nations, it may be said that acceptance was only general because the implications of this policy were not realized. Everyone was agreed that the Arabs and the Czechs and the various negro tribes under German rule were entitled to self-government: it did not at the time occur to anyone that if this were true the subject peoples of the British Empire must possess a similar right.

Inevitably much misunderstanding and confusion resulted. Most confused of all were the Irish who jumped to the conclusion that their right to freedom from British rule, for which they had struggled in vain for centuries, had at last been admitted. Sternly admonished not to obstruct a crusade for the liberty of small nations by putting forward selfish claims, the Irish broke into revolt. The ruthless crushing of the Easter Rebellion proved beyond question that in practice the methods and outlook of British Imperialism remained quite uninfluenced by the acceptance in theory of any new political conceptions.

In fact, it may be maintained that no real transformation in outlook of any kind took place in Great Britain during the First World War. The outbreak of war quickly generated a frenzy of self-righteousness and pugnacity in which thought of any kind was impossible. The British public learnt and repeated parrot-wise a succession of political slogans because the politicians assured them that these would embarrass the Germans and so pave the way for ultimate victory. If these slogans achieved this purpose, their meaning was of no importance. When at last peace came and the frenzy gradually ceased, the British public discovered that it had been committed to an entirely novel political outlook which was in every way the opposite to the outlook of the Kipling age. Seen in this new light the ideals which had inspired the founders of the British Empire seemed obsolete and even discreditable conceptions inherited from a remote past.

Outwardly, indeed, the British Empire emerged from the First World War greater in extent and more powerful than ever.

Chapter 5 — Civilized Warfare (The Second Phase)

"We have got most of the things we set out to get," declared Mr. Lloyd George in a rare moment of candour. "The German Navy has been handed over, the German merchant shipping has been handed over, and the German colonies have been given up. One of our chief trade competitors has been most seriously crippled and our Allies are about to become Germany's biggest creditors. This is no small achievement!"[58]

In fact, however, the British Empire had received a mortal blow. No longer could the possession of an empire be regarded as a subject for pride. The ideals proclaimed during the war for the purpose of bringing about the downfall of the German Empire could not be reconciled with the existence of any empire. As far as Great Britain was concerned the history of the next fifty years may be summarised by saying that it consisted of the story of the gradual dissolution of the British Empire as the natural and inevitable consequence of the acceptance of these ideals. In 1960 Mr. Harold Macmillan caused a sensation by a speech in which he declared, "the wind of change" was blowing through Africa, but it had been blowing with destructive force throughout Europe and Asia ever since the First World War.

Only the empire of the Czars, newly labelled a proletarian dictatorship, survived the storm. The successors of the Czars, Lenin, Stalin, Khrushchev and Kosygin, all cheerfully adopted in turn democracy, anti-militarism, self-determination and the other catchwords of the First World War as useful slogans for the embarrassment of their opponents, in short for the simple purpose for which these slogans had originally been designed. Whereas the British Government felt compelled to attach a meaning to these slogans, and only acted in defiance of them with reluctance and shame, the Soviet Government used them only as a standard by which could be denounced the conduct of their opponents, a standard having not the least application to their own conduct. In consequence the Soviet Government was able wholeheartedly to repress the revolts of subject peoples, to carry out mass-deportations and to wage a series of aggressive wars with the result that the empire of the Czars, far from breaking up, gradually evolved into a communist empire far stronger than its imperial predecessor had ever been. The British Empire, on the other hand, simply crumbled to pieces, the spirit which had created it being no longer in existence to inspire its defence.

Advance to Barbarism

Men like John Nicholson or Lord Kitchener never doubted for an instant the right of the British Empire to subjugate and rule weaker peoples or their own plain duty to crush ruthlessly any attempt by them at revolt. In exactly the same spirit when the Soviet generals dealt with the heroic attempt of the Hungarian people in 1956 to free themselves from the Russian yoke, a doubt never crossed their minds as to the justification of repressing ruthlessly a little people venturing to oppose the will of a Communist dictatorship. But from the Sinn Fein revolt in Ireland in 1919 to the terrorist campaign of EOKA in Cyprus in 1955, the efforts of the armed forces of the British Empire were paralysed by the subconscious conviction that their opponents had right on their side. In 1848 General Cavaignac declared that a social order which permits its principles to be examined and rejected is already lost. The British Empire was doomed during the First World War when to obtain a temporary political advantage it expressly repudiated the principles upon which its existence depended.

Seen in perspective it is now clear that the First World War was an unqualified disaster for the White Race. The first and greatest sufferers were the German people who after passing through a decade of humiliation and acute economic distress entered a decade of feverish activity and reckless political ambitions culminating in 1945 in a far greater and more complete disaster than that of 1918. The Nazi regime of Adolf Hitler was in essence a natural reaction to the flagrant injustice and hypocrisy of the Versailles Treaty.

Sooner or later all the peoples of Europe were destined to suffer from the consequences of the First World War. The military, moral and economic supremacy of Europe over Asia and Africa was lost for ever. The Yellow Race and Black Race no longer regarded the White Race as a distinct kind of superior being, invincible on the battlefield and guided by higher moral standards than those of coloured peoples. After 1945 the intelligence of the White Man was assessed by reference to his indulgence in two suicidal world wars for no rational purpose and in which victors and vanquished were obviously both bound to be losers: the White Man's claim to be guided by higher moral standards was judged by reference to the abominable atrocities which White peoples had committed on each other during two world wars. To an impartial observer whether an Asiatic or an African it was clear

Chapter 5 — Civilized Warfare (The Second Phase)

from the joint testimony of both sides that the White peoples had behaved to each other with ruthless cruelty and reckless perfidy and it was hard for onlookers to say which group of antagonists was the worst.

Only in regard to the gigantic scale on which it was fought did the First World War surpass all previous conflicts. No leader of genius arose on either side to direct the fighting. Huge masses of men, mostly hurriedly trained civilians, were blindly hurled against each other supported by an unprecedented expenditure of ammunition. Naturally the loss of life resulting from the employment of such tactics was on a scale hitherto unimaginable. On the first day of the great Somme Offensive in 1916, the casualties of the British alone amounted to 60,000. After four months of continual and furious fighting both sides were utterly exhausted but no noteworthy advantage had been gained. Sir Douglas Haig complacently reported that the powers of resistance of the German Army must have been substantially reduced by such a slaughter, and set about preparing for a similar mass-offensive next year. It is estimated that during the Somme Offensive, three million men, the flower of the young manhood of the three leading European races, took part and over a million of them became casualties.

It can hardly be said that the First World War led to any fundamental developments in the art of war. The recently invented aeroplane was rapidly improved in order to serve as a weapon of war; the invention of the tank restored to the attacking side the advantage it had enjoyed over the defence before the introduction of quick-firing weapons and barbed wire. Surgery made great advances; those injured by the new scientific methods of destruction were patched up by new scientific methods of treatment. Only in one respect did the First World War initiate an entirely novel development and this was a political and not a military development. Until 1914 wars had been fought to secure some specific and limited aim. War propaganda had consisted of little more than vague assertions of the essential justice of this aim and haphazard abuse of the leaders of the enemy state. Although officially encouraged and inspired, it entirely lacked official planning and direction. It was intended merely to intensify normal patriotic feeling. The actual fighting was of course done by professional soldiers who obeyed their orders and needed no propaganda fictions to stimulate their zeal. But in 1914 an entirely novel situation arose. It was not only necessary to work out a plausible explanation of Britain's participation in the war. It was imperative to develop a technique of presenting this explanation so skilfully and convincingly that nation-wide enthusiasm for the war would be generated.

In due course the Fourteen Points were propounded to an admiring world. The method of presentation adopted was an entirely new departure in international politics but the principles upon which this presentation was based had long been partially understood. For many years before 1914, a mass of empirical knowledge concerning the reactions of the human mind to certain astutely applied stimuli had been gradually accumulating and had been frequently turned to account for personal gain by various gifted individuals. As long before as the time of Charles II, Titus Oates had achieved results which in their way have never been surpassed. No emotional engineer of modern times can be compared with that French woman of genius, Madame Therese Humbert, who, at the end of the nineteenth century, for nearly twenty years kept the most astute bankers and financiers of Paris under her spell to her own great profit and their great loss. The celebrated Tichborne case of 1872 and the equally remarkable Druce case of 1907, the two most celebrated English fraud cases, both promoted by publicity, demonstrated how limitless is the credulity of the general public and what an imposing structure can be erected from a scientific blending of distorted facts and skilful fabrications.[59] It was not, however, until 1914, that it was realized that what could be achieved by Orton the Wagga Wagga butcher and by Druce the Melbourne carpenter for their own personal advantage could be achieved on a far wider scale for the national good by persons of the highest integrity employed by the State and with all the resources of the State behind them. As so frequently happens in contemporary life, the haphazard lessons learned by private enterprise were adapted, systematized, and developed by the community. In this instance, at least, nationalization was triumphantly vindicated by the decisive results achieved.

It was the opinion of two such dissimilar observers as Lord Northcliffe and Adolf Hitler that the war of 1914-1918 was won by the war propaganda of the Allies. On the one hand, the peoples of the Allies were inspired in their war efforts by loud professions of genuine, if vague, ideals. On the other hand, the German

Chapter 5 — Civilized Warfare (The Second Phase)

people were never clear for what exactly they were fighting. When hostilities were progressing favourably they were told their reward would be the annexation of some foreign territory; when hostilities took an unfavourable turn, they were told that they were fighting for their existence—although their enemies were pledged to conclude a peace to which no reasonable objection could be made.

By winning the war, Allied propaganda can be said to have fully justified itself and yet it entailed serious drawbacks, the full effects of which were not experienced until afterwards. Obviously, this propaganda campaign violated two of the principles upon which Emeric de Vattel had been most insistent. In the first place, as we have seen, he had laid down that "all offensive expressions indicating sentiments of hatred, animosity and bitterness" must be avoided so that the way to a negotiated settlement might not be closed. Secondly, he had insisted that war aims must be limited and specific and should "not be mixed up with Justice and Right nor any of the great passions which move a people."

In support of these contentions, Vattel had, in brief, argued that the only justification for any war is that it will lead to a lasting peace. Now a lasting peace can only arise from a freely negotiated settlement. Emotion in any form is an impediment to negotiation. Offensive expressions and appeals to abstractions arouse emotion. Therefore, offensive expressions and appeals to abstractions must be avoided in warfare.

The war of 1914-1918 may be said to have been won by copious and adroit use of offensive expressions and appeals to abstractions. In accordance with Vattel's argument, it did not lead to a lasting peace. Further, Vattel contended that a harsh dictated peace must inevitably rouse a determination in the defeated side to reverse it. Adolf Hitler can best be interpreted as the incarnation of this determination.

During the course of the struggle, one final opportunity was vouchsafed the peoples of Europe by indulgent destiny to escape the natural penalty of disunity and disorder. In European Civil War No. 8a, the belligerents proved so equally matched that after three years of desperate conflict no decisive advantage had been gained. Truculent self-confidence had been everywhere abashed; the German Army had achieved no second Sedan at the Marne and no second Trafalgar had been achieved by the British

Advance to Barbarism

Navy at Jutland; far from reconquering Alsace, the French Army had failed to protect Northern France from enemy occupation; the Russian Army and the Austrian Army had each sustained a series of humiliating defeats; and the Italian Army had recently demonstrated at Caporetto how far and how fast panic-stricken human beings can run. In every country and among all classes, realization had come that war was no longer the polite orderly sport of kings as it had been in the eighteenth century, but had become a tedious, costly, and murderous business; in every country and among all classes war-weariness and disillusionment had become predominant. To those who objected that three years of frantic endeavour and terrible slaughter must not be wasted, it could be answered that the best and, in fact, the only justification of so much toil and bloodshed would be not some petty territorial annexations or frontier adjustments but an enduring peace, securely based on the realization by all concerned that in a present-day war no one benefits. Had peace been concluded in 1917, for several generations at least the militarists and armament manufacturers would have striven in vain to banish the memory of such an experience.

    The golden opportunity to establish a lasting settlement must have been obvious to many at the time. It was left, however, to the Marquess of Lansdowne alone to draw public attention to it. Representing not merely sane public opinion in Great Britain or even sane contemporary opinion in Europe, but voicing the protest against futile squabbling which had been so often expressed by isolated European thinkers since the dawn of the Middle Ages, on November 27, 1917, Lord Lansdowne wrote a letter to *The Times* urging that negotiations for peace should be commenced. "The prolongation of this war will spell ruin for the civilized world," he wrote. "If the war is to be brought to a close in time to avoid a world-catastrophe, it will be because on both sides the peoples realize that it has already lasted too long."

    In attempting to influence a public suffering from acute paranoia by an appeal to reason, Lord Lansdowne displayed the highest moral courage. He also displayed keen political foresight, although we may not be able to credit him with vision of all that was at stake. If a peace without victors and without vanquished had been concluded in 1917, it would have been a peace primarily the work of and, consequently, there would have been no occasion

Chapter 5 — Civilized Warfare (The Second Phase)

to pay humble homage to President Wilson and his gospel of "self-determination" which inevitably entailed an early dissolution of the British Empire; Germany's Unknown Soldier would have remained merely one of the obscure millions who had fought in the front line for their fatherland; the return of Alsace by Germany to France would have removed the principal subject for ill-feeling between the two chief European states; the ruling classes in Russia would have quickly regained the upper hand; Russia would have remained a member of the European family of nations and Lenin's attempt to restore the Eurasian Empire of Genghis Khan in the shape of a militant communist commonwealth would have been stifled at its inception; and unthinkable would have remained such features of contemporary life as the indiscriminate killing of civilians by terror attacks from the air, the mass deportations of populations numbering millions, the official looting of private property, the systematic sabotage of enemy industries, and the consignment of prisoners of war to the gallows or to slavery of indeterminate duration. Perhaps of even greater interest to many in the future will be the fact that Asia would have remained a vast but remote area beyond the Urals and not, by swallowing half Europe, have extended to the banks of the Oder within four flying hours of London. No date in human history suggests more pregnant might-have-beens than the date of Lord Lansdowne's letter.

But habits engrained during a thousand years are not easily overcome. The editor of *The Times*, before falling into a swoon, consigned the letter, albeit it was the letter of a peer and an ex-cabinet minister, to his wastepaper basket. The editor of *The Daily Telegraph* was, however, made of sterner stuff: greatly daring, he published the letter. Before writing it, Lord Lansdowne had disclosed his intention to a number of prominent statesmen — including Mr. Balfour, Lord Hardinge and the American, Colonel House — who had whispered approval of his views. But when the storm broke, these gentlemen preserved a discreet silence. The British Government expressed horror at the mere suggestion that the objects of the war should be disclosed; the emotional engineers were given their orders and, in a few days, Lord Lansdowne was the most unpopular man in the country. Thereafter, those who continued to fight for European sanity were fighting a battle finally lost.

Advance to Barbarism

In retrospect, the decline in the standards of warfare during the war of 1914-1918 appears less than might have been expected under all the circumstances. There was a marked but not a headlong decline. In essence, this conflict remained a European civil war and the traditions of European civil warfare which had then existed for two centuries were, on the whole, maintained. This is best seen by contrasting the behaviour of the troops who entered Germany in 1918 with that of those who invaded the country in 1945. Cut off by four years' service at the front from the home population, the troops of Foch and Haig had acquired, to a great extent, the outlook of professional soldiers. In contact with facts, they were little influenced by the fictions of propaganda, and sympathy and respect had grown up between them and their opponents as between men facing the same dangers, enduring the same hardships, and performing the same duties. Their discipline, when they entered enemy territory in 1918, was not undermined by official exhortations to refrain at all costs from "pampering" the enemy. Looting of civilian property by soldiers was still a major military crime — as it remained until it was announced, that after hostilities enemy civilian property would be officially looted. They had not before them the example of the troops of non-European Powers, indifferent to the rules of European civil warfare, nor of the gangs of auxiliaries from the underworld of countries recently under German occupation, bent on paying off old scores. Their leaders were men of strong character — it is recorded that, soon after the Armistice, General Plumer informed Whitehall that he must decline to remain responsible for discipline in Cologne if his troops continued to be followed by bands of starving children for whom no provision had been made by the politicians. With complete disregard for the feelings of propaganda-befuddled civilian opinion at home, General Plumer did not disguise his sympathy with the attitude of his men.

Admittedly, episodes of this kind were not frequent. The reception accorded to the German peace delegates at Compiègne was without precedent in the long annals of European civil war for its chilly severity. Marshal Foch was an unamiable personality, cold, precise, and stern. His attitude throughout was harsh and unbending. But he never forgot that he was a professional European soldier, familiar since youth with the rules and etiquette of the European civil war game. After the Armistice, a noisy clamour

Chapter 5 — Civilized Warfare (The Second Phase)

was raised in civilian circles that a number of distinguished professional soldiers, including Marshal von Hindenburg, should be penalized. The usual complete unanimity between the military and the civilian outlook was, of course, preserved: But the clamour mysteriously subsided and died away. One can but suspect that a heavy foot or feet was or were put down by a person or persons unknown.

There were during the struggle few deliberate breaches of the Rules of Civilized Warfare: the fighting was limited to the uniformed armed forces of the combatants, prisoners and wounded were treated with humanity, the rights of enemy civilians in occupied territory were preserved and enemy civilian property was not wantonly destroyed. There were no organised campaigns of murder and sabotage behind the enemy lines carried out by armed civilians and consequently no savage reprisals by the security forces. The Germans temporarily terrorized Paris by firing a few shells into the city by use of an improvised long range cannon, but the damage to life and property was slight. Much damage was, of course, done to French and Belgian cities as a result of artillery bombardment during the advance of the German armies westward but this occurred only in connection with direct military operations, as was sanctioned by the European code of civilized warfare. The main onslaught upon civilian life was a product of the British blockade of Germany, which was continued for nearly a year after the Armistice and led to the starvation of nearly a million German non-combatants. On the whole, however, the old European code of civilized warfare dominated military strategy and operations during the conflict.

Few would now have the hardihood to deny that the peace settlement of Versailles in 1919 was a complete and tragic failure. It failed completely for precisely the reason so lucidly set forth and explained by Vattel 150 years before. Its failure was tragic because the principles upon which it was professedly based justified the highest hopes. Admittedly, it is impossible to reconcile the terms of the Treaty with the Fourteen Points in accordance with which the Allied pledge was given at the time of the Armistice. But we are not, therefore, compelled to accept the view, so passionately urged by Adolf Hitler, that the Treaty of Versailles was merely the culmination of a gigantic swindle intended from the start. The Fourteen Points were not a collection of dishonest verbiage like the

Advance to Barbarism

Atlantic Charter. Certainly they were used later for propaganda to beguile the German people, but they were not designed for this purpose by their author, President Wilson.

It is a curious fact that the Versailles Treaty actually came to grief upon the very point on which it followed most strictly orthodox practice. For centuries, it had been the accepted principle of European civil warfare that the vanquished side should pay to the victors the cost of the war. The same principle is adopted in the legal systems of all countries in litigation between individuals. Costs follow the event. The man who goes to law and fails must pay the cost of the proceedings. With equal reason the country which goes to war and is defeated should be called upon to pay the cost of hostilities.

So long as warfare was waged on a small scale and was comparatively inexpensive, this principle was so obviously reasonable that the payment of war indemnities gave rise to little difficulty or ill-feeling. In litigation, a taxing master sees to it that the successful side does not give free rein to its imagination when drawing its bill of costs. In warfare, indeed, there has never been an international taxing master. Still, the war indemnities demanded in the eighteenth and nineteenth centuries do not seem to have been extortionate. It was once the custom to denounce the indemnity demanded by Bismarck after the defeat of France in 1870 as severe. To our eyes it seems moderate in the extreme. Surely, this is proved by the fact that France was able to pay the whole sum demanded within five years and, within ten years of Sedan, was once again a rich and prosperous state and one of the three great military powers of Europe.

By 1919, however, warfare had become so fabulously costly that, even if the expenses of the Allies had been assessed by a fair-minded tribunal, the sum payable would have been utterly beyond the capacity of the vanquished to pay and, further, if by some miracle it had been paid, the entire economic structure of the world would have been upset. Payment in full—although everyone admitted this to be impossible—was insisted on. Of course, promiscuous looting of public and private property, as provided by the Potsdam Agreement of 1945, would have been unthinkable to the mind of President Wilson who had formerly been a professor of jurisprudence. Not one single penny must be taken from Germany, he repeatedly insisted: all that could

Chapter 5 — Civilized Warfare (The Second Phase)

be required of Germany was that she should comply with the principle that costs follow the event. That compliance would mean the payment of vastly more than the total wealth of Germany must not be allowed to disturb this well-established legal principle.

The result was a succession of futile conferences, each conference leading to a settlement of the "reparations problem" which everyone knew to be impossible. The only result was that war-time bitterness was repeatedly aggravated and perpetuated. At long last, the Allies grew weary of insisting upon performance of the impossible, and tacit cancellation of one section of the treaty naturally encouraged the Germans to go on to repudiate the balance.

For a brief spell, round about 1925, it seemed possible that, once again, Europe would escape the natural penalty for indulging in civil war. The United States had ostentatiously repudiated further interest in European affairs. Few believed that Lenin's successors would succeed in keeping together the Soviet State which he had created out of the ruins of the Empire of the Czars. At Locarno, M. Briand, Herr Stresemann, and Sir Austen Chamberlain met together and cordially agreed henceforth to work together for the common good. The lamps which, in 1914, Sir Edward Grey had watched being extinguished one by one were to be re-lit, contrary to his lugubrious prediction, and the prosperity and happiness of the Edwardian Age was to return.

But habits dating back a dozen centuries are not so easily shaken off. In Europe, in the past, political differences had always led ultimately as a matter of course to civil war. Never before had there existed in Europe so many and so acute political differences. As Vattel in the Age of Reason had pointed out, a treaty imposed by force can only be maintained by force. The Treaty of Versailles had imposed harsh dictated peace terms upon the vanquished, thereby inevitably arousing in them a determination to reverse its decisions, regardless of the risks involved. Between 1933 and 1938, Adolf Hitler, the incarnation of this determination, by threats of force set aside one by one the main provisions of the Versailles Treaty. Throughout this time the Soviet Union continued to consolidate into a great military Power, with all the far-reaching territorial ambitions of the Czars combined with the political and economic ambitions of Karl Marx. Between Western Europe and the Soviet Union lay the newly re-created state of Poland. To

Germany, in particular, Poland served as an invaluable buffer state. Self-preservation linked Poland with Germany, since the Polish ruling classes depended for their existence on being able to keep Communism in check. But among the major absurdities of the Versailles Treaty had been the creation of the so-called Polish Corridor. To rectify this wrong, of much greater emotional than practical importance, Hitler was prepared to sacrifice the protection of this buffer state. For their part, the Polish ruling classes were prepared to defend the Corridor by force, although the price of victory would inevitably entail the ultimate absorption of Poland by the Soviet Union and their own ruthless liquidation.

The preservation of peace was so obviously of paramount importance to both the German and Polish Governments that each, quite naturally, became convinced that the other must be bluffing. Accordingly, in September, 1939, the first steps were taken which were finally to lead Hitler to suicide in the ruins of the burning Reich Chancellery and the Polish ruling classes to that systematic extermination which was destined to begin less than a year later in the Katyn forest.

Undeniably in 1939 by risking another world war leading the possible complete destruction of all he had achieved over relatively so small an issue as the liberation of Danzig, Hitler displayed a lack of any sense of proportion well justifying the odium in which his memory is now held by mankind in general and by his countrymen in particular. He acted, however, strictly in accordance with one of the most firmly established principles of traditional European diplomacy, which, as we have seen, laid down that if a statesman muddled himself into a position from which withdrawal was impossible, he was bound to resort to war to preserve his country's honour.

It has been argued that this principle in 1939 had become obsolete because the conscience of mankind had ceased to recognise warfare as a means of settling international disputes. With regard to what was then and is now the current attitude to warfare, it is hardly possible merely to appeal to higher authority than that of the leading contemporary champion of non-violence and conciliation, the disciple of the saintly Ghandi, the late Pandit Nehru. In 1961 Pandit Nehru, finding himself unable verbally to coerce the Portuguese Government to cede to India the port of Goa, a Portuguese possession on the Malabar Coast for four hundred

Chapter 5 — Civilized Warfare (The Second Phase)

and fifty years, ordered his troops to occupy Goa by force. The two cases are exactly parallel except that in 1939 Hitler had an undeniable moral claim to Danzig, and Pandit Nehru in 1961 had no claim at all to Goa, moral or otherwise. At a Press conference held shortly after the resistance of the tiny Portuguese garrison had been overcome, Pandit Nehru justified his action by declaring blandly, "The use of force was of course open to us according to suitability and opportunity."

According to this weighty authority, therefore, Hitler's offence in 1939 was not that he ordered his troops to occupy Danzig by force, but that he did so at a moment lacking suitability and opportunity.

In the final analysis the outbreak of war in 1939 will be found to be the last and culminating episode of a political chain reaction which had been set in motion in August 1914. Between these dates each successive development followed naturally and inevitably from the one before it.

The Treaty of Versailles, almost from the date it was signed, was condemned by many as a compound of injustice, perfidy and stupidity: the statesmen responsible for it have been derided as self-satisfied charlatans who, for motives of greed and spite, betrayed the hopes of mankind for a just and lasting peace settlement.

Few can now be found to defend the Treaty of Versailles. On the other hand, it was exactly the peace settlement which might have been expected to result from the spontaneous irrational frenzy of pugnacity which led to the outbreak in 1914 of a war which was continued for four years in an equally irrational frenzy of obstinacy. To us it may seem clear that the poet Rupert Brooke was in urgent need of expert psychiatric treatment when he wrote in 1914, "Now God be thanked who has matched us with this hour!" but all over Europe hundreds of thousands of young men were expressing the same thankfulness although few of them had any clearer idea than Rupert Brooke what the war was about.

Surely if all this blind, hysterical activity had led to the conclusion of a sane, balanced and just peace settlement it could only have been because a sudden and miraculous change of heart took place in 1919. No such miracle, however, took place. The struggle which was long known as the Great War led inevitably to the Treaty of Versailles.

Equally inevitably the Treaty of Versailles led to a period of growing tension as the vanquished, gradually recovering their strength, began to agitate for the redress of their wrongs. If, between the Treaty of Locarno in 1925 and the assumption of power by Hitler in 1933, the victors could have brought themselves to make reasonable concessions, it is possible that the Treaty of Versailles might have been replaced by a lasting peace settlement. But this again could only have come about through a belated change of heart in the victorious countries. Such a development would have been so entirely contrary to the natural trend of events as to have required some supernatural intervention. No such intervention took place.

It followed naturally as part of the political chain reaction that frustration brought militant nationalism to power in Germany. Thereafter the chain reaction proceeded with ever increasing speed. Not one of Hitler's demands taken alone seemed worth going to war about. One propaganda delusion after another concerning the so-called Great War had had to be abandoned, but the belief was still held with pathetic insistence that a struggle lasting four years and costing ten million lives had at least banished warfare for ever from the world. Few were ready to demonstrate that this belief was also a delusion by resorting to war over an issue which in itself was not of vital importance to the victorious Powers.

Once the process had started, the shackles imposed on Germany by the Treaty of Versailles were broken one by one in rapid succession. But this process could not go on indefinitely: as Shakespeare says, even time must have a stop. Hitler gave a classic example of "brinkmanship", but his success made it inevitable that ultimately his opponents would adopt the same dangerous policy. The last phase of the chain reaction occurred in 1939 when Hitler ordered his troops to cross the border of the Polish Corridor.

No difficulty arose in 1939 about finding a convincing war aim such as had arisen in 1914. The necessity for preserving the integrity of Poland was not a war aim likely to arouse much enthusiasm in either Britain or France, but this explanation for the outbreak of war was quickly superseded by attributing to Hitler precisely the same plans for world conquest which had been attributed to Kaiser Wilhelm. To make plausible this charge against the latter elaborate fictions had had to be invented, but in the case of Hitler it was only necessary to stress the undeniable

Chapter 5 — Civilized Warfare (The Second Phase)

fact that he had repeatedly disturbed the *status quo* by unilateral action.

So closely interlocked are the First and Second World Wars that it seems likely that future historians will regard them as merely episodes of the same struggle. The interval of twenty-one years between them will be dismissed as a period of feverish but futile activity during which it proved to be impossible to control the irrational passions which had been released in 1914. If this view be ultimately accepted, the Armistice signed on November 11th, 1918, which at the time seemed an epoch-making event in the history of mankind will be regarded as a mere truce which allowed the victors to despoil the vanquished to their heart's content for a limited time: when the German troops crossed the border of the Polish Corridor in 1939 they were merely resuming a struggle which exhaustion had brought to a halt in November 1918.

The immediate outcome of this resumption of hostilities was the first break in the political chain reaction which had started in 1914. When Great Britain and France declared war on Germany in 1939, professedly to preserve the integrity of Poland, they did so confidently believing that the task before them would be swiftly and easily accomplished. Facts and figures were produced in abundance proving that Germany lacked money and supplies of essential war materials; the Reichwehr was said not only to lack equipment and training, but a fighting spirit. The German people were said to be groaning beneath the tyranny of the Nazi regime and to be waiting impatiently for a favourable opportunity to revolt. The slightest set-back would provide such an opportunity by shattering Hitler's prestige for ever. On the face of it, was it possible to believe that the hastily trained and unwilling conscripts of the Third Reich could defeat the combined armies of Great Britain and France, a task which had been beyond the strength of the magnificent Imperial Army of the Kaiser? We now know that several of the ablest of Hitler's military advisers shared this doubt. In British and French military circles there seems to have been no doubts at all as to the outcome. No serious fighting was to be apprehended; it was merely a question of putting the clock back to the 11th November, 1918.

This indeed would have been the only outcome which would have been consistent with the political chain reaction which had begun in 1914. Contrary, however, to all expectation, the issue was not simply decided by such factors as more numerous and better weapons, superior organization and vastly greater resources. These factors were outweighed by a factor which had been overlooked, although perhaps Napoleon's oft-quoted dictum should have provided a warning. The outcome proved that a decision by politicians to resort to war to preserve an admittedly unsatisfactory *status quo* does not produce a fighting spirit equal to that generated by a blind fanatical determination to avenge at all costs past defeats and humiliations.

Chapter 6 — The Splendid Decision

The war which began in September, 1939, and ended in June 1940, was in all essentials a typical European civil war. Of absorbing interest to students of strategy and tactics, it offers no exceptional features of any kind except that the point at issue was rather more frivolous than usual; its duration was unprecedentedly brief; and it caused comparatively little loss of life and damage — in the Battle of France the Germans lost 27,074 killed and 129,418 wounded and missing, in all therefore some 150,000 casualties. In 1914 the Kaiser's armies had overrun Northern France and Belgium at the cost of 638,000 casualties, including 85,000 killed. The total casualties of both sides in the great Somme offensive in 1916 reached nearly 1,000,000 men: on the first day of this offensive Sir Douglas Haig sacrificed over 60,000 men.

Because the Battle of France ended so quickly — the actual fighting lasted only two months — a war psychosis had no time to develop. Before the emotional engineers could work up their respective publics into a frenzy of hatred, it was all over. The decision of 1918 had been reversed, the French Army had surrendered and the B.E.F. had withdrawn, minus its tanks, artillery, stores and equipment, across the Channel.

Intoxicated by the speed and completeness of their triumph, the victors were in no mood to set about paying off old scores. Clemenceau's deliberate humiliation of the German delegates at Versailles, the garrisoning of German towns with negro warriors, and M. Tirard's campaign to annex the Rhinelands by violence and intrigue were forgotten. With his highly developed sense of historical fitness, Hitler indeed insisted that the famous railway coach in the Forest of Compiègne, in which Marshal Foch had dictated terms of surrender so harshly some 22 years before, should be the scene of the surrender of the Army which Foch had then led to victory. All the forms of military etiquette, however,

Advance to Barbarism

were again punctiliously observed. Marshal Pétain was treated with the respect which his record as a soldier deserved. In spite of the boasted modernity of their outlook, it does not seem to have occurred, even to the most extreme of the Nazis that Pétain's heroic defence of Verdun in 1916 justified his condemnation as a war criminal. Not until five years later, and then at the hands of his own countrymen, was the gallant old Marshal to experience what Dante called "the horrid art of justice".

It is, of course, the unchallengeable right of every sovereign state to deal with its own citizens according to its own ideas of justice. The administration of justice in France is the exclusive concern of Frenchmen. Still, the spectacle of the Hero of Verdun (alias the Prisoner of Yeu), the man who saved France and the cause of the Allies when the French army mutinied after the failure of the offensive on the Chemin des Dames, and the general whose strategy defeated Ludendorff in 1918, dying at the age of 95 after enduring six years of rigorous imprisonment on a bleak little island off the Atlantic coast, is a matter of general interest. It is not open to question that Marshal Pétain took command in France in 1940 entirely from a soldierly sense of duty, and in a completely constitutional manner. It is equally unquestionable that he did his best to serve France in hopeless circumstances. When disaster came, he considered it his duty to remain at the helm of state. In 1919, Field Marshal von Hindenburg, like Marshal Pétain a soldier of the old school, had come to the same decision and won thereby universal respect. Both acted in accordance with the ancient tradition that the captain should be the last to leave a sinking ship. This traditional role has often been contrasted with the behaviour of rats who, according to a popular belief of equal antiquity, will leave a ship which they know by instinct is about to sink. It is curious that these traditions seem never before to have been combined in a single legend of a captain going down with his ship and later surviving to be traduced and reviled by those who judged it more prudent or less unpleasant to make a timely departure.[60]

The role played by Marshal Foch, in 1918, was played in 1940 by the Chef des Oberkommandos der Wehrmacht, Generaloberst Wilhelm Keitel, shortly afterwards promoted to Field Marshal. An unknown captain in the Artillery commanding a battery in 1914 but shortly transferred to the General Staff, Keitel

Chapter 6 — The Splendid Decision

had progressed steadily and inconspicuously thenceforth from one staff appointment to another until, while still practically unknown outside military circles, he had reached the front rank of his profession. At that historic spot in the Forest of Compiègne on June 22, 1940, Keitel crowned his military career by accepting the surrender of the beaten French Army, thereby securing an assured place in the annals of modern warfare alongside Grant, Moltke, and Foch.

For the leading role which he played in the Forest of Compiègne in 1940, the name of Field Marshal Keitel will live in history. For this reason only, if for no other, it has become a subject for regret that destiny had reserved for him a grim sequel, a sequel which was enacted some six years later on a scaffold at Nuremberg, in accordance with a decision reached shortly before the end of the war by the heads of state attending the Yalta Conference. From all accounts it would seem that Keitel was neither a strong personality nor a gifted soldier like his colleagues, Field Marshal von Runstedt or Field Marshal von Manstein. He was widely despised in German military circles as Hitler's "Yes-man" on the General Staff and there is no doubt he gave his formal approval to a number of crimes against humanity committed on the Eastern Front. His defence to the charges later brought against him, he himself summarised in a single sentence, "The struggle against the Red Army was not a knightly combat (em ritterlicher Krieg): at stake was the entire way of life of one side or the other." It is a matter for speculation what his fate would have been if he had been tried by an impartial court. Still at least it cannot be said that his death by hanging was an example of judicial murder like the hanging of General Yamashita, the gallant conqueror of Singapore.

Whatever view be taken of Keitel's fate, it certainly marked a turning point in history. Unsuspected by him and by his contemporaries in 1940 Nemesis was about to overtake the nations of Europe after so many centuries of indulgence with impunity in civil strife. The old standards, the old restraints, the old decencies, with so much else, were destined to disappear. Being done to death upon being taken prisoner was not included among the legitimate risks of soldiering at the time Keitel joined the army in 1901 — unless, of course, one served against savages like the Dervishes or the Abyssinians. By, suffering death as a prisoner of war, Keitel achieved a far wider historical significance than he had achieved during his career. If and when the art of war becomes obsolete, his military achievements will be of interest only to antiquarians: his death by violence when a prisoner of war at Nuremberg in 1946 will be remembered as an event marking an important deviation in the development of human civilization.

As remarked above, the war of 1939-40 had, in itself, no outstanding characteristics. From outside, however, its course was dominated by an entirely new factor. Across the eastern frontier of Poland had arisen the Union of Soviet Socialist Republics, a gigantic quasi-Asiatic totalitarian military power with unlimited natural resources and a rapidly developing industrial system, "profoundly" (to quote General J. F. C. Fuller) "anti-Occidental in outlook."[61]

With this military colossus watching and waiting so near, civil war was no longer a domestic concern to be conducted at leisure, a mere matter of adjusting some frontiers and paying off a few old scores. Even the briefest civil war entailed serious consequences. Immediately hostilities had started, the U.S.S.R. set about realizing far-reaching plans for expansion at the expense of Europe. First, about one-third of Poland was annexed with bland indifference to the fact that Great Britain and France professed to be fighting to preserve the integrity of Poland. Then Finland, "sublime in the jaws of peril", to quote Mr. Churchill, was attacked and subdued. Next, Esthonia, Latvia and Lithuania were overrun and the leading members of the bourgeois classes liquidated or deported to the interior of Russia. With the collapse of France and the withdrawal of the British across the Channel, two urgent problems arose for the consideration of all Europeans—first, whether domination of Europe by the Soviet Union was too heavy a price to pay for the continuance of the civil war, and secondly, if this price was not too heavy, by what means was the war to be continued. Germany with a navy negligible in size could not send an army across the sea to invade Great Britain; single-handed Great Britain could never hope to invade Europe with an army strong enough to avoid its being immediately attacked and overwhelmed.

To put the problem in a nutshell: the essential rule of civilized warfare laid down that hostilities must be limited to the combatant forces. But, as from June 25th, 1940, the combatant

Chapter 6 — The Splendid Decision

forces were separated by the sea. How in such circumstances could hostilities be continued?

Hitler's solution of this problem was an offer to negotiate peace. We need not consider whether this offer was sincere, since any other course from his point of view, would have been madness. He had achieved all and much more than all he had set out to achieve and Germany lay under the shadow of the Red Army.[62] Nor need we consider what terms he would have been willing to offer since his proposal was not even accorded a reply. In their speeches to the House of Commons justifying the silent rejection of Hitler's peace offer both the Prime Minister, Winston Churchill, and the Foreign Minister, Lord Halifax, followed the precedent set by the British Government during the First World War, and gave no indication of any basis upon which a peaceful settlement could be discussed.

But a sulky silence by Hitler's opponents offered no solution to the problem as to how hostilities were to be continued and the war prevented from stagnating until boredom should overcome public opinion. Half a century before, the only means available would have been to launch a series of tip-and-run naval raids on the coasts of Europe. Now, however, the conquest of the air had provided a new method by which not only could boredom be combatted but a war psychosis created. The indiscriminate dropping of bombs at night on enemy centres of population would be bound, sooner or later, to call forth reprisals of a similar nature, and the resulting slaughter of innocent civilians could not fail to inflame warlike passions on both sides.

Certainly it is hard to imagine any other course of action which would have produced the result desired. The only drawback to this course was that the Luftwaffe at the moment was numerically much superior to the R.A.F. Hitler was threatening that, if the British air attacks on the German civil population continued, he would drop ten bombs on Britain for every bomb dropped on Germany. Consequently, the trials of the British civilian population would temporarily, at least, be severe if this policy were persisted in.

It is one of the greatest triumphs of modern emotional engineering that, in spite of the plain facts of the case which could never be disguised or even materially distorted, the British public, throughout the Blitz Period (1940-1941), remained convinced that the entire responsibility for the sufferings it was undergoing rested on the German leaders. Faith is prized by theologians as one of the three cardinal virtues and accepting the definition that "faith is believing what one knows isn't so", it can truly be said that never before had this cardinal virtue been displayed so steadfastly by so many for so long. The practical value of this steadfast faith for the war effort can hardly be exaggerated: the Blitz was unanimously accepted as proof positive of the innate wickedness of the Nazi regime and, as such, endured as something inescapable. General recognition of the fact that it could be brought to an end at any moment might well have had a decisive influence on the public attitude. Too high praise cannot, therefore, be lavished on the British emotional engineers for the infinite skill with which the public mind was conditioned prior to and during a period of unparalleled strain.

It was not until April, 1944, by which time the Luftwaffe had become paralysed from lack of petrol and the issue of the struggle was no longer in doubt, that the strict taboo on all mention of the facts was lifted in favour of Mr. J. M. Spaight, C.B., C.B.E., former Principal Secretary of the Air Ministry, who was permitted to publish a book entitled *Bombing Vindicated*. The title in itself came as a surprise, since few until then had any idea that any vindication for bombing was needed. In this book the man in the street learned for the first time that he had made an heroic decision on May 11, 1940. The man-in-the-street had, of course, no recollection of having made any decision, heroic or otherwise, on this particular date; in fact, he could not recall having made a decision of any kind for a very long time, since in a democracy decisions are not made by such as he, but by international financiers, Press barons, permanent officials and even, occasionally, by Cabinet Ministers. No wonder the man in the street was perplexed.

Mr. Spaight, C.B., C.B.E., resolved this perplexity in the following lyrical passage:

"Because we were doubtful about the psychological effect of propagandist distortion of the truth that it was we who started the strategic bombing offensive, we have shrunk from giving our great decision of May 11th, 1940, the publicity which it deserved. That, surely, was a mistake. It was a splendid decision. It was as heroic, as self-sacrificing, as Russia's decision to adopt her policy of 'scorched earth'. It gave Coventry and Birmingham, Sheffield

Chapter 6 — The Splendid Decision

and Southampton, the right to look Kiev and Kharkov, Stalingrad and Sebastopol, in the face. Our Soviet Allies would have been less critical of our inactivity in 1942 if they had understood what we had done."[63]

In passing, the comment must be made that Mr. Spaight in this passage does much less than justice to the services rendered to him and his colleagues of the Air Ministry by the emotional engineers of the Ministry of Information. Without their aid, this splendid decision might well have led to disastrous consequences; it was entirely thanks to what he is pleased to term "propagandist distortion" that the inhabitants of Coventry, for example, continued to imagine that their sufferings were due to the innate villainy of Adolf Hitler without a suspicion that a decision, splendid or otherwise, of the British War Cabinet was the decisive factor in the case. Had this suspicion existed, their reaction might have been somewhat different. Is it fair for the famous surgeon to sneer at the contribution of the humble anaesthetist which alone renders possible his own delicate operations? Without previous conditioning by the emotional engineer would the activities of the "block-buster" have been tolerated by public opinion?

Contemporary publications on the war may be scanned in vain for a clue why the date May 11, 1940, is in any way memorable. A very close search will, however, bring to light the fact, at the time obscured by far more sensational news, that on the night of May 11th, "eighteen Whitley bombers attacked railway installations in Western Germany." Naturally this announcement when made aroused little interest since it was only claimed these installations had been attacked; it was not suggested that they suffered any injury thereby.

The full significance of this announcement, first disclosed nearly four years afterwards by Mr. Spaight, only appears after further investigation and reflection. Western Germany in May 1940 was, of course, as much outside the area of military operations as Patagonia. Up to this date, only places within the area of military operations or such definitely military objectives as the German air base on Sylt or the British air base on the Orkneys had been attacked. This raid on the night of May 11, 1940, although in itself trivial, was an epoch-marking event since it was the first deliberate breach of the fundamental rule of civilized warfare that hostilities must only be waged against the enemy combatant forces.

In default of any further details it must be left to the imagination to picture the eighteen bombers setting forth on the night of May 11th from their base with instructions to drop their bombs when they found themselves over Western Germany in the hope that some of them might land on railway installations. To achieve this modest purpose they would have to cross the battlefront, extending from the North Sea to Switzerland, which had suddenly blazed into frantic activity as the German armies hurled themselves to the attack from the Zuider Zee to the Maginot Line in Lorraine. As nothing to the contrary has been recorded, it may be assumed that the eighteen bombers all returned safely and that some of their bombs damaged something somewhere. To the crews of these bombers it must have seemed strange to fly over a battlefield where a life and death struggle was taking place and then on over country crowded with columns of enemy troops pouring forward to the attack, in order to reach the peaceful countryside of Westphalia on the off-chance that some of their bombs dropped there would land on railway installations. The value of their contribution to the great battle in which the fate of France was being decided must indeed have seemed to them obscure. Yet without realising it they were turning a major page of history. Their flight marked the end of an epoch which had lasted for two and one-half centuries.

How many times during this long period must Mars have sadly reflected on the words of King Draco the Great in Anatole France's *Penguin Island*: "War without fire is like tripe without mustard: it is an insipid thing." What use the great conquerors of the past could have made of these new-fangled flying machines. They themselves had achieved much certainly, but how sadly they had been hampered by the limited powers of destruction at their disposal. We may picture the shadowy figures of the great conquerors in the days when war had really been war as admiring and envious spectators of the doings of those eighteen bombers on that memorable May night: against a background of prosaic twentieth century railway installations we can imagine the grim forms of Asshurnazirpal and Sennacherib stroking their square-cut, curled and scented beards with dignified approval; the squat figure of Attila, the King of the Huns; the awe-inspiring shape of the great Mongol conqueror, Genghis Khan, and the forms of his successors, Hulagu, whose destruction of the irrigation system of

Chapter 6 — The Splendid Decision

the Euphrates Valley was so thorough that what for thousands of years had been one of the most prosperous parts of the earth became a desert, the mighty Tamerlane, and a score of others. To these men, at least, the limitless possibilities of this new method of achieving an ancient purpose would have been clear.

These possibilities, however, were at the time realized by few. It was not until much later that it became necessary to find justification for such horrors as took place on that night when the most densely populated parts of Hamburg became a roaring furnace in which thousands of men, women and children were throwing themselves into the canals to escape the frightful heat. The stock apology then put forward was that it was only a reprisal for the German bombing of Warsaw and Rotterdam. Mr. Spaight dismisses this argument with the contempt it deserves. "When Warsaw and Rotterdam were bombed," he points out, "German armies were at their gates. The air bombardment was an operation of the tactical offensive."[64] Captain Liddell Hart accepts the same view. "Bombing did not take place," he writes, "until the German troops were fighting their way into these cities and thus conformed to the old rules of siege bombardment."[65]

Bombing Vindicated is a remarkable book: in fact, an amazing book having regard to the date when it was written.[66] Mr. Spaight is not content merely to admit that upon Britain rests the responsibility for starting the practice of bombing civilian populations, but insists that to Britain must be awarded the entire credit for conceiving and carrying into effect this practice. He derides (p. 149) the suggestion rather half-heartedly put forward at the time by the Ministry of Information that "the whole majestic process had been set in operation" because an unidentified plane had dropped some bombs on a wood near Canterbury. Nor will he admit the splendid decision of May 11, 1940, "was unpremeditated". On the contrary, he insists hotly (p. 38), that this decision can be traced "to a brainwave which came to British experts in 1936," when the Bomber Command was organized—"The whole raison d'être of Bomber Command," he tells us (p. 60), "was to bomb Germany should she be our enemy". Further, he says it was obvious that Hitler realized that this was Britain's intention in the event of war, and that he was, in consequence, genuinely anxious to reach with Britain an agreement "confining the action of aircraft to the battle zones". Finally, he agrees that Hitler only undertook the bombing of the British civilian population reluctantly three months after the R.A.F. had commenced bombing the German civilian population, and expresses the opinion (p. 47) that after it had started Hitler would have been willing at any time to have stopped the slaughter — "Hitler assuredly did not want the mutual bombing to go on." The reader will find the facts of the case set out with frank jubilation by Mr. Spaight in the above-mentioned book, and with the objective detachment of a veteran historian by Captain Liddell Hart in his *Revolution in Warfare*. They are repeated by Air Marshal Sir Arthur Harris in his book,*Bomber Offensive* (1947) by that time much tinged by a marked petulance arising from the dawning realization of the far-reaching consequences of the precedent created by "the splendid decision of May 11, 1940". And truly it is a disturbing precedent for the inhabitants of a small, densely populated island, now that all the military might, air prowess, and boundless resources of Asia have become no further distant than the Oder.

Air Marshal Harris joins with Mr. Spaight in pouring contempt on the shortsightedness of professional soldiers throughout the world, and in particular in Germany, for not perceiving in the years before 1939 that the heavy bomber would be a far more effective weapon against civilians than against combatant forces. The issue for what purpose an air force should be designed to serve was hotly debated in Britain immediately after the First World War. Germany had been disarmed but France had emerged from the struggle with the largest air force in the world and was bitterly aggrieved at British opposition to her plans for annexation in the Middle East. The question was, what type of plane would Britain need in the event of another war? The professional soldiers in the War Office naturally took the traditional view; the chiefs of the newly created air force, unhampered by tradition, took an entirely novel view. In 1923 Air Marshal Sir Hugh Trenchard, Chief of the Air Staff, exactly summarized the point at issue when he wrote, "The Army policy was to defeat the enemy army; our policy was to defeat the enemy nation."

Far from planning a Blitz, Air Marshal Harris declares that Germany lost the war because, when compelled in September 1940 to carry out the Blitz, she found that the generals who dominated the Luftwaffe and regarded the bomber as merely a form of

Chapter 6 — The Splendid Decision

long-range artillery for use in battle, had neglected to equip the Luftwaffe with heavily armed bomber planes designed for a Blitz. "The Germans," writes Air Marshal Harris, "had allowed their soldiers to dictate the whole policy of the Luftwaffe which was designed expressly to assist the army in rapid offensives.... Much too late in the day they saw the advantage of a strategic bombing force ... the outcome was the German Army had to be deprived of air cover and air support on every front to provide some defence for Germany against independent strategic action in the air."[67]

Mr. Spaight puts the matter in a nutshell when he writes (p. 144): "In Germany and in France the air arm never cut adrift from the land arm: it was tethered to the Army in these countries. In Britain it was free to roam." To this it may be replied that orthodox military opinion holds that it is the duty of a soldier to fight and not to roam. "For Germany," Mr. Spaight continues, "the bomber was artillery for stationary troops dug fast into the Maginot Line; for Britain, it was an offensive weapon designed to attack the economic resources of the enemy deep within his country."

It is important to note that the "splendid decision of May 11, 1940" was put into effect "General Gamelin notwithstanding". "The French General Staff," remarks Mr. Spaight sadly (p. 70), "had all along a conception of air warfare broadly similar to that of the German General Staff and divergent from that of the British Air Staff. They viewed with the greatest misgivings any plan by which bombers were to be used for attacks on German industry, and did not hesitate to say so. In their considered opinion the main, indeed the only, use to which a bombing force should be put was to extend the range of artillery supporting armies in the field."

From every point of view Air Marshal Harris' book, *Bomber Offensive*, is a much less illuminating work than Mr. Spaight's *Bombing Vindicated*. Writing in the same spirit, his tone is much more subdued. Substantially, however, he is in complete agreement with Mr. Spaight. He also attributes the failure of the Blitz to the shortsightedness of the Luftwaffe chiefs in not providing themselves in peace time with long-distance bomber planes designed for attacks on an enemy civilian population, an omission, he declares, which lost Germany the war. Had the Germans been able to persist in their attacks, he writes, London would unquestionably have suffered the terrible fate which over took Hamburg two years later. But in September 1940 the Germans found themselves "with almost unarmed bombers ... so that in the Battle of Britain the destruction of the German bomber squadrons was very similar to shooting cows in a field."

Only with regard to the justification of attacks from the air on civilians can the Air Marshal be said to go one better than the Principal Air Secretary. When reproached for the inhumanity of this form of warfare, he tells us complacently, it is his practice to confound his critics by quoting to them a British Government White Paper which estimates that the blockade of Europe by the British Navy between 1914 and 1918 "caused nearly 800,000 deaths, mainly women and children," while, on the other hand, indiscriminate bombing by the R.A.F. between 1940 and 1945 probably did not in his opinion kill more than 300,000. He assures us that this retort invariably left his critics dumfounded and abashed.

Certainly this is a novel line of argument which, if it ever secured acceptance in criminal law, would lead to strange consequences. For example, a person accused of a single murder could by this argument claim acquittal on the ground that there have been cases of persons guilty of wholesale murder.

In passing it may be noted that the Air Marshal's estimate of the civilian casualties resulting from the British air offensive against Germany is far below the figure now generally accepted. At the Manstein Trial in Hamburg in 1949 the figure of 250,000 was put forward as the probable total of casualties from one air raid, that on Dresden on the night of February 13th, 1945. While declaring that the casualties in this raid will probably always remain a subject for speculation, General Hans Rumpf, after a careful examination and analysis of all the available evidence, comes to the conclusion that in Germany between 1940 and 1945 some 600,000 were killed and 800,000 were wounded in air attacks — see his *Das war der Bombenkrieg*, (Gerhard Stalling Verlag, Oldenburg, 1961, page 114).

Messrs. Spaight and Harris speak with the authority of a Principal Secretary to the Air Ministry and of an Air Marshal respectively. The facts which they set forth are not open to question by persons who lack the expert and inside knowledge which they possess. Yet some may find it hard to credit their interpretation of these facts. According to their joint testimony, prior to 1939

Chapter 6 — The Splendid Decision

the General Staffs of Great Britain, Germany and France were composed entirely of elderly professional soldiers whose brains, rendered senile by routine and red tape, were incapable of grasping so obvious a fact that if bombs were showered from the air upon an enemy power's chief centres of population, its war effort would be affected. Only in the British Air Ministry, and then only thanks to a memorable "brain-wave" in 1936, did this fact dawn, with the result that for three years before the outbreak of war Britain alone was planning accordingly. As a result of the opposition of the French General Staff, it was not until May 11, 1940, that the Bomber Command was permitted to fulfil the purpose for which it was built. Thereafter it was free "to roam" — with consequences with which we are all familiar.

It may seem presumptuous but, it is submitted, there is an alternative interpretation which has escaped the attention of Messrs. Spaight and Harris. The men who had risen to the leadership of the General Staffs of Great Britain, Germany and France may not have been congenital idiots unable to perceive the obvious; they may have fully realized the effect which could be produced by bombing an enemy civilian population and yet have deliberately ruled out the adoption of this policy as contrary to the first principle of civilized warfare. In taking up such an attitude they would only have been following the example of the statesmen of all the nations of Europe for the preceding two hundred years. Frequently tempted to depart from it to gain manifest but temporary advantage, European statesmen since the time of Louis XIV had consistently maintained the principle that hostilities must be confined to the combatant forces of the belligerents.

They did so because they realized that civilization is a fragile structure, inevitably subjected to severe strain even by a war limited by strict rules — by mere "fooling with war" as Mr. Spaight calls it. The exclusion of non-combatants from the scope of hostilities is the fundamental distinction between civilized and barbarous warfare. All other restraints had followed naturally from acceptance of this first principle. If it were abandoned, all else would quickly disappear. Subconsciously, at any rate, it may have been realized by them how thin and fragile was the partition separating civilized man from the passions of the jungle: how civilization itself might not survive the release of the dark forces which would be set free by warfare waged in the manner

Advance to Barbarism

of primitive times. Victory would then indeed be barren. At all events, rightly or wrongly, wisely or unwisely, the fundamental principle of civilized warfare was repudiated on May 11, 1940 — according to Mr. Spaight, as a result of a "brain-wave" in the British Air Ministry in 1936 — and, with the keystone removed, the whole structure of civilized warfare as it had been gradually built tip in Europe during the preceding two centuries collapsed in ruins.

The assumption became general that a war waged by barbarous methods must inevitably end in a barbarous peace. Faced with this appalling prospect, each side felt any act was justified, provided only that it served even remotely to stave off defeat. As the war proceeded and the prospects darkened, this became more and more openly the German attitude. The entry of the United States and the Soviet Union accelerated the head long decline of civilized warfare, since, as non-European powers, neither felt in any way bound to observe the rules of civil war adopted by the European aborigines. In happier days, Europeans had cheerfully disregarded their own rules in warfare outside Europe with non-Europeans; now, for the first time in Europe, Europeans found these rules disregarded by non-Europeans. The entry of the Soviet Union into the war, of course, completely transformed its original character.

In a marginal note which was fatuously brought up against him at Nuremberg, Field Marshal Keitel drew attention to the obvious fact that the struggle with the Red Army was not "ein ritterlicherKrieg" — "Hier handelt es sich um die Vernichtung einer Weltanschauung." ("This is no knightly combat: it involves the destruction of the whole life philosophy of one side or the other.") It is characteristic of primary wars that they are never "ritterlich" (knightly) or at most only superficially. The campaigns on the Eastern Front were primary warfare in its grimmest aspect.

The above outline of the facts relating to the Bombing Campaign during the Second World War summarises all that was known on this subject in 1953 when the first edition of *Advance to Barbarism* (from which these paragraphs are reproduced) was published. After what Mr. Spaight had disclosed in 1944 it was impossible for anyone, however credulous, to accept the repeated and solemn assertions of His Majesty's Ministers in Parliament that the bombing of Germany was being carried out with strict

Chapter 6 — The Splendid Decision

regard to the dictates of humanity in accordance with the rules of civilized warfare. But only those who had actually taken part in this bombing campaign or those having had access to official documents knew exactly what had taken place. Serious students of the subject indeed had no doubt that "unrestricted" or "indiscriminate" bombing (these terms were regarded as synonyms) had been deliberately adopted as a means of winning the war. The full truth was not disclosed until 1961: it far surpassed the worst suspicions of those who at the time condemned what Mr. Spaight has called "the splendid Decision" as a relapse into barbarism.

As stressed earlier in these pages the essential principle, of the Rules of Civilized Warfare was that military operations should be restricted to overcoming the uniformed armed forces of the enemy, and on no account should the enemy civilian population be attacked or molested.

As we have seen, the main difficulty which arose from the start with regard to the application of this simple principle was in connection with siege operations. Everyone was agreed that places on a battlefield held by enemy troops could be attacked without regard to the lives of civilians living in them, and besieged towns could be bombarded in order to force their garrisons to surrender. Differences of opinion soon arose whether it was justifiable to use a defended town itself, as distinct from its fortifications, as a target for bombardment, as Copenhagen was used by the British Navy in 1807, or Strasburg was used by the German Army in 1870. But it was generally agreed that this was justifiable provided that the town in question was within the theatre of military operations, that it was defended and that it contained military objectives. In theory the projectiles were aimed at these military objectives even if the chance of hitting them was small and it was certain that those which missed would kill innocent civilians. Casualties so caused were dismissed as deeply regrettable happenings unavoidable in warfare.

Such were the recognized conditions of warfare from the beginning of the 18th century down to and including the First World War. A commander who ordered his men to destroy a hospital or a school in preference to a fort or a barracks would have been regarded not only as a sadistic monster, but as a fool. A belated echo of this point of view was expressed by Air

Marshal Harris in his notorious broadcast to the German people on the 28th July, 1942, when he said, "Obviously we prefer to hit factories, shipyards and railways. But those people who work in these plants live close to them. Therefore we hit your homes and you." Until shortly before this contention would have seemed such obvious common sense that it would have carried instant conviction with everyone. Of course, at the time it was spoken Air Marshal Harris knew that he was expressing the attitude of a bygone age. Four months previously, the British Government had accepted the Lindemann Plan by which the killing of civilians was made a military objective which henceforth was to be given, to use the official jargon of the time, "top priority".

Although throughout the First World War the Rules of Civilized Warfare were observed in so far as attacks were always directed against recognized military objectives, yet these attacks were delivered with an ever increasing disregard for the safety of civilian life. The outstanding example of this disregard was the Zeppelin Air Offensive against Great Britain in 1915-17. Examining this offensive Sir Charles Webster and Dr. Noble Frankland, the joint authors of the officially published work *The Strategic Air Offensive against Germany, 1939-45* (H.M. Stationery Office, London, 1961), admit frankly these raids were all aimed at military objectives, but comment soberly, "The Zeppelin commanders often did not know where they were and their bombs were dropped largely at random. They did on occasion, more by luck than management, cause some damage." (Page 34.)

It is no subject for surprise that the civilian casualties resulting were relatively slight. What is surprising is that military objectives were so frequently hit. Thus, for example, on the night of June 17th, 1917, the Fish Market at Ramsgate in which were stored mines swept up by the mine-sweeping flotilla operating from Ramsgate was hit by a bomb and widespread damage was caused: another bomb from a Zeppelin made a direct hit on a crowded naval dormitory at Chatham Barracks causing great loss of life. Such results were made possible by the slow speed at which the airships flew and the low altitude at which they were able to fly owing to the ineffective anti-aircraft fire of the time. But far more, such results were due to luck, if luck be the right word. The Kaiser and his advisers were like children with a new toy. They were justifiably proud of the Zeppelin Airship, the product of Count

Chapter 6 — The Splendid Decision

Zeppelin's inventive genius. There were undeniably numerous military objectives in Britain, the destruction of which would serve a military purpose. So they ordered the Zeppelin commanders to fly over Britain and destroy with bombs these military objectives. They callously ignored the fact that not one bomb in a hundred, dropped at night by crews with no experience of bombing and using primitive instruments, was likely to hit a military objective and that bombs that missed would endanger civilian life. The Zeppelin commanders no doubt did their best to carry out their orders. When they returned they reported, no doubt in good faith, that they had achieved the missions assigned to them.

Their will to believe being strong, the Kaiser and his advisers accepted these reports as true. Similarly, for eighteen months after the "Splendid Decision" to bomb industrial targets in Germany had been taken, Winston Churchill and his advisers were kept happy by the reports of the R.A.F. pilots announcing in perfect good faith the destruction of the targets assigned to them. Aerial photography had by that time, however, been brought to a high state of perfection. All doubts on the subject were laid to rest by the Bensusan-Butt Report dated the 18th August, 1941. The British Cabinet were horrified to learn that aerial photographs taken of the targets described as having been completely demolished disclosed that most of them showed no signs of damage; of all the aircraft credited with having bombed their targets, only one-third had, in fact, bombed within five miles of them.

Until April 1961 everyone believed that what was called "the strategic air offensive" against Germany which started in May 1940 was an offensive carried out in a spirit similar to that of the Zeppelin offensive of 1915-17 against Britain. Both offensives were directed against military objectives with the same callous disregard for the lives of the civilian population. The fact that the British offensive was carried out on a vastly greater scale and owing to the enormously improved aircraft and bombs employed incomparably greater destruction was caused, made no essential distinction between them. It was maintained that because the R.A.F., like the Zeppelins, directed their bombs against specified targets, the use of the term "indiscriminate bombing" was a slanderous misnomer. Some maintained, however, that the official use of the term "saturation bombing" to describe the dropping of enormous quantities of bombs on a selected area justified the use of the word "indiscriminate" with regard to R.A.F. bombing. Within this selected area, often of considerable extent, such bombing was certainly both indiscriminate and unrestricted.

One essential distinction, however, existed between these air offensives. When the British air offensive was launched against Germany in May 1940 Winston Churchill and his advisers extended the definition of "military objectives" which had been accepted for two and a half centuries, to include factories, oil plants, public buildings and any structure which contributed or was of use, if only indirectly, to the war effort of the enemy.

This extension was the essence of "the Splendid Decision" which filled Mr. Spaight with such pride. Many maintained that this extension rendered the definition of "military objectives" meaningless, since there was not a city, town or village in the industrial areas of Western Europe which did not possess a building of some kind which came within this definition — a railway station, a post office, a police station, a bridge or an electrical power plant. The existence of any of these in a place rendered that place with all its inhabitants liable to be obliterated by bombs. Thus, accepting the definition which included all public buildings as military objectives, if a bomb was aimed at a village which contained for example a police station, missed its mark and killed people in that village, no breach of the Rules of Civilized Warfare would take place, because it had long been agreed that when a missile which had been aimed at a military objective caused civilian casualties, such casualties could be attributed to a regrettable, but in no way blameworthy, accident.

Not unreasonably, it is submitted, many people maintained that bombing carried out in accordance with this novel definition of military objectives was, in fact, unrestricted bombing. No part of the enemy civilian population was excluded from the scope of the military operations, and therefore the Rules of Civilized Warfare were in practice, although not expressly, repudiated. Apologists for the Air Offensive argued that as the definition of "military objectives" had always been somewhat vague and elastic, the British Government was entitled to amend the current definition as it pleased, and anyway there had been no express repudiation of the Rules of Civilized Warfare.

All arguments concerning the British bombing of Germany during the Second World War were brought abruptly

Chapter 6 — The Splendid Decision

to an end in April 1961 by a single paragraph in a little book with the uninspiring title *Science and Government*.[68] The author was Sir Charles Snow, scientist and novelist. His purpose in writing it was to assess the respective achievements of two rival physicists, Professor Lindemann and Dr. Henry Tizard. The book was primarily concerned to show that when the opinions of these two men conflicted, Dr. Tizard always proved to be right and Professor Lindemann always wrong. To do this he was compelled to disclose the truth concerning one of the principal issues which arose between them.

This paragraph will be found quoted verbatim on page 18 in the Introduction to this book. In a nutshell Sir Charles Snow disclosed that early in 1942 — the exact date, it now appears, was March 30th, 1942 — Professor Lindemann submitted a Minute to the War Cabinet in which he urged that bombing henceforth should be directed against German working-class houses in preference to military objectives, which were much too difficult to hit. He claimed that given a total concentration of effort on the production of aircraft suitable for this work, 50% of all the houses in the cities and towns in Germany with over 50,000 inhabitants would be destroyed. Sir Charles declared that the Lindemann Plan to initiate terror bombing against Germany was adopted by the British Government "and put into action with every effort the country could make."

It was everywhere expected that these assertions of Sir Charles Snow would at once be rebutted by categorical and emphatic denials. No attempt at denial was made, however. Lord Birkenhead indeed hurriedly produced a biography of Professor Lindemann in which he rebutted at length and with indignation the popular belief that Lindemann was a Jew, a point of no relevance or interest to anyone, but he had nothing to say with regard to the suggestion that Lindemann was a war criminal responsible for a ghastly crime against humanity. In October, 1961, six months after the publication of Sir Charles Snow's book, the full truth was disclosed in the above mentioned official publication, *The Strategic Air Offensive against Germany* (H.M. Stationery Office, London, 1961).

It has thus now become possible to trace in detail the development of air bombing during the Second World War. This development took place in three clearly marked stages, during the first of which starting with the outbreak of war on the 3rd September 1939 and lasting until the 11th May 1940, the air forces of both sides attacked only military objectives strictly in accordance with the Rules of Civilized Warfare.

The second stage began on the 11th May, 1940, when the R.A.F. launched its first attack on industrial areas in Germany, the British Government having adopted a new definition of military objectives so that this term included any building which in any way contributed, directly or indirectly, to the war effort of the enemy. The R.A.F. attacked "military objectives" as so defined in accordance with the orders of the War Cabinet, but very soon the Air Staff chiefs began to permit themselves greater and greater latitude in carrying out their orders. Thus, as early as the 16th December, 1940, a moonlight raid by 134 planes took place on Mannheim, described in the above mentioned official British history of the air offensive as "the first 'area' attack of the war." The object of this attack, as Air Chief Marshal Peirse later explained, was "to concentrate the maximum amount of damage in the centre of the town." As early as this therefore, all pretence of attacking military, industrial or in fact any particular targets was in practice abandoned.

The British air offensive launched on the 11th May 1940 against industrial objectives in Germany continued without retaliation for nearly four months. During May and June the Luftwaffe was fully occupied taking part in the campaign in France. After the surrender of France on the 22nd June, for a month Hitler clung to the delusion that the struggle could be brought to an end by a negotiated peace. Realising at last this hope was vain, Hitler launched a massive air attack on Britain in order to win command of the air preparatory to an invasion. This was a purely military operation, carried out mainly in daylight, against airfields, docks and shipping. The Battle of Britain ended with a defeat for Germany as decisive as the Battle of Stalingrad. It was not until September that the Luftwaffe was ordered to cease its costly efforts to win command of the air over the English Channel, and to launch a reprisal air offensive against Britain exactly similar to the British air offensive against Germany which had been going on ever since May 11th. On the 6th September London was subjected to a mass attack by 270 bombers, the greatest concentration of air power collected up to that time, and great damage and many casualties

Chapter 6 — The Splendid Decision

were caused. Thereafter every night favourable for bombing the chief industrial cities of Britain suffered the same fate. Until the following Spring when the Luftwaffe was withdrawn to take part in the invasion of Russia, the two air offensives continued concurrently. The British air offensive during this period must be set down as a failure to the extent that it achieved nothing towards crippling the war production of Germany but as a success to the extent that it prevented the war stagnating and it generated a frenzied war psychosis. The German air offensive, on the other hand, must be dismissed as a complete failure since it did not achieve its only purpose, namely, to induce the British Government to discontinue the air offensive against Germany.

Throughout this period the British public believed without question that the British air offensive against Germany was a reprisal for the attacks of the Luftwaffe on Britain which, it was said, began with the dropping of bombs by an unidentified plane on a wood near Canterbury. A faint echo of this belief will be found in the official history of the air offensive where it is stated that the destructive raid on Coventry on the 14th November, 1940, decided the chiefs of Bomber Command to launch the attack on the centre of Mannheim above mentioned. Indisputably, of course, both Coventry and Mannheim possessed "military objectives" according to the new definition of this term adopted by the British Government in the previous May.

In passing it may be observed that the question which air offensive was a reprisal for which has now long ceased to be a subject for dispute. As early as 1953 H.M. Stationery Office published the first volume of a work *The Royal Air Force, 1939-1945* entitled *The Fight at Odds*, a book described as "officially commissioned and based throughout on official documents which had been read and approved by the Air Ministry Historical Branch." The author, Mr. Dennis Richards, states plainly that the destruction of oil plants and factories was only a secondary purpose of the British air attacks on Germany which began in May 1940. The primary purpose of these raids was to goad the Germans into undertaking reprisal raids of a similar character on Britain. Such raids would arouse intense indignation in Britain against Germany and so create a war psychosis without which it is impossible to carry on a modern war. Mr. Dennis Richards writes:—

Advance to Barbarism

"If the Royal Air Force raided the Ruhr, destroying oil plants with its most accurately placed bombs *and urban property with those that went astray,* the outcry for retaliation against Britain might prove too strong for the German generals to resist. Indeed, Hitler himself would probably head the clamour. *The attack on the Ruhr, in other words, was an informal invitation to the Luftwaffe to bomb London."* (Page 122).

This passage, of course, merely confirmed what Mr. Spaight had so incautiously disclosed in 1944 in his by then forgotten book *Bombing Vindicated*. The popular belief that Hitler started unrestricted bombing still persisted and is, in fact, widely held even at the present day.

The third and last phase of the British air offensive against Germany began in March 1942 with the adoption of the Lindemann Plan by the British War Cabinet, and continued with undiminished ferocity until the end of the war in May, 1945. The bombing during this period was not, as the Germans complained, indiscriminate. On the contrary, it was concentrated on working-class houses because, as Professor Lindemann maintained, a higher percentage of bloodshed per ton of explosives dropped could be expected from bombing houses built close together, rather than by bombing higher class houses surrounded by gardens. Neither was it unrestricted bombing, except, of course, in the sense that it was not restricted to military objectives as originally defined by the Rules of Civilized Warfare, which in practice had been found difficult to hit and therefore wasteful of bombs. The bombing during this period was simple terror bombing designed to shatter the morale of the civilian population and so to generate an inclination to surrender.

The adoption of the Lindemann Plan produced no startlingly obvious changes in bombing tactics perceptible even to the German civilian population. Ever since the first "area" bombing, the above mentioned raid on Mannheim in December 1940, the British air chiefs on their own initiative had been carrying out their orders to reduce German industrial production by an easier method than by dropping bombs through the roofs of factories. They argued that the desired result would be more readily achieved if the homes of the workers in the factories were destroyed: if the workers were kept busy arranging for the burial of their wives and children, output might reasonably be expected

Chapter 6 — The Splendid Decision

to fall. Thus the adoption of the Lindemann Plan merely gave express government sanction to tactics which had long been adopted with semi-official approval.

The Lindemann Plan was first carried into effect on the 28th March, 1942, when Lilibeck was attacked by 234 aircraft of Bomber Command. This beautiful old Hanseatic port had no military or special industrial importance but was chosen because, as Air Marshal Harris subsequently described it, the city was "built more like a firelighter than a human habitation." The focus of the attack was the Altstadt composed of medieval houses with narrow, tortuous streets; some 30,000 people lived in an area of two square kilometres. Photographic reconnaissance showed the raid had been "a first class success." From 45% to 50% of the city was totally destroyed, together with the Cathedral and the Market Hall.

During the last seven years full particulars with copious official statistics have been published concerning the subsequent course of the great Air Offensive. The grisly story can be read elsewhere. Here it will be sufficient to say that one "first class success" followed another. The climax of the offensive was reached on the night of February 13th, 1945, when a mass raid by several thousand heavy bombers was directed against Dresden. The result of this air raid was indisputably a first class success, far surpassing all previous first class successes. Naturally there was jubilation at Supreme Allied Headquarters in Paris which approved a despatch from the Associated Press correspondent announcing that "Allied war chiefs have made the long awaited decision to adopt deliberate terror bombing of German population centres as a ruthless expedient to hasten Hitler's doom.... The all-out air war on Germany became obvious with the unprecedented assault on the refugee-crowded Saxon capital two weeks ago." The text of this sensational announcement will be found quoted more fully earlier in this book.

Almost at once, however, it was realised that if the decision to adopt ruthless terror bombing was held up for public glorification, the question would be asked, When had this decision been reached? Remembering that this was not, as stated, "a long-awaited decision", but a decision taken nearly three years before, which had been repeatedly and solemnly denied by Ministers of the Crown in Parliament, Commander Brabner, Under Secretary of State for Air, was instructed to repeat these denials and to assure the House of Commons that the statement approved by the Supreme Allied Headquarters in Paris was incorrect. Officially no crime against humanity had been committed. A stringent taboo prevented the publication of details and the matter was quickly forgotten by the public. Indisputably, the destruction of Dresden was not only an outstanding event of the Second World War but an outstanding event of European history, an event which was the culmination of that fatal addiction to civil war in which the nations of Europe had been indulging for centuries. Those at the time who desired information concerning the destruction of Dresden naturally consulted the monumental work in four volumes of Sir Winston Churchill which purported to give a complete record of the events of the Second World War, and found what they sought on page 470 of Volume IV, *Triumph and Tragedy*. They had however to be content with twenty-two words — "Throughout January and February 1945 our bombers continued to attack, and we made a heavy raid in the latter month on Dresden." Sir Winston has nothing further to say on the subject.

The following account of the bombing of Dresden was first published in 1953 in the American edition of the present book.[69] For ten years, until the publication of a book entirely devoted to this subject and based on British official records (*The Destruction of Dresden* by David living, Kimber, London, 1963), it remained the only account in the English language of the Schreckensnacht of February 13th, 1945. It was mainly based on *Der Tod von Dresden* by Axel Rodenberger (*Das grüne Blatt*, Dortmund, 1951) the first German writer to collect all the then available facts concerning this holocaust. No material facts have come to light since 1951 which make revision necessary of what the present author wrote in 1953.

Reverting to the authoritative work of Air Marshal Harris, *Bomber Offensive*, it is noteworthy that even the gallant Air Marshal's hardihood falters in regard to the mass bombing by some two thousand heavy bombing planes of Dresden on the night of February 13th, 1945, when the normal population of "this large and splendid city" was swollen by a horde of terrified women and children from the eastern provinces of Germany in flight from the most dreadful fate which had ever confronted a large European population since the Mongol invasion of 1241. In February, 1945, the war had, of course, long ceased to be a military

Chapter 6 — The Splendid Decision

operation and had become merely the breaking of the desperate but hopeless resistance of a defeated people, the leaders of which faced death and the remainder slavery. Selecting his words with obvious care, the Air Marshal writes, "I will only say that the attack on Dresden was at the time considered a military necessity by much more important people than myself."[70]

It will be noted that the Air Marshal pointedly refrains from endorsing the opinion of these important people. He leaves it open to speculation whether this was due to a modest shrinking from associating himself with so much importance or whether, after reflecting on the facts and circumstances, to sheer horror. It is further to be noted that he attributes this opinion to these important people as held by them only "at the time", from which it may be deduced that he cannot bring himself to believe that any sane person could still hold such an opinion. Finally, it will be noted that he loyally refrains from disclosing the identity of these important people.

An examination of the situation existing at the time of this great mass air raid will provide an explanation of the Air Marshal's studied reticence. In February, 1945, the war had been won and no military purpose remained to be served by indiscriminate bombing. From the East, the Russian hordes were advancing steadily and irresistibly. In the centre, they had reached the Oder on a wide front on each side of Frankfurt-an-der-Oder, only 50 miles east of Berlin; on the right wing, the greater part of East Prussia which for seven hundred years had served as an advanced bastion of Europe against Asia, had been subdued; on the left wing, Lower Silesia had been overrun, although the capital, Breslau, closely surrounded, continued to offer a resistance as heroic as this city had offered the Mongol hordes of Batu almost exactly seven hundred years before.

In the West, the armies of General Eisenhower were advancing on a wide front to the Rhine. The surviving German armies in the field continued to resist, not from any lingering hope that defeat could be averted but because their enemies' insistence on unconditional surrender made it seem preferable to a people brought up for generations on the tradition of Frederick the Great to go down fighting to the last. The publication of the infamous Morgenthau Plan had left it in no doubt what were the conqueror intentions whether Germany surrendered at once or a final stand

Advance to Barbarism

was made. The only military problem remaining in February, 1945 (if such it can be called) was the question along what line running North and South across Germany the invaders of Germany from the West would meet the invaders of Germany from the East. In fact, the campaign which had commenced on the Normandy beaches in the previous summer had become a mere race with the Soviet hordes, a race in which anything which the Germans could do to retard the progress of the latter, although of no practical benefit to themselves, would be of enormous political value to the Western Powers. Nevertheless, the British and Americans decided to launch a mass air attack on Dresden: then about 70 miles behind the scanty German forces resisting desperately the Russian advance across Lower Silesia.

Very little authoritative information has been available until very recently concerning this mass air raid. In the earliest books which dealt with the last stage of the war, the course usually adopted was to refer airily to the bombing of Dresden as the last of a long series of mass air raids in which it happened that an exceptionally large number of people were killed. As a result of this general reticence little could be added for a long time to the following reference to this air raid published in *The Times* three days after it had taken place:

"Dresden, which had been pounded on Tuesday night by 800 of the 1,400 heavies sent out by the R.A.F. and was the main object of 1,350 Fortresses and Liberators on the following day, yesterday received its third heavy attack in thirty-six hours. It was the principal target for more than 1,100 United States 8th Army Air Force bombers."[71]

Other British newspapers reported similarly. In none of them was any attempt made to explain why Dresden should have been selected as the target for such a terrific concentration of force. Reference to a guide book will provide no clue. The modern city of Dresden has grown up round the medieval town, now known as the Altstadt which lies at the southern end of the bridge crossing the Elbe. In the eighteenth century Dresden became one of the great show cities of the world through the construction of a number of magnificent public buildings, all of which were erected in the Altstadt district of the city. Within a radius of half a mile from the southern end of the Augustus Bridge was built a unique group of palaces, art galleries, museums and churches—the

Chapter 6 — The Splendid Decision

Schloss, containing the famous Grünes Gewölbe with its priceless art treasures; the beautiful Brühl Terrasse extending along the left bank of the Elbe; the beautiful Catholic Cathedral; the domed Frauen Kirche; the Opera House; the Johanneum Museum and, above all, the famous Zwinger Museum containing one of the finest collections of pictures in the world, including among its many treasures Raphael's Sistine Madonna, purchased by the Elector, Augustus II, in 1745, for 20,000 ducats. Within this small area, so well known to British and American travellers on the continent, there were, and could be, no munition factories or, in fact, industries of any kind. The resident population of this district was small. The main railway station of Dresden is situated a mile away to the South and the railway bridge which carries the main line to Berlin is half a mile away down the river.

The following brief details of this raid, which are now well established, are added in amplification of the contemporary report from *The Times* set out above.

On the morning of the fateful February 13, 1945, fast enemy reconnaissance planes were observed flying over the city. The inhabitants of Dresden had had no experience of modern air warfare and the appearance of these planes aroused curiosity rather than apprehension. Having been for so long outside any theatre of war, the city lacked anti-aircraft defences and these planes were able to observe in complete safety all that they desired. No doubt, they observed and reported that all the roads through and around Dresden were filled with dense throngs moving westward. It is impossible, however, that these throngs could have been mistaken for troop concentrations. It was common knowledge that the German High Command had thrown in its last reserves to reinforce the crumbling battlefronts and consequently there existed no troops which could possibly be massing so far from any fighting. It was also common knowledge that a frantic orgy of murder, rape and arson was taking place in those districts of Silesia which had been overrun by the Soviet hordes. It should not have been difficult to deduce in these circumstances that many people in districts threatened by the Russian advance would decide to try to escape westwards.[72]

Some hours after night had fallen, about 9.30 p.m., the first wave of attacking planes passed over Dresden. The focus of the attack was the Altstadt. Terrific fires soon broke out which were still blazing when the second wave of attackers arrived shortly after midnight. The resulting slaughter was appalling, since the normal population of the city of some 600,000 had been recently swollen by a multitude of refugees, mostly women and children, their menfolk having remained behind to defend their homes. Every house in Dresden was filled with these unfortunates, every public building was crowded with them, many were camping in the streets. Estimates of their number vary between 300,000 and 500,000.

There were no air raid shelters. There were, in fact no air raid defences of any kind, unless we so regard the enormous cloud of stifling black smoke which, after the first attack, covered the city and into which the second and third waves of attackers dropped their bombs. Adding a unique touch to the general horror, the wild animals in the zoological gardens, rendered frantic by the noise and glare, broke loose; it is said that these animals and terrified groups of refugees were machine-gunned as they tried to escape across the Grosser Garten by low-flying planes and that many bodies riddled by bullets were found later in this park.[73]

Long after the bombing crews had comfortably eaten their breakfasts and retired to rest, having carried out their orders without the loss of a single plane, Dresden remained completely hidden by a vast cloud of black smoke. Parts of the city continued to burn for days. Not one of the famous buildings in the Altstadt mentioned above escaped destruction. Fortunately some time before the raid the priceless art treasures in the Zwinger Museum, including Raphael's masterpiece of the Virgin and Child, had been removed and hidden in a place of safety.

A few weeks after the raid the Russian forces occupied the ruins of Dresden. It is possible to claim that this raid achieved the result of accelerating by a few days the progress of the Russian advance. This is satisfactory to some since, otherwise, the painful admission would be unavoidable that the raid had no influence whatever on the contemporary course of events.

The number of casualties will probably always remain a subject for speculation. Most of the victims were refugee women and children escaping from Silesia. The homes which they left behind them have since been confiscated and are now occupied by foreign squatters. The circumstances made it impossible for the authorities to undertake the task of trying to identify the victims.

Chapter 6 — The Splendid Decision

So enormous were the number of bodies that nothing could be done but to pile them on timber collected from the ruins and there to burn them. In the Altmarkt one funeral pyre after another disposed of five hundred bodies or parts of bodies at a time. This gruesome work went on for weeks. Estimates as to the total number of casualties vary between very wide limits. Some put the figure as high as a quarter of a million, and this figure was put forward as the probable total at the Manstein Trial in 1949, when the court was solemnly considering the charges of inhumanity brought against the German Field Marshal.

The Swiss paper, *Flugwehr und Technik*, writes, "In the three great attacks on Dresden the number of dead from reliable sources is reported at 100,000." Air Marshal Sir Robert Saundby in his preface to David Irving's above-mentioned book accepts the estimate of 135,000. Having regard to the fact that there were at the time over a million people crowded into the city and to the complete lack of air raid shelters, this would appear an absurdly conservative estimate. Generalmajor Hans Rumpf mentions an estimate of 250,000, but says that "we do not know and never shall know how many perished." At that time hundreds of thousands of families living in Silesia and Pomerania disappeared without trace and are no doubt dead, but it is impossible to say whether they were massacred in their homes by the advancing Red Army, were butchered on their flight by the Polish and Czech partisans operating behind the German lines, or were slaughtered in Dresden by the bombs of the R.A.F.

The late Father Ronald Knox once confessed himself somewhat disturbed by the thought that the atomic bomb dropped on Hiroshima sent thousands to their death without an opportunity to offer a prayer. To the secular mind it may seem that the best that can be said for the dropping of the first atomic bomb is that sudden death literally fell from a blue sky on the doomed city. What took place there may seem far less "disturbing" than what had taken place a few months before in Dresden, when dense crowds of homeless women and children had surged this way and that for hours in search of a place of safety in a strange city amid bursting bombs, burning phosphorus and falling buildings.

In his above cited preface to David Irving's book Air Marshal Saundby writes, "I am still not satisfied that I fully understand why it happened.... That the bombing of Dresden was a great tragedy none can deny; that it was really a military necessity few, after reading this book, will believe. It was one of those terrible things that sometimes happen in wartime, brought about by an unfortunate combination of circumstances. Those who approved it were neither wicked nor cruel, though it may well be that they were too remote from the harsh realities of war to understand fully the appalling destructive power of air bombardment in the Spring of 1945."

All very true, no doubt, except, of course, the Dresden Massacre was not one of those terrible things which are brought about by an unfortunate combination of circumstances. It was the final outcome of a policy deliberately chosen three years before when the Lindemann Plan was adopted: a great number of working-class homes were indeed destroyed in this mass air raid in accordance with the plan. The origin of the Dresden Massacre can, however, be traced back for another two decades when what was regarded as a novel conception of warfare was put forward by the chiefs of the newly established Air Force, relatively youthful men who were intoxicated by the military possibilities of the heaver-than-air flying machine, an invention dating only from the experiments of the Wright brothers at the beginning of the century. This novel conception of warfare which was, in fact held and practised by the ancient Assyrians, was well expressed by Air Marshal Sir Hugh Trenchard in 1923 when he wrote: "The Army policy is to defeat the enemy army: our policy is to defeat the enemy nation."

The Dresden Massacre was the result of the gradual conversion by the Air Force chiefs of the politicians to this primitive conception of warfare. During the period between the world wars little progress had been made, but immediately war broke out in September 1939 the Air Staff began to clamour for leave to carry their ideas of warfare into practice. When Winston Churchill became Prime Minister in May, 1940, they obtained his permission to adopt a definition of military objectives so wide as to render the term in practice meaningless: their final triumph came two years later with the adoption of the Lindermann Plan which initiated terrorism as a means to victory, terrorism, as employed by King Sennacherib.

Although one of his first acts when he took office was to give way to the frantic entreaties of the Air Staff for a free

Chapter 6 — The Splendid Decision

hand, there is some evidence that Churchill gave way with some reluctance, and thereafter was never free from twinges of conscience This is not really surprising. Churchill had started his career in the Victorian Epoch as a professional soldier, and never lost the traditional outlook of the professional soldier of his youth. He had an unrivalled knowledge of every campaign fought in the civil wars of Europe during the previous two and a half centuries, all of which had been fought in accordance with the Rules of Civilized Warfare. Regarding history from an early age as a drama in which it was his ambition to play a leading role, he was deeply concerned with what view future historians would take of him, unlike so many of his colleagues who were indifferent to the judgment of posterity so long as they successfully performed the task which at the moment they had in hand.

Strange as it may seem, Churchill appears to have been one of those of whom Air Marshal Saundby speaks who were too remote from the harsh realities of war to realise exactly what the adoption of the Lindemann Plan entailed. The Australian diplomat Lord Casey, who was sent to Washington in December, 1940, to sabotage in advance any attempt it was feared Lloyd George might make to induce President Roosevelt to support a negotiated peace, in his memoirs entitled *Personal Experiences* (Constable, London, 1962) records the following entry in his diary for the 27th June, 1943, on which day he visited Chequers where a film of the bombing campaign was shown for the entertainment of the Prime Minister and his guests: "In the course of the film showing the bombing of German towns from the air, very well and dramatically done, W. C. suddenly sat bolt upright and said to me: 'Are we beasts? Are we taking this too far?'"

Of the innumerable anecdotes told of Sir Winston Churchill, this is likely to become the most frequently quoted by his admirers. There is no reason to question its authenticity since its narrator, Lord Casey, was clearly surprised that "a very well and dramatically done" film should disturb the Prime Minister's equanimity. It is consistent also with the minute dated the 28th March 1945, which Sir Winston Churchill sent to the Chief of the Air Staff, Sir Charles Portal, six weeks after the mass raid on Dresden:

"It seems to me that the moment has come when the question of bombing of German cities *simply for the sake of increasing the terror, though under other pretexts* should he reviewed. The destruction of Dresden remains a serious query against the conduct of Allied bombing. I am of the opinion that military objectives must henceforth be more strictly studied in our own interests rather than that of the enemy. I feel the need for more precise concentration upon military objectives, such as oil and communications behind the immediate battle-zone, rather than on mere acts of terror and wanton destruction, however impressive."

Naturally, Air Marshal Portal, one of the foremost champions of the bombing policy which had been carried out for the previous three years with the Government's entire approval, expostulated at the frank wording of this minute. The Prime Minister withdrew it and substituted one tactfully worded, but nevertheless referring to "the question of *so-called* 'area bombing' of German cities."

In fact, as Sir Charles Webster and Dr. Noble Frankland say in their official history of the Air Offensive, that immediately after victory became certain, "The Prime Minister and others in authority seemed to turn away from the subject as though it were distasteful to them and as though they had forgotten their own recent efforts to initiate and maintain the offensive."

No shorthand notes are taken of the proceedings at British cabinet meetings and consequently we are dependent on the memory and the veracity of those ministers taking part who later see fit to disclose their recollection of what occurred. We do not know therefore what took place at that momentous cabinet meeting in March 1942 when it was decided to adopt the plan submitted by Professor Lindemann to win the war by terror bombing: we do not know what objections, if any, were raised to the adoption of this plan and by which ministers present. It has all along been certain that Winston Churchill, the Prime Minister, overcame his natural scruples and supported the adoption of the plan, otherwise of course it would not have been adopted.

Since the publication in 1961 of the official history of terror bombing, *The Strategic Air Offensive against Germany, 1939-45*, it has become clear that adoption was also supported by the Foreign Secretary, Sir Anthony Eden. On the 15th April, 1942, only a month after its adoption, Sir Anthony wrote to the Air Minister, Sir Archibald Sinclair, expressing the view that "the psychological effects of bombing have little connection with the military and

Chapter 6 — The Splendid Decision

economic importance of the target." He went on to suggest that the psychological effects of attacking a medium-sized town were greater than those of attacking, with equal force, a larger town, and added:

"I wish to recommend therefore that in the selection of targets in Germany, the claims of smaller towns of under 50,000 inhabitants which are not too heavily defended, should be considered, even though those towns contain only targets of secondary importance."

"There is no reason to suppose," comment the joint authors of this authoritative work, "that Sir Archibald Sinclair found these views morally repugnant." Quite the contrary in fact! They proceed to quote a letter written the following month by Sir Archibald declaring that he was "in full agreement" with the views of an unnamed M.P. who had written him emphatically supporting terror bombing and proclaiming that he was "all for the bombing of working-class areas in German cities. I am a Cromwellian—I believe in 'slaying in the name of the Lord'."[74]

One is left wondering what was the reaction of this Honourable Gentleman when on the 30th March, 1943, he heard Sir Archibald Sinclair, in reply to a question by Mr. Richard Stokes, solemnly assure the House of Commons, "The targets of Bomber Command are always military."[75] Presumably he regarded this ministerial departure from the truth as relating to mere "operational details", which according to David Irving was the attitude of the hundred thousand airmen who ever since the great raid on Mannheim on the 16th December 1940 had known that night after night aircraft had been despatched against German civilian centres.[76]

In a letter to the *Daily Telegraph* of the 1st March 1963 Dr. Noble Frankland put forward what seems to be the only plausible justification for terror bombing. He pointed out that in 1914 the submarine, and in 1939 the long-range bomber, were recently perfected but hitherto untested weapons of war. The British adopted the unrestricted use of the long range heavy bomber in the Second World War for exactly the same reasons as the Germans had adopted the unrestricted use of the submarine in the First World War, because they realised that the employment of this novel weapon would ultimately be of greater use to them than to their opponents. "Naturally," he writes, "the Germans detested the idea of 'strategic bombing' in 1942 just as the British deplored the unrestricted submarine warfare of 1917."

Probably in default of anything more convincing, a defence along these lines will finally be adopted by apologists for terror bombing. Reflection will show, however, that an important distinction can be drawn between the two cases. The Germans torpedoed merchant ships in the First World War, not for the purpose of drowning their civilian crews, but in order to enforce a blockade of the British Isles as a countermove to the blockade of Germany which the British, thanks to their command of the sea, were successfully enforcing with ultimately decisive results. The intention of terror bombing during the Second World War, on the other hand, it is now officially admitted, was to kill as many civilians as possible until the survivors had been terrorised into unconditional surrender. Everything here turns about the intention. In all such cases the true test is to decide whether the act in question was contrary to the accepted standards of conduct at the time it was committed. With regard to terror bombing it is difficult to maintain that terror bombing was in accordance with the standards accepted in 1942, otherwise obviously it would not have been necessary to carry out terror bombing behind a screen of indignant and mendacious official denials.

Exposure of the truth, firstly by Sir Charles Snow in March 1961 and then in a voluminous official record published in September of the same year, naturally caused a sensation throughout the civilized world and particularly in Great Britain. The subject of the terror bombing of Germany which came to an end in May 1945 had been driven from the minds of the British Public by the dropping of the first atomic bomb on the Japanese on the 5th August, 1945. At first the news of the devastation of Hiroshima was received with gloating satisfaction as a fitting retribution upon the presumptuous Yellow people who had challenged White Supremacy in the Far East. But after the secrets of nuclear fission had been betrayed to Stalin by the Communist espionage network in the United States, the spy ring led by Julius and Ethel Rosenberg taking the leading part, misgivings concerning the use of the atomic bomb to terrorise the Japanese into surrender became widespread. No one could doubt that Stalin would without hesitation drop an atomic bomb on Great Britain if it happened to suit his plans. The public conscience

Chapter 6 — The Splendid Decision

became deeply stirred: the use of atomic weapons was declared to be morally wrong, even for so worthy a cause as the defence of Colonialism in Asia. Overshadowed by the horrible possibility that London might one day suffer the fate of Hiroshima, the terror bombing of Germany a few years before quickly came to be regarded as an episode of the remote past. The great four-engine bombers with their loads of high explosives which had devastated Dresden in 1945 began to seem as obsolete and out-of-date as the mighty galleons which Philip II had despatched against England in 1588.

Disclosure of the truth concerning this episode of recent history had been delayed for nearly two decades during which public opinion had undergone a complete change. In 1942 when the Lindemann Plan was adopted by the British Government, terror bombing was unquestionably contrary to the accepted standards of the time. Enlightened opinion would have dismissed it as unthinkable. After twenty years, however, enlightened opinion had grown accustomed to the idea. By 1962 terrorism as an instrument of policy had gradually become accepted by public opinion as a natural method by which one state could impose its will upon a rival state. A long-range bomber could indeed be used for terrorism as Professor Lindemann had pointed out, but it could also be used as a weapon for use against the armed forces of the enemy strictly in accordance with the Rules of Civilized Warfare. An atomic bomb, on the other hand, was simply an instrument of terror: it would be useless on a battlefield against the armed forces of the enemy: it was designed solely to blot out the enemy civilian population. Everyone in 1962 knew that the United States and Russia were collecting huge stock piles of atomic bombs, and no one could be in any doubt that in the event of war they would adopt terrorism as a means to victory. Public opinion everywhere had become resigned to this assumption. In 1962 it was assumed by everyone that if President Kennedy persisted in his declared intention of stopping by armed force Khrushchev's convoy transporting atomic missiles and reinforcements to the rocket bases which he had secretly established in Cuba, the inevitable result would be an exchange of salvoes of rockets with atomic warheads across the Atlantic.

Owing to this change of outlook, in the violent and protracted controversies which raged in the British Press following the disclosure of the truth concerning the terror bombing of Germany during the Second World War twenty years before, hardly any reference was made to the ethical aspects of the subject. The leading Socialist politician and Labour M.P. Richard Crossman who in 1964 became Minister for Housing in Harold Wilson's Labour Cabinet, indeed spoke severely of the screen of lies behind which the terror bombing campaign was carried out. "One of the most unhealthy features of the bomber offensive," he wrote, "was that the War Cabinet — and in particular the Secretary for Air Sir Archibald Sinclair (now Lord Thurso) — felt it necessary to repudiate publicly the orders which they themselves had given to Bomber Command."[77]

Some may think that a lack of a sense of proportion on the part of the future Labour Minister for Housing is shown in this observation. No doubt mendacity was an unhealthy feature of the so-called "strategic air offensive against Germany" and as such deserving of censure, but surely to a less extent than the ruthless savagery, unnecessarily protracted to the end of the war, which resulted in the death of 600,000 innocent people, an aspect of the matter which seems to have escaped Mr. Crossman's attention.

Although this is an age in which so many loudly profess deep concern over such moral questions as social justice and racial discrimination, the majority remain content to judge every action by applying the simple test, whether or no it has achieved its purpose.

The essential nature of the terror bombing campaign escaped the attention of the British public because the moral aspect was obscured by the outburst of dismay aroused by the considered opinion expressed by the joint authors of the official history of the campaign, Messrs. Charles Webster and Noble Frankland, that the campaign must be regarded as a failure since it did not justify its nature by bringing the war to an early end; it neither succeeded in paralysing German war production nor in breaking the morale of the German people.

Many bitterly resented the official publication of facts and figures indicating that more useful results could have been achieved if the enormous concentration of industrial output and the sacrifice of highly-trained personnel had been expended, not on terror bombing but on attacking such military objectives as the U-Boat bases from which the submarines of Admiral Donitz were

Chapter 6 — The Splendid Decision

causing devastating losses to Allied shipping. "We were in danger of losing the war," wrote Admiral Sir William James, "for lack of planes to fight the submarines in the Atlantic. These planes were made available only just in time."

In the opinion of Albert Speer, the brilliant German Minister of War Production, the terror bombing of the British caused less dislocation of German industry than the "precision bombing" of the Americans which was directed against specific targets. The astonishing fact was only disclosed long after the end of the war that throughout the bombing offensive the production of German armaments continued to increase steadily until the last year of the war; thus, after the frightful air raid on Hamburg in July 1943 which caused the death of over 50,000 of its inhabitants, war production was cut to half for only a month and was soon restored to its former level.

This issue is important because only if it succeeded in shortening the war could some sort of justification for the policy of terror bombing be found. In the opinion of the authors of the official record of the terror bombing campaign it failed to achieve this purpose.

Perhaps the most hotly disputed issue of the controversy aroused by the publication of the official history of the terror bombing campaign was whether Air Marshal Sir Arthur Harris, Commander-in-Chief of Bomber Command, was unjustly treated by the British Government after victory had been achieved. At the end of the war Winston Churchill made no attempt to disguise the distaste which he had come to feel for the subject of terror bombing of which the Air Marshal had been a fanatical advocate; his successor, Clement Attlee, who had been a member of the War Cabinet at the time of the adoption of the Lindemann Plan, naturally felt the same distaste for the subject as Winston Churchill. As a consequence, a peerage was not conferred on Air Marshal Harris in 1945 as one of the successful war leaders; he was not even awarded a special medal for his services; he was even prohibited from using official records when writing his account of the campaign. Conscious of official disapproval, unobtrusively within a year of the end of the war he left England to take up a commercial appointment in South Africa.

On the one hand it seems clearly unjust to hold Air Marshal Harris responsible for terror bombing. Certainly he

Advance to Barbarism

strongly advocated it, like most of the other leaders of the R.A.F., but he carried it out in accordance with the orders of the executive government. In 1960, Mr. Clement Attlee, when challenged on the subject, observed that in his opinion a more effective use could have been made of his bombs by Air Marshal Harris if he had directed them against military targets instead of devastating German cities. This observation stung the Air Marshal into pointing out acidly that "the decision to bomb industrial cities for morale effect was made, and in force, before I became C.-in-C., Bomber Command."

That this is true there can be no question. On the other hand, after he obtained command Air Marshal Harris conducted the campaign with ruthless zeal, and strongly opposed any relaxation of the attack. By sheer force of character he dominated the politicians, so that, as one critic puts it, the official history of British bombing during the Second World War is less the story of Bomber Command than the story of Harris' campaign against the German civilian population. Yet, as the authors of the official history observe, in terms of his own strategy, Harris is proved wrong on almost every major decision.

A comparison between Air Marshal Sir Arthur Harris and Field Marshal Sir Douglas Haig is irresistibly suggested. Both were men of the strongest character; neither enjoyed the confidence of the politicians from whom they received their orders. Both advocated policies which they guaranteed would bring swift and complete victory. Haig was certain in 1916 that his great offensive on the Somme would break through the German front and drive the enemy in rout back to their own frontier: Harris in 1942 was equally confident that if he were given a free hand and a sufficient number of long-range bombers he could break the morale of the German people and bring the war to a victorious conclusion in a few months.

Neither man was able to fulfil his assurances and when they failed, neither of them had any new suggestions to make but merely asked permission to try again and the politicians were afraid to dismiss them. Haig repeated his performance on the Somme by a similar attempt in 1917 to break through at Passchendaele and with the same result. Harris was allowed to continue his destruction of German working-class dwellings until the very end of the war. Both were prodigal of the lives of their men.

Chapter 6 — The Splendid Decision

Perhaps no revelation of Messrs. Charles Webster and Noble Frankland more shocked the British public than the disclosure that the Terror Bombing Offensive cost the air crews of the R.A.F. no less than 58,888 lives, nearly the same number of casualties as those suffered by British junior army officers during the First World War. Attention has often been drawn to the fact that the pick of an entire generation perished in the trenches in France as junior officers under the command of Sir Douglas Haig; we now know that approximately the same number perished over Germany during the Second World War, an even more calamitous loss since the standard of health and intelligence required for the men of Bomber Command was far higher than that of the junior officers who served in the trenches in France twenty years before.

The question whether the tremendous concentration of men and material for the purpose of bombing the German civilian population during the Second World War could otherwise have been more effectively employed will probably always remain a matter for speculation. We now know exactly what this great air offensive achieved in the form of destruction of human life and property and the price which had to be paid for this achievement, but we can only speculate as to what would have been achieved if this great effort had been directed against military objectives in accordance with the rules of civilized warfare, or if it had been employed to carry out a campaign of "precision bombing" of selected targets on the lines successfully adopted by the American Air Force.

Naturally the conclusion of Messrs. Charles Webster and Noble Frankland that nearly sixty thousand young and valuable lives were sacrificed to carry out a policy which failed in its declared purpose, namely to bring about a collapse of the morale of the German people, seems intollerable to many.

Yet the most that can be claimed for the Lindemann Plan is that it contributed to some indefinable extent to the final outcome of the war although it was certainly not the decisive factor or perhaps even a decisive factor. Terror bombing however was a logical and perhaps inevitable extension of the "Splendid Decision" by the British Government in May 1940 to repudiate the rules of civilized warfare and to adopt the policy advocated by Air Marshal Trenchard in 1923 when he declared that the purpose of war was not merely to defeat the armed forces of the enemy but to defeat the enemy nation. Terror bombing was a logical application of this view of warfare which is in complete conformity with the maxim of Clausewitz, "War is an act of violence pushed to its utmost limit."

The "Splendid Decision", carried out to its utmost limit in the form of terror bombing, failed to defeat the enemy nation by bringing about a collapse of its will power to resist. It had nevertheless decisive consequences not only on the course of the Second World War but on subsequent world history. Its immediate effect was to keep alive the conflict which had started in 1939 as a European civil war of the usual type and to prevent it from petering out in stagnation and general boredom, so that Roosevelt was given time to involve the United States and transform it into a global conflict.[78]

This momentous result has been closely studied by many historians from various conflicting points of view. It is a strange fact however that no one has yet drawn attention to the decisive influence, if only a negative influence, which the "Splendid Decision", within a week of its being taken, had on the course of the Second World War.

Although hundreds of books have been written concerning that great conflict yet not one of them has drawn attention to the 14th May 1940, as a date on which Hitler's triumphal progress which, thanks to the outcome of events on that day he was able to continue for the following two years, came so near to being brought to an abrupt and final halt. The facts are not in dispute, and it is submitted, only one conclusion can be drawn from them.

The following dates should be carefully noted. On the 10th May 1940, the Germans launched a great offensive along the whole front in the West from the North Sea to Switzerland. On the 13th May, troops belonging to the army group commanded by General von Kleist, having occupied Sedan on the right bank of the Meuse the previous day, crossed the river in pneumatic boats, stormed the French pill-boxes on the left bank, and by the evening had established a bridgehead south of Sedan, about four miles deep and about four miles wide.

During the night of the 13th the work of repairing the bridge at Gaulier, a mile west of Sedan, and building pontoon bridges, was pushed forward in desperate haste in order to reinforce with tanks and artillery the infantry precariously holding the bridgehead.

Chapter 6 — The Splendid Decision

Obviously it was a vital matter for the Allies to prevent this being carried out: a critical situation for both sides had arisen.

While this great conflict was raging along the Meuse, another conflict of a different kind was raging between the French and British High Commands. The breakthrough south of Sedan had been so swift and so unexpected that no concentration of heavy artillery was at hand to cut off the bridgehead with a barrage of shell fire. Regarding the primary purpose of the heavy bomber to be that of long-range artillery, the French clamoured for an immediate concentration of bombers for a mass attack on the crossings of the Meuse. They found however the chiefs of the R.A.F. were reluctant to cancel the plans which they had made for large scale air attacks on German industrial centres in accordance with Air Marshal Trenchard's conception of the role of the heavy bomber in warfare.

The situation which existed on the 14th May is best described by Dennis Richards in his previously cited book, *The Fight at Odds*. He sets out the facts and the points of view of the disputants fairly and lucidly although, writing thirteen years after the event, he remained completely oblivious to the fact that the outcome proved that the French High Command was completely right in their contentions and chiefs of the R.A.F. were completely wrong. Having outlined the decisive results which the British air chiefs expected to follow from air attacks on the main centres of German industry, he complains bitterly, "The French however remained obstinately unconvinced. Whatever might be the merits of bombing German industry, they entirely doubted whether the correct time to begin was the opening of a great land battle. And as for the idea that an air attack on the Ruhr would impose any immediate or material delay on the advancing enemy (which after all was the main point) seemed to them fantastic."

"Our air leaders," Mr. Richards comments, "could hardly take these views at their face value, for they were painfully aware that the views of the French were coloured by an apprehension which was sometimes expressed and sometimes concealed, but never absent. Not to put too fine a point on it, our Allies were desperately afraid of the Luftwaffe." (Page 111).

If Dennis Richards is justified in ascribing to the R.A.F. chiefs this ungenerous attitude to their French allies, it is hardly surprising that they acceded to the French appeal for help reluctantly and, as he later disclosed in his book, to a very restricted extent.

Reverting to the progress of the great battle raging south of Sedan, during the night of May 13th, the German pioneers working with frantic haste, finished repairing the Gaulier Bridge over the Meuse, and on the 14th the heavy tanks of the 1st Panzer Division under General Guderian crossed the river and then with incredible and, some would say, reckless daring, swung westward in that headlong drive which was to take them to the English Channel, leaving their exposed left flank to be protected by a screen of infantry. Facing this screen was the French 3rd Armoured Division of heavy tanks, hitherto unengaged, ready poised for a counter stroke which would have cut the supplies crossing the river for Guderian's tanks. Obviously until the bridgehead had been consolidated, the German tank spearhead would be in acute danger. It was imperative for the Allies that Guderian's communications should be cut by the destruction of the bridge over the Meuse.

"Upon the destruction of Gaulier Bridge depends victory or defeat," declared General Billotte in a frantic message to General d'Astiere de la Vigerie imploring that every available bomber should be assigned this vital task. Throughout the 14th May desperate efforts were indeed made to destroy the bridge by bombing. Protected by French fighters, 170 French and British bombers, of which about 100 were Blenheims, swept in waves over the Meuse Valley at Sedan and plastered the area of the bridge with bombs in order to cut the panzers' vital artery.[79]

The attack failed. The German anti-aircraft fire proved to be unexpectedly accurate; 85 bombers were shot down of which 35 were British. "The British and French airmen attacked heroically," writes General Guderian, "but did not succeed in hitting the bridge. Flak had its day of glory."

Great credit is no doubt due to the German anti-aircraft gunners, but obviously the Germans were amazingly lucky on this occasion. With so many bombers unloading their bombs in the neighbourhood of the bridge, it is astonishing that no direct hit was made. And obviously every additional bomber which had joined in the attack would have made the chances of scoring a hit more likely. We now know that 96 heavy bombers were at this vital moment available to join in the attack. While this supreme

Chapter 6 — The Splendid Decision

effort was being made to cut the communications of the German tank spearhead advancing towards the English Channel, these 96 heavy bombers were waiting passively on nearby airfields in preparation for a mass attack on the factories and oil plants in the Ruhr which had been planned to take place on the evening of the following day.

This mass attack, the greatest air raid which had ever taken place down to that time, duly took place. Concerning it, Dennis Richards writes:

"After the intensity of the struggle to persuade the British War Cabinet, the Army and the French that heavy bombers would be best employed against the Ruhr, the result of the operations came as something of an anti-climax. On the night the 15th/16th May, 96 heavy bombers took off for objectives east of the Rhine: 78 were directed against oil plants. Only 24 of the crews ever claimed to have found them."

With regard to the results in practice of the application of Air Marshal Trenchard's views of the role of the heavy bomber in warfare, Dennis Richards concludes as follows:

"In sum, the heavy bombers achieved none of their objects. Industrial damage was negligible; whatever delay was inflicted on the German Army was insignificant; not a single German fighter or anti-aircraft gun was withdrawn from the Western front to protect the Reich; and not a single German bomber was diverted from attacking the French armies and their communications to reply to the provocation from England. The assault on the Ruhr, most cherished of all Air Staff projects, was a failure." (Page 124).

No doubt the great air offensive against industrial objectives in Germany which the R.A.F. chiefs insisted on launching at the most vital moment of the Battle of France, was a failure in the sense that it failed to achieve the results which according to Air Marshal Trenchard's theories concerning air warfare it should have had. Nevertheless it had decisive results in a negative sense on the course of the campaign in France and on the whole course of the war for the next two years. A heavy price had indeed to be paid for the granting by Mr. Churchill to the R.A.F. of that "freedom to roam" of which Mr. Spaight speaks with such pride. One extra load of bombs on the crossing over the Meuse by Sedan — let alone ninety-six loads — might have made all the difference between victory and defeat as General Billotte pointed out at the time.

Advance to Barbarism

Had the supplies of Guderian's Panzers been cut off, he would soon have been brought to a halt from lack of petrol and then forced to surrender when his ammunition was exhausted. The great German offensive in the West upon which Hitler had staked the survival of his regime would have ended with a humiliating disaster. Hitler's prestige, the product of an unbroken succession of diplomatic successes, would have been ruined. The German General Staff which had undertaken this offensive with many dire forebodings would have compelled his retirement: the National Socialist movement would have collapsed. Britain and France would then have been in a position to dictate terms of peace. No doubt these terms would have been a repetition of the terms of the Treaty of Versailles, but at least the war would have ended in a peace settlement in which some regard would have been paid to the lofty principles of justice and humanity which the victors professed.

In short the clock would have been put back two decades if the first military campaign launched by Hitler had ended in early and complete disaster. Europeans would have been able to make a fresh start as from 1919 without interference by non-European Powers. Neither the Soviet Union, the United States nor the Japanese Empire would have been involved in what would have remained a European civil war. The discovery of the atomic bomb might have been postponed indefinitely or at least delayed until the outbreak of another war since it is unlikely that any country in peace time would have undertaken the enormously expensive tests necessary to establish that it was a practicable possibility, as distinct from a theoretical possibility, to bring about a nuclear explosion. There would have been no terror bombing, no extermination campaign against the Jews, no mass-deportations, no mock-trials of prisoners of war by their captors. Last but not least the British Empire, instead of collapsing from exhaustion, might have gradually evolved into a federation of self-governing states, admission to which would have been dependent on the attainment of a certain level of civilization.

The Battle of France must rank as one of the decisive battles of history because it so transformed the character of the conflict which had broken out in 1939 that it led to an outcome five years later which was equally disastrous to the victors as to the vanquished.

Chapter 6 — The Splendid Decision

The Battle of France indeed ended in a complete German victory. Hitler took enormous risks—some would say insane risks—and his gamble succeeded. But a slight change in the fortunes of war—in particular, by a lucky bomb hit on the Gaulier Bridge—and the result might so easily have been a complete German disaster. If the Allied bombers had concentrated on the enemy armed forces, their proper function according to orthodox military opinion, the outcome might have been very different.

Only gradually, it seems, did Mr. Churchill become converted to the Trenchard conception of warfare. After the failure of the great mass attack by Bomber Command on the Ruhr on the night of May 15th, he at first accepted the French view that bombing should be concentrated against the crossings of the Meuse. "From then onwards however," writes Dennis Richards, "the efforts of the heavy bombers were either divided, or else pursued in uneasy alternation, between the objectives east of the Rhine favoured by the Air Staff and the objectives nearer the battlefield proposed by the French."

A month later however Mr. Churchill had gradually reverted to the Trenchard conception of warfare. On the 12th June he visited French Headquarters at the Chateau du Muguet. At that time the military situation had become most grave but not desperate. German tank spearheads were advancing on each side of Paris; on the right General Rommel had trapped the remnants of the B.E.F. under General Fortune at St. Valery on the Normandy coast; and on the left General Guderian was striking south-westwards towards Chalons-sur-Marne with the intention of isolating the Maginot Line. Nevertheless we hear that Churchill was furious at the refusal of the French to allow the R.A.F. to use their airfields in the south of France for an attack on Genoa as a reprisal for Italy's entry into the war.

Admittedly Italy deserved retribution in 1940 for stabbing France in the back in her hour of desperate need —-as much as Italy had deserved retribution in 1915 for stabbing in the back her ally, Austria—but the doubt may well be felt whether it was a moment to indulge in killing Italian civilians when every bomber was needed to hold up the advance of the German armies in France.

Probably future historians will agree with the learned authors of the official history of the British strategic air offensive that the Second World War was not won by British terror bombing.

Advance to Barbarism

On the other hand, terror bombing, officially adopted in March 1942, was only the logical outcome of Churchill's "Splendid Decision" of May 1940. Future historians may well reach the conclusion that although the "Splendid Decision" did not bring victory, it protracted the struggle for five years and transformed it from an orderly European civil war into a global conflict conducted by both sides with unrestricted barbarity and ending, as Churchill himself described it, in tragedy.

As long ago as 1948 General J.F.C. Fuller summarised this view of the subject in his authoritative study *The Second World War* (Eyre and Spottiswoode, London, 1948) in which on page 89 he commented on Air Chief Marshal Dowding's assertion that the lesson to be drawn from the victorious outcome of the Battle of Britain was that in long-range aerial warfare "the defence has a basic advantage which increases with the distance between the attackers and the target." General Fuller wrote:

"This lesson was lost on the British Air Force which continued to hold that 'strategic bombing' was the be all and end all of air power. This fallacy not only prolonged the war, but went far to render the 'peace' which followed it unprofitable to Britain and disastrous to the world in general."

Chapter 7 — The Nuremberg Trials

Regarded as an isolated phenomenon the initiation in 1945 of the practice of disposing of prisoners of war by charging them with "war-crimes" and then finding them guilty at trials in which their accusers acted as judges of their own charges, was one of the most astonishing developments in the history of mankind.

Regarded, however, merely as the last link in a chain of developments all entirely consistent with each other and all displaying the same general trend, the initiation of trials for "war-crimes" seems the natural and inevitable outcome of a war in which one side had officially adopted a policy of systematically slaughtering a hostile racial minority without regard to age or sex and the other side had officially adopted a policy of slaughtering the enemy civilian population by dropping bombs on the most densely populated residential areas in order to terrorise the survivors into unconditional surrender. A struggle conducted in such a spirit could have no other sequel.

Enough has already been said in these pages concerning terror bombing. In essence it also was merely a reversion to ancient practice. In savage warfare no tactics are more frequently adopted than sending out raiding parties to attack the women and children of the enemy in order to engender a disposition to surrender.

It would indeed be a subject for surprise if a war conducted in accordance with the most ancient traditions had ended without a reversion to primitive practice in regard to the disposal of captured enemy leaders. To the savage mind the natural and proper way to deal with a captured enemy in one's power is to kill him.

If the "advance to barbarism" examined in these pages proves to be only a temporary fluctuation in the course of human progress followed by a return to civilized standards, no doubt historians will express surprise and indignation at the depths to which mankind sank during the fifth decade of the 20th century.

It was, however, a case of chain reaction; each lapse from accepted standards of conduct led inevitably to the next. Finally a stage was reached when moral indignation became irrelevant because all moral standards had disappeared. The penalty of defeat had become so frightful that the leaders on both sides considered that any act was justifiable that might in any way, directly or indirectly, help to avoid defeat. Viewed in this way, even the plans associated on the one side with Eichmann and on the other side with Lindemann can be said to be justified on the ground that they were bona fide designed to aid the war effort.

On reflection it will become obvious that a struggle waged in this spirit could end in no other way, whichever side won, but with a massacre of the leaders of the defeated side. What is far from obvious, however, is the reason why it was decided that this inevitable massacre should be preceded by the performance of trials for alleged war-crimes. At first sight it is hard to see what purpose this entirely novel deviation from primitive practice was intended to serve. The obvious course for the victors was to publish a list of their leading opponents and to announce that everyone whose name was on this list was *hors la loi* and as such liable on capture to immediate execution on proof merely of identity. It would then have been easy later to have excused such summary treatment by saying it was a natural if perhaps excessive expression of emotions inflamed by a protracted and sanguinary conflict.

Among the simple-minded the explanation has won wide acceptance that Roosevelt, Stalin and Churchill did not adopt this summary procedure because they were so overcome by sincere moral indignation at the shortcomings of their captive opponents that they determined that the full facts should be disclosed at a trial as a warning to posterity. Cynics, on the other hand, have suggested that the real purpose of the trial was to divert attention from the conduct of the victors by a public investigation of the conduct of the vanquished.

Neither explanation, however, offers an answer to the question why, when it was decided to put the leaders of the vanquished side on trial, the obvious course was not adopted of establishing an impartial court to try them, whose verdict would carry weight with posterity. It would have been an easy matter to have created an impartial court consisting of leading jurists, men

Chapter 7 — The Nuremberg Trials

of integrity and repute, known to be without personal political bias, from the countries which had been neutral during the war, such as Switzerland, Sweden, Spain, Turkey and the Argentine. Such a court would probably have convicted most of the accused on one charge or another, and its findings of fact would have been readily accepted by future historians.

The only possible objection to having the charges against the accused decided by a court composed of neutral jurists was that such a court could not have been relied on to bring in exactly the verdict the victors required and could not have been precluded from investigating the surrounding circumstances of the offences alleged which would obviously entail an investigation of the conduct of the victors. Having decided that before execution the prisoners should be subjected to "a form of trial" (to quote the Soviet judge, General Nikitchenko), the victors realised that the only way out of their difficulties was to create a special court composed of their own nationals to try "the major war criminals of the European Axis countries". It was agreed that minor war criminals should be tried and disposed of in whatever manner might be decided by their captors in the country in which they were held as prisoners of war.

This novel deviation from primitive practice certainly achieved its purpose to the extent of providing for the disposal of captured enemies with a minimum of friction between the victorious Powers. "The major war criminals" (so described months before any specific charge was made against them) were duly liquidated after a trial at Nuremberg lasting a year; the fate of all the other captives numbering many hundreds of thousands, depended entirely on chance, speaking, generally, those who found themselves on the western front at the time of Germany's unconditional surrender, had reason to consider themselves relatively fortunate as compared with those who found themselves on the eastern front. No prisoner charged with a war-crime by the Czechs, Poles, Serbs or Greeks ever survived to describe the trial to which he was subjected and consequently posterity has been spared numberless gruesome stories.

The subject of war-crimes can be dealt with from a number of distinct aspects. To historians war-crimes trials are of particular interest as an aftermath of a great war without a parallel in civilized times. To sociologists they are also of special interest as a unique

Advance to Barbarism

variation in the development of human relations. To students of the science of war propaganda they are a novel and daring experiment designed to befuddle public opinion. To politicians they are of deep personal concern since, however insignificant and inoffensive a state may be, there is always a possibility that it may be drawn against its will into a war between its neighbours when, if it finds itself on the losing side, its rulers become, *ipso facto*, war-criminals in accordance with the law laid down in effect at Nuremberg that being on the losing side is the supreme international crime. Finally, to jurists war-crimes trials offer a wide variety of legal problems never before raised, such as, for example, whether an accuser ought to be debarred as such from acting as the judge of his own charges; whether it is just that a person should be convicted of an act which was not declared to be a crime until after its alleged commission, and whether the rules of evidence for so long regarded by all lawyers as indispensable for ascertaining the truth can, on occasion, be entirely disregarded without injustice resulting.

In this book we are dealing with that abrupt reversion of the course of human progress which began in 1914 and which the present author writing in 1946 labelled "the advance to barbarism". From this point of view the introduction of war-crimes trials in 1945 was only the last phase of this reversion, a phase which followed naturally from the phase of wholesale terror-bombing and genocide which preceded it. It would be out of place to attempt to describe here the course of the Nuremberg Trials or of the other war-crimes trials which followed them. Voluminous details of these proceedings can be found in the official records and several books have already been written devoted to one or other of these so-called trials.[80]

Less horrible indeed, but owing to the smug self-satisfaction of those who conducted them, war-crimes trials described in detail make almost as repulsive reading as accounts of the doings in such concentration camps as Auschwitz or descriptions of one of the terror raids carried out in accordance with the Lindemann Plan. War-crimes trials, genocide and terror-bombing were alike symptoms of the same world-wide reversion.

Indisputably a war conducted in the spirit in which the Second World War was waged was bound to end in the putting to death of the leaders of the vanquished in the event of either

Chapter 7 — The Nuremberg Trials

side succeeding in forcing the other to surrender unconditionally. This putting to death might well have been a swift, crude and informal process. The method actually adopted was the result of the combined effect of a number of quite fortuitous circumstances. For reasons of political expediency no spectacular mass war-crimes trial of the Italian leaders was ever staged, and if Stalin immediately after the Yalta Conference had dropped the pretence of being a loyal ally and disclosed his real ambition to subjugate the whole of Europe, it is most unlikely there would ever have been a mass trial of the surviving German political and military leaders. At most, prosecutions would probably have taken place of prisoners notoriously responsible for specific crimes against humanity. Guilt in such cases would have been proved in accordance with the accepted rules of evidence. There would have been no occasion to invent new crimes in order to provide an excuse to punish them retrospectively. And, of course, it would have occurred to no one to bring obviously fictitious charges such as those brought at Nuremberg against the German naval leaders, Grossadmiral Raeder and his successor, Gross-admiral Dönitz.

Apart from the attempt made by the present writer in the little booklet entitled *Advance to Barbarism* published in 1948, no attempt has ever been made to explain why such elaborate and cumbrous means were adopted in 1945 to dispose of captured enemy leaders. Investigation will show that war-trials were initiated as a compromise between two entirely irreconcilable points of view.

When, at last, the end of the war came in sight, there was naturally worldwide speculations as to the conditions of the coming peace. In 1918, the question had been merely how exactly certain well-defined principles should be carried into effect: a quarter of a century later, all principles had been specifically repudiated, so that the public imagination had an absolute free rein. It was generally agreed that a demand for reparations based on the legal maxim "costs follow the event" would be out of place at the end of an orgy of violence, and that the victors should act on the assumption that victory had automatically vested all enemy property in them. There was also general agreement that Adolf Hitler and the members of his Government should be punished by death, although the expectation was that, when further resistance became impossible, they would follow the advice of Brutus:

"Our enemies have beat us to the pit:
It is more worthy to leap in ourselves
Than tarry till they push us."

In primary warfare between civilized states and barbarian invaders, this course has usually been adopted. Thus, in the thirteenth century when China was being overrun by the Mongol hordes of Genghis Khan and his successors, the Chinese leaders invariably killed themselves and their families rather than fall into the hands of the savages. The Chinese persisted in this practice long after the unrestrained ferocity of Mongol methods of warfare had become considerably tempered by contact with civilized nations. It is recorded that Kublai Khan, the grandson of Ghengis Khan, resenting his troops being still regarded as savages, ordered his generals, when a city was captured and the Chinese leaders were found to have committed suicide, personally to visit the bodies in order to demonstrate by a public act of respect that the Mongols had become a civilized people.

The question of the treatment to be accorded to prominent Germans after the downfall of the Third Reich, seems first to have been mentioned publicly at the Teheran Conference in November 1943. Elliott Roosevelt, the son of the American President, was present at a banquet given by Stalin at the conclusion of the Conference and, three years later, published a very frank account of what passed in his presence between his father, President Roosevelt, Mr. Stalin and Mr. Winston Churchill.[81]

According to Elliott Roosevelt, this topic was first broached to everyone's surprise by Stalin at the end of a magnificent banquet at which, Elliott tells us, Stalin had partaken of vodka, "100% proof", while Mr. Churchill "had stuck to his favourite brandy". Rising to propose "the umpteenth toast" Stalin said, "I propose a salute to the swiftest possible justice for all of Germany's war criminals — justice before a firing squad. I drink to our unity in dispatching them as fast as we capture them, all of them, and there must be at least 50,000 of them."

These words appear to have roused something in Mr. Churchill — perhaps a remembrance that he was a European and the only prominent European present. "The British people," he declared roundly, "will never stand for such mass murder! I feel most strongly that no one, Nazi or no, shall be summarily dealt with before a firing squad, without a proper legal trial!"

Chapter 7 — The Nuremberg Trials

Thus began the first exchange of views on the then startling and seemingly original suggestion that, after a victory, there ought to be a grand massacre of the vanquished. It must be stressed that Elliott Roosevelt does not suggest or hint that one of Mr. Churchill's eyelids flickered humorously when he used the word "trial". On the contrary, he says that Stalin's proposal caused Mr. Churchill to lose his temper hopelessly. The warmth of the British Prime Minister's feelings, he says, amused Stalin, who seemed "hugely tickled", and surprised everyone present including Anthony Eden.[82] In fact, so exaggerated did his reaction seem over a suggested mass murder of 50,000 persons, that Elliott is reduced to hinting in his book at an extraneous cause for Mr. Churchill's "mounting fury". Far from suggesting Mr. Churchill's indignation was simulated, the whole incident is narrated expressly to contrast the antiquated, pedantic, unreasoning prejudices of the British Prime Minister with the broadminded, man-of-the-world outlook of his father, the President, the crude simplicity of Stalin, and his own consummate tact in an awkward moment.

According to his son, the American President had hidden a smile when this proposal to mass-murder 50,000 Europeans was made. "Perhaps," he remarked genially, "we could say that instead of summarily executing 50,000 we should settle on a smaller number. Shall we say 49,500?"

Elliott Roosevelt hoped that, with this delightfully humorous observation, the subject of mass murder would be allowed to drop, but Stalin stuck to his point and appealed to Elliott for his own views, thus presenting him with a golden opportunity to display his diplomatic tact.

"Isn't the whole thing pretty academic?" Elliott tells us that he replied. "Russian, American and British soldiers will settle the issue for most of those 50,000 in battle, and I hope that not only those 50,000 war criminals will be taken care of, but many hundreds of thousands more Nazis as well."

Elliott's answer pleased Stalin: "Stalin was beaming with pleasure. Around the table he came, flung an arm around my shoulders. An excellent answer! A toast to my health! I flushed with pleasure." It failed, however, to please Churchill. "He was furious, and no fooling."

There is, of course, no obligation to accept Elliott's story as an accurate objective account of what took place that evening at Teheran, since it is obviously written to glorify President Roosevelt's statecraft, urbanity, and tact at the expense of Mr. Churchill, whom Elliott evidently disliked heartily. Still, in its main outlines, no doubt, Elliott's story should be accepted as approximately accurate.

The contrast which he draws between the European attitude and the American attitude rings true. Mr. Churchill's alleged behaviour would have been quite natural in the circumstances in which he found himself — as a European, he was in a false position, knew it, and the knowledge frayed his nerves. Intending to caricature Mr. Churchill, Elliott Roosevelt has drawn a picture of him which will be much more acceptable to Mr. Churchill's admirers in the future than the picture which Elliott at the same time drew of his own father will be to the latter's admirers, or to the latter's European admirers at least.

What Elliott Roosevelt says took place at Teheran is entirely consistent with what we all know took place later. At Nuremberg, the proceedings were outwardly European, but throughout the driving force behind them was Russia. At Teheran, Stalin proposed a mass murder of 50,000 persons — a round figure. President Roosevelt suggested that Mr. Churchill's objection might be overcome by reducing the mass murder by five hundred — another round figure. Elliott Roosevelt, thereupon, expressed the hope that the number of victims would, in fact, be increased to hundreds of thousands — that is to say, substituting an indefinite figure for a round figure. Finally, the subject was dropped as "academic". So long as a sufficient number of victims died, preliminary procedure was not worth quarrelling about. The result was a compromise by which all three parties carried their points. Ultimately, the American solution was carried out; Mr. Stalin had his mass murder and Mr. Churchill his trial.[83]

When the first edition of this book was published in July, 1948, no other record of this memorable episode of the Teheran Conference existed than that of Elliott Roosevelt. In the British Press at the time his version was by common consent dismissed as inherently improbable. In 1948, the illusion was still rigidly maintained in Great Britain that Stalin was inspired by the same lofty principles by which Mr. Roosevelt and Mr. Churchill were supposed to be inspired. It was therefore held to be unpatriotic even to mention that Elliott Roosevelt had attributed so outrageous

Chapter 7 — The Nuremberg Trials

a proposal to a hero who was considered to have atoned for a murky past by his noble conduct during the war. Although Stalin had of late been acting strangely, as one of the leading figures in the great and glorious anti-Nazi crusade, he was still entitled to claim that his loyal allies should disbelieve any facts to his discredit.

Six years after the publication of Elliott Roosevelt's version, however, an alternative account of this episode has become available from the pen of Mr. Winston Churchill himself, in the installment of his war memoirs entitled *Closing the Ring* (1952). True, Mr. Churchill complains that Elliott's version is "highly coloured and extremely misleading", but, in fact, his own version confirms Elliott's account of the essential point of the story. At this banquet at Teheran, Mr. Churchill says that Stalin pointed out that Germany's strength depended upon 50,000 officers and technicians and, if these were rounded up and shot, "German military strength would be extirpated." In spite of Mr. Churchill's indignant protest, however, these 50,000 must be shot, Stalin insisted.

The two versions therefore agree that a massacre of 50,000 persons when victory was achieved was proposed by Stalin at the Teheran Conference but, whereas Elliott says these 50,000 were to be "war criminals", Churchill says they were to be the officers and technicians upon whom Germany's strength depended.

On the latter detail—a significant detail certainly—Mr. Churchill's version is greatly to be preferred. What Stalin clearly had in mind was a massacre similar to the Katyn Forest Massacre which the Soviet authorities had carried out only three and a half years before. Except that it would have been on a far greater scale, what Stalin proposed when German resistance should be overcome, was a massacre which would have served the same purpose and have had the same justification as the Katyn Massacre—these German officers and technicians, like the Polish victims at Katyn, were members of a class which was unassimilable by Communism. As a Marxist it was natural that Stalin should frame his proposal in the way in which Mr. Churchill says he framed it. It was equally natural that Elliott Roosevelt, knowing nothing of Marxian ideology, should quite guilelessly have assumed that Stalin must have intended to propose the mass execution of criminals, and so, without intending to mislead, he interpreted Stalin's words in his own bourgeois phraseology.

Advance to Barbarism

Although conflicting in several other details, the version of Elliott Roosevelt regarding the issue which caused such sharp dissension at Stalin's alcoholic orgy at the Teheran Conference is in essence confirmed by the version of Mr. Churchill. His habitual surly reticence mellowed by drinking repeated toasts in neat vodka, Stalin proposed that victory should be celebrated by an initial massacre of 50,000 Germans. Mr. Churchill, speaking as a civilized European, retorted indignantly that such a massacre would be mass murder to which he would never consent unless the victims wet first given a trial.

It is fortunate that this incident has been recorded in such detail by two independent witnesses whose testimony is on the essential point so exactly in agreement. From their joint testimony it is possible to state with certainty that to this brief but angry altercation between two elderly men, one of whom had been drinking "umpteen toasts" in vodka and the other in brandy, can be clearly traced the first conception of war-crimes trials, a conception later solemnly upheld and defended by many leading jurists of learning and renown as the most brilliant innovation in the administration of swift and certain justice conceived in modern times.

No doubt Stalin spoke without due regard to the bourgeois prejudice against mass murder, and it happened that this bourgeois prejudice was particularly strong in the British delegation to the Teheran Conference owing to the fact that a mass murder of outstanding enormity had recently been engaging the attention of the British Foreign Office. When Hitler invaded Poland from the west in September 1939, Stalin immediately invaded Poland from the east. Over 200,000 Polish troops surrendered to the Russians and were sent to various prisoner of war camps in the interior of Russia, the officers to the number of some 15,000 being sent to three camps near Smolensk. When Hitler invaded Russia in June 1941, it was naturally decided to arm and equip these Polish prisoners and to form a Polish army under Russian command. The discovery was then made that the officers had disappeared without trace; nothing had been heard of any of them since April 1940. The Soviet Government was, however, blandly reassuring; the missing men would be quickly found and released. For nearly two years the British Foreign Office, under constant pressure from the indignant Poles, sent repeated appeals to the Soviet

Chapter 7 — The Nuremberg Trials

Government to expedite this pretended search. Stalin, appealed to personally, declared that the search was being extended to the remotest parts of the Soviet Union including Nova Zembla in the Arctic Ocean. At last, in April 1943, the bodies of 5,000 of the missing men were found by the Germans in a huge grave in the Katyn Forest near Smolensk, an area by that time in German occupation. Each had been murdered by a revolver shot in the back of the head. The circumstantial evidence as to their fate in the possession of the British Foreign Office was overwhelming; they had been in Russian custody when last heard of alive in April 1940, and the Russian authorities had shown guilty knowledge of their fate by giving lying and contradictory explanations of what had occurred. When, therefore, the British delegates set forth for the Teheran Conference in November 1943, only six months after the discovery of the bodies, the subject of the Katyn Forest Massacre was fresh in their minds. When Stalin found himself an ally of Great Britain as a result of the German invasion, they had done their best to convince themselves that as a consequence his character and the character of his regime had undergone a miraculous reformation. This delusion was abruptly shattered when, at the Teheran Conference, Stalin announced his intention to massacre 50,000 German soldiers and technicians. Obviously he had not changed in the least since the days when he had taken a leading part in the Red Terror following the Russian Revolution in 1917. Naturally Mr. Churchill who for thirty years, had been exposing in the strongest terms the character of the Communist regime in Russia, reacted strongly to Stalin's proposal.

In passing it may be noted that the memory of Katyn Forest Massacre which had caused such heated dissension at the Teheran Conference two years later acutely embarrassed the Nuremberg Tribunal. With breathtaking effrontery the Soviet Government insisted that among the charges brought against the captured German leaders should be a charge that the Katyn Forest Massacre had been perpetrated by the Germans!

Vainly Stalin's allies expostulated with him, pointing out that it would make the judges on the Tribunal look ridiculous if they were forced to consider charges which everyone in court would know were fictitious, since the real culprits had long been known by everyone. Stalin remained adamant for reasons which to this day are obscure. Probably to the Red Dictator's macabre

Advance to Barbarism

sense of fun those who for a year had to sit through the Nuremberg proceedings are indebted for one episode which certainly had a humorous side, however exasperating it must have been to the presiding judges.

It was, of course, extremely tactless of Stalin to recall to the minds of the British delegation to the Teheran Conference the painful subject of the Katyn Forest Massacre by proposing a similar massacre on a much larger scale of German prisoners. Presumably he had forgotten that only a couple of years before he had personally assured the Polish Ambassador and General Anders, the Polish Commander-in-Chief, that the intensive search for the missing Polish officers had been extended to Nova Zembla. Stalin should surely have assumed that the British delegates, and particularly the Foreign Secretary, Anthony Eden, must feel some resentment for being duped so long and so outrageously. For nearly two years the British Foreign Office had been kept busy passing on various mendacious explanations received from the Kremlin to the Polish exiled Government in London. Anthony Eden had had to profess a belief in these explanations so that when at last the truth came to light he knew that he must be set down by the Poles as a credulous fool. In the circumstances, therefore it is difficult to maintain that this unnecessary reference to the Katyn Forest Massacre reflects less credit on Stalin's diplomacy than on his sense of humour.

On the other hand, infamous as Stalin's artless proposal seemed to Mr. Churchill, it was strictly in accordance with orthodox Marxian theory. As the main driving force throughout the proceedings at Nuremberg came from the Soviet Government, to understand these proceedings it is imperative to understand the Marxian viewpoint with regard to the liquidation of political opponents. A great deal of nonsense has been talked in capitalist circles, partly deliberately and partly from ignorance of Marxian ideology, concerning the liquidation of individuals and classes by Communist authorities. The raison d'être of a Communist government, according to Karl Marx, is to build up a proletarian system of society. When persons or classes of persons are found who cannot be fitted into such a society, they are "liquidated", that is to say, put to death. No more question of justice enters into the matter than when, for example, a botanist who is trying to establish a new variety of flower with certain qualities of colour, height, shape of petals, etc., by selecting specimens possessing the desired qualities, ruthlessly throws aside those specimens lacking those qualities. If he is seeking a variety with, say, a long stem, he has no intention of punishing short-stemmed specimens when he tears them up and discards them. Now, obviously, a man like Hermann Göring could not be made to fit into a proletarian system of society. What else, therefore, could be done with him but eliminate him? No question of punishing him enters into the matter. In fact, in the abstract, a Communist might even admire him as an individual in the same way as one might admit that a lion roaming about Piccadilly Circus was a noble animal, a masterpiece of nature produced by ages of evolution which was only devouring people in accordance with its perfectly natural instinct. One might become lyrical concerning its courage and beauty and yet quite reasonably maintain that there was no alternative to removing by violence a creature which would obviously be a disturbing influence to the human life around it.

In this entirely passionless spirit, Lenin and Dzerzhinsky had eliminated the aristocratic and plutocratic classes of Czarist Russia together with tens of thousands of Orthodox bishops and priests after the Revolution of 1917. To complain that many innocent persons perished in the Red Terror is entirely to miss the point. The great majority perished, not because they were deemed guilty of any particular offence, but because they could not be assimilated by the new proletarian state then being created.

It must surely be conceded that Hermann Göring and his colleagues had demonstrated that they were opponents of Communism. This being so, no further argument or justification was needed. How could they expect a different fate from that which, for example, had recently overtaken the anti-communist classes of such tiny and inoffensive states as Esthonia, Latvia, and Lithuania, when these states were overrun by the Soviet armies in 1939?

When, therefore, Mr. Stalin suggested at Teheran that the German leaders should be shot by a firing squad, as and when captured, he was speaking with the strict orthodoxy which might be expected from one upon whom the mantle of the great Lenin had descended. As an Asiatic, Stalin was also, of course, following faithfully in the tradition of Genghis Khan, Hulagu, and Tamerlane.

Unfortunately, from the point of view of the ultimately predestined victims, this simple, logical, expeditious and even humane solution did not appeal to Mr. Stalin's allies. If Hermann Göring would be an anachronism in a proletarian paradise, so, equally, would Mr. Churchill and Mr. Roosevelt. These gentlemen could hardly subscribe to the view that the liquidation of Hermann Göring was merely a matter of biological selection — the elimination of an unwanted type.

Possibly, it was this humorous aspect of the matter which caused Mr. Stalin's eyes to twinkle so merrily. Further, in capitalist societies, the conventional practice demands that before a man can be done to death, he must be accused of something, tried, and pronounced guilty. The Soviet Government proved most accommodating: so long as liquidation was reached in the end, it was of no consequence what preliminary judicial fooleries were indulged in to satisfy capitalist susceptibilities.

An obvious alternative to the carrying out of Mr. Stalin's proposal for a summary mass-slaughter on the lines carried out by the medieval Mongols, was a mock-trial along the lines which may be said to have originated, or at least to have been perfected, during the preceding twenty years in Soviet Russia. But disposal by mock-trial was a conception both novel and repugnant to contemporary. European juristic thought. Finally, as a compromise, it was decided that the prisoners should be charged with certain specific offences, that the changes should be heard by a tribunal composed of representatives of the four chief victorious Powers, and that the prisoners should be heard in their own defence in accordance with normal practice, excepting only they should be debarred from challenging the jurisdiction of this tribunal to try them, and at their trial the rules of evidence should be suspended.

As supremely able opportunists, neither Mr. Roosevelt nor Mr. Churchill was interested either in the theoretical justification for this solution or in the consequences which, in the fullness of time, must inevitably flow from it. His cheerful acceptance of the Morgenthau Plan[84] shows that Mr. Roosevelt felt no compunction at the idea of reducing, by systematic looting and sabotage, a prosperous industrial state of eighty million inhabitants to a defenceless and poverty-stricken agricultural community. Why then should he shrink from the proposal to put out of their misery

Chapter 7 — The Nuremberg Trials

by shooting some 50,000 individuals, some of whom may not have deserved much of their fellow-men? As a practical politician, his natural inclination was towards ruthless measures which, it might be safely assumed, would be welcomed by several very powerful sections of the American electorate as a reprisal for the ruthless anti-Jewish and anti-democratic policies of the Nazi Government. He was also deeply concerned to prevent any difference of opinion between his cantankerous allies standing in the way of victory.

On his part, Mr. Churchill's sole concern was to avoid anything which might weaken the joint war effort. Unlike the President, he entertained no fatuous illusions concerning the Communist rulers of Russia: for over twenty years he had been denouncing them as "bloody baboons", "crocodiles with masterminds", and as "the foul, filthy butchers of Moscow". But not least among his many gifts was a remarkable capacity to dismiss from his mind previously expressed opinions, if the occasion and expediency required it.

Two years before he had convinced himself that no price — not even the dissolution of the British Empire — was too high to pay to achieve victory. This unsatisfactory compromise with Stalin seemed in comparison a very small concession. His mind had always been the exact opposite to the judicial: he knew nothing and cared less about the legal difficulties in the way of a trial in which the victors would sit in judgment and decide their own charges against the vanquished.

No doubt, he had genuinely convinced himself at the moment that Hitler and his colleagues were guilty of abominable crimes. Should they escape punishment through the lack of a court with jurisdiction to try them?

With a score of urgent problems demanding his immediate attention, was it not natural that Mr. Churchill should dismiss the subject with the reflection that, when the time came, it should not be beyond the capacity of his legal advisers to work out a scheme for the proposed trials which would be free from technical objections and, while upholding the proud traditions of British justice, would satisfy Mr. Stalin by providing for the liquidation of many prominent opponents of Communism, and would satisfy Mr. Roosevelt by assuring for him and the Democrat Party a solid bloc of gratified voters in doubtful states at the next Presidential Election?

Advance to Barbarism

It need hardly be added that it occurred to no one at Teheran to suggest that all persons, whatever their nationality, accused of committing crimes during the war, should at its conclusion be put on trial. How Mr. Churchill would have flared up at any such suggestion can be deduced from his heated reaction at Yalta on February 9, 1945, when the question arose of establishing trusteeships for backward peoples. According to notes taken then by Mr. James F. Byrnes, Mr. Churchill declared:

"After we have done our best to fight in this war and have done no crime to anyone I will have no suggestion that the British Empire is to be put into the dock and examined by everybody to see whether it is up to their standard. No one will induce me as long as I am Prime Minister to let any representative of Great Britain go to a conference where we will be placed in the dock and asked to justify our right to live in a world we have tried to save."

It should not be overlooked that, when the term 'war-criminal' was used at the Teheran Conference in 1943, it was a legal term long recognised with a precise and definite meaning. A 'war criminal' was one who had committed a 'war crime', and a 'war-crime' as defined in the military manuals of all civilized countries, was a breach of the rules of civilized warfare, that is to say, a breach of those rules adopted at the end of the seventeenth century by the European nations for the conduct of their wars with each other. It comprised such matters as the ill-treatment of prisoners, hostilities committed by individuals not being members of the armed forces, espionage, and looting. The term was strictly limited to specific acts committed in the conduct of a war; it was never applied to the aims and objects of those responsible for commencing a war, however indefensible these might be.

Eighteen months were to pass before the compromise agreed upon at Teheran could be put into effect but, in due course, the Law Officers of the Crown received instructions to consult with the American, Russian, and French legal authorities, in order that a plan might be prepared for the trial of the German leaders after unconditional surrender had taken place. For learned and experienced lawyers, the task was both invidious and thankless. It was invidious because it entailed setting at naught the principles in which they had been trained throughout their professional lives. It was obvious that only a small proportion of the prisoners were war-criminals according to the accepted definition of the term.

Chapter 7 — The Nuremberg Trials

The only way out of the difficulty was to create new offences and then to assert that anyone who had in the past committed these new offences should be deemed a war-criminal. Retrospective legislation has always been abhorrent to lawyers and it must, in consequence, have been particularly distasteful to the learned Law Officers of the Crown to frame charges alleging that criminal acts had been committed before these acts had been declared crimes. Even more distasteful must have been the necessity of giving effect to the decision of the politicians that at the coming trials "the tribunal should not be bound by technical rules of evidence" but could admit "any evidence which it deemed to have probative value," that is to say, might help to support a conviction.[85]

Obviously, this innovation, if regarded otherwise than as a temporary expedient to secure convictions, would place lawyers generally in an embarrassing dilemma. The accepted rules of evidence had been gradually established through the centuries with the express purpose of arriving at the truth of a charge with as much certainty as was humanly possible. Regarded in this light, the rules of evidence had, for hundreds of years, been jealously guarded by the courts of law in England and America. Did this decision to dispense with the rules of evidence entail an admission that these rules did not really help in arriving at the truth? But, in that event, these rules should obviously be declared obsolete and abolished henceforth in all courts of law. The only possible alternative to this far-reaching and, to lawyers, painful conclusion was that, although the rules of evidence were still necessary for arriving at the truth in all judicial trials, yet in a trial of a prisoner of war by his captors they were out of place, since in such a trial the object was not to ascertain the truth but to secure a conviction.

Naturally, no professional lawyer is willing to admit that the truth in a normal judicial trial could just as readily be ascertained without the rules and safeguards which centuries of experience have proved so necessary. On the other hand, it was imperative to repudiate at all costs the suggestion that there was a fundamental distinction between a judicial trial and the trial of a prisoner of war by his captors.

For months, the eminent lawyers instructed to prepare for the trial of the German leaders struggled with their task which, as above remarked, was not only invidious to them as lawyers but entirely thankless, since in the eyes of the man-in-the-street the task presented no difficulties whatever. Who could doubt the guilt of the German leaders when the Press and the Radio unanimously asserted it! That the persons whom it was proposed to try were criminals, even before the charges against them had been decided, was as clear to the man-in-the-street as it was to Dr. Garbett, the Archbishop of York, who on March 20, 1945, in an outburst of enthusiasm, explained to the House of Lords: "It is for the sake of justice, for the vindication of that underlying sense of the difference between right and wrong, which makes us demand that these criminals should receive their punishment."

What need was there, in such circumstances, for complicated arrangements and technicalities? What better precedent could be adopted, slightly adapted perhaps to comply with present-day susceptibilities, than that provided in 1539 by that great English man King Henry VIII, equally distinguished as a pious defender of the faith, and as a tireless wielder of the sword of justice. Having detained the aged Richard Whiting, Abbot of Glastonbury, in the Tower for many months without preferring any charge against him, Henry at length decided it was time that "the criminal should receive his punishment" for which purpose he should be returned to his native Somerset. The order to His Majesty's judges has been preserved; it is in the handwriting of Henry's chief minister, Thomas Cromwell, and reads:

"The Abbot of Glaston to be tried at Glaston and also executed there with his complycys. See the evidence be well sorted and the indictments well drawn."

It must be acknowledged that this direction is a model of brevity and lucidity. The stupidest judge could have been in no doubt as to what was required of him. A slight but unmistakable note of menace may be detected in the last sentence and we may be sure that the evidence was "well sorted" and that there was no slipshod work in the drawing of the indictments. In fact no hitch of any kind delayed the fulfilment of the royal wishes. Very shortly afterwards, on a grey November morning, the underlying sense of the difference between right and wrong was vindicated by the hanging, disembowelling and quartering of Abbot Whiting "and his complycys" on Glastonbury Tor.

Possibly the promoters of the Nuremberg trials were unfamiliar with this striking Tudor precedent: or perhaps they rejected it as too simple for service at the present day. At all events,

Chapter 7 — The Nuremberg Trials

the unfortunate lawyers were directed to ransack the pages of history for more modern precedents. No doubt in their search they came across and noted with approval the dictum of Oliver St. John, the Solicitor-General, during the debate in the Commons preceding the judicial murder of Thomas Wentworth, Earl of Strafford, in 1641: "No evidence is necessary if each man *feels* in his mind that the accused is guilty." And St. John provided a precedent for the Nuremberg distinction between the victors and losers in the war by his statement that: "We give law to hares and deer because they be beasts of chase, it was never accounted cruelty or foul play to knock foxes and wolves on the head as they can be found, because they be beasts of prey".

The only really recent precedent which existed for the proposed proceedings at Nuremberg were the various political mock-trials which had taken place in Russia from the Revolution in 1917 onwards. It is, therefore, necessary to glance briefly at these mock-trials in Russia in order to realise how widely they departed from judicial trials in other countries and to consider to what extent they differed from the procedure later adopted at Nuremberg.

In a normal judicial trial, the result depends on the impartial judgment of independent third parties no more connected with the prosecution than with the defence. In a political trial in Soviet Russia, on the other hand, the judges and the prosecuting counsel together form a team; the proceedings are an act of state, and the result is a foregone conclusion. Neither the victim nor the prosecution are concerned with the figures duly arrayed as judges on the bench. The role of the latter is purely ornamental: their only active part is to read, when all is over, the judgment and sentences previously decided upon by the executive government. The speeches for the prosecution are political manifestoes, designed to justify the action of the government in instituting the proceedings and are directed, not to the Court, but to the outside public. At times, even a communist dictatorship must justify its actions to its subjects.

Thus, in 1936, when it was decided to liquidate Zinoviev, Kamenev, Smirnov, and other prominent Soviet leaders whom the Russian public had long been taught to revere as heroes of the revolution, some kind of explanation for a political somersault of this magnitude had to be offered to the man-in-the-street. It was found that the most convenient manner of putting forward such an explanation was in the form of a speech for the prosecution, delivered after dictated confessions of guilt had been recited by the accused and before the death penalty had been recited by the Court. In normal mock-trials, all other roles are ancillary to that of the public prosecutor. The judge is a mere lay figure who recites a few set words when all is over.[86] Occasionally, as at the mock-trial of the G.P.U. chief, Henry Yagoda, charged with the murder by poison of the novelist Maxim Gorky, the judge enlivens the proceedings by what in the parlance of the music halls is termed "gagging". But "gagging" by judges in a normal mock-trial is exceptional and irregular and is tolerated only as a relief from the tedium of long proceedings or when the public prosecutor fails to put over the Government manifesto as well as might be desired.

It would be futile to attempt an enquiry whether Stalin really believed, for example, that Yagoda was guilty of the crimes of which he was accused. That Yagoda was guilty of countless crimes there can be no doubt—Mr. Stephen Graham calls him "the worst villain of the Revolution"[87]—but it is difficult to see what motive Yagoda could have had to finish off by poison a septuagenarian novelist already dying of senility. Probably Stalin troubled himself very little on the point, on which he may have had no definite opinion. To him it was merely a matter of routine practice that a G.P.U. chief, discarded as no longer useful to the regime, should be liquidated.

In *Russian Purge*[88] the authors, themselves prominent Soviet citizens who were victims of the Great Purge of 1936-1938 but escaped with their lives, express surprise that the delusion should persist in the West that, in Soviet Russia, there exists any necessary connection between a man's arrest and any particular offence alleged against him. In the vast majority of cases, persons were arrested during the Purge for having "objective characteristics" which means, in Marxian legal jargon, that they belonged to one or another of a dozen categories which the executive government had decided "as a measure of social security" to eliminate or suppress.

The precise charge, bringing these unfortunates within the Soviet Criminal Code and on which, in due course, they would be sent to a term of forced labour or to execution, was decided much later. In the United States and in Great Britain, the functions of

Chapter 7 — The Nuremberg Trials

the judiciary and the functions of the executive are kept rigidly distinct. But, under Soviet law, the executive exercises the widest judicial powers. The vast majority of political prisoners are dealt with by the executive; only one case, here and there, is passed on to the judiciary for what is called in the above-mentioned book "a show trial". In these cases, the duty of the judiciary is limited in practice to rubber-stamping, for propaganda purposes, the judgment of the executive government.

Handicapped, on the one hand, by their own legal learning and, on the other, by their profound ignorance of Marxian ideology, the English and American judges were pained and puzzled by the Alice-in-Wonderland atmosphere which, as a result of the dual character of the proceedings, prevailed at Nuremberg and which they strove in vain to dispel. Yet nothing, in fact, could have been simpler or more logical than the Marxian attitude to the trial. The prisoners were members of a political party established by Adolf Hitler for the express purpose of combatting Communism. Their "objective characteristics" could not, therefore, be in dispute. No punishment was called for in such a case but the exercise of "the supreme measure of social security", which in Marxian terminology means the carrying out of a sentence of death.

It was easy enough for the politicians to agree that the war should end with a liquidation, in accordance with Marxian ideology, of all persons with undesirable objective characteristics, preceded, however, by a trial in accordance with established principles of justice.

It would, however, be hard to exaggerate the difficulties which faced the lawyers entrusted with the task of devising a procedure which would carry out this agreement. Lawyers instinctively turn to precedents for guidance, but intensive searching of the legal records of ancient and modern times disclosed no exact precedents, but only a few cases containing helpful suggestions. Of these it could at least be claimed that the prosecution, conviction and execution of the Persian satrap, Bessos, by Alexander the Great at Zariaspa in Bactria in 329 B.C. was a precedent of classical antiquity.

Bessos was a Persian patriot who led the last resistance to the victorious Macedonians after the overthrow of King Darius at Arbela. Having been subjected to various tortures, and having had his nose and ears cut off as a pre-conviction punishment, Bessos was condemned to a formal trial. Alexander the Great assumed the role of prosecutor and delivered an eloquent speech demanding conviction. He then assumed the role of judge, declared himself convinced by his own arguments and sentenced the unfortunate Oriental to a death by torture. In A.D. 1945, the case of Bessos in 329 B.C. was triumphantly cited by eminent jurists as an authority for the contention that an accuser was a fit person to act as judge of his own charges.

Until the close of the Second World War it had not indeed occurred to anyone to attach significance to this episode in the life of the great soldier and conqueror which had been generally regarded by his biographers as a discreditable lapse revealing the latent streak of savage cruelty in his character. Admirers of Alexander have always contended that he was prone to histrionic gestures and that there is no reason to doubt that he sincerely believed Bessos was a villain richly deserving severe punishment. With complete sincerity and characteristic vanity he was convinced that no one could plead for a conviction more forcibly than himself, and no one could more ably discharge the duties of a judge or find a penalty more neatly fitting the crime.

Whether or not the trial of Bessos can be regarded as a precedent justifying the trial of the German leaders after the Second World War, it must be conceded that it contained all the essential characteristics of the "war-crimes trial" as practised in recent times. It is distinguishable on the one hand from the ancient mock-trial in which the victim suffers as a symbol for the shortcomings of his race or party, and on the other hand, from the mock-trial of the type which evolved in Russia after the Bolshevik Revolution and which, as explained above, is in essence a political manifesto by the party in power expressed for convenience or effect in the form of a trial at law.

Having discovered a trial in the year 329 B.C. which could be plausibly cited as a precedent for the trial which the chiefs of state at the Yalta Conference had decided should take place before the liquidation of the captured German leaders, the eminent British, French and American lawyers entrusted with the task of making the necessary arrangements searched in vain the records of the following two thousand years for another helpful precedent.

In deference to French public opinion it was clearly inexpedient to cite the trial of Joan of Arc in 1431. In any case

Chapter 7 — The Nuremberg Trials

the nature of this trial and the form in which it was conducted distinguished it sharply both from a symbolic mock-trial and from a war-crimes trial of the Bessos type, although the English Government had undoubtedly decided beforehand that the outcome of the proceedings must be the death of the prisoner. The question which faced the English Regent, the Duke of Bedford, was in fact exactly the same as that which faced the chiefs of state at Yalta five hundred years later. Three courses were open to him.

A majority of the Great Council of England recommended that when she had been purchased from her captor, the Duke of Luxembourg, she should be sewn in a sack and surreptitiously dropped in a river. If that course had been adopted Joan would now only be remembered as a peasant girl who, according to popular belief at the time, had played the leading part in the relief of Orleans in 1429. Alternatively he could have ordered her to be tried on a charge of war-crimes by a selection of the disgruntled warriors who had fled before her at Patay. The Regent, however, decided to take advantage of Joan's capture to stage what would now be called a propaganda stunt. In the 20th century it has become customary to regard a successful political opponent as a criminal; in the 15th century it seemed natural to ascribe one's defeats to the use of witchcraft. So the Regent decided to hand Joan over to an ecclesiastical court presided over by the Bishop of Beauvais in whose diocese she had been captured, there to be tried on charges of "divers superstitions, false teachings and other treasons against the Divine Majesty."

Although useless as a precedent, the trial of Joan of Arc provided the team of lawyers preparing in 1945 for the trial of the captured German leaders with many valuable lessons. In 1431 the Regent decided that the prisoner should be tried by an independent tribunal over which he could exercise no direct control. The ecclesiastical court which tried Joan of Arc was in theory at least far above mere political considerations and acted in accordance with an elaborate and well-established system of law, clarified by copious precedents, which for centuries had been accepted by every Christian country. No question arose, therefore, as at Nuremberg in 1945 of inventing a novel system of law in order to establish breaches thereof. Also the jurisdiction of the court to try her on charges of offences against God, and the accepted beliefs and morality of Christendom could not be challenged. It is unnecessary to speculate here as to what the English Government might have done if this ecclesiastical court had acquitted her and ordered her release. The court convicted her, largely on her own admissions, on the charges brought against her. As Bernard Shaw says in *Saint Joan*: "She was condemned after a very careful and conscientious trial."

While it convicted the accused, however, the ecclesiastical court did not bring in exactly the verdict which the Regent's policy required. In place of public burning as "a Heretic, Relapsed, Apostate, Idolatress", she was sentenced to life imprisonment. As Lenin once said: "Who troubles about imprisonment when a change of fortune may bring swift release?" As a result of his decision to have Joan tried by an independent court, the Regent Bedford failed to get the judgment he desired. In order to achieve his purpose he had to exercise strong pressure behind the scenes to have the sentence of imprisonment passed by the ecclesiastical court on Joan replaced by a sentence of death by burning at the stake. Evidently the War Crimes Commission in 1945 took this lesson to heart and so avoided the mistake made in 1431. Probably at Nuremberg an impartial court, composed of neutral judges, would have convicted most of the prisoners on one charge or another. Most certainly, however, they would not have rubber-stamped the verdict of guilt already pronounced by the chiefs of state at the Yalta Conference.

One lesson, however, from the records of the past was overlooked by politicians and lawyers in 1945. Almost without exception trials of which the main object is political, whether they be grotesque mock-trials or "careful and conscientious" judicial trials, fail dismally in their two main objects. Instead of discrediting the accused in the eyes of posterity, they bestow on them fame, publicity, interest and sympathy. Not her actual achievements, but the decision of the English Government to bring about her death in a strictly legal, orderly and public manner, established the fame of Joan of Arc, enriched the history of the Middle Ages with their most picturesque figure, gave France a national heroine and ultimately added her name to the Calendar of the Saints.

Similarly, political trials designed to establish for all time the victors' point of view have the opposite result. If they do not always arouse sympathy for the vanquished, distaste and resentment is inevitably generated against the victors. Self-

Chapter 7 — The Nuremberg Trials

satisfied rectitude, even when justified, is rarely an attractive spectacle, and moral indignation, when clearly not disinterested, is very liable to be mistaken for hypocrisy.

The latter drawback to political trials was demonstrated in 1648 by the trial of King Charles I by a court composed of his political enemies and having not a shadow of jurisdiction to sit in judgment on him. Few can now read an account of this trial without becoming insensibly influenced in Charles' favour. The verdict itself, of course, has not the faintest weight with historians. Opinions are still divided concerning Charles; some consider him, in the main, a well-meaning monarch, more sinned against than sinning; others consider him, on the whole, a weak and irresponsible tyrant. No one would dream of quoting the verdict of John Bradshaw and his fellow regicides as having decided the matter.

It had no doubt been hoped that a diligent search of the annals of the Revolutionary and Napoleonic wars would provide authority for the contention that civilized victors have recognised an unescapable duty placed upon them by their victory to punish the shortcomings of the vanquished. But, as pointed out in the chapter of this book dealing with civilized warfare, the victors in 1815 recognised no such duty. Their forbearance, which seems so astonishing at the present day, was certainly not due to any lack of deeds of violence by the vanquished French which could have been made the subject of criminal charges. Marshal Blücher, remembering the ruthless treatment of Prussia by Davout after the battle of Jena, urged with soldierly directness that Napoleon should be shot on capture and the traitor Talleyrand heartily approved. The victorious allies, however, not only refused to countenance such summary treatment of a fallen foe but rejected the demand of the restored Bourbons that Napoleon should be put on trial by a French court for the shooting of the Duc d'Enghien in 1804.

During the twenty-three years during which the struggle had raged French armies had overrun all Western Europe from Cadiz to Moscow, and had committed wholesale every variety of violent crime. In Germany, in Russia, and particularly in Spain guerilla bands had harried the French troops with a ferocity hardly surpassed even by the gangs of Partisans which harried the German troops during the Second World War, with the result that equally savage reprisals had been provoked. In particular,

Advance to Barbarism

Marshal Suchet had made himself notorious while in command in Aragon by the severe methods which he employed to protect the lives of his men from treacherous attacks by armed Spanish civilians. Evidence for a dozen charges against him of having been responsible for war-crimes could easily have been collected and his conviction by a Spanish court would have been a certainty. Nevertheless no action of any kind was taken against him and he was allowed to end his days in honourable retirement.

Between 1815 and 1918 no European war ended with the victorious side finding itself in a position to dictate the terms of peace entirely as it suited them, regardless of the rights of the vanquished. Excessive demands might have provoked intervention by neutral Powers: world opinion had to be taken into account by the victors. All the wars between these dates were wars between individual Powers like the Franco-German war of 1870 or small groups of Powers like the Crimean war of 1854. They all ended with negotiated peace treaties which, because they were negotiated treaties, proved lasting. No precedents for the disposal of captured enemies even of the most shadowy kind were to be found in the records of the wars of the 19th century. It is amusing to note however that if Queen Victoria had been allowed to have her way in 1882 the lawyers planning the Nuremberg trials in 1945 would have been provided with a really helpful precedent. Seventy years before Nasser's seizure of power in Egypt, another junior officer, Colonel Ahmed Aribi, led a similar revolt against the corrupt rule of the Khedive Ismail, but which ended very differently. To protect the interests of the Christian holders of Egyptian bonds, Alexandria was bombarded, a British army was landed and Aribi Pasha's troops defeated at Tell-el-Kebir. Aribi Pasha became a prisoner of war and the question then arose what should be done with him.

The Khedive insisted strongly that the prisoner should be handed over to him so that his fate might serve as a lesson for all time to mutinous junior officers — a lesson indeed which, if administered, might have helped three quarters of a century later to keep in order a certain junior officer named Nasser. The decision rested with Mr. Gladstone. Although, as he characteristically expressed it, he "was almost driven to the conclusion that Aribi Pasha was a bad man", Mr. Gladstone hesitated to hand over the captured officer to the Khedive. Queen Victoria, however, had

Chapter 7 — The Nuremberg Trials

no doubts whatever on the subject. She was, as she herself put it, "distressed and alarmed" at the mere possibility that "the arch-rebel and traitor Aribi" should escape the fate which he deserved which she "believed everyone, including Mr. Gladstone himself, wished him to suffer." In the end Mr. Gladstone, in spite of her expostulations, decided to send Aribi into exile in Ceylon. When she was asked to send a personal message to the Khedive to help him soothe the ladies of his harem who were "frantic with indignation" at this leniency, she flatly refused, declaring that the Khedive's wives "show a right feeling in being frantic" at this display of weakness by the British Government of which she herself "so highly disapproved".

The lawyers entrusted with the task of preparing for the Nuremberg Trials had, of course, very clear and recent precedents ready to hand in the various "show-trials" (to use Marxian terminology) staged by Stalin during the Great Purge (1936-38). Unfortunately in 1945 it was impossible for them to cite these precedents because a stringent taboo was in force prohibiting all mention of the Great Purge, which, at the time it was carried out, had aroused worldwide surprise, consternation and horror, especially in those Leftist circles in Britain and the United States which regarded the Russian Revolution as a great landmark in the course of human progress. That Stalin should order the death of his closest colleagues, the men who had helped Lenin to Confer the blessings of Communism on the Russian people, was of course entirely consistent with all that was known concerning his personal character. Nevertheless the Great Purge came as a shock to all those who cherished delusions concerning the nature of the Soviet Regime.

When Hitler's invasion of Russia in June 1941 transformed Stalin from a confederate of Hitler into an ally of Britain, it became imperative to expunge from public memory all recollection of what was known concerning him and the grim police state which he had established in Russia. This was successfully accomplished by the invention of the Great Stalin Myth. In place of the ruthless tyrant whose character was finally revealed to the world in 1956 by his successor, Nikita Khrushchev, there was held up for public admiration the benign figure of "Uncle Joe Stalin", the champion of liberty and lover of all mankind, the loyal ally who was inspired by the same lofty ideals as Churchill and Roosevelt. To preserve public belief in the Stalin Myth it was absolutely imperative that no mention of any kind should be made of the Great Purge.

Deprived of the only set of useful precedents for the coming trials of the captured German leaders, the group of international lawyers preparing for these trials had no choice but to present them as a completely novel departure in the administration of justice. They received with shocked silence General Nikitchenko's unwelcome assertion that the coming trials to be held in Nuremberg would be merely an adaptation of the show-trials carried out during the Great Purge, and they proceeded to make arrangements which would disguise this fact so far as it was possible. The result of their intensive labours was the production of the London Agreement which was made public on the 8th August, 1945. The details of this remarkable production require brief examination here.

The London Agreement was an agreement between the British, American, French and Russian Governments to establish a body to be called the International Military Tribunal for the trial of "the major war criminals whose offences have no particular geographical location." No definition was given of the term "major war criminals" except that the right was reserved by each victorious state to try, according to its own laws, any war criminal in its hands for offences committed on its own territory. Attached to the Agreement and forming an integral part of it was a sort of schedule, grandiloquently labelled "The Charter", which purported to define the powers of the Tribunal and the procedure which it was to adopt.

On the face of it, therefore, the London Agreement was nothing more than a private arrangement between four sovereign states to put on trial captured subjects of another sovereign state. Had the contracting parties been, say, Costa Rica, Nicaragua, Honduras and Salvador, such an agreement would only have been of interest as an indication of how little the elements of jurisprudence were understood in these countries. The fact that the four parties to the London Agreement happened at the time to be the four most powerful states in the world, clearly could have no bearing on the question whether its terms were in accordance with international law. The tribunal which it created was not an international body, except in the sense that more than one state was represented on it. It was simply a gathering of legal officials

Chapter 7 — The Nuremberg Trials

appointed by four states in accordance with a private arrangement between themselves.

The most important part of the so-called Charter is Article 6, which purports to create two new crimes against international law. The first is labelled, "Crimes against peace", which it defines as "planning, preparing or waging a war of aggression or a war in violation of international treaties." The second is labelled "Crimes against humanity", which it defines as "inhumane acts against any civilian population before or during the war and persecutions on political, racial or religious grounds."

With regard to the first of these novel creations, the framers of the Charter had abandoned in despair a desperate attempt to define "a war of aggression" without impliedly condemning Russia for her numerous unprovoked attacks on her neighbours, beginning with her attack on Finland in 1939 and ending with her declaration of war on Japan in 1945 in defiance of the Non-aggression Pact which she had signed with the latter country. The chiefs of state at the Yalta Conference had cheerfully convicted their captured enemies of having plotted and waged a war of aggression and set the framers of the Charter the utterly impossible task of defining this alleged offence. Of course they failed. As long before as 1933, Edwin M. Borchard, the famous professor of international law at Yale University, had dismissed the word "aggression" as "an essentially dishonest and mischievous term calculated to mislead the uninformed."[89]

With regard to the second novel crime created by the London Agreement precise definition was obviously equally impossible at a moment when the victors were carrying out mass-deportations of populations totalling some fourteen millions and entailing indescribable misery. In most cases these deportations followed wholesale mass-murders carried out in the homelands of the populations condemned to deportation.

It is, perhaps, hardly necessary to comment on the fundamental injustice of inventing an *ad hoc* law and then bringing charges alleging acts in breach of this law committed before this law existed. In the United States this injustice was widely recognised. As the leading Republican Senator, Robert A. Taft, a politician respected by all parties, pointed out, "It is completely alien to the American tradition of law to prosecute men for criminal acts which were not declared to be so until long after the fact. The

Advance to Barbarism

Nuremberg Trials will for ever remain a blot on the escutcheon of American jurisprudence."

However grave and however numerous may be the technical objections which can be raised against it, the London Agreement from a practical point of view was undeniably a very workmanlike production, admirably devised to carry out the purpose which it was intended to fulfil. It left the judges of the International Military Tribunal in no possible doubt as to what was expected of them. It gave them an absolutely free hand.

Thus the vitally important Clause 18 of the Charter empowered the Tribunal "to rule out irrelevant issues and statements of any kind". By reference to this clause, the Tribunal could not only reject any evidence or submission by the Defendants simply by declaring it "irrelevant"; it entitled the Tribunal to refuse to hear any evidence concerning the background against which the alleged offences of the Defendants were committed. In short, it precluded the Defendants from proving that the acts, now declared criminal, of which they were accused, were concurrently being committed by their opponents. Thus, as we shall see later, Grossadmiral Raeder, in answer to the charge that he had planned the invasion of neutral Norway, was prevented from calling evidence to prove that at precisely the same time the British Admiralty was taking active steps to invade Norway.

Clause 19 released the Tribunal from any obligation to enforce "the technical rules of evidence." It expressly directed the Tribunal "to admit any evidence which it deemed to have probative value". To bolster up any charge which could not be proved by admissible evidence, the Tribunal was directed to accept hearsay evidence. In accordance with this clause a quantity of second and third hand statements, documents the authenticity of which no attempt was made to prove, and other inadmissible evidence was cheerfully accepted by the Tribunal. For the first time in legal history, the mere fact that an allegation was made or suggested was held to have "probative value" of its truth.

The Tribunal saw fit to exercise rigorously the powers given by Clauses 18 and 19. On the other hand the Tribunal to a great extent ignored Clause 21 which directed them "to take judicial notice of facts of common knowledge" and to dispense with formal proof. That this clause might cut both ways was probably overlooked by the framers of the Charter. On several occasions

Chapter 7 — The Nuremberg Trials

the Tribunal was caused grave embarrassment by Clause 21. Thus regarding the invasion of neutral Norway, Mr. Churchill had told the Commons on the 11th April 1940 that Britain had infringed Norwegian neutrality before the German invasion was launched, and his speech had been reported in full in the Press. By the time of the Nuremberg Trials in 1945 the truth had become common knowledge. The Tribunal, however, insisted on being judicially ignorant of what they could have read in Hansard.

Naturally the peculiarities and eccentricities of the London Agreement were of interest only to lawyers. The general public accepted its provisions complacently, regarding it merely as a formal direction setting out the preliminaries to be observed before the execution of the prisoners. This complacency was not disturbed by objections of mere lawyers, an appearance of apparently unanimous approval by the legal profession being created by the policy adopted by the Press not to report any expression of dissent. Occasionally, indeed, adverse opinions reached the public; for example in the little book by Montgomery Belgion previously cited entitled *Epitaph on Nuremberg*, and again when Serjeant Sullivan was roused to indignant protest by a ruling of the Bar Council that it was "undesirable" that a member of the English Bar should appear for the defence before the Nuremberg Tribunal. "If indeed the Tribunal and its task", wrote the veteran barrister, "are such that self-respecting Counsel should not lend himself to the proceedings, it is undesirable that an English judge should sit and an English law officer as such should prosecute". Naturally, however, the lay public disregarded such lonely protests at the adoption of novel legal conceptions which were supported by legal opinion of the greatest weight. Foremost among the eminent lawyers who defended the practice of holding war trials of captured enemies was Lord Justice Wright, unquestionably one of the ablest lawyers of his generation.

After a distinguished career at the Bar during which he is said to have earned £25,000 a year, he was made a judge in 1925, a Lord of Appeal in 1932 and presided at many famous trials. After the War he accepted the appointment of chairman of the War Crimes Commission and later defiantly defended the arrangements for war-crimes trials made by himself and his colleagues. The essence of his contentions was that if an accused person was, in fact, guilty no injustice could be done by convicting him. In the memorable debate on the 19th May 1949 in the House of Lords, following an attack by Lord Hankey on the Tokyo War-Crimes Trial, Lord Wright complained bitterly, "It was very unfair and irrelevant to criticise war-crimes tribunals as conqueror's law. The only question was, did the accused have a fair trial?"

Looking back on the subject unclouded by the war-time passions which still survived in 1949, the fallacy of this argument is apparent. Of course a guilty man, that is to say, a man who in fact is guilty and admits that he is guilty, has no ground for complaint if he is convicted. But if an accused person, whether guilty or innocent, elects to deny the charge, how are his fellow citizens to decide what is the truth? The essential question then is, how and by whom is it to be decided whether he is guilty or not? A fair trial means a trial before an impartial court at which the rules of evidence are observed. No man living knew better than Lord Justice Wright the meaning of the term 'a fair trial': when presiding in the Court of Appeal he had unhesitatingly reversed judgments given in lower courts following trials in which inadvertently had been infringed the principles which Clauses 18 and 19 of the London Agreement authorised the Nuremberg Tribunal to disregard. Another stalwart upholder of the validity of war-trials was Professor Arthur Goodhart, Professor of Jurisprudence at Oxford University. This may now seem not less astonishing than would be a declaration by the Astronomer Royal that he had become convinced that the earth was flat. Naturally however the lay public in 1945 was gratified to hear that an innovation that seemed on the face of it a flagrant repudiation of the fundamental principle of jurisprudence had the emphatic approval of so many eminent judges and learned jurists.

Whatever shortcomings may now be obvious to everyone in the London Agreement, it cannot be denied that the procedure which it laid down succeeded in achieving one of the main objects of its framers: it provided for the disposal of the captured enemy leaders with a minimum of friction between the victorious Powers. Although the British, French and American judges on the Nuremberg Tribunal considered that the task of the court was to decide whether the accused were guilty of the offences alleged against them and the Soviet judges considered that the task before the court was simply to order the elimination of a group of avowed opponents of Communism, yet this complete divergence

Chapter 7 — The Nuremberg Trials

of outlook never during the hearing became obtrusively apparent. In public at any rate complete harmony prevailed.

There was never unseemly bickering between the members of the Tribunal, although in fact the only link between them was a common determination that no hitch should arise from their irreconcilable outlooks. Later, this determination was strengthened by the personal goodwill and respect which grew up between the members of the Court. It is no matter for surprise that the proceedings ended with a mass-hanging of the prisoners, but, in view of the composition of the Court, it is remarkable that there was so little friction during the trial, there being at the end a perfect crescendo of mutual congratulation. The Judges, Marxian and non-Marxian, praised each other and Counsel; Counsel thanked the Judges and each other. The British representatives paid the time-honoured tributes to British Justice and generously admitted the merits of the various foreign legal systems, and the foreign representatives praised British Justice and each spoke favourably of his own country's system of administering justice. To the extent, at least, of the four countries taking part, rarely has there been such a demonstration of international amity.

Nevertheless, there is reason for doubting whether the non-Marxian members of the Tribunal ever comprehended the distinctive outlook of their Soviet colleagues. How genuine was the goodwill and how complete this incomprehension were strikingly demonstrated some three years after the close of the Nuremberg trials. Although, by this time, public opinion in Great Britain and in the United States with regard to the Soviet Union had completely changed, we find Lord Justice Lawrence, now become Lord Oaksey, who had acted as President of the Tribunal, hotly resenting an attack on Russia's participation in the proceedings as a reflection not only on himself but on his Soviet colleagues. Speaking in the House of Lords on May 5, 1949, Lord Hankey had declared that "there was something cynical and revolting in the spectacle of British, French and American judges sitting on the Bench with colleagues representing a country which before, during and since the trials had perpetrated half the political crimes in the calendar." Speaking in reply, on May 19th, Lord Justice Lawrence declared that Lord Hankey's observations were "insulting to my Soviet colleagues, to Mr. Justice Birkett and myself. The Soviet judges demonstrated their ability and fairness."

Advance to Barbarism

The relevance of this reply may appear obscure. Lord Hankey had merely expressed the surprise, long felt by many, that the Soviet Union, having so recently wantonly attacked Finland, conquered and annexed Esthonia, Latvia and Lithuania, and deprived Roumania by force of Bessarabia, should, nevertheless, have been considered eligible to participate in a trial of the leaders of another Power, charged with having waged a single war of aggression. Lord Justice Lawrence's reply was that there was no ground for surprise, because the individuals sent to represent the Soviet Union at the trial turned out to be able and fair-minded.

We may, of course, readily accept Lord Justice Lawrence's testimony that his two Soviet colleagues impressed him as able and fair-minded men. Lord Hankey had, in fact, expressly admitted that they may have been "impeccable as individuals". For all we know to the contrary, they may also have been excellent husbands and fathers, profound students of botany, expert mountaineers, or ardent philatelists.[90] But what bearing could their personal gifts, virtues and tastes have on Lord Hankey's contention that the participation in the Nuremberg Trials of a state with the record of the Soviet Union was "cynical and revolting"? Even Lord Justice Lawrence must surely have become gradually conscious of the Alice-in-Wonderland atmosphere that the participation of the Soviet Union conferred on the proceedings, and which platitudes about humanity and denunciations of aggressive warfare as the supreme international crime, however impressively and pompously expressed, failed utterly to dispel.

It is hard to believe that Lord Justice Lawrence had never heard of that series of political trials which began in Russia, in 1936, known to history as the Great Purge. Apparently, however, he was not aware that these trials were conducted in accordance with a novel and distinctive system of law, of which the only effective principle familiar to jurists in the rest of the world was the Roman maxim, *Salus populi est suprema lex*, adapted to mean, "What in the opinion of Joseph Stalin is necessary for the safety of the Communist Party is the paramount law."

In the years following 1936, Joseph Stalin came repeatedly to the opinion that the safety of the Communist Party necessitated the liquidation of one or other of the famous men who had helped Lenin to bring about the Russian Revolution twenty years before. Included among them were Lenin's personal assistant Gregory

Chapter 7 — The Nuremberg Trials

Zinoviev; Leo Kamenev, the president of the Moscow Soviet and, like Zinoviev, one of the original members of the Politbureau; Ivan Smirnov, once acclaimed "the Lenin of Siberia"; Nikholai Bukharin, the editor of "Izvestia"; the once powerful journalist, Alexei Rikov; Marshal Mikail Tukhachevsky, the most successful leader of the Red Army during the Civil War; Karl Radek, once director of Bolshevik foreign propaganda; and even the dreaded chief of the G.P.U., Henry Yagoda. The trial and execution of these men duly followed. There is no reason to think that the judges who condemned them were not able and fair-minded; in accordance with their legal training they accepted the guidance of the Marxian legal maxim quoted above.[91]

Similarly, at the Teheran Conference, Joseph Stalin, in the name of the executive government of the Soviet Union, expressed the opinion that certain German opponents of Communism, to the number of 50,000, should be liquidated "as fast as we capture them before a firing squad." As a concession to the bourgeois scruples of his Allies Stalin, indeed, agreed that a trial should, in each case, precede execution, but his decision that these men must die remained unaltered. Did Lord Justice Lawrence imagine that the Soviet Judges who tried any of these cases in Moscow or in Nuremberg were at liberty to reverse Joseph Stalin's decisions on this subject or on any other? His speech in the House of Lords, quoted above, clearly indicated that this was his belief, since otherwise the importance which he attached to the fairness of his Soviet colleagues is quite incomprehensible.

In one sense, of course, the learned English judge may have been right in his belief. In the same sense no doubt, Henry VIII's judges may be said to have been at liberty to reverse the decision of their royal master that "the Abbot of Glaston should be tried at Glaston and also executed there with his complycys". There is no reason to think that the judges who condemned Abbot Whiting to the lingering horrors of an English execution for high treason were not able and fair-minded men.

But, as loyal and obedient servants of His Majesty, they would have had little difficulty in convincing themselves that the opinion of their sovereign lord, the king, was well founded. Similarly, a Soviet judge would, naturally, feel it presumptuous on his part to investigate too deeply the grounds upon which "our great wise Leader, Lenin's true pupil and successor," had formed an opinion. Soviet law gives the widest judicial powers to the executive government, and the duty of a Soviet judge is to administer, not to reform, Soviet law. Joseph Stalin, like Bluff King Hal, was notoriously impatient with subordinates who failed on any pretext to carry out his instructions, and was very likely to regard anyone who disagreed with him as a self-confessed counter-revolutionary. In Tudor times, those who had the honour to serve Bluff King Hal lived under the shadow of the Tower, just as those who, four hundred years later, served Joseph Stalin, lived beneath the shadow of the Lubianka Prison.

"Stuff and nonsense," exclaimed Alice when the Queen demanded, "Sentence first—verdict afterwards." The members of the International Military Tribunal at Nuremberg can be divided into two distinct groups, according to their attitude to this celebrated passage in Lewis Carroll's classic story. To the Soviet judges, the Queen's demand for "Sentence first—verdict afterwards" was a perfectly rational requirement supported by numerous weighty precedents. To Lord Justice Lawrence and his non-Marxian colleagues, as to Lewis Carroll's contemporaries, it was nothing but brilliant nonsense, a whimsical extravagance so wildly fantastic as to be humorous.

Neither group had the slightest comprehension of the legal concepts of the other. Lord Justice Lawrence's tribute to the fairness of his Soviet colleagues proves, for example, that no less than three years after the Nuremberg Trials the leading British representative on the tribunal had still not grasped the Marxian significance of the word "fairness". In Marxian legal ideology, the word "fairness" means fairness to the proletarian state; fairness to an unrepentant opponent of Communism is simply a contradiction in terms. All the occupants of the dock were undeniably guilty of being anti-Communists and, as such, required elimination.

Whether they deserved execution for certain specific acts was a question of no practical importance. When a majority of the Tribunal in a fleeting spasm of self-assertion decided to acquit von Papen, the Soviet Government lodged a strong protest. His acquittal might have been "fair" in a non-Marxian sense, meaning that he was not guilty of the acts of which he was accused, but it was obviously "unfair" to Communism that an outspoken opponent of Communism should be allowed to survive. Some may think that the above protest of Lord Justice Lawrence showed undue

Chapter 7 — The Nuremberg Trials

touchiness to reasoned and moderately expressed criticism. Full credit should, however, be given him for the loyalty displayed by him to his foreign colleagues who, no longer seated on the Bench at Nuremberg secure from challenge or objection, were, like himself, standing before the bar of history awaiting judgment. But what is really significant in the episode is that the English judge should assume that Soviet judges should need or desire any defence from charges of having outraged established principles of justice which he himself, of course, accepted without question but which had long come to be regarded as obsolete bourgeois prejudices in the Soviet Union.

Concerning Lord Justice Lawrence, afterwards Lord Oaksey, it can at least be said of him that he stood out head and shoulders above the motley team of judges, barristers, investigators, warders and executioners, which gathered among the ruins of the beautiful medieval city of Nuremberg in October 1945. It was entirely owing to the fact that he was chosen to act as Chairman of the so-called International Military Tribunal that the proceedings were conducted with decorum and decency. His gifts and limitations combined to make him the ideal man for the post. His dignity was never shaken even when the most embarrassingly absurd situations arose, and his unquestionable integrity and sincerity cast a much needed cloak of respectability over the protracted proceedings. Thanks entirely to the unruffled courtesy and firmness with which he conducted the trials, it can be said without fear of contradiction that if a stranger, say, from Patagonia, who knew nothing of the circumstances and spoke no language but his own, had happened one day to visit the Justizpalast in Nuremberg during a hearing, he might well have imagined a normal judicial trial was in progress—providing, of course, that he did not tarry too long.

Some of Lord Justice Lawrence's colleagues may have equalled him in legal learning and judicial experience, but none could rival his guileless sincerity. His outstanding characteristic was simplicity. His mind was one that might have been cited by propaganda specialists as a perfect example of what the well-conditioned mind of a patriotic citizen ought to be. Having accepted without question at its start the contention that the Second World War was a conflict between Good and Evil, nothing that happened later disturbed this conviction. It may seem strange that travelling about Germany for over a year and seeing everywhere scenes of ghastly devastation, his faith remained unshaken in the official explanation that it was all a reprisal for a bomb said to have been dropped five years before by an unidentified plane near Canterbury.

It must be remembered, however, that relatively few people in Britain at that time had ever heard of the Lindemann Plan and there is no reason to think Lord Justice Lawrence was in possession of what was then inside information. A busy man with many responsible duties, he seems to have taken little interest in current affairs and so it may well be that his recollection of what he had read in the Press at the time concerning the Great Purge in Russia had become dim. Consequently he found no difficulty in believing even the ridiculous Stalin Myth. He accepted the appointment to represent Britain on the International Military Tribunal as a patriotic duty. He envisaged the task before him as in no way different in essentials from that of presiding over a trial of some criminal at the Old Bailey. All he imagined he would have to do was to listen to the evidence laid before the court by the prosecution and then to decide whether the charges had been established. The praise which the representatives of the Press lavished upon him for his dignified bearing filled him with surprise and irritation. Did these journalists imagine that he would sit with his feet on his desk, exchanging wisecracks with the gorilla-faced guards surrounding the prisoners in the dock! Naturally he behaved on the Bench like an English gentleman: it was regrettable that so many found his accent affected and irritating but he spoke like anyone else educated at Haileybury and who for twenty years had been a member of the Inner Temple. The reason why he never showed embarrassment when awkward situations occurred was that he never noticed anything which could embarrass him.

Thus he listened with unwearied patience to the evidence which the Communist chief prosecutor laid before the court concerning the Katyn Forest Massacre. He repressed the least sign of surprise that such transparent rubbish should be put forward as evidence. Unfortunately, however, the matter could not be disposed of simply by acquitting the prisoners of this charge. As no doubt his colleagues pointed out to him, if the Germans had not murdered these unfortunate Polish officers, then the Russians must have murdered them, since clearly these Poles could not

Chapter 7 — The Nuremberg Trials

have committed suicide and then buried themselves in a mass grave. An acquittal of the Germans would therefore be equivalent to a conviction of the Russians. The jurisdiction of the Tribunal was strictly limited by the Charter "to crimes committed in the interest of the Axis Powers".

If the Tribunal by implication convicted the Russians of this crime, Stalin would undoubtedly regard it as a flagrant breach of the London Agreement and would withdraw his representatives from the Nuremberg Trials. The result would assuredly have been an acute international crisis: the Trials which had been designed to demonstrate the unshakable unity of the Grand Alliance would have shown that unity to have been a propaganda fiction. The situation would have come about which did not in fact come about until 1948 when Stalin ordered the blockade of West Berlin.

For the first time probably it then dawned upon the mind of Lord Justice Lawrence that the proceedings over which he was presiding with such dignity had nothing to do with the administration of justice but were simply a political gesture, a move in the game of high international politics. The fate of the Nuremberg Trials hung in the balance. In spite of the (to him) unfamiliar circumstances Lord Justice Lawrence rose grandly to the occasion. Perhaps indeed the brilliant solution of what had seemed a hopeless predicament did not originate in his decidedly unoriginating mind; probably it was suggested to him by one of his colleagues, possibly by his British colleague, the far from guileless Mr. Justice Birkett. True, this solution entailed defiance of the elementary principle of justice that when the prosecution fails to establish a charge, the defendant is entitled as of right to have the charge dismissed. Such considerations of elementary justice, however, never troubled the International Military Tribunal. From the start they had acted in accordance with principles of justice which they invented in accordance with the requirements of the moment. When the time at last arrived to deliver judgment, Lord Justice Lawrence with unshakable dignity avoided all mention of the charge relating to the Katyn Forest Massacre. The Tribunal left this charge in the air and acted as if it had never been brought!

The judgment of the International Military Tribunal which was delivered on the 1st October 1946 after a hearing lasting a year, was a truly remarkable production. No doubt all the members of the Tribunal, each assisted by his team of legal

Advance to Barbarism

advisers, took a hand in drafting it. It may be that Lord Justice Lawrence did not take a leading part in this delicate work, but the duty of reading it fell upon him as chairman of the Court, and it was universally agreed that he performed this duty with an awe-inspiring gravity which almost carried conviction amongst those who heard him. The principal charge against the accused was the commission of the newly invented crime of planning and waging a war of aggression, to which charge all the other charges made were ancillary.

As previously stated, the Tribunal had utterly failed to find and agree upon a definition of "war of aggression" which would on the one hand include Hitler's invasion of Poland in 1939 and, on the other hand, would exclude the half dozen invasions launched by Stalin against the territories of the states bordering the Soviet Union. The Tribunal had given up the task of finding a definition in despair. "Aggressive war has not been and perhaps never will be adequately defined," brazenly declared Whitney R. Harris, the assistant American prosecutor at Nuremberg, "and it may be contended that the very indefiniteness of the concept makes difficult its prohibition.

But it does not follow that so elusive a concept may not afford an adequate judicial basis for criminal prosecution." Without indicating what this judicial basis was, the Tribunal decided that in view of the conviction recorded against the defendants by the chiefs of state at the Yalta Conference the defendants were clearly guilty of the offence alleged, although they were unable to say exactly what this offence was. The Tribunal was unanimously agreed that whatever this offence exactly might be, it was a very grave offence. With a solemnity which held the Court spellbound, Lord Justice Lawrence declared:

"The initiation of a war of aggression is not only an international crime, it is the supreme international crime, differing only from other war crimes in that it contains within itself the accumulated evil of the whole."

With unruffled dignity the learned chairman of the Tribunal then proceeded to deal with other matters, leaving "a war of aggression" undefined. No better example can be cited of the preeminent services rendered by Lord Justice Lawrence to the promoters of the Nuremberg Trials than the fact that this passage from the judgment of Tribunal as read by him was received at the

Chapter 7 — The Nuremberg Trials

time with general approbation as marking a memorable advance in the development of international law.

In 1962 the Oxford University historian and leading anti-German publicist, Dr. A. J. P. Taylor, sixteen years after the close of the Nuremberg Trials, ventured to express his opinion as to their nature.[92] He described the Nuremberg Tribunal as "a macabre farce" and expressed surprise that an English judge should have been found to preside over it, and that English lawyers, including the then Lord Chancellor, should have pleaded before it.[93] Many may now think "a macabre farce" an apt description of what actually took place. But for Lord Justice Lawrence's firm and dignified handling of this macabre farce, however, it would have quickly degenerated into a sordid burlesque.

Lord Justice Lawrence's outstanding services at the Nuremberg Trials were rewarded by a well-deserved peerage. How vital to the outcome of these proceedings were these services was not generally recognised at the time, and particularly by his colleague, Mr. Justice Birkett, who failed to understand that Lawrence had not been made a baron merely for spending a year among the ruins of Nuremberg, taking part as a judge at the trials. He felt strongly that he also was entitled to a peerage since, as he recorded in his diary, he, just as much as Lawrence, had had "to sit in suffering silence listening to clouds of verbiage, mountains of irrelevance and oceans of arid pomposity." When he learned that Lawrence had been made a baron, Birkett remained silent in public but he wrote privately to Lord Chancellor Jowitt: "I spent a day nursing my most grievous hurt, for it is idle to deny that I am hurt, deeply and grievously."

One may sympathise with his outraged feelings while remembering that it is a common experience of many people in this world to receive less than the justice which they think they deserve. At the time Birkett was "nursing his most grievous hurt" in comfortable retirement, others concerned in the Nuremberg trials were suffering far more acutely from injustice, as for example Grossadmiral Raeder who had been condemned to nurse the grievous hurt of having been condemned as a criminal on a transparently frivolous charge to spend the rest of his life in the gloomy horrors, humiliations and hardships of Spandau Prison.

In a nutshell the business of the International Military Tribunal was to investigate and punish war-crimes, and one may

Advance to Barbarism

pause here to consider briefly what meaning the Tribunal at length came to attach to the term, war-crime. They made no attempt to define it and no one has attempted to define it since. Originally, as we have seen, the term meant breaches of that unwritten code of civilized warfare which was adopted by the European nations in their wars with each other towards the end of the 17th century. The deliberate bombing of an enemy civilian population was obviously a breach of this code but the promoters of the Nuremberg Trials decided not to prefer charges of indiscriminate bombing against the captured enemy leaders.

This omission caused great astonishment at the time since in popular opinion this was the crime of which the Germans were most flagrantly guilty. We now know why no such charge was preferred. The Chief American Prosecutor at Nuremberg, Robert H. Jackson, many years later explained the mystery. The decision not to prefer any such charges, he tells us, was reached after long and anxious deliberation because of the difficulty of distinguishing between "the military necessity" which was accepted as justification for the destruction by British and American airmen of the cities and towns of Germany and "the military necessity" for similar destruction by German airmen. Raising this subject, he tells us naïvely, would have been *"to invite recriminations which would not have been useful at the trial."*

As a result of this decision reached after long and anxious deliberation, the Tribunal was spared any mention of the Lindemann Plan and was not therefore compelled to give any ruling on terror bombing. With regard to unrestricted submarine warfare, however, the Tribunal gave an important ruling. Grossadmiral Dönitz was charged with waging unrestricted submarine warfare, and the Tribunal reluctantly admitted that in assessing this crime an order of the British Admiralty, dated 8th May 1940, directing that all ships in the Skagerrak should in future be sunk without warning, combined with the admitted fact that the United States had waged unrestricted submarine warfare from the first day the United States had entered the war, could not be left out of account.

This ruling established the novel principle that, whether a particular act was a crime or not depended on whether the victors could be shown to have committed it. If the victors had committed it, it could not be a crime.

Chapter 7 — The Nuremberg Trials

In order to discover what meaning the Tribunal ultimately came to attach to the word "war-crime", several other factors have to be taken into consideration. First and foremost, the London Agreement made it clear that to render a person liable to punishment for a "war-crime" he must be a citizen of a state on the vanquished side. The jurisdiction of the Tribunal was strictly limited to offences committed in the interests of the Axis Powers. The moment it appeared that the offence had been committed in the interests of the victorious opponents of the Axis Powers — as happened in the case of the charges relating to the Katyn Forest Massacre — the Tribunal was forbidden to consider the subject any further. In all trials for "war-crimes" therefore, the prosecution had first of all to prove the accused was on the losing side and then, having done this, proceed to prove the accused committed the act in question.

Secondly, it is agreed that political expediency may qualify the guilt of an accused person. Thus, for example, Italian subjects admittedly committed acts which have been labelled "war crimes" and for which Germans and Japanese have been done to death. No international mass-trial of Italian subjects on the lines of the Nuremberg and Tokyo mass-trials ever took place.

Taking into account the above-mentioned exclusion of Italian subjects from prosecution for war-crimes, and the omission to include the indiscriminate bombing of civilians as a war-crime even when committed by German subjects, the following definition of a war-crime is reached:

"A war-crime is an act committed by a member of a vanquished state but not a vanquished state wholly or partially absolved from war guilt for political expediency, which in the opinion of the conquerors of that state is a war-crime, but which act is not an offence which has been so flagrantly and openly committed by the conquerors themselves that mention of it would cause them embarrassment."

A further amendment may be considered necessary, if one weighty *obiter dictum* be accepted. In the war-trials at Tokyo, in 1947-1948, the Indian representative, Mr. Justice Rahabinode Pal, delivered a brilliant dissenting judgment in which he laid down that "the farce of a trial of vanquished leaders by the victors was itself an offence against humanity", and was, therefore, in itself, a war-crime.

Advance to Barbarism

With due respect to that profound student of international law, Mr. Justice Rahabinode Pal, it is submitted that this contention would only become true if, later, the members of the tribunal found themselves on the losing side. All the authorities are agreed that being on the losing side is an essential element in a war-crime. The trial of prisoners of war by their captors may be, and generally is, a crime against humanity, but, according to the definition laid down in the London Agreement and accepted at Nuremberg, a crime against humanity is only a war-crime if it be committed "in the interests of the vanquished side".

No passage in the Nuremberg Judgment had been more frequently quoted than the passage describing the initiation of a war of aggression as "the supreme international crime, differing only from other war-crimes in that it contains within itself the accumulated evil of the whole."

Standing by itself with the words "a war of aggression" undefined, this description means nothing whatever and it is hard to explain how it came about that two experienced and learned English High Court judges were brought to endorse such pompous and meaningless verbiage. Can it, however, be a coincidence that the fundamental principle upon which the Nuremberg war-trials was based and by which the International Military Tribunal was guided, is exactly defined if the wording be altered to, "Being on the losing side is the supreme international crime, differing only from other war crimes in that it contains within itself the accumulated evil of the whole"?

It would be consistent with the terms of the Charter, the rulings of the Tribunal, and all the surrounding circumstances, if, as originally drafted, the judgment had in fact contained this illuminating definition. It is, however, easy to understand why, to the majority of the members of the Tribunal, it appeared on consideration much too illuminating. No doubt, proud of his own eloquent phraseology, the author of this particular passage, whichever member of the Tribunal it may have been, strongly objected to its elimination, and his colleagues at last came to accept the view that the passage could do no harm, provided that it was deprived of all meaning.

In fact, this celebrated passage in the judgment reads equally well if the words "To initiate a war of aggression" be substituted for the words "Being on the losing side".

Chapter 7 — The Nuremberg Trials

Except that all twenty-one accused were undeniably guilty of being on the losing side, there was no connecting link between them. The charges brought against Ernst Kaltenbrunner, the head of the Security Forces, were entirely different from those brought against Julius Streicher, the anti-Semitic editor of *Der Stuermer* and neither group of charges was even remotely connected with the charges, such as they were, brought against Grossadmiral Raeder, the commander-in-chief of the German Navy. Each day the twenty-one accused were forced to sit in the dock to listen to all the evidence collected by the prosecution, although only a small fraction of it had any bearing on any of the charges brought against any individual. Mr. Justice Birkett, as we have seen, complained bitterly at having, day after day, "to sit in suffering silence listening to clouds of verbiage, mountains of irrelevance and oceans of arid pomposity."

He was a trained lawyer, accustomed to listen to involved evidence and legal argument; he could doze when he was bored. The accused were laymen and much of what went on must have been completely incomprehensible to them. Nevertheless, being on trial for their lives they could not afford to miss any point which might possibly have a bearing, however remote, on the charges made against them personally.

To disentangle the twenty-one cases from each other and then to sketch the course of each even in outline would be a lengthy and profitless undertaking; to sketch in outline the course of the proceedings as a whole would be impossible, since the Tribunal gave no indication as to what evidence they accepted and what they rejected. All that can be done here is to trace the course of one trial so as to show how the procedure laid down by the Charter to the London Agreement worked in practice. The trial of Grossadmiral Raeder is chosen as illustrating this most clearly. The charge against Grossadmiral Raeder was under Article 6 of the Charter. It was alleged that he had committed a crime against peace by planning and directing the invasion of Norway in 1940. Undeniably as commander-in-chief of the German Navy he had taken a leading part in planning and directing this invasion. Admittedly no quarrel of any kind existed between Germany and Norway. On the face of it, therefore, this invasion was plainly an aggressive war and the London Agreement had declared that to wage an aggressive war was a crime. If it be admitted that this declaration had retrospective effect, conviction after a hearing lasting only a few hours would seem inevitable.

The case, however, was not so simple as this. No one suggested that Germany had any grievance against Norway. In a nutshell Grossadmiral Raeder's defence was that the invasion of Norway which admittedly he had planned and directed, was not undertaken as a result of any quarrel with Norway, but in order to forestall a British invasion of Norway which was on the point of being launched.

The business of the Tribunal was to punish various acts, hitherto regarded as innocent but which had been pronounced criminal by the London Agreement. In theory the Tribunal had the right to interpret the London Agreement as they pleased and to hold any act criminal subject only to the express limitation of their jurisdiction to punishing only such acts as were committed in the interests of the European Axis Powers. The Tribunal interpreted this limitation of its powers as imposing on it a duty to act on the assumption that the victorious Powers were, one and all, incapable of committing war crimes. From this as it followed logically that if one of the victorious Powers could be proved to have committed a certain act, the Tribunal had no power to declare that act a crime. The act in question received, as it were, a certificate of innocence. With remorseless logic the Tribunal decided that an act which must be regarded as innocent as having been committed in the interests of the Victors could not at the same time be pronounced a crime if committed in the interests of the vanquished.

The promoters of the Nuremberg Trials had foreseen that the Tribunal might take this view and consequently, as we have seen, no charges of indiscriminate bombing were preferred against the captured enemy leaders. Rather incautiously, however, charges of waging unrestricted submarine warfare were preferred with the result the Tribunal held that as both the Americans and British had undeniably waged unrestricted submarine warfare, it was entitled to a certificate of innocence and consequently Admiral Dönitz was entitled to be acquitted on this charge.[94]

Upon this ruling of the Nuremberg Tribunal in the Dönitz Case the fate of Admiral Raeder depended. The main charge against him was that he had planned the invasion of Norway in 1940. If he was allowed to prove that this invasion was launched to forestall a British invasion of Norway, he would be entitled

Chapter 7 — The Nuremberg Trials

to an acquittal. By the same reasoning as had led to unrestricted submarine warfare being granted a certificate of innocence, an invasion of Norway in 1940 would have to be pronounced innocent.

During the first month of the war the suggestion was made and freely discussed in the British Press that a British army should be landed on the northern coast of Norway and from there should strike across northern Sweden to the port of Lulea on the Baltic, from which port the Swedish iron ore upon which the Germ armament industry was largely dependent, was exported to Germany. If supplies from the Gallivare iron mines were cut off, Germany's output of munitions would be dealt a paralysing, perhaps ultimately a fatal, blow. To many this seemed a promising way of winning the war, far less costly than a mass attack on the Siegfried Line. The prospect of a repetition of the Somme Offensive appalled everyone. It occurred to no one at the time that there would be anything unethical, much less criminal, in invading two small neutral countries. Many felt, as Mr. Churchill put it in a Memorandum to the War Cabinet dated the 16th December, 1939, that small neutral countries ought to be glad to put up with some temporary inconvenience in order that a war being fought to preserve the rights of small countries could be won. "Humanity, not legality, should be the guide," declared Mr. Churchill. When, twenty-four hours before the German invasion of Norway was launched on April 9th, 1940, the news arrived that British minefields had been laid in Norwegian territorial waters, it was generally assumed — and, as it later proved, rightly assumed — that this was a prelude to the long discussed Norwegian invasion. In a speech on April 9th Mr. Churchill told the House of Commons that just before the German invasion British mine-fields had been laid in Norwegian territorial waters and so this fact at least could be proved by reference to Hansard.

It was not indeed known at the time of Raeder's trial that some units of the British expeditionary force had actually been embarked when the German expeditionary force left for Norway, but it was common knowledge that the British Government was planning an invasion and as a preliminary step had laid minefields near Narvik. The Tribunal reluctantly admitted that laying mines in Norwegian territorial waters was an infringement of Norwegian neutrality, but refused to accept as a fact of common knowledge that this was an overt act indicating an intention to invade Norway.

Abundant evidence as to British intentions in regard to Norway of course existed but Admiral Raeder, a closely guarded prisoner in a country in enemy occupation, had no possible means of obtaining it. There were scores of highly placed persons in Britain who knew the full truth, but there was no way of forcing them to attend the trial at Nuremberg to tell it. The Tribunal insisted on being judicially ignorant of what, as Lord Hankey wrote afterwards, "had long been a matter of public knowledge". The Tribunal dealt with the German invasion of Norway as if it had been a single isolated act without regard to current events or to the surrounding circumstances. Admiral Raeder was convicted and sentenced to life imprisonment.

It was not until he had endured for several years the carefully devised humiliations, hardships and deprivations of Spandau Prison, that the full truth gradually began to come to light. Following a brilliant outline of the events leading up to the German invasion of Norway, Lord Hankey, in his book, *Politics: Trials and Errors*[95] summarises the facts as follows:

"By the beginning of April 1940 the preparations for the major offensive operation in Norway had been completed both by the British and the Germans. Neither side had given the other an easy excuse for launching their expedition, and by a coincidence the two operations were launched almost simultaneously without any pretext having been found. The actual German landing did not take place until April 9th. Twenty-four hours before that, namely between 4.30 and 5.00 a.m. on April 8th, the British minefields had been laid in the West Fjord near Narvik."

Lord Hankey then proceeds as follows:

"From the start of planning to the German invasion, Great Britain and Germany were keeping more or less level in their plans and preparations. Britain actually started planning a little earlier, partly owing to Mr. Churchill's prescience, and partly perhaps because she had a better and more experienced system of Higher Control of the War than Germany. Throughout the period of preparations the planning continued normally. The essence of the British plan was to stop the German supplies of Gallivare ore during the winter. Both plans were executed almost simultaneously, Britain being twenty-four hours ahead in this so-

Chapter 7 — The Nuremberg Trials

called act of aggression, if the term is really applicable to either side."

Only two years after the publication of Lord Hankey's memorable work the full truth was disclosed in the first volume of a series of military histories of the Second World War entitled *The Campaign in Norway*.[96] The author, Dr. T. K. Deny, from official sources presumably not available to Lord Hankey, disclosed that as early as November 1939 the British Admiralty began to push forward in earnest plans for an invasion of Norway as a result of a report by the Ministry of Economic Warfare that if Germany's supplies of Swedish iron ore were cut off, within twelve months Germany would be unable from lack of munitions to wage active warfare. When the Soviet Union launched an unprovoked attack on Finland in November 1939, to the original purpose which an invasion of Norway and Sweden was intended to serve was added the quite distinct purpose of providing help to the gallant Finns, "sublime in the jaws of peril", as Mr. Churchill put it. On February 6th, 1940, the Supreme War Council approved detailed plans to land an army in Norway which "on its way to rescue the Finns" as Dr. Derry demurely expresses it, would seize the Swedish ore fields and the Baltic port of Lulea. The most startling revelation in this official record of the Norwegian Campaign is best summarised in the following passage from a remarkable review of this book by "Our Special Correspondent" published in *The Times* of December 10th 1952 under the title, *A Gallant Fiasco*:

"Britain was dickering with a modified version of the original scheme for securing Narvik and some troops had actually been embarked in warships when, in the early hours of April 9th, Hitler struck.

"With the exception of Oslo, which had never figured in our plans, the immediate German objectives in Norway were precisely (and inevitably) the same ports whose seizure the Allies had been assiduously plotting for many months."

The cool cynicism of this reference to "plotting for many months" will only be realised if it be remembered that when these words were written Admiral Raeder had for six years been enduring the horrors of Spandau Prison after condemnation as a criminal for exactly the same plotting.

No doubt the Special Correspondent of *The Times* when he wrote this review had forgotten completely the conviction of

249

Admiral Raeder. By the British public in general Admiral Raeder was remembered, if at all, as one of the German leaders who had been convicted at Nuremberg. Although the trials had started in the full glare of publicity, the proceedings each day being fully reported in the Press, public interest quickly faded in spite of desperate efforts to keep it alive. After the first couple of months reporting became more and more brief. Few readers attempted to work out what exactly were the charges being brought against each defendant individually.

At the end Admiral Raeder's name was just one on a list of names of defendants who had been convicted of something or other. Consequently when the full truth concerning the intended British invasion of Norway was published, there was no public outcry over what was now clearly a gross miscarriage of justice. Admiral Raeder remained in Spandau Prison until the 25th September 1955 when he was released on the ground of ill-health, having spent almost exactly nine years there "in very hard and inhumane conditions", to quote Mr. Churchill. Far more than Mr. Justice Birkett he had reason to consider himself a victim of grievous injustice since, as it has now been disclosed, he was only included in the list of major war-criminals because, as Whitney R. Harris, the assistant American prosecutor at Nuremberg, long afterwards cynically explained, "Raeder was a not illogical defendant-counterpart to Field Marshal Keitel".

While the trial of Admiral Raeder was in progress the British politicians who had "plotted" the invasion of Norway and the generals and admirals who had been given the command of the Norwegian Expeditionary Force left the International Military Tribunal to deal as best they could with the carefully selected facts produced in evidence by the prosecution. If some consciences were disturbed during this time or at Admiral Raeder's conviction, no outward sign of this disturbance was given. In fairness to the Tribunal, the extreme delicacy of the task given them should be pointed out.

How delicate this task would be was clearly overlooked by Whitney R. Harris and his colleagues when they decided to prosecute Admiral Raeder as "a not illogical defendant-counterpart to Field Marshal Keitel. It was one thing for the Tribunal to grant certificates of innocence to indiscriminate bombing and to unrestricted submarine warfare on the ground

Chapter 7 — The Nuremberg Trials

that both these forms of warfare had been waged by the victors. It was quite another thing to grant a certificate of innocence to an unprovoked invasion of Norway by Germany on the ground that this invasion was to forestall an unprovoked invasion of Norway by Britain. Such a ruling by the Tribunal would have been universally denounced, especially in small countries, as the aggressors' charter! Thenceforth every great Power would have had a ready excuse for an attack on a small state by alleging that it was intended simply to forestall an attack by another great Power. It is perhaps not entirely irrelevant to note that without any ruling by the Nuremberg Tribunal this excuse was put forward by Anthony Eden in 1956 when he claimed that the Franco-British invasion of Egypt in that year was intended to protect Egypt from an invasion by Israel.

The Tribunal could of course have resolved their difficulties by accepting Admiral Raeder's evidence that the German invasion of Norway was a countermove intended to forestall a pending British invasion, no evidence contradicting the Admiral's testimony having been tended by the prosecution, and then to have ruled that there was a fundamental distinction between the two invasions, the British invasion being intended to further a just cause and the German invasion an unjust cause. Admiral Raeder in accordance with this ruling could then have been convicted of planning and directing an invasion in an unjust cause.

Having failed however to define 'a war of aggression', the Tribunal foresaw that the same difficulty would arise in distinguishing between a just cause and an unjust cause. In fact the difficulty would be essentially the same. It would obviously be impossible to define an unjust cause without impliedly condemning the invasion of Finland by Soviet Russia in November 1939 and thereby arousing Stalin's dreaded anger. Very prudently the Tribunal decided to take no such risk.

In all criminal trials there is invariably one outstanding figure upon whom all interest centres. Generally this is the accused person in the dock. In the "Great Business" in Westminster Hall in 1649 all attention centred on "The Grand Delinquent" standing trial for his life. Few now remember anything in particular about the pack of vindictive weasels which conducted the prosecution of Charles I. The promoters of the trial, Oliver Cromwell and his "grim colonels", preferred to lurk unobtrusively in the background. In the dock at Nuremberg in that year of grace, 1945, there were twenty-one persons alleged to be delinquents, but only one who could be regarded as a Grand Delinquent. The figure of Field Marshal Herman Göring towered not only above all the other accused, but over everyone else taking part in the proceedings. This was not simply due to his recognised position as, next to Hitler, the most influential leader in the Nazi Party, the only one of the accused whose name was known throughout the world. The other occupants of the dock had little to say for themselves.

The generals and admirals, men brought up from youth in the traditions of European civilized warfare, found it hard to believe that their captors really intended to put them to death. They were prisoners of war and as such were entitled to be treated in accordance with international law codified by treaties to which the victorious Powers had been parties. But long before the Geneva Convention it had been the custom in Europe for two and half centuries to treat captured enemy military and naval leaders with respect and honour. Any act of violence against their persons would cast an indelible slur on the profession of arms. Probably they relied on their professional brethren serving in the armies and navies of the victorious Powers to veto any secret plan for their elimination which the politicians might have arranged. Anyway the novel charges probably seemed so fantastic to them as to be incomprehensible.

The other German political leaders in the dock with Göring were demoralised by the completeness of the disaster which had overtaken them and sought to meet the charges brought against them by denials, explanations, excuses and regrets. After the trial Göring is reported to have commented on Ribbentrop's appearance in the witness box, "I was sorry to see Ribbentrop break down. If I had been Foreign Minister I would have said, "That was my foreign policy and I stick to it. If you want to put me on trial for it, go ahead. You've got the power: you are the victors!'"

Whether this observation is authentic or not, it exactly expresses Göring's own attitude to the Nuremberg Trials. As an intelligent man he knew that whatever he said, he was doomed. He had not followed the example of Hitler, Goebbels and Himmler and escaped the ordeal of "a form of trial" (once again to quote General Nikitchenko's description of the proceedings)

Chapter 7 — The Nuremberg Trials

by committing suicide, because he was determined that at least someone should put on record the defence of the German people to the charges of their enemies.

In his evidence he was speaking not to the Tribunal but to posterity. Whether or not posterity will find it convincing, it was without question a masterly presentation of the German point of view. The chief American prosecutor, Robert H. Jackson, began his cross-examination with a series of carefully prepared questions, which he imagined Göring would meet with blunt denials, and so would soon entangle himself with damaging contradictions. But Göring frankly admitted the suggestions made to him. Of course from the first he had set out to bring about the downfall of the Weimar constitution. Certainly he had planned to free Germany from the unjust restrictions imposed by the dictated Treaty of Versailles. Obviously his re-creation of the Luftwaffe was a breach of the clauses of that Treaty.

So, of course, also was the re-occupation of the Rhinelands. Yes, he had been prepared to use armed force to recover the German city of Danzig, annexed by Poland in 1939. Yes, in common with statesmen of all countries in all ages, he had been willing to resort to war to achieve a political purpose. Completely baffled, Jackson lost his temper, but soon found that bullying could not shake the witness's iron self-control. In the end he was driven to appeal to the protection of the Tribunal from his intended victim.

Mr. Justice Birkett noted in his diary, "the cross-examination of Göring had not proceeded more than ten minutes before it was seen that Göring was the complete master of Justice Jackson. Suave, shrewd, adroit, capable, resourceful, he quickly saw the elements of the situation and, as his confidence grew, his mastery became more apparent. For almost two days he held the stage without interruption of any kind."

Birkett then made the ingenuous comment, astonishing from one purporting to sit in a judicial capacity, that the Tribunal should have intervened to protect bullying Counsel from this unyielding witness. Intervention, he notes, would have had the happy result of restoring Jackson's lost confidence and so would have been "for the ultimate benefit of all concerned in the trial".

Writing nearly twenty years later, the chief British prosecutor at Nuremberg, Sir David Maxwell Fyfe, in his book *Political Adventure*[97] expresses the opinion that on this point

253

"Birkett's judgment was seriously at fault. If Göring could run rings round prosecuting Counsel, that was a matter for Counsel to put right without assistance from the Tribunal". He himself then adds a glowing tribute to what he calls "Göring's insolent competence" and declares that Göring was "the most formidable witness I have ever examined."

From his book, cited above, it is clear that Sir David Maxwell Fyfe looks back with complacent satisfaction on the humiliating discomfiture of his American colleague, Jackson, as providing him with an opportunity to pay himself a glowing tribute for what he describes as his own masterly cross-examination of the fallen Nazi leader. Resolutely ignoring Göring's "jibes and insolence, his sallies, his wit and sneers," he concentrated on the charge which most deeply interested the British public, the charge that Göring was personally responsible for the shooting of some fifty British airmen who had effected a mass escape from a prison camp known as Stalag Luft III. He suggests that he succeeded in establishing this charge although not apparently to the Tribunal's satisfaction, judging from the fact the Tribunal followed the practice they had adopted in the case of the Katyn Forest charges and omitted all reference to this charge in the judgment, the accused on this charge being neither convicted nor acquitted.

Perhaps the failure of the Tribunal to recognise that he had succeeded where Jackson had so signally failed may account for Sir David's rather tart references to the British judge, Birkett. He consoled himself for this disappointment by claiming that he extracted damaging admissions by Göring with regard to the treatment of captured Allied airmen, shot down when carrying out the Lindemann Plan, of partisans operating behind the German lines, and of the inhabitants of the countries in German occupation. And even Sir David, with his unlimited capacity for self-congratulation, could not claim that Göring's conviction was due to his brilliant cross-examination since the judgment of the Tribunal, read with special solemnity by Lord Justice Lawrence, stressed that Göring was being convicted on the charges which he himself had contemptuously admitted. The wording of the judgment is as follows:

"Göring was often, indeed almost always, the moving force, second only to his leader. He was the leading war aggressor both as political and as military leader; he was the director of the slave-labour programme and the creator of the oppressive programme against the Jews and other races, at home and abroad. All of these aims he has frankly admitted. On some special cases there may be conflict of testimony, but in terms of the broad outline his admissions are more than sufficiently wide to be conclusive of his guilt. His guilt is unique in its enormity. The record discloses no excuses for this man."

The objections to the Nuremberg Trials as a whole are so many, so grave and so unanswerable that if an international court of appeal composed of judges from neutral countries had been in existence in 1946, before which the doings of the International Military Tribunal could have been brought, no doubt the judgments delivered at Nuremberg would have been quashed *in toto*, including the conviction of Hermann Göring. Without going into the details of particular charges against particular individuals, an impartial court of appeal would have declared the proceedings *void ab initio* as based on contentions repugnant to the fundamental principles of justice.

That the Tribunal's findings of fact, apart from findings of guilt, carry no weight has now become generally recognised. How utterly discredited the Nuremberg Trials have become was strikingly demonstrated during the heated controversy which arose in 1961 between the rival Oxford University historians, Trevor Roper and A. J. P. Taylor, following the publication of the latter's book in which he refuted the propaganda fiction that Hitler was solely responsible for the outbreak of the Second World War. Trevor Roper had declared that this exposure of the truth would do "irreparable harm", and on the 9th July, 1961, the B.B.C. arranged a televised debate between these two learned gentlemen.

Taylor in his book had not troubled to mention the findings of the Nuremberg Tribunal on the subject of war guilt and it was confidently expected that Trevor Roper would summarily dispose of his opponent's contentions by drawing his attention to these findings and pointing out that the questions dealt with in Taylor's book were *res judicata*, having been settled once and for all by the judgment of the Tribunal.

To the general surprise, however, Trevor Roper did not once refer to the judgment. Tacitly, therefore, he accepted Taylor's view that the unanimous findings of the eight learned judges reached after what purported to be an investigation of the facts lasting a year, were not worth citing even as a pointer in the direction of the truth.

Unquestionably any conviction following a trial conducted on the lines of the Nuremberg Trials would in any civilized Western country be quashed without hesitation by a court of criminal appeal. Unquestionably also many of the convictions pronounced by the International Military Tribunal were in themselves undeniably gross miscarriages of justice: perhaps of these the conviction of Admiral Raeder may be cited as the most indefensible. On the other hand it does not necessarily follow from this that all the accused convicted at Nuremberg were wrongly convicted. Several of them were clearly guilty of abominable crimes against humanity.

When condemning a lynching one is apt to regard the person done to death as the victim of lawless violence although probably in the majority of cases the victims of lynching deserve their fate. Similarly in regard to many of the accused at Nuremberg. The case of Field Marshal Hermann Göring is one in which it can be reasonably argued that on the facts proved his conviction was wrong, while it is possible also to argue that no injustice resulted from his conviction and that he richly deserved his fate.

The principal charge on which Göring was convicted was that he had planned and waged an aggressive war. This admittedly was not a crime when allegedly he had committed it but was declared to be a crime by the London Agreement of the 8th August 1945, a declaration which was treated as having retrospective effect.

Göring frankly admitted planning and waging a war for a political purpose and since as we have seen the Tribunal deliberately refrained from defining an aggressive war, we are left without guidance as to the nature of the war for which Göring was admittedly partly responsible. Of course if one accepts the view that any resorting to war to achieve a political purpose is *per se* a crime, then clearly Göring's conviction was justified.

One hesitates to accept this view since it entails the admission that Anthony Eden was a criminal in 1956 when he ordered a British army to invade Egypt in alliance with France and Israel, the saintly Pandit Nehru was a criminal in 1961 when he invaded and annexed the four hundred year old Portuguese possession of Goa, and the Sectariat of U.N.O. were criminals in

Chapter 7 — The Nuremberg Trials

1963 when they ordered their forces in the Congo to invade the province of Katanga!

Apparently the Tribunal came to the conclusion that the prosecution had failed to establish Göring's personal responsibility for any of the specific crimes against humanity brought against him or for any of the specific war-crimes as defined under the unwritten code of European civilized warfare, as for example the alleged shooting of the British airmen escaping from Stalag Luft III. Very reasonably however they held that Göring as a leading member of a government which had authorised wholesale crimes against humanity of the most frightful description must be deemed to bear a share of the burden of the collective guilt. They rejected his claim that the Air Ministry of which he was the head was not concerned with the doings of Himmler and the S.S., and that although he knew of the existence of the concentration camps to which Jews and others were being sent, he had no knowledge of what was going on in these camps. It was as if a member of the British Cabinet in 1942 who was able to prove that he had not been present at the cabinet meeting at the end of March of that year when the Lindemann Plan was adopted, subsequently maintained that he had no personal knowledge that a terror bombing campaign in accordance with this plan was being conducted against the German civilian population. For once taking up a position on firm ground, the Tribunal convicted Göring, as the judgment expressed it, "in terms of the broad outline."

The trial of Field Marshal Hermann Göring owes its unique interest among the trials of modern times not certainly to the legal technicalities which arose during its course, most of which indeed arose during the concurrent trials of the other twenty defendants, nor to the discomfiture of the bullying prosecutor, Robert H. Jackson, nor to the demonstration, to his own satisfaction, of Sir David Maxwell Fyfe's gifts as a cross-examiner, nor even to the unruffled dignity of the president of the Tribunal, but to the colourful personality and unflinching courage of the defendant.

Success, political power and wealth had brought all the faults and weaknesses of Göring's character uppermost. Those who remembered the handsome young flying officer who in 1918 had taken over the command of Baron von Richthofen's Jagdgeschwader I of the famous 'Flying Circus' on the death of the Red Baron, hardly recognised as the same man the corpulent

Advance to Barbarism

figure, bedecked with medals, of the most powerful man in the Third Reich next to the Führer himself. He had in the course of twenty years become self-indulgent, vulgar, unscrupulous and ruthless, a braggart and a bully. Disaster brought about an equally astonishing transformation. The semi-starvation to which like all the other prisoners he was subjected during his captivity — the reader will remember the pre-conviction punishment inflicted on Bessos before his trial — worked a miracle on his appearance and in his character. He faced his accusers with the same dauntless spirit with which during, the First World War he had set forth in his plane against the overwhelming air strength of the Allies. In June 1918 he knew that the war was lost but at least he could bring down a few more enemy planes: in October 1945 he knew that he was doomed and that nothing he could do or say would avert his fate but at least he could score a few last triumphs, if only verbal ones, over his captors.

As a youth Göring had been prone to making defiant gestures. In 1918 after the signing of the Armistice he received orders to fly his squadron to some airfield in France and there surrender it: risking a well-deserved court martial, he refused to obey and led his squadron back to its base in Germany as a protest, a rather futile protest, it must be admitted, against fate. In 1946 after he left the dock in Nuremberg for the last time it must have seemed that there remained nothing further for him to do but to wait until the hangman was ready to deal with him. Ever since his arrest at Kitzbuhel his enemies throughout the world had been gloating over the prospect of his execution as some compensation for their disappointment over the suicide of Hitler about which they could only comfort themselves by pious reflections on the sanctity of human life and the enormity of the sin of self-destruction. The execution of Göring was to have been a sort of sacramental act: it was intended that in his person the whole National Socialist Party should expiate its shortcomings, follies and crimes by an ignominious death on a gallows. Extraordinary and most stringent precautions were taken to make it absolutely certain that Göring possessed no means of committing suicide and that no such means should reach him.

How Göring, shortly before midnight and less than an hour before the time fixed for his execution, succeeded in committing suicide remains after over twenty years a mystery. Charles Bewley

Chapter 7 — The Nuremberg Trials

in his biography of Göring[98] assures us that all the guesses made to date as to what happened have been baseless and that the truth has not been disclosed by the surviving members of Göring's family because the essential role was played by "a non-German in the prison" whose identity must be kept secret.

It seems indeed scarcely believable that among Göring's carefully selected guards was a foreign sympathiser with the Nazi movement. On the other hand we know that the accused when they were removed from the dock to the cells beneath were subjected to the harshest, if not brutal, treatment. This fact is made clear by the complaint made in open court by Julius Streicher to the Tribunal that he had been violently assaulted by his jailers who among other indignities had forced him to drink his own urine. The truth of this complaint finds some confirmation in the fact that not only did the Tribunal refuse to order an investigation but on the application of Rob H. Jackson, the chief American prosecutor, they ordered that this complaint should be deleted from the record of Streicher's evidence, so that future historians, studying the Nuremberg Trials, and imagining the shorthand notes of the proceedings were complete, would not know that this complaint had been made. It is not unlikely that this incident suggested to George Orwell the periodic re-writing of history to suit the political requirements of the moment which he describes in *Nineteen Eighty-four*. Whether Streicher's complaint be accepted or not, it is at any rate certain that no control was exercised over the treatment of the prisoners and it is therefore just conceivable that some witness of this treatment may have been inspired by disgust and sympathy to intervene.

Whatever the motives of this unknown person may have been, the Grand Delinquent of Nuremberg found himself literally at the eleventh hour in possession of what before anything else in the world he desired to have. His jailors found him lying on his plank bed as if asleep with an amused smile on his lips and an empty file of cyankali on the floor beside him. Even many who attributed their wrongs to him have come to the conclusion that this was a fitting end to the career of the famous fighter pilot for which the most hackneyed lines in literature might well have been expressedly written, "Nothing in his life became him like the leaving it."

Chapter 8 — The Last Phase

The mass-trial of the leading German politicians and service chiefs at Nuremberg was the natural outcome of a war in which one side had adopted terror bombing and the other genocide as part of their war effort. No other outcome was to be expected. It was just one stage of the chain reaction which had started in 1914. The Nuremberg mass-trial however was only one episode of this stage in the chain reaction which included not only the equally significant mass-trial of the Japanese leaders at Tokyo, but many thousand war-crimes trials of prisoners of war which took place in widely separated places in Europe and Asia and continued for a period of half a dozen years.

The Nuremberg War-crimes Trial overshadows all other war-crimes trials held after 1945 because, when it started, all the manifold resources of the science of modern propaganda were concentrated upon it in order to implant in the public mind the conviction that the disposal of the leaders of a defeated and discredited political party was an event of unique significance for all mankind. In itself of course it mattered nothing whether these ill-fated men died on a scaffold or were allowed to die a natural death in their beds, but the promoters of the trial had determined to represent their disposal as a symbolic act which could be made the subject for worldwide jollification.

Consequently no pains were spared to give the proceedings the widest publicity. While at first the reaction of the public was all that could have been desired, the arrangements made were so clumsy and elaborate that the proceedings dragged on for nearly a year and the public became bored with so protracted a performance. One cannot remain in a state of joyful ecstasy for eleven months! Nevertheless the conviction was successfully planted in the public mind that the Nuremberg War-crimes Trial was of unique importance.

No comparable attempt was made to give publicity to any of the other war-crimes trials which took place from 1945 onwards. Not one of these war-crimes trials, even the great Tokyo War-crimes Trial, was reported in any detail in the British Press. Every few days over a period of half a dozen years the execution of some prisoner of war was announced unobtrusively as an item of news on the back pages of the newspapers but the victim was merely described as a war-criminal and rarely was any mention made of his alleged offence. The vast majority of war-crimes trials were never reported at all.

It will be remembered that the Nuremberg Tribunal was created by Article I of the London Agreement to try "war-criminals whose offences had no particular geographical location." This Article referred only to prisoners who before their trial were labelled 'major war-criminals'. In the preamble to the Agreement reference was made to the Moscow Declaration of the 30th October 1943 by which it had been agreed that prisoners who were responsible for crimes committed in a particular country should be sent back to that country "to be judged and punished according to the laws of that country." It was assumed that prisoners already in captivity in the country where they were alleged to have committed crimes would be dealt with by their captors as the latter saw fit and so no international agreement was needed to provide for their liquidation.

So long as Germany remained able to resist, fear of reprisals offered protection to German prisoners of war. The moment unconditional surrender had taken place, this protection was removed and the work of disposal was gleefully undertaken in all the victorious countries. Not only did executions commence but in accordance with the Moscow Declaration a brisk traffic of prisoners of war began. It frequently happened as had been foreseen at the Moscow Conference in 1943 that several of the victorious Powers would claim the right to bring to trial and to liquidate the same prisoner of war. Keen bargaining then often resulted. Thus, for example, it might happen that Czechs held some officer of high rank as a prisoner of war against whom they had no particular grudge but against whom both the Poles and Serbs had laid distinct sets of charges. Each claimant would then make an offer for the victim. Thus the Poles might offer to hand over in exchange to the Czechs an officer of equal rank whom the

Advance to Barbarism

Czechs wanted to hang while the Serbs would offer to hand over a dozen S.S. men of a unit upon whom the Czechs particularly desired to lay their hands. Like antique dealers, the victorious Powers exchanged lists of the human commodities which they had for barter. Once a claim had been laid the victim was handed over unless the Power whose prisoner he was happened to have charges of its own against him. The principle upon which the Moscow Declaration was based was that the accusers of a prisoner were not only eligible to try their own charges against him but were the parties most eligible to try these charges. It was argued that as conviction and justice were in practice synonymous, the swiftest and surest way of ensuring a conviction must also be the swiftest and surest way of dispensing justice. None of the victorious Powers acknowledged any obligation to investigate any charge made by one of its allies against a prisoner of war in its custody. The fact that a charge was made was accepted as evidence of sufficient 'probative value' to indicate the victim's guilt. The only obligation admitted once a claim had been laid for the surrender of a prisoner of war was to take all necessary precautions to prevent the victim from committing suicide.

The official attitude in such cases is well expressed in the following extract from a letter dated the 19th December 1960 from a high official in the British Foreign Office in reply to an appeal for intervention by Britain to secure the release by Italy of Major Walter Reder, a German prisoner of war who after being in British custody for over a year had been handed over to the Italians so that they could try their own charges against him. An outline of the facts of this remarkable case will be given later in this chapter. This illuminating extract reads as follows:

"When you wrote in March 1958, Mr. David Ormsby-Gore said in reply that we were afraid that we were unable to help; that Reder had been handed over to Italian jurisdiction and from that moment the case had become one for Italian penological and clemency procedures; and that the fact that we had handed Reder over did not give us any say in these procedures. I am afraid that the situation is unchanged. At the end of the war, there were, as you know, a great number of war-Criminals whom two or more countries wanted to try, and the decision in each case had to be taken on an *ad hoc* basis. It was of course very much a matter of chance whose forces originally captured any particular war-

Chapter 8 — The Last Phase

criminal, and the fact that Reder was originally in our hands does not, I am afraid, give us any right to intervene on his behalf with the Italians. Once he had been handed over, he was removed entirely from our jurisdiction."

This letter left unanswered the question why the British military authorities in Italy handed Major Reder over to the Italians in order that they might try their own charges against him instead of putting him on trial before a British military tribunal as they had done with his superior officers, Field Marshal Kesselring and General Max Simon, under whose orders Major Reder had acted. To this day the reason why this extraordinary procedure was adopted remains a mystery: to this day also after over twenty years Major Reder remains in captivity.

War-crimes trials took many different forms. In fact the only characteristic common to all of them was that they were all based on the principle that an accuser is a fit person to act as judge of his own charges. In accordance with the Moscow Declaration, each country dealt with its prisoners of war according to its own notions of justice, however vague these notions might be. The procedures adopted even by the civilized Powers varied greatly. Thus the Americans followed to a large extent the terms of the Charter of the London Agreement and in accordance therewith prosecuted Field Marshal Sperrle and eleven other generals for the 'ersatz' crime of planning, preparing and initiating aggressive warfare: they also prosecuted a group of German Foreign Office officials on the same charge.

Most grotesquely of all they even undertook the prosecution of the directors of Krupps in an effort to establish by a judicial decision a factual basis for the Krupp Myth, the most celebrated myth of the First World War.[99]

The British, on the other hand, very wisely ignored the creation of such newly invented crimes and prosecuted their prisoners of war only for "violations of the laws and usages of war," — that is to say, of breaches of that code of civilized warfare first tacitly adopted at the end of the 17th century which was examined at length in Chapters 4 and 5 of this book. This course was possible without blatant absurdity at the time because the adoption of the Lindemann Plan by the British Government in March 1942 was not disclosed until 1961, long after the last war-crimes trial had ended. The adoption of terror bombing as a

Advance to Barbarism

means of winning a war was of course the most flagrant breach conceivable of "the laws and usages of war."

War-crimes trials carried out in the years immediately following 1945 may be roughly classified into four main groups under the following headings, The *Spectacular War-crimes Trial*: the *Informal War-crimes Trial*: the *Show War-crimes Trial* and the *Routine War-crimes Trial*.

In the previous chapter a description was given of the first and most celebrated Spectacular War-crimes Trial, the mass-trial of the captured German leaders at Nuremberg. In a war-crimes trial of this type the leaders of a vanquished Power are disposed of with the maximum publicity. The view that the aim of such a war-crimes trial is to wreak vengeance on hated national enemies is inadequate and superficial. The immediate purpose is to establish conclusively the fact that the vanquished Power had been completely defeated so that no question of this could possibly later arise as it did after the First World War when many Germans persuaded themselves that Germany had not been overcome by force of arms but had been beguiled into signing the Armistice on the promise that the peace treaty would be based on the Fourteen Points.

The ultimate purpose of a Spectacular War-crimes Trial is to stifle future investigation by historians of the rights and wrongs of the struggle in question by a formal verdict by a Court appointed by the victors which lays the entire blame on the vanquished. After the First World War it was hoped to achieve the latter purpose by inserting an admission of guilt by the vanquished in the peace treaty which they were compelled to sign without discussion. It was soon found, however, that Clause 231 of the Versailles Treaty had become generally dismissed as worthless as having been extorted under duress. After the Second World War the victors decided to achieve the same object by staging a lengthy investigation of carefully selected evidence leading to a solemn verdict proclaiming the guilt of the vanquished. After the passage of twenty years, however, it has become open to doubt whether the verdict of the International Military Tribunal will carry any greater weight with posterity than the notorious Clause 231 of the Versailles Treaty.

The only other Spectacular War-crimes trial which has taken place since 1945 was the great mass war-crimes trial held

Chapter 8 — The Last Phase

in Tokyo of the vanquished Japanese leaders. It was an even more grandiose affair than the Nuremberg Trials; whereas at Nuremberg there were 21 defendants and the trial lasted 331 days, at Tokyo there were 27 defendants and the trial lasted 417 days. "At Tokyo," commented Lord Hankey, "most of the weaknesses of the Nuremberg Trials were repeated and exaggerated". The Tokyo mass-trial was presented to the American public as a subject for rejoicing but by the time it started the British public had become utterly bored by war-crimes trials in general and no attempt was made in Britain to arouse interest in what purported to be legal proceedings in far-off Japan. It happened that while the trial was in progress Stalin abandoned the pretence of being a friendly ally by establishing by force a Communist dictatorship in Czechoslovakia and by blockading West Berlin, and with the prospect of a third world war starting at any moment, few interested themselves in the liquidation of the Japanese leaders. Dr. Bell, the Bishop of Chichester, who, during the war, alone among the prelates of the Church of England, had raised a voice in protest against terror bombing, dismissed the proceedings in one short sentence, "As at Nuremberg, so at Tokyo, the victors tried and condemned the vanquished."

Summarising this mass-trial in more detail and from an American point of view, Mr. George F. Blewitt writes:

"The basic fact of this war-trial is that the victorious Powers tried twenty-seven leaders of the defeated nation for violation of *ex post facto* law. Because the charter of the Tribunal was issued by a General of the U.S. Army; because the defendants were in the custody of the U.S. Army; because the Chief of Prosecution was a prominent American; because the costs of the trial were met by funds from the U.S. Treasury; and because the seven found guilty by a majority verdict were hanged by Americans—for all these reasons—the long-run effects of the trial are likely to be far more damaging to the prestige of the United States than to any other Nation represented on the Tokyo Tribunal."[100]

Some have even maintained that the conviction of Mamoru Shigemitsu at the mass-trial in Tokyo was an even grosser and less excusable miscarriage of justice than the conviction of Admiral Raeder at the mass-trial at Nuremberg. This may seem to be putting the matter impossibly high but there are facts to support it. At the outbreak of war Shigemitsu was the Japanese

Ambassador in London. All his life he had opposed the dominant group of militarist politicians which plunged Japan into war in December 1941, and it was not indeed alleged at his trial that he was in any way responsible for this disastrous decision. After the outbreak of war he returned to Japan, but it was not until after the tide of war had definitely turned against Japan that he joined the Japanese Cabinet, by which time no other course was open to him or any other Japanese politician than to do everything possible to maintain so stout a resistance that reasonable terms of peace would be offered. Unconditional surrender was, however, demanded. Shigemitsu was charged with the crime of being a member of the Japanese Cabinet at the time of Japan's surrender after the explosion of the first atomic bombs. The French and Dutch judges on the Tokyo Tribunal delivered dissenting judgments acquitting him on all counts, but the majority judgment found him guilty and he was condemned to seven years' imprisonment.

It is some consolation for the fact that the British representatives on the Tribunal were among the majority of the judges which reached this absurd conclusion, that the speedy rectification of this glaring miscarriage of justice was mainly due to the efforts of Lord Hankey, who crowned his long career of outstanding public service by devoting his tireless energies to obtaining justice for the victims of war-crimes trials. In a memorable speech in the House of Lords on the 19th May 1949 Lord Hankey delivered a scathing attack on the condemnation of Shigemitsu, making public for the first time the details of his so-called trial. These details were then quite unknown in Britain; only three weeks before the debate in the House of Lords the transcripts of the Tokyo war-crimes trials had arrived in London consisting of "a pile of double-spaced foolscap 30-feet high, including 48,000 pages of evidence, the Majority Judgment of 1,600 pages and the Minority Judgments of 1,500 pages."[101]

In reply for the Government the Lord Chancellor, Viscount Jowett, expressed serene confidence that everything had been done in accordance with the high standards of British justice and was at pains to defend the integrity of the judges conducting the trials at Tokyo, in particular the British judge, Lord Patrick, although, of course, in fact no one had called their integrity in question. The House of Lords however languidly declined to interest itself in the question of justice to war-criminals. To break

Chapter 8 — The Last Phase

down this indifference, Lord Hankey then proceeded to set out the facts in his book, *Politics: Trials and Errors*, a work memorable as the only book written after the war which had a definite influence on the course of contemporary events. As a direct result of the publicity given to his case by this book, combined with the support of General MacArthur which Lord Hankey managed to enlist, Mamoru Shigemitsu was shortly released.

In passing it may be observed that the attitude of Viscount Jowett to the question of tempering justice with mercy was, to say the least, peculiar. "He did not say in so many words that he supported the conviction of Shigemitsu," writes Lord Hankey, "but he gave that impression." On the other hand, Viscount Jowett later wrote a book concerning the conviction of the communist spy Alger Hiss in which, while carefully avoiding saying that he believed Hiss was innocent, he urged that if only the Americans had been wise enough to have adopted the same rules of evidence as those in force in England there was a good chance that Hiss would have escaped justice, an outcome of the trial he clearly thought would have been very desirable. While strenuously defending the belated trial of Field Marshal von Manstein on transparently frivolous charges, he supported the great communist propaganda campaign to secure a reprieve for Julius and Ethel Rosenberg, the New York Jews who betrayed the secrets of the atomic bomb to the Soviet Union.

The most outstanding feature of the Tokyo war-crime trials was the brilliant dissenting judgment of Mr. Justice Radhabinode Pal, the representative of India on the Tribunal, who was, says Mr. Blewitt, "the only deep student of international law on the Bench". In a 1,900-page judgment Mr. Justice Pal tore in shreds one by one the various charges against the accused. "A mere declaration of intent," he declared "could not give the Allies any legal right to define war-criminals in a manner which suited their policies at the moment." He held that there was no evidence to show that any of the accused were war-criminals according to the previously accepted definition of the term, and declared, regardless of the feelings of his colleagues on the Bench, that *"to purport to put on trial and then to hang prisoners of war was in itself a war-crime of peculiar gravity."*

Nothing illustrates more vividly how complete has been the reversal of public opinion which has taken place during the past twenty years concerning racial equality than the reference in the charges against the defendants at Tokyo to the war commenced by Japan in December 1941 as "an aggressive war conducted for the purpose of securing military and political domination of East Asia."

Few at the present time would venture so to describe this war because they have been subconsciously conditioned by the now widely accepted axiom of so-called progressive thought that in any conflict between the White Race and the Black or Coloured Races, the White Man is always in the wrong, and they feel it would somehow be disgracefully "reactionary" to dispute this axiom. Certainly no responsible politician in any country would now dare to brave the wrath of the Afro-Asian bloc in the Assembly of UNO by referring in such terms to a struggle which brought about the downfall of Colonialism in Eastern Asia and led to independence being achieved by half a dozen coloured nations from the bondage of Western Imperialism. Contemporary opinion, however, regarded the Tokyo war-crimes trial as well-merited retribution on a race of presumptuous yellow dwarfs for daring to challenge White supremacy in the Far East and, while the struggle remained on equal terms, for proving themselves more than a match for the White Race.

Informal war-crimes trials, the second of the four classes into which war-crimes trials may be divided, are the exact opposite of *Spectacular War-crime trials*. War-crimes trials of this kind seem to have been particularly common in the Soviet Union. The first step in such a trial is a decision by the officials of the government department which had been entrusted with the task of disposing of prisoners of war, that a particular enemy unit should be held responsible for the commission of a certain alleged crime. Once this decision had been reached nothing remained to be done but to order that parades should be held of the inmates in all the prisoner of war camps in the country so that the members of this unit could be picked out. The unfortunates in each camp so picked out would then be paraded separately from their comrades when they would be informed that they had been collectively judged guilty of the offence in question and had been sentenced to a long term of forced labour in Siberia.

It may perhaps be argued that *Informal War-crimes Trials* are not really trials at all. The decision of a government department cannot be described as a judicial verdict. To this objection the reply can be made that in a rough and ready way this procedure followed the august precedent established at Nuremberg where "the major war criminals of European Axis Powers" had already been adjudicated and found guilty (to quote once again the Russian judge at Nuremberg, General Nikitchenko) by the Chiefs of State at the Yalta Conference. The only distinction which can be drawn between the two cases is that the decision to convict the prisoners at Nuremberg was reached by a group of powerful politicians representing their respective countries, while in cases of *Informal War-crimes Trials* a similar decision to convict is reached by a committee of obscure bureaucrats. It can at least be said in favour of informal War-crimes Trials that the victims are spared the ordeal of having to listen to pompous speeches, and no pretence is made that strict justice is being meted out to individuals.

For the third class of war-crimes trials the name *Show War-crimes Trial* has been suggested. This procedure seems to have been most frequently adopted in Czecho-slovakia. The prisoner is taken to the place where he is alleged to have committed his crime and the trial takes place there publicly before a jury composed of the relations and friends of his alleged victims and is followed by his execution amid general rejoicings. This procedure has in recent years been employed in an elaborated form in Cuba by Fidel Castro for the disposal of adherents of the fallen Batista regime, following the precedent already set in China after the establishment of a communist regime by Mao Tse Tung. In China, after 1949, persons accused of being anti-Communist were tried in the place where they resided by a mass jury composed of their neighbours.

All the forms of a judicial trial are strictly observed. The proceedings are commenced by a speech by the prosecuting official in which the offences of the accused are graphically described at length amid great applause. The accused then recites his confession amid demonstrations of popular indignation and anger. The judge then solemnly announces his verdict which is of course loudly cheered. The execution then follows amid a general jollification that the punishment should so satisfactorily fit the crime. This class of war trial puts into practice the suggestion of W. S. Gilbert in *The Mikado* that each prisoner pent should provide the community with innocent merriment.[102]

The vast majority of war-crimes trials form a distinct group which, for want of a better term, may be labelled *Routine War-crimes Trials*. Outwardly most of them took the form of normal criminal prosecutions. The two *Spectacular War-crimes Trials* which followed the Second World War were essentially political demonstrations in the form of a legal trial in accordance with the principle adopted in the Yalta Conference which was well summarised by Field Marshal Montgomery in a speech he made in Paris on June 9th, 1948, "The waging of an unsuccessful war is a crime; henceforth generals on the defeated side will be tried and then hanged."

As we have seen, to date only two examples of this type of trial have taken place; the murder of Benito Mussolini by a communist liquidation squad "at least spared the world an Italian Nuremberg," to quote Winston Churchill's comment in his book, *Triumph and Tragedy*, and Stalin disposed of the leaders of the other vanquished Powers, Hungary, Roumania and Bulgaria, without inviting the participation of his allies. The practice of disposing of prisoners of war after Informal War-crimes Trials does not seem to have been widely adopted outside the Soviet Union while only in semi-civilized countries were Show War-crimes Trials carried out and no statistics are available to provide a basis even for a guess as to the total number of victims. On the other hand, many thousands of prisoners of war were done to death in Europe and Asia after Routine War-crimes Trials.

War-crimes Trials of this type were all conducted on the lines of a court-martial in accordance with the military law of the country in which they were held. Generally they concerned such undoubted criminal acts as robbery, looting, or the murder or maltreatment of prisoners or civilians, acts which would be criminal if committed by anyone but are dealt with under military law when the alleged offenders happen to be soldiers and who, as prisoners of war, remain under military discipline. The same military courts also dealt with alleged breaches "of the laws and usages of war", to quote the phrase adopted by the British military authorities. Occasionally, as we have seen, the American authorities brought to trial before their military courts enemy prisoners of war and even enemy civilians charged with the commission of one or other of the newly invented "ersatz" crimes, such as planning or waging a war of aggression.

Chapter 8 — The Last Phase

Unlike the so-called International Military Tribunal which sat at Nuremberg, most of whose members were civilians, the adjudicating body in Routine War-crimes Trials was invariably composed of three or more army officers generally assisted by a lawyer who advised the court on military law. Rarely in cases of this type was an attempt made to interest the general public in the proceedings, and only in cases when the accused was a well known enemy leader did the British Press, at any rate, spare more than a few lines to record that the prisoner had been tried and executed. Particulars of his alleged offence were rarely supplied. Naturally, the treatment accorded to the accused at the hearing varied widely according to the standard of civilization reached in the country in which the trial took place, the extent to which that country had suffered during the war, and to the national temperament.

British military tribunals carried out their duties in a brisk, business-like way, carefully avoiding the appeals to emotion and flights of eloquence in which, for example, French military tribunals indulged. A routine procedure, more or less based on the Charter of the London Agreement, was soon established and thereafter punctiliously observed. Conviction before British courts was not automatic as it was in Routine War-crimes Trials conducted beyond the Iron Curtain. The issues to be decided by the military tribunals were simple issues of fact: should the evidence for the prosecution be accepted or the denials of the accused? Objections raised to the jurisdiction given to the Tribunals by a Royal Warrant to try foreign subjects were curtly dismissed: it was not until one of the last war-crimes trials, that of Field Marshal von Manstein in Hamburg in 1949, that these objections were permitted to be urged at length with the result that prosecuting counsel in this trial was reduced to arguing that as it had long been the established practice to reject these objections, to admit them now would amount to admitting that all the many hundreds of convictions recorded by British military tribunals of prisoners of war were invalid.

Naturally the Hamburg tribunal recoiled from coming to so far-reaching and distressing a conclusion, and therefore decided to dispose of the matter by acting on the assumption that the Warrant of King George VI. had somehow conferred on them jurisdiction to adjudicate on charges brought against foreign subjects. They tried and convicted Field Marshal von Manstein accordingly.

No doubt the great majority of the British officers called upon in the course of their duties to serve on war-crimes tribunals were fair-minded men who did their best to dispense justice and at the same time to carry out what they conceived to be the wishes of their superiors. How often and how grossly they failed in the general run of the unrecorded cases which came before them can only be deduced from the glaring miscarriages of justice which resulted from carefully recorded prosecutions as that of Field Marshal Kesselring and Field Marshal von Manstein. Having regard to the state of public opinion at the time it was inevitable that when forced to choose between the evidence for the prosecution and the evidence for the defence, they invariably accepted the former. In brief, their attitude to the prisoners of war brought before them was similar to that of a bench of sporting country magistrates in England a century ago when forced to choose between the evidence of a gamekeeper and the evidence of an alleged poacher.

It might well be imagined that the course of all war-crimes trials would be governed by the provisions of the Geneva Convention of 1899 and the Hague Convention of 1907 which (*inter alia*) laid down clearly defined rules as to the treatment of prisoners of war. In brief it had been solemnly agreed by all civilized countries that prisoners of war had a right to be treated similarly to the members of their captors' armed forces: that offences committed by them when in captivity should be dealt with in accordance with the military law of the country holding them captive: and that they were entitled to release as soon as practicable after hostilities ceased.

During the Manstein Trial, defending counsel for the accused, Mr. R. T. Paget, clearly summarised Article 63 of the Geneva convention as follows, "The Convention provides that when a prisoner is tried by his captors, he shall have a fair trial, and defines a fair trial as a trial which the captor himself considered fair for his own troops."

When these international treaties were ratified they were acclaimed as outstanding landmarks in the course of human progress: no longer would the rights of prisoners of war be based on a mere tacit understanding between civilized peoples: these

Chapter 8 — The Last Phase

rights had become defined and codified by treaty and consequently these rights would henceforth be unassailable.

It is distressing to record that when in 1945 the matter was first put to the test it was found that rights granted by international treaties were illusory if the will to disregard them existed. By a pettifogging quibble which would have delighted the hearts of those astute legal practitioners, Dodson and Fogg, late of Freeman Court, the obligations imposed at Geneva and the Hague were summarily set aside. It was pointed out that a prisoner of war was a captured enemy soldier and therefore if he ceased to be a soldier he would lose the unassailable rights of a prisoner of war. All that the captors of a prisoner of war had to do was to declare that he had become a civilian by announcing that he had been 'demobilised', a transformation which was carried out by formally depriving him of his uniform or by simply depriving him of his insignias of rank: Once he had become a civilian, his captors could treat him as they pleased. All the victims of war-crimes trials were tried and condemned as civilians.[103]

It only remains to illustrate by examples how in practice a Routine War-crimes Trial was conducted. Five examples have been chosen, two British, one American, one Italian and one French. It cannot be claimed that any of these five trials can be regarded as representing the average Routine War-crimes Trial. In all of them the adjudicating military tribunal took its duties seriously and listened carefully to the evidence placed before it both by the prosecution and by the defence. In the American example chosen, the Trial of General Yamashita, the judgment of the military tribunal was reviewed by the Supreme Court of the United States.

Although this trial resulted in what was perhaps the most flagrant miscarriage of justice of the five trials selected, it can at least be said that the accused was given a right of appeal from the military tribunal which condemned him to the highest civilian court of the country of his captors. None of the other victims of military courts enjoyed any such right of appeal. The details of this case are well known because, as in the case of Field Marshal von Manstein, defending counsel was moved to express his indignation with the verdict by writing a book describing the trial. A White Book has been published by the Italian Ministry of the Interior on the facts of the Italian example chosen, the trial of

Major Walter Reder, while the French example, the trial of General Ramcke, has been brilliantly described in a book by the victim himself. Only the details of the trial of Field Marshal Kesselring remain obscure. None of the promoters of these war-crimes trials, nor counsel for the prosecution in any of them, have felt impelled to write books justifying what took place, no doubt feeling that the sooner the subject was buried in oblivion the better.

The average Routine War-crimes Trial was very different in practice, but not in theory, from the five celebrated trials described below. Except in the case of these five trials no details have been published and no records have been made public concerning any of these prosecutions before military tribunals. Most of the victims were obscure individuals whose fate was of no interest to anyone but their relations and friends. The verdicts carry no weight and would be promptly quashed by any court of appeal reviewing them judicially in accordance with established legal principles because in all these proceedings hearsay evidence had been freely admitted in reliance on the authority given in the London Agreement. Only if and when the records are made available for investigation will it be possible to form an opinion as to the proportion of these cases where it can be claimed that a sort of rough justice was probably done.

THE TRIAL OF FIELD MARSHAL KESSELRING

When the Nuremberg Trials commenced on the 20th November 1945, all the manifold resources of propaganda were mobilised to focus public attention on this great Spectacular War-crimes Trial. In consequence the numerous Routine War-crimes Trials which were taking place contemporaneously were allowed to pass unnoticed. Only occasionally was space on the back pages of the newspapers spared for a brief announcement that some war-criminal had been tried and executed somewhere or other. After a few months however the British public became heartily bored by the slow progress of the mass war-crimes trials going on at Nuremberg.

When desperate efforts to retain public interest in these proceedings had failed the promoters wisely decided to discontinue their intensive propaganda campaign. Finally, when after some eleven months it could be announced proudly that the Nazi war-criminals had been at last convicted, it was decided in deference to the growing public distaste to withdraw unobtrusively the subject of the disposal of the prisoners taken in the late war behind an Iron Curtain of Discreet Silence. War crimes tribunals continued to function as briskly as ever but no details of their doings were published and the British public gradually forgot what was going on and turned its attention to more pleasant subjects.

The Iron Curtain of Discreet Silence remained unbroken in Britain until May 1947, when it was casually disclosed in the Press that Field Marshal Albert Kesselring, the commander-in-chief of the German forces in Italy, had been sentenced to death by a British military court in Venice, after a hearing lasting three months, for being responsible for the shooting of certain hostages and various Italian partisans and bandits who had been caught operating behind the German lines.

The storm of protests which this unobtrusive announcement aroused seems to have filled the British authorities with genuine surprise. Other generals of equal standing to Field Marshal Kesselring had been quietly liquidated by courts having no more jurisdiction to enquire into their doings than the court in Venice which had condemned this particular prisoner of war. Field Marshal Kesselring was unquestionably a general on the defeated side. Why then, it was asked plaintively, should he, contrary to all democratic principles, be treated as an exception? Why should he alone be allowed to enjoy the rights of a prisoner of war?

Certainly no fault can be found in this reasoning. Besides, it was pointed out, into this particular case political considerations entered; it was known that Italian public opinion would be favourably influenced if the German general who had defended Italian soil so long and so gallantly were hanged. The fact was overlooked that many people in Great Britain, both influential and obscure, were extremely proud of the campaign in Italy, a campaign waged by both sides with but few lapses from the highest standards of civilized warfare—apart, of course, from the numerous outrages committed on prisoners and wounded by the Italian partisans and the ruthless reprisals of the German security police, similar to those of the Black-and-Tans in Ireland, in 1920. In fact, apart from that one "tragic mistake", the wanton destruction of the Monte Cassino Monastery—the blame for which still remains a subject of dispute between the American, General Mark

Advance to Barbarism

Clark, and the New Zealander, Lieut.-General Bernard Freyberg — the campaign in Italy was one of which both sides might be justly proud. It was felt in wide circles in Great Britain that if Field Marshal Kesselring were hanged, the laurels of his victorious opponents would be irredeemably sullied. It was realised that, in the eyes of posterity, so monstrous an act of barbarism would cast a shadow over the whole allied campaign in Italy.

As the result of a single official indiscretion there collapsed that Iron Curtain of Discreet Silence behind which Britain's enemies in Germany were being quietly liquidated without too great a strain being placed upon the famed British love of justice and fair play. Lieut.-General Sir Oliver Leese, the commander of the Eighth Army, declared in an interview in the Press that had it been his fate to have been on the defeated side, the same charges as those brought against Field Marshal Kesselring could have been established against himself.

"Kesselring was a very gallant soldier who fought his battles well and squarely," General Leese declared. "With regard to the treatment of prisoners, I think that Kesselring, like Rommel, set a very good example — a far better example than the Italians." In support of this opinion, the General quoted Viscount Alexander as saying, "I think that the warfare in Italy was carried out fairly, and from a soldierly point of view, as well as it could have been done"[104]

These and similar protests were from persons so eminent and influential that it was impossible to dismiss them summarily by neither publishing nor commenting on them. The British authorities had brought this storm on themselves by their own blunder but it must be admitted that they succeeded in extricating themselves from an awkward situation with considerable skill. No attempt was made to justify the trial of the German field marshal; no attempt was made to defend the unfortunate military court at Venice which, after all, had only administered what they were assured was the new law governing the matter before them. The unanswerable denunciations of Field Marshal Kesselring's trial at Venice applied equally, of course, to war-crimes trials generally, but few of those who denounced this particular war-crimes trial were in the least interested in Kesselring personally, still less in abstract questions of justice. British public opinion had been roused simply because the honour and reputation of the Eighth

Chapter 8 — The Last Phase

Army had been made dependent on the saving of Field Marshal Kesselring from the hangman.

The obvious solution of the difficulty was to grant the Field Marshal a reprieve. But an unexpected difficulty then arose. The Field Marshal declined to lodge an appeal. His resolution was only overcome by appeals from brother professionals of the highest rank among his captors not to allow the military profession to be discredited by the carrying out of the sentence. It is not known what assurances were at the same time given him that he would receive honourable treatment if he went to reside in a British military prison: if given, these assurances were certainly not carried out. In due course, the British public learned with relief that the Field Marshal had lodged an appeal and had been duly reprieved; it was cheerfully assumed, but quite erroneously as it later proved, that the faces of the British military authorities would be saved by a short detention as a nominal prisoner. The whole subject was dismissed thankfully from mind, the Iron Curtain of Discreet Silence descended once more, and the work of "putting to death our enemies in Germany"[105] continued, as before. England is a land of many creeds but whatever his creed may be, every Englishman firmly believes that what is not discussed or thought about has no existence: Quod non apparet non est.

Nevertheless, it is most remarkable how easily and quickly the Kesselring war-crimes trial was completely dismissed from mind immediately after it was announced that it had been decided not to hang the Field Marshal. Unquestionably this war-crimes trial was one of the most memorable of all that long series of such trials which began after the conclusion of hostilities in 1945. The facts of this case have since attracted little or no attention and remain curiously little known. During the hearing, only brief, disconnected and generally inaccurate details were published in the Press. Only when the astonishing verdict was announced was public attention aroused.

Four years later, no book giving even an outline of this war-trial had been published so that when in June, 1951, an appeal was made to Field Marshal Viscount Alexander to give his support to an agitation which had started in Germany to obtain belated justice for his gallant opponent in the campaign in Italy, Viscount Alexander was forced to admit, "I cannot make any statement on Field Marshal Kesselring's court-martial as I don't know the facts." All he could do in response to this appeal was to confirm "what I have already said," namely, "I fought against the Field Marshal for a considerable period, both in North Africa and Italy, and I never had anything to complain of in his conduct of operations. He was a very able opponent and he and his troops fought a perfectly straight forward and fair fight against us."[106]

So much at least is common knowledge to those familiar with the facts of the campaign in Italy. Less well known is the fact that the "pro-Italian sentiment of Kesselring" ("italophile Gesinnung Kesselrings") frequently aroused angry comment at the Führer's headquarters where Kesselring's disposition to forgo military advantages rather than bring destruction upon the irreplaceable historical, architectural, and artistic treasures of Italy was regarded with little favour by Hitler and his entourage. Thus, thanks to his express orders, Rome was evacuated without resistance, with the consequence that the Allied tanks and mechanised columns were able to sweep through the city, unhampered by ruins and broken bridges, in pursuit of his hard-pressed troops.

It must be left to future historians to decide whether General Mark Clark or the jaunty General Bernard Freyberg must bear the chief responsibility for that "tragic mistake, psychologically and militarily", which led to the destruction of the Monte Cassino Monastery, but it is at least certain that Kesselring did all in his power to prevent this "tragic mistake" by refraining from occupying this famous shrine of Christendom with his troops, having previously arranged for the removal of its most precious treasures to a place of safety in the Vatican City.

Posterity will undoubtedly acknowledge a debt of gratitude to Field Marshal Kesselring for the preservation of so much which would otherwise have been destroyed when the allied war chiefs saw fit, as Mr. Churchill cheerfully puts it, "to drag the hot rake of war up the length of the Italian peninsula." Like Hitler and his advisers at German G.H.Q., the Allied military leaders regarded the campaign in Italy from an entirely military point of view. Had not Kesselring been one of the few who, in the general frenzy then prevailing, retained some sense of proportion, who can doubt that many other "tragic mistakes" would have taken place?[107] There is one good reason for thinking that, in regard to this subject, even Italian public opinion will change in time. If only ruins could be

Chapter 8 — The Last Phase

shown to foreign tourists where Milan Cathedral, St. Peters, and the Uffizi Galleries now stand, the Italian tourist trade would suffer enduring and incalculable loss. Even future generations of Italians may thus be led to recall Kesselring's memory with gratitude.

The facts which led up to this war-crimes trial are not in dispute and make the attitude of the British authorities even more inexplicable. Italy had entered the war, in 1940, with no more justification or excuse than when, in 1915, she had declared war on her ally, Austria. On both occasions, she was undeniably guilty of embarking on a war of aggression, defined by Lord Justice Lawrence as "the supreme international crime". In 1940, as in 1915, her motive was simply to be found among the victors at the end of the war. In 1915, her guess as to which side would be victorious proved right, and she was rewarded by being permitted to annex the Austrian Tyrol; in 1940 her guess proved wrong and, with a naiveté not lacking a certain charm, Italy then set about doing her best to change sides. Unfortunately, large forces of German troops had already entered Italy as allies, at the invitation and request of the Italian Government. This circumstance was, however, turned to account since it provided an opportunity to demonstrate by acts of violence to the men who had recently been allies and who had now become unwelcome guests, that Italy had changed, or desired to change, sides.

The spectacle of German troops defending Italian soil from invasion, a task from which he and the Italian Army had ingloriously retired, seems to have filled Marshal Badoglio with violent emotions, among which was possibly shame. At all events, from the security of Brindisi, this Italian "warrior" occupied himself sending forth wireless appeals to the Italian civilian population, calling upon them to murder every German within reach whenever possible and without mercy. When the probability that Germany would ultimately be defeated became a certainty, the response to these appeals, at first timid, rapidly gathered strength, although less, apparently, among Badoglio's own political supporters than among his bitterest opponents, the Italian Communists. Thousands of German soldiers were stabbed or shot in the back, bombed or blown up by land-mines. All the time-honoured practices of the Spanish guerillas in their campaign against Napoleon's armies were adopted by the Italian partisans, together with such innovations as the construction of

Advance to Barbarism

grim booby-traps consisting of the severed heads of slaughtered prisoners fixed on stakes in such a way that if touched a hidden land-mine would be exploded. The German regular forces reacted to this campaign in precisely the same way as regular forces in the past had reacted when subjected to similar attacks by a civilian population. As in Spain during the Peninsular War and in Ireland during "the Troubles" of 1920, the troops frequently got out of hand, in modern terminology, "saw red", and savage reprisals unquestionably took place. At the same time, the German authorities carried out official reprisals: hostages were taken and, after each outrage, a number were shot.

Two charges were made against Field Marshal Kesselring. First, he was accused of supporting drastic measures by his subordinates, and against him was quoted a general order issued by him authorising local commanders to take such measures as, at their discretion, they might consider necessary to protect the lives of their men. Secondly — and this seems to have been regarded as the main charge against him — he was accused of approving an order from Hitler himself that, following the explosion of a land-mine in the Via Rasella in Rome, by which 32 German soldiers were killed and 68 wounded, besides ten Italian civilians killed, including six children, a number of Italian hostages, held in custody as supporters of Badoglio, should be shot in the ratio of ten for every soldier murdered.

Had the court which tried Kesselring been composed of civilians, it would be easy to understand why it should appear outrageous in any circumstances that an innocent person should be executed for the crime of another. But the court was composed of experienced soldiers and the execution of hostages is unanimously upheld by the military authorities of all civilized countries as a coercive measure. Articles 453 and 454 of the British Manual of Military Law are explicit on the subject. Article 454 explains that "the coercive force of reprisals arises from the fact that in most cases they inflict suffering on innocent individuals." Article 358 of the American Military Manual also authorises the execution of hostages as a necessary measure to safeguard the lives of combatant forces. If it be thought that Kesselring was condemned because the tribunal considered the ratio of 10 to 1 excessive, it becomes necessary to state that, when the French occupied Stuttgart in April, 1945, it was announced that hostages would

Chapter 8 — The Last Phase

be shot in the ratio of 25 to 1 for every French soldier murdered by the German civilian population; and that when the Americans entered the Harz district, execution was threatened in the ratio of 200 to 1 for every American soldier murdered.

The reason why it was considered so desirable to hush up the facts of this war-crimes trial are sufficiently obvious. The verdict was quite indefensible. The reason why it was possible to keep the facts from the public so long is also open to a very simple explanation. At his war-crimes trial at Manila in the previous year, General Tomoyuki Yamashita was provided with a team of American lawyers who not only ably defended him but carried his appeal to the Supreme Court of the United States. While they failed to save his life, one of his lawyers, Mr. A. Frank Reel, cleared his memory by writing a classic study of the case in which the full facts are set forth.[108] Similarly two years later, Field Marshal Fritz Erich von Manstein was provided with English Counsel to defend him at his trial at Hamburg in 1949; to their efforts he owed his life, and one of them, Mr. R. T. Paget, Q.C., has since written an account of the proceedings which leaves in no doubt the grounds upon which and the methods by which a conviction was obtained.[109]

Field Marshal Kesselring, in contrast, was denied the services of English lawyers to defend him before the English military court instructed to try him. He was forced to rely on German lawyers quite unfamiliar with English legal conceptions and English military legal procedure. As citizens of a defeated state, his defenders were not free, like Mr. Reel and Mr. Paget, to carry on the struggle for justice after their professional services were completed. Victimisation for what the occupying authorities might consider excessive zeal was an ever-present possibility. It is, of course, a characteristic of all war-crimes trials that, usually, only those concerned with the defence show any disposition to dwell afterwards on the facts. In the Kesselring war-crimes trial, those concerned with the defence lacked the means to make known the facts, at least to the world outside Germany; and those concerned otherwise than with the defence have ever since rigidly preserved a prudent silence.

Unlike in most Routine War-crimes Trials, those dealing with the prosecution of Kesselring seem to have regarded a conviction as a necessary formality, a mere repetition of what

Advance to Barbarism

had already been decided. The reason for this attitude was that three months before two of Kesselring's colleagues, General von Mackensen and General Mälzer, had been sentenced to death in Rome on the same charges arising from the same facts as those now brought against Kesselring Although the military tribunal which assembled in Venice to try Kesselring was not the same as that which had so recently adjudicated in Rome, the Advocate General, the functionary whose role it was to advise the tribunal on points of law, was the same. It was obvious, of course, to everyone in court that an acquittal of Kesselring would amount to an admission that the Rome tribunal had erred—a simply unthinkable conclusion. Having advised on the same evidence once, the Judge Advocate saw no reason to change his mind. "His prejudice" writes Kesselring, "was glaring." Comparing him with the official prosecutor, a Swiss newspaper commented tersely, "The Judge Advocate was the second, and the better, prosecutor."

From one point of view, in particular, the Kesselring war-crimes trial is far more remarkable than the Nuremberg war-crimes trial. The tribunal which purported to adjudicate at Nuremberg was composed of lawyers sitting only six months after the termination of hostilities. Inevitably, their minds were still under the influence of wartime passions, and, if they erred deplorably in the case of Admiral Raeder, it can at least be said they meted out a sort of rough justice to some of the accused. As lawyers, they had no reason for feeling any particular understanding or sympathy for sailors like Admiral Raeder or Admiral Donitz, or for soldiers like Field Marshal Keitel or General Jodl.

On the other hand, the military court at Venice which tried Field Marshal Kesselring, was composed of soldiers of standing and repute, sitting two years after the conclusion of hostilities. They had before them a brother professional, not only a soldier of the highest rank but the hero of one of the greatest fighting retreats in military annals.

At any other period of history, the minds of such a body would have been dominated by sympathy for a commander who, faced by an enemy superior in numbers, vastly superior in equipment, and enjoying undisputed command of the sea and air, had maintained an unbroken resistance, step by step, from the southern shores of Sicily to the foothills of the Alps, until his gallant troops, deprived of air support by lack of petrol and hampered at

Chapter 8 — The Last Phase

first by cowardly and later by treacherous allies, were engulfed, still undefeated, in the general ruin.

What is so particularly remarkable is that the charge against Field Marshal Kesselring was the one least likely to appeal to military minds — the charge that he had adopted severe methods to protect his hard-pressed troops from treacherous attacks from the rear by gangs of armed civilians. Most of the members of the Court were aware from personal observation of the nature and methods of the Italian underground movement against which Kesselring had had to contend. In similar circumstances they themselves would have adopted similar measures, measures which were, in fact, adopted without hesitation by the Americans six years later in the campaign in Korea in 1950, when their lines of communication were being raided by communist irregulars.

Very different had been the reaction of British officers in the past when the same circumstances had arisen. Thus, for example, Professor Charles W. C. Oman, in his *Peninsular War*, complains that, as a consequence of having witnessed the atrocities of the Spanish guerillas, many of Wellington's officers developed a distinctly pro-French bias. In particular, he complains that one of Wellington's officers, Sir William Napier, in his military classic, *War in the Peninsula*, became so biased that he was "over-hard on the Spaniards and over-lenient to Bonaparte ... he invariably exaggerates Spanish defeats and minimises Spanish successes."[110]

There was nothing exceptional or unique in the situation which led to Field Marshal Kesselring finding himself at the disposal of the foreign enemies occupying his country. Thus, France, in 1814, was as completely at the mercy of her conquerors as was Germany in 1945, and most of the French Generals had, at one time or another, faced the task of coping with the Spanish guerillas during the Peninsular War. But, although he had been much assisted in his operations by their activities, the Duke of Wellington felt himself under no obligation to avenge the execution of the assassins and saboteurs who had occupied themselves behind the French lines sniping isolated detachments, stabbing sentries, torturing prisoners, and mutilating the wounded. On the contrary we hear of him, only two years after the termination of hostilities, when commander-in-chief of the army of occupation in France, paying Marshal Massena a friendly visit at the house of

Advance to Barbarism

another "war-criminal", Marshal Soult, and exchanging with him reminiscences of the campaign in Spain. The idea that either of these famous soldiers ought to be put on trial for their handling of the Spanish "underground movement" apparently never entered Wellington's mind. Even Marshal Suchet, who had particularly distinguished himself by the energy[111] by which he had repressed the gangs of Spanish civilians which had harried his troops in Aragon, was permitted to end his days in honourable retirement in Paris without molestation by the foreign occupiers of his country.

Perhaps the most fitting concluding observation on the subject is that, although Field Marshal Kesselring was unfortunate not to have lived in earlier and more civilized times, he was, on the other hand, fortunate to have lived before the reversion to barbarism had proceeded so far that it had become a universal rule (to quote, once more, Field Marshal Montgomery): "after a war, generals on the defeated side are tried and hanged."

In the autobiography which Field Marshal Kesselring wrote in retirement after his release in 1952, he deals with his treatment as a prisoner of war in British hands with remarkable reserve and moderation. When possible he pays tribute to the conduct of his captors, in particular to the officer to whom he surrendered, General Taylor, afterwards commander-in-chief in the Korean War, and to Colonel Scotland, the commandant of the notorious 'Kensington Cage' in London in which he was subjected to "interrogation". He discloses that before his trial started in Venice in February 1947 he endured a period of solitary confinement lasting five months in Nuremberg waiting to be called to give evidence at the mass-trial there taking place, and refutes the comfortable belief held in Britain that after the sentence of death passed on him in Venice had been commuted to a sentence of imprisonment for life, he was detained in nominal detention for a short period as a face-saving measure to preserve the credit of the British military authorities. In fact, however, he was treated as a common criminal in Werl Prison where he spent his time, he tells us, gumming paper bags: he was not set free until the 24th October 1952 by what was called "an act of clemency." He died on the 15th July 1960.

It must be confessed that in few respects can the Kesselring Trial be regarded as a typical Routine War-crimes Trial. Its purpose was entirely political, although it may at first be hard to see what political purpose could be served by paying attention to the complaints of the Italians against the Field Marshal. No one indeed was concerned to placate Italian public opinion but the very powerful Communist Party in Italy enjoyed the special patronage of Stalin whose menacing figure then overshadowed Europe. The trial took place during the early months of 1947 when the Stalin Myth was still almost universally believed and the British and American Governments still clung to the hope that by continued subservience to the wishes of the communist dictator he could be induced to act as a loyal and friendly ally in the crusade for the liberty and welfare of mankind.

It was not until the following year that this pathetic delusion was shattered by the establishment by force of communist rule in Czecho-slovakia and the blockade by the Red Army of West Berlin. When in 1948 the grim prospect had to be faced that at any time Europe might be invaded and occupied by the Red Army, the scandal of Kesselring's conviction was quickly driven from the attention of the public and the victim soon became a forgotten prisoner, gumming paper bags, in Werl Prison.

THE TRIAL OF MAJOR WALTER REDER

The trial of Major Walter Reder before an Italian military tribunal at Bologna in the autumn of 1951 may be regarded as a belated sequel to the trial of Field Marshal Kesselring before a British military tribunal in Venice in the spring of 1947, that is to say, four and half years before. Major Reder was charged with offences alleged to have been committed by him when commanding the Reconnaissance Panzer Unit No. 16 of the 16th Panzer Division, forming part of the German forces in Italy of which Field Marshal Kesselring was commander-in-chief.

This trial was one of the last of the series of war-crimes trials which began in 1945 immediately after the unconditional surrender of Germany. After the passage of six years wartime passions had to a considerable extent subsided and the trial in itself may be considered as a very favourable example of a Routine War-crimes Trial. The Italian army officers who composed the military tribunal in Bologna took their duties very seriously and listened carefully to all the evidence, not only for the prosecution but for the defence. Unfortunately, an acquittal was impossible owing to the political situation existing in Italy at the time. The trial took place in Bologna, a stronghold of the Italian Communist Party, and throughout the hearing angry mobs demonstrated outside the court house demanding the blood of the accused. An acquittal would have been widely resented in Italy as a deliberate affront to the Italian Partisan movement and might well have so aroused popular feeling as to have brought about the downfall of the weak coalition government then in power. Had a communist government then taken office, the officers composing the tribunal would probably have been charged with acquitting the accused owing to their secret sympathy with Fascism. In these difficult circumstances the tribunal did their best to administer justice: probably they thought that by condemning Reder to imprisonment they were saving his life by putting him out of harm's way for a time, assuming that when he had been forgotten by his communist enemies, he would be surreptitiously set at liberty.

No doubt this would have been the ultimate outcome of his conviction but unfortunately for Major Reder, Marzabotto, the place nearest to the scene of his alleged offences, was chosen by the Communist Party as a place of pilgrimage at which Communist Partisans could gather annually to honour the memory of that heroic Resistance fighter Mario Musolesi (alias 'Major' Lupo) and his Red Star Brigade of Communist Partisans who died fighting to the last man against troops commanded by Major Reder, and at the same time to mourn the abominable massacre of the said Mario Musolesi and his gathering of unarmed, peace loving Italian civilians, known as the Red Star Brigade, by the troops of the said Major Reder.

Accounts of the war-crimes trials which followed the Second World War are rendered tedious by the fact that precisely the same issue arose in so many of them. Exact statistics are not available but probably in at least three quarters of these prosecutions the complaint against the accused was that he had dealt harshly with civilian irregulars and terrorists who had been attacking his troops in the rear. In all these cases there was generally only one issue to be decided: were the victims of the accused in offensive civilians so unfortunate as to have found themselves in the midst of hostilities or were they really combatants in civilian dress? War-crimes tribunals invariably accepted the former contention.

The Italian war-crimes tribunal which tried the Italian charges against Major Reder adopted the novel course of accepting both contentions. The gallant but muddle-headed officers who composed this tribunal held as a fact that the inhabitants of a few tiny villages in the mountains south of Marzabotto in which a gang of communist terrorists was surrounded and annihilated by troops some of whom were under the command of Major Reder, were ruthlessly slaughtered as a reprisal for the atrocities previously committed by this gang of terrorists. At the same time the tribunal held that the inhabitants of these mountain villages had well earned the Gold Medal for Valour collectively awarded them posthumously "for heroically resisting the Fascist attack."

Major Reder was born in Freiwald in Bohemia in 1915, a subject of the Austro-Hungarian Empire. He had a distinguished career in the German Army as leader of front-line troops, serving in France in 1940 and later in Russia where at the battle of Kharkov in March 1943 he was so severely wounded that his left forearm had to be amputated. For his services in Russia he was awarded the Knight's Cross of the Iron Cross. In May 1944 he was sent to Italy and there took part in the desperate battles in Tuscany, fought to hold up the advance northward of the Allies. The division to which he belonged was signalled out for special and generous praise by Field Marshal Lord Alexander in his report on the operations between the 3rd September 1943 and the 1st July 1944. (See the Supplement to the *London Gazette* dated the 4th June 1950, No. 38937). In particular, speaking of the fighting at Cecina on the 29th June to the 1st July 1944, the British commander-in-chief observes, "The 16th Panzer Division had been brought in here to strengthen the German defence and fought with skill and fanaticism." Later, referring to the struggle for Rosignano during the first week in July, Lord Alexander records, "the town was defended by the 16th Panzer Grenadiers against the 34th United States Division with the same stubbornness as they had shown at Cecina."

As winter approached the desperate attempts of the Allies to achieve a breakthrough were intensified. Nevertheless at this critical moment Major Reder and his unit of crack troops had to be withdrawn from the front line facing the 34th U.S. Division in order to deal with a strong group of Communist Partisans called the Red Star Brigade which from a stronghold in the mountains south of Marzabotto was threatening the main road and railway communications between the front and the German headquarters at Bologna. Major Reder performed his mission brilliantly and swiftly.

The Red Star Brigade, numbering over 2,000 civilians armed with heavy machine guns and mortars, under the command of the celebrated Communist Partisan leader who called himself 'Major' Lupo, was encircled and annihilated. It was with reference to this operation on the 29th September 1944 that the main charge against Major Reder was brought. Upon it was based the notorious propaganda myth called the Marzabotto Massacre.

Major Reder remained in Italy throughout the following autumn and winter. In February 1945 he was transferred to Hungary across which Stalin's hordes were then sweeping in overwhelming strength. He was again severely wounded. After the general capitulation of the Axis Powers, he returned to his mother's home in Salzburg. Here he was arrested by the American occupying forces on complaints lodged with them against him by the Italians.

For two years — from September 1945 to September 1947 — Major Reder was a prisoner in an American concentration camp at Glasenbach in which were detained some 7,500 men and 500 women kept prisoner on one pretext or another. Presumably the lengthy task of investigating so many distinct cases provides the reason why the Americans took so long in reaching a decision with regard to the charges against Major Reder. When at last his captors found time to investigate his case they decided that he had no case to answer. As however the charges had been lodged by the Italians and the British were in military occupation of Italy, they rid themselves of responsibility for his fate by handing him over to the British.

The British military authorities investigated the Italian charges against Major Reder with praiseworthy care. At first his interrogation was carried out by a Major J. E. McKee. Later his interrogation was completed by a Major W. G. Aylen. Neither of these gentlemen spoke German so that the services of an interpreter, a Dr. Hans Susseroth, was necessary. At Major Reder's trial in Bologna, this man Susseroth gave evidence that he himself had interrogated the accused who had denied taking part in any operations against the Italian Partisans.

In affidavits sworn for Major Reder's appeal to the Supreme Italian Military Court in Rome, both Major McKee and

Major Aylen swore that Susseroth had given false evidence. He had been employed, they both testified, only as an interpreter, never as an interrogator. Further, they both testified that Major Reder had freely admitted having directed the operations against the Red Star Brigade south of Bologna in which its commander, 'Major' Lupo was killed. In fact Major Reder had claimed that his detachment had borne the brunt of the fighting on that occasion.

Major McKee concluded his affidavit by stating: "Throughout his interrogation by me, Major Reder behaved with dignity. He repeatedly affirmed his innocence. He denied ordering excesses against the Italian civilian population or having received orders from his superiors to carry out excesses. On one occasion Major Reder could without difficulty or danger have escaped from British custody. He explained that he had refrained from escaping as he was quite prepared to face a trial on the charges made against him."

As we have seen, the British military authorities had already brought to trial and convicted Major Reder's commander-in-chief, Field Marshal Kesselring. They had also afterwards disposed of his immediate superior, the divisional commander, General Max Simon, at a war-crimes trial at Padua in January 1948 at which he had been sentenced to death and then sent to join Field Marshal Kesselring in Werl Prison. With regard to Major Reder therefore two obvious courses were open to the British military authorities. If they came to the same conclusion as the American authorities that he had no case to answer, their plain duty was to release him at once. If however they were satisfied that a *prima facie* case against him had been made out, they could put him on trial before a British military tribunal as they had done with his superior officers, Field Marshal Kesselring and General Max Simon.

Neither of these courses were adopted. On the 13th May 1948 Major Reder was handed over by the British military authorities to the Italians so that the latter might try their own charges against him.

The present writer regrets that he has been unable to find any clue suggesting an explanation for this extraordinary procedure. In itself, this is not perhaps remarkable. The working of the British military-legal or legal-military mind during the post-war years is generally quite beyond mere human comprehension.

Possibly closer investigation of the political situation in May 1948 would disclose that there was some special reason at that moment for making a gesture which would conciliate Italian public opinion. Some cynical politician in London may have decided that an obscure German officer would conveniently serve as a subject for such a gesture. But a simpler but adequate explanation would be that the British authorities in charge of Major Reder's case had got themselves in a muddle and therefore decided that the easiest way out of it was to follow the precedent set by Pontius Pilate long ago. It was at any rate clear that the Italians were convinced of Major Reder's guilt. If therefore the case was handed over to the Italians so that they could act as judges of their own charges, the British could wash their hands of the matter with the confident assurance that it would be quickly disposed of by the prisoner's death.

Even from a strictly technical legal point of view the procedure adopted in the case of Major Reder seems utterly indefensible. It is true that by the Moscow Declaration of the 30th October 1943 the victorious Powers had conferred on themselves the right to swop prisoners of war between each other in disregard of their treaty obligations under the Hague and Geneva Conventions. Even assuming this swopping of prisoners of war was justified as between the victorious Powers, no authority existed for handing prisoners of war over to a defeated Power. In October 1943 Italy was an ally of Germany and the fortunes of war had turned finally against them. Shortly afterwards Italy abjectly surrendered and her efforts to join the winning side were coldly rebuffed. It is not easy to define what exactly was her status when Reder was handed over to the Italian authorities in 1948 but by no stretch of imagination can it be said that Italy emerged from the Second World War as a victorious Power!

Earlier in this chapter a letter dated the 19th December 1960 written by a high official of the British Foreign Office was quoted verbatim. It sets out clearly what is the official attitude of the British Government to this distressing subject. It may be summarised as follows: "No doubt our military authorities in Italy in 1948 made a grave and deplorable error of judgment when they handed over this prisoner of war in British hands to our former enemies, the Italians. No doubt Major Reder was treated with callous indifference as to his fate: probably his surrender by us to the Italians was contrary to international law. But this regrettable error having been made, no good purpose would be served now by investigating it because once this prisoner of war had passed out of our hands we ceased to have any rights concerning him. The Italians found their own charges proved against him and if they had shot him we could not have complained. In that case he would by now be entirely forgotten and we should not now be troubled to find excuses for the inexcusable. As it is, he unfortunately still lives, a prisoner in an Italian prison, but as we can do nothing to secure his release, there is no good talking about the subject."

That Major Reder is not now a completely forgotten prisoner in an Italian prison is owing to a fortunate chance. It happened that the present writer was instructed professionally by Reder's legal advisers to trace and obtain affidavits from the two British officers above mentioned who had interrogated him while he was in British custody, for the purpose of an appeal against conviction which was being made to the Supreme Italian Military Court in Rome. In this way the present writer learned the facts of this case which he later set out in a chapter of a book which received wide publicity not only in Britain and the United States but in Germany and Spain.[112] Many influential people have since interested themselves in securing Reder's release—including in Britain, the late Lord Hankey and Field Marshal Lord Alexander, and in Italy, the late Pope Pius XII. So far the only result of these appeals for justice has been repeated soothing assurances that Reder would be released immediately a propitious moment arrived. Having waited in captivity for twenty years, Major Reder is still waiting for this propitious moment to arrive.

The above mentioned book, published in 1958, gave the first outline of the facts of Major Reder's case, hitherto entirely unknown outside Italy. Necessarily it was a one-sided account since it was based entirely on information supplied by the lawyers who had defended him at his trial. In 1961 however the Italian Ministry of the Interior took the unparalleled step of publishing a White Book setting out in full the judgment of the military tribunal in Bologna which convicted Major Reder in 1951 and the judgment of the Supreme Military Court in Rome in 1954 which rejected his appeal.

By publishing this White Book the Italian Government conferred on Major Reder a unique distinction: in his case, alone of all the thousands of cases of prisoners of war subjected to trials for alleged war-crimes, was it considered desirable by his captors to issue an official statement justifying their treatment of him. However contradictory the facts found by the tribunal and muddled its reasoning from these facts, the publication of this White Book at least shows that the Italian legal authorities, unlike the legal authorities of other countries responsible for showing that justice had been done, felt in this case they had nothing to hide. It had long been the invariable practice of war-crimes tribunals at the end of the hearing simply to announce that the accused had been found guilty, leaving this conclusion a subject for guesswork. Often when the indictment contained a number of distinct charges the victim was left in complete doubt whether he had been convicted on all or only some of them. The verdict in fact merely intimated that the adjudicating tribunal had reached the opinion that he deserved to be hanged. The Italian military tribunal which tried Major Reder, on the other hand, stated clearly in their judgment their findings of fact and the reasons which had led them to convict him. Their painstaking and conscientious judgment contrasts strikingly with the vague and slipshod judgment delivered in the relatively well-conducted war-crimes trial before a British military tribunal of Field Marshal von Manstein in Hamburg in 1949.

A judgment which merely pronounces a defendant guilty without stating the facts upon which this conclusion is reached is immune from adverse criticism. It reflects therefore the highest credit on the Italian military authorities that they have dealt with the charges against Major Reder, if belatedly, in so judicial a manner. On the other hand, by conducting his trial in a judicial manner and later publishing the findings of fact and the reasoning of the tribunal which led them to convict him, they exposed the weakness of the case against him.

As is usual in war-crimes trials, a number of ancillary charges were made against Reder, such charges being generally intended to make the indictment seem more formidable. The main charge against him upon which his fate depended related to the encirclement and annihilation of the above mentioned group of Communist Partisans known as the Red Star Brigade. The headquarters of this group of heavily armed civilians was at Caprara, a tiny village on the upper slopes of Monte Sole, a mountain, 2,190 feet high, on a ridge between two mountain streams, the Reno and the Setta, running parallel with each other about four miles apart north-eastward from the Apennines into the Po Valley. From this stronghold the Red Star Brigade struck at the German lines of communication by road and railway along the valleys of the Reno and the Setta. Convoys were continually ambushed, railway bridges and tunnels damaged by sabotage, isolated German garrisons attacked. The methods of Red Star Brigade were similar to those of other Communist bands operating in Italy in the rear of the German armies: in order to shake the morale of the regular troops opposed to them, individual soldiers caught unawares were shot or stabbed, prisoners were tortured and then murdered, the bodies of the dead were mutilated.

On the 29th September 1944 the stronghold of the Red Star Brigade was attacked by converging columns. The attack was under the general direction of General Max Simon: Major Reder directed the attack from the east from across the Setta. The Partisans to the number of some two thousand armed with machine guns and mortars offered a desperate resistance which was quickly broken. The Red Star Brigade was annihilated: its leader "Major" Lupo was killed.

In its findings of fact the adjudicating military tribunal, as the White Book now discloses, accepted two contradictory contentions. The tribunal held that Reder's men ruthlessly slaughtered the unarmed and inoffensive inhabitants of three small villages, Caprara, Casaglia and Cerpiane, lying on the upper slopes of Monte Sole. It had been pointed out by the defence that the inhabitants of these places had afterwards been collectively awarded the Gold Cross for Valour in recognition of their heroic resistance "to the Fascist invaders". With the howls of the communist mob demonstrating in the street outside the courthouse, the tribunal could hardly be expected to disparage this award. The tribunal held, therefore, that the inhabitants of the three villages had defended themselves heroically, while at the same time they had allowed themselves to be butchered like helpless sheep.

A half-hearted attempt was indeed made to reconcile these contradictory findings by holding, without a shred of evidence in support, that a complete separation took place between the local inhabitants and the civilian warriors of the Red Star Brigade.

Advance to Barbarism

They declared that "Major" Lupo, finding himself surrounded, withdrew his men from the three villages above mentioned to the summit of Monte Sole for a last stand, leaving the inhabitants of these places "to the chivalry and humanity of the enemy:"

Examination of a large scale map will immediately disclose that this contention is nonsense. Caprara, the headquarters of the Red Star Brigade, is only 548 yards from the summit of Monte Sole, from which the other two places mentioned are less than half a mile away. No separation of the civilian warriors of the Red Star Brigade from the local inhabitants of the area, as found by the tribunal, was therefore possible. Also the suggestion is fantastic that an experienced guerilla fighter like Lupo would withdraw his men from the shelter of these places in order to concentrate them on the bare summit of Monte Sole, where they would have been quickly obliterated by artillery fire.

There can be no reasonable doubt the last stand of the Red Star Brigade took place in Caprara and the two neighbouring villages, Casaglia and Cerpiane. It may well be believed that the German troops took little trouble to distinguish between civilians using their weapons and civilians who had thrown away their arms. There is no reason to doubt also that when the Partisans in houses in these villages refused to surrender the attacking forces threw grenades through the windows regardless of any women and children who might be sheltering therein.

The tribunal expressed horror at such ruthlessness. No doubt some women and children lost their lives although the number must have been small since these places near the summit of Monte Sole, described in the White Book as villages, were in fact mere clusters of huts inhabited by goatherds and shepherds who browsed their flocks on the barren mountainside. A prominent feature, it may be noted, of the Marzabotto Myth was the burning of Marzabotto Church to which "the entire population of the town to the number of 1,700 had fled, and there perished, including the priest"[113] The White Book makes it clear that no fighting took place in Marzabotto: in the judgment of the tribunal the Church of Marzabotto reappears as the tiny shrine or chapel at Cerpiane in which, so the tribunal held, fifty persons lost their lives.

Judging from the White Book the tribunal took no account of the surrounding circumstances existing at the time, and the methods by which warfare had come to be waged in Europe. It

Chapter 8 — The Last Phase

was no doubt a dreadful thing that on the 29th September 1944 women and children should have lost their lives from bombs thrown into their homes in order to compel the defenders of the village in which they lived to surrender. But in that year and during the previous two years, on every night suitable for air attack, hundreds, and often thousands, of civilians, men, women and children, had been killed throughout Germany not by mere hand grenades but by "block-busters", deliberately dropped on crowded working-class areas in accordance with the Lindemann Plan adopted by the British Government in March 1942. The story of what took place in the mountains south of Marzabotto should be judged against the background of contemporary events.

In conclusion, it was proved at the trial that whatever excesses might have been committed on the upper slopes of Monte Sole, Major Reder took no personal part in them. Owing to a recent wound, throughout the action he remained on a hillside on the other side of the Setta and directed the advance of his men by wireless.

No admissible evidence that he personally had directed, ordered or countenanced reprisals against civilians was proved against him. As a one-armed man he would have been easily identifiable. No evidence of such identification was given.

The claim is often made that this is a Humanitarian Age in which not only the thought of capital punishment is repugnant but also long terms of imprisonment. Thus in 1962 the British public was shocked to learn that a Greek communist terrorist, Tony Ambatielos, still remained in captivity after sixteen years. The fact was ignored that the reason for his continued detention was his refusal to give an undertaking not to resume his efforts to establish a communist dictatorship in Greece. The general view, even in circles hostile to Communism, was well expressed by *The Times* which declared that, however heinous this man's crimes may have been, sixteen years was too long to keep a criminal in captivity.

In response to public opinion in Britain at the present time, sentences of imprisonment for life are carefully reviewed after only twelve years and the culprit, however conclusive his guilt, is released. Major Reder has been in prison now for over twenty-two years after a war-crimes trial in which his accusers acted as judges of their own charges.

It may perhaps seem that the attention paid here to the case of Major Reder is disproportionately long. It has been dealt with in some detail, partly because it is a favourable example of a Routine War-crimes Trial, but more because it happens the victim is still alive and is still suffering from the miscarriage of justice committed against him. Nearly all the other victims of war-crimes trials are either dead or have long ago been released. Responsibility for his fate rests fairly and squarely on the British Government. In a professedly humanitarian age, a further recital of the facts should lead to belated rectification of an indefensible miscarriage of justice.

THE TRIAL OF GENERAL YAMASHITA

The trial of General Tomoyuki Yamashita was in several important respects very unlike the trial of Field Marshal Kesselring. The issues in the trial of "the Tiger of Malaya" were not overshadowed by the knowledge that an acquittal of the accused would discredit the previous judgment of a tribunal of brother officers, dealing with the same facts, in an earlier prosecution.

Field Marshal Kesselring was at least tried by a court composed of fellow Europeans belonging to a nation which only since 1914 could be described as national enemies: General Yamashita, on the other hand, was a member of the Yellow Race and he was tried by a court composed of members of the White Race by which at the time the Japanese were regarded as presumptuous Oriental dwarfs who had dared to challenge White supremacy. Although during recent years, beginning with the trial of the two anarchists Sacco and Vanzetti in 1927 down to the trial of the communist traitor, Alger Hiss, in 1949, American methods of administering justice have been subjected to much patronising criticism by British lawyers, the trial of General Yamashita in many ways compares very favourably with the trial of Field Marshal Kesselring. Under the American legal system this distinguished Japanese prisoner of war was provided by his accusers with American Counsel to defend him, lawyers familiar with American legal procedure, and it was made possible for him on conviction to appeal to the American Supreme Court. Kesselring, on the other hand, had to rely on German lawyers who knew nothing about British military legal procedure. No possibility existed for him

Chapter 8 — The Last Phase

to appeal against conviction to the House of Lords, since, by an amusing legal fiction, British military tribunals, so far as prisoners of war are concerned, are deemed infallible.

These trials are alike in that they both ended in grave and indisputable miscarriages of justice, Yamashita being hanged and Kesselring being condemned as a result of his conviction to gum paper bags in the company of common criminals until after five years he was released by what was called "an act of clemency". The ultimate consequences of the conviction of Yamashita, however, are certain to be graver and far more enduring than the conviction of Kesselring. By posterity Kesselring will be remembered merely as one of a number of able European soldiers who were wrongly convicted by courts composed of other European soldiers during a period of acute mental disturbance following a European civil war which was conducted by both sides with hitherto unparalleled barbarity. Yamashita, on the other hand, will be remembered as a member of the Yellow Race who was wrongly convicted by a court composed of members of, at that time, dominant White Race. In a world which has come to profess abhorrence of racial discrimination in any form, his trial will long be cited, rightly or wrongly, as an example of the methods by which Western Imperialism strove to keep in subjection the coloured peoples of Asia.

Without question General Yamashita was one of the most gifted military leaders who fought in the Second World War. It has been customary to attribute the disastrous outcome of the Malayan Campaign to the mistakes of Yamashita's British opponents. This is unfair both to them and to him. The task entrusted to him at the outbreak of war by the Mikado might reasonably have been dismissed as impossible by the British High Command. In brief, he was ordered to land an army of some 50,000 men on the north-eastern coast of the Malay Peninsula, a distance of 1,700 miles from the nearest Japanese territory, the island of Formosa, in spite of the fact that he enjoyed no assured command of the sea; then to advance southward down the entire length of the peninsula, a distance of over 350 miles, along roads through dense jungle, overcoming on the way the resistance of the defending forces, numbering nearly 100,000 men; and finally to capture the great fortress of Singapore on an island separated from the mainland by a deep channel half a mile wide.

Advance to Barbarism

It only remains to add that the Malay Peninsula at its widest part is only 150 miles across from east to west and the main road running southward crosses half a dozen streams, each one of which offers a good defensive position to a defending army. No blame therefore attaches to General Percival and his advisers if they dismissed this operation as too hazardous for any sane general to undertake.

Nevertheless General Yamashita achieved what might reasonably have been regarded as the impossible. On the seventieth day after the first landing of Japanese troops on the coast of Malaya; the fortress of Singapore, after an assault lasting eight days; surrendered. 90,000 British, Indian and Australian troops laid down their arms.

This astonishing triumph shattered for ever the legend of the invincible military supremacy of the White Race which dates from the days of Marathon. The consequences of this were not expunged by the fact that four years later the Japanese were forced by the overwhelming military and industrial strength of Great Britain and the United States, aided by a stab in the back by Soviet Russia and the dropping of the first atomic bombs, to sign humiliating terms of surrender. No triumph, however spectacular, could restore the prestige of the White Man upon which Western Imperialism in Asia had for so long securely rested. As a consequence of Yamashita's campaign in Malaya the peoples of India, Pakistan, Ceylon, Burma, Malaya, Cambodia, South Vietnam, North Vietnam, Laos and Indonesia now enjoy — if enjoy be the right word — independence. Only the inhabitants of Japan have failed to benefit from their own achievements. Like the German troops who invaded Russia in 1941, and who were first received with joy as liberators from the tyranny of Stalin, the Japanese soon made themselves hated by the inhabitants of the countries which they overran by their arrogance and brutality. In consequence, although the peoples of Asia owe their present freedom from Western Imperialism to General Yamashita's victories, they entertain no gratitude or kindly feelings for the Japanese. The Japanese Empire, deprived of all its overseas possessions, is now a satellite state of the United States.

The trial of General Yamashita in Manila in the autumn of 1945 was fully and lucidly recorded in a book written shortly afterwards by his leading Counsel, A. Frank Reel.[114] It begins

Chapter 8 — The Last Phase

with a brief outline of Yamashita's career. He was the son of a country doctor in a remote district of Japan and although without wealth or family influence he won a place in the Cadets' Academy after a brilliant career at school. Yamashita owes his place in history entirely to his epoch-making campaign in Malaya which culminated after ten weeks with the capture of Singapore on the 15th February 1942. For two and a half years thereafter, during which the fate of Japan was decided, his career was uneventful. Owing to the jealousy of his rivals at Army headquarters in Tokyo, and in particular of the all-powerful General Togo, he was removed from the direction of active operations and sent to command the Japanese forces in garrison in Manchuria. It was not until the fortunes of war had irrevocably turned against the Japanese that Japan's most brilliant general was sent to take command in the Philippines, by then threatened by an American invasion in overwhelming strength. Yamashita arrived in the Philippines on the 7th October 1944. Ten days after his arrival the American landing took place.

The charges brought against General Yamashita did not relate to his direction of the Malayan Campaign, although no doubt the resentment felt for the humiliation of the dominant White Race by an upstart people of yellow dwarfs inspired these charges. Neither was it suggested that he was in any way responsible for the enormities committed during the building of the Burma Road or in the Japanese prisoner-of-war camps. The charges related solely to happenings in the Philippines between the 7th October, 1944, and the 3rd September, 1945, when Yamashita on the express command of the Emperor surrendered.

There is no dispute concerning the situation which existed in the Philippines when Yamashita took over the command of the 14th Army Group garrisoning this American overseas colonial possession.[115] After the fall of Corregidor on the 5th May, 1942, and the surrender of the American regular troops, resistance was continued by irregular units of Filipinos armed and financed by the Americans. Most of the aboriginal inhabitants of the Philippines were what was then described by their White rulers as heathen savages, a term which has fallen into disuse as wounding to the susceptibilities of the Afro-Asian bloc in U.N.O. For centuries down to 1899 they had waged guerilla warfare against the Spaniards, and for four decades after that against their new

Advance to Barbarism

American masters. After 1942 they continued this struggle, this time against the Japanese invaders and now armed with modern weapons. Their methods of waging guerilla warfare were those which might be expected of heathen savages but which, it must be confessed, were not fundamentally different from those being employed by those Christian peoples of contemporary Europe who were subject to enemy occupations. Japanese units were ambushed and massacred; prisoners and wounded were tortured and murdered.

The Japanese, as might be expected, retaliated with energy and enthusiasm. For two years one horrible atrocity was matched by another; terrorism was met by terrorism. After years of inconclusive guerilla fighting in China, the Japanese had become accustomed to dealing drastically with partisan irregulars. Like the French ten years later when faced with insurrection in Algeria, the Japanese regularly employed torture when interrogating suspects, burned villages and massacred their inhabitants. When it became clear that Japan's defeat was certain, the irregulars intensified their ferocious attacks and the Japanese reprisals became even more wholesale and savage.

This admittedly was the situation in the Philippines which Yamashita found when he arrived there in October 1944. He was handicapped from the outset by the fact that he had never even set eyes on the Philippines before, and knew nothing of the inhabitants or the geography of these islands. He was further handicapped by contradictory and often impossible orders from the Japanese army headquarters in Tokyo, and by the fact that the naval forces and the air force units defending the Philippines were under separate commands.

When, ten days after his arrival, the American invasion began, the combined effect of intensive bombing by the American Air Force which held undisputed command of the air and sabotage of the roads and railways by the irregulars, quickly led to Yamashita being completely cut off from most of the units under his command. In these circumstances it is hardly surprising that the discipline of many of the Japanese troops gave way. They defended themselves blindly and savagely. Undeniably horrible atrocities were committed. There is no reason to reject the allegation that 25,000 unarmed non-combatant civilians were slaughtered. Yamashita was gradually driven back into the

Chapter 8 — The Last Phase

mountainous northern end of the island of Luzon. He continued to resist stubbornly until Japan's surrender in September 1945.

General Yamashita surrendered on September 3rd. On September 25th he was charged with being a war-criminal: two weeks later he was arraigned and served with an indictment with sixty-four particulars. His trial was fixed for October 29th, so his defenders were given less than three weeks to study this lengthy document and to prepare his defence. It is thus hardly surprising that Mr. Justice Rutledge of the United States Supreme Court in his dissenting judgment commented that "the accused had been rushed to trial with needless and indecent haste." Mr. Frank Reel does not hesitate to attribute the refusal of the tribunal to grant proper time to prepare the defence to express orders sent them by General MacArthur, the supreme Military Authority in the Far East, to proceed with the work of liquidating the prisoners without delay.

It was not suggested by the prosecution that General Yamashita had been personally present at any of the numerous atrocities which were commited in various parts of the Philippines between October 1944 and September 1945, or that he had ordered or incited their commission. The prosecution maintained that as he was commander-in-chief in the Philippines he was responsible for everything his troops did during the period he commanded them.

The Tribunal convicted General Yamashita of having "failed to provide effective control over his troops", a crime hitherto unknown in the annals of jurisprudence. He was not convicted of having done anything or ordered or incited anything to be done: he was convicted of failing to do something. The Tribunal did not find that it was within his power to do what they found he had failed to do, namely to control his troops. So it would be more accurate to say he was convicted not for *doing* or *failing to do* anything, but for *being* the commander of demoralised troops who, without his knowledge or approval, committed crimes.

To do them justice the Tribunal made no pretence of being an impartial body. Their duty was to carry out the wishes of the American Commander-in-Chief, General MacArthur. Several times, Mr. Reel tells us, he and the other defence counsel were rebuked behind the scenes for being obstructive. "You men are not knights in armour jousting," General Reynolds told them, "You are officers of the Army and of this court and you are detailed to help us find the facts, not score points over the prosecution".

General Yamashita's calm dignity seems to have aroused the personal hostility of the prosecuting counsel. Contrary to the accepted practice in war-crimes trials, the prisoner appeared in court in his uniform as a general of the Japanese army with four rows of campaign ribbons. Colonel Meek, one of the prosecuting counsel, said to Mr. Reel, "Damn it, it makes me mad, seeing him decked out in uniform. He steals the show: he dominates the court room! If I had my way I'd put him in prison overalls and put chains on him."

Mr. Reel observes, "Even in overalls and chains General Yamashita would have stolen the show and dominated the court room. He personified dignity and serenity."

So outraged were Mr. Reel and the other counsel for the defence at the way the trial had been conducted that they determined not to give up the fight as lost after the verdict and the sentence, death by hanging, had been pronounced. Nominally, there is no right of appeal from a verdict of a court martial to a civil court. In this case, however, the court had convicted the prisoner of an offence for which no one had ever been convicted before. Further, the court had admitted hearsay evidence which made it possible to maintain that the trial was a breach of the Fifth Amendment of the American Constitution which guarantees a fair trial to any person accused of a crime by the Federal Government. It was decided, therefore, to apply to the Supreme Court of the United States for its ruling on these and other objections and for a stay of the execution until this ruling had been obtained.

A frantic race against time ensued. Application had first to be made to the Supreme Court of the Philippines and then when this application was inevitably rejected, to appeal against the rejection to the Supreme Court in Washington. The prosecution was deliberately obstructive, evading service of notices and omitting to supply copy documents. In the end the Supreme Court, which grants on an average only one application made to it out of seven, was induced to act. As General MacArthur refused point-blank to postpone the execution, the Supreme Court ordered a stay of further proceedings. Thereafter the War Department granted every assistance. Air transportation—"No. 1 priority"—was given to Mr. Reel and two of his colleagues. On December

Chapter 8 — The Last Phase

25th, 1945, they set off on a flight half way round the world from the Philippines to Washington. On January 7th, 1946, General Yamashita's appeal was heard by the Supreme Court.

It is often said the Supreme Court upheld the verdict of the Manila military tribunal. This is incorrect. Seven judges adjudicated and five of them held they had no jurisdiction to enquire into the findings of a court martial. The court, they maintained, could not concern itself "with the guilt or innocence of General Yamashita". If a wrong decision had been made on disputed facts, correction was the duty of the superior military authority, that is to say, of the Commander-in-Chief, General MacArthur. In the majority judgment the objection was evaded that the fundamental legal rights guaranteed by the Fifth Amendment had been disregarded by the admission of hearsay evidence. "It is unnecessary to consider here what in other situations the Fifth Amendment might require. Nothing we have said here is to be taken as indicating any opinion on the question of the wisdom of considering such evidence."

Only an American lawyer is competent to express an opinion whether this majority judgment of the Supreme Court was technically justified. Mr. Frank Reel maintains strongly that it was not. In his brilliant book, however, he gives no indication that he realised that far more was at stake than the life of a single Japanese general. To have granted the appeal would have led to the most far-reaching and most serious political consequences. One member of the Court was Mr. Justice Felix Frankfurter who was no mere learned lawyer, but as the intimate friend and confidant of the late Franklin D. Roosevelt, had for many years advised the President on the latter's tortuous foreign policy, and knew all there was to know concerning the international political situation. Although Frankfurter took no active part during the hearing of the appeal in court, we may be sure that he dominated his colleagues in their deliberations behind closed doors afterwards. To him it would have been clear that expediency demanded that the Supreme Court should reject General Yamashita's appeal and above all refrain from expressing any opinion on the legality and advisability of ignoring rules of evidence and admitting hearsay testimony. The contention of Yamashita's defenders that by ignoring rules of evidence and admitting hearsay testimony the military tribunal at Manila had failed to give Yamashita the fair trial to which he was entitled under the American Constitution might be described as veritably political dynamite. The tribunal had admittedly done this in accordance with the regulations for the disposal of Japanese prisoners of war drawn up by General Douglas MacArthur on the authority conferred on him by the President. Now MacArthur, a professional soldier with no knowledge of law, had merely adopted the innovations laid down for the trial of the major Nazi war-criminals at Nuremberg in the Charter of the London Agreement.[116]

Naturally he felt himself justified in assuming that the team of eminent jurists who had drafted the Charter knew their business. No doubt he felt he could hardly go wrong if he adopted the conclusions reached by such legal experts as Lord Justice Wright, one of the most distinguished members of the British Court of Appeal, and Ivan Nikitchenko, whose knowledge of Soviet law had so won him the esteem of Joseph Stalin that he had entrusted him with the task of preparing for the trial of the major Nazi war-criminals and had later sent him to represent the Soviet Union at the Nuremberg Trials in order to ensure that the verdict reached would confirm the verdict of guilt already pronounced by himself and the other chiefs of state at the Yalta Conference. No blame certainly could attach to General MacArthur for blindly following such eminent legal authorities.

The consequences, nevertheless, were extremely embarrassing, as no doubt Mr. Justice Frankfurter pointed out to his colleagues. In the circumstances, can it be doubted that he urged his learned colleagues not to waste their time debating whether one Japanese general should be hanged or should be allowed to end his days in retirement. They should realise, he no doubt pointed out, that it would be impossible to condemn MacArthur's regulations for Yamashita's trial without condemning the almost exactly similar regulations laid down in the Charter to the London Agreement under which at that very moment the mass trial of the major Nazi war-criminals was taking place at Nuremberg.

Their distinguished colleague, Mr. Justice Jackson, was at Nuremberg acting as chief American prosecutor. Would he not regard it as an undeserved affront if he was told that the Supreme Court, of which he was a member, had ruled the proceedings in which he was taking a leading part was not a fair trial within the meaning of the Fifth Amendment because of the rules under which it was being conducted. Far more important, however, was

Chapter 8 — The Last Phase

what would America's mighty ally, Joseph Stalin, think of such a finding. Already he was showing a disposition to be hostile. If they accepted Yamashita's appeal a grave international crisis would result, the consequences of which no man could foresee.

To avoid precipitating an international crisis, five of the seven judges of the Supreme Court hearing Yamashita's appeal very prudently held that if the Manila tribunal had been at fault in convicting him, it was not within their jurisdiction to set matters right, which was the business of the supreme military authority in the Far East, in other words, of the Commander-in-Chief, General MacArthur.

As so often happens in war-crimes trials, the dissenting judgments delivered are the most memorable features of the proceedings. Thus the dissenting judgment of the Indian representative on the Tokyo War-crimes Tribunal, Mr. Justice Rahabinode Pal, will be remembered long after the majority judgment delivered at that notorious war-crimes trial has been forgotten. Similarly the dissenting judgments which Mr. Justice Murphy and Mr. Justice Rutledge delivered regarding General Yamashita's appeal to the U.S. Supreme Court will always be honoured as emphatic re-assertions of long established legal principles.

Mr. Justice Murphy in his judgment declared: —

"The Fifth Amendment guarantee of due process of law applies to 'any person' — American citizens, aliens, alien enemies or enemy belligerents — who is accused of a crime by the Federal Government or any of its agencies.

General Yamashita was therefore entitled to a fair trial as to any alleged crimes and to be free from charges of legally unrecognized crimes that would only permit his accusers to satisfy their desires for revenge.

General Yamashita was, however, rushed to trial under an improper charge, given insufficient time to prepare an adequate defence, deprived of the benefits of some of the most elementary rules of evidence and summarily sentenced to be hanged. In all this needless and unseemly haste there was no serious attempt to charge or to prove that he committed a recognised violation of the laws of war. He was not charged with personally participating in the acts of atrocity or with ordering or condoning their commission. Not even knowledge of these crimes was attributed to him. It was simply alleged that he unlawfully disregarded and failed to discharge his duty as commander to control the operations of the members of his command."

With regard to General Yamashita's alleged failure to control the operations of the members of his command, Mr. Justice Murphy summarised the case for the prosecution in the following scathing and oft-quoted passage:

"The charges amount to this, 'We, the victorious American forces, have done everything possible to destroy and disorganise your lines of communication, your effective control of your personnel, your ability to wage war. We have defeated and crushed your forces. And now we charge and condemn you for having been inefficient in maintaining control of your troops, during the period when we were so effectively besieging and eliminating your forces and blockading your ability to maintain effective control. Many terrible atrocities were committed by your disorganised troops. Because these atrocities were so wide spread we will not bother to charge or prove you committed, ordered, or condoned them. We will assume that they must have resulted from your inefficiency and negligence as a commander. In short, we charge you with inefficiency in controlling your troops. We will judge the discharge of your duties by the disorganisation which we ourselves created in large part. Our standards of judgment are whatever we wish to make them';"

Mr. Justice Rutledge then read his dissenting judgment which confirmed and amplified the conclusions of Mr. Justice Murphy. He was particularly scathing regarding the complete disregard of the rules of evidence. "The tribunal has accepted," he declared, "every conceivable kind of statement, rumour, report, at first, second, third, or further hand, and even one propaganda film as evidence." He proceeded: "A more complete abrogation of the customary rules could hardly have been made. So far as the admissibility and probative value of evidence was concerned, the directive (of General MacArthur) made the tribunal a law unto itself and it acted accordingly."

Mr. Justice Rutledge concluded by declaring that so flagrant were the tribunal's departures from justice that "it was without jurisdiction from the beginning, and if it acquired jurisdiction, then its power to proceed was lost in the course of what was done before and during the trial." In passing, regret may be expressed

Chapter 8 — The Last Phase

that no means were available to bring the doings of the so-called International Military Tribunal at Nuremberg to the attention of the Supreme Court of the United States. Of course the majority of the Court would have timidly declined to express any opinion as they had done in the case of General Yamashita, but we may be sure that Mr. Justice Murphy and Mr. Justice Rutledge would have delivered dissenting judgments exposing with devastating logic and clarity the absurdities and iniquities committed at that macabre farce.

Although two judges of the Supreme Court had condemned the conduct of Yamashita's trial by the Manila tribunal in the most scathing terms and the other five judges had merely said that if the tribunal had erred it was the duty of the military authorities to rectify any wrong it had done, General MacArthur did nothing. On February 23rd, 1946, General Yamashita was hanged. Needless to say, he met his fate with stoical courage and dignity. The execution of General Yamashita is an indelible blot on the otherwise stainless career of General Douglas MacArthur, the last of that long line of Western empire-builders and colonial administrators who created, extended and maintained that White supremacy in Eastern Asia which had begun with the great naval victory of the Portuguese Viceroy Dom Francisco d'Almeida at Cannanore on the west coast of India over the Arab and Indian fleets in 1506.

When MacArthur died at an advanced age in 1964 the Eastern Asia he had known, dominated by Western Colonialism, had become a faded and discredited memory, a subject for the quite unjustified shame for many members of the formerly dominant White Race and for the equally unjustified hatred of the formerly subject Coloured Races. It may be true that White Supremacy in East Asia was bound to disappear in the course of time. White Supremacy, however, depended less on actual military strength than on White morale. No man contributed more to the shattering of White morale than General Tomoyuki Yamashita by his epoch-making capture of Singapore.

THE TRIAL OF GENERAL RAMCKE

A brief outline of the trial of the famous leader of paratroops, General Bernard Ramcke, is included here because it illustrates so vividly the hardships and injustice inflicted on prisoners of war by the Moscow Declaration of the 30th October, 1943, by which, it will be remembered, the victorious Powers conferred on themselves the right, in defiance of the Geneva Convention, to swop prisoners of war with each other.

Secondly, it demonstrates, if this really requires any demonstration, that a prisoner of war on trial before a war-crimes tribunal had a negligible chance of being acquitted, however threadbare the case for the prosecution. In this war-crimes trial the absurdity of the charges against General Ramcke was obvious to everyone in court long before the case ended. Nevertheless the Tribunal decided to convict in accordance with the principle that a war-crimes trial ought to end with a conviction, although this particular tribunal upheld the credit of French justice by imposing a nominal penalty which resulted in the release of the prisoner after the elapse of only a few months.

This trial also confirms the view that war-crimes tribunals often adopted one of the principles on which trials before the Inquisition were conducted. A person charged with heresy before a court of the Holy Office who conclusively proved his complete innocence was indeed acquitted of heresy but was convicted of having incurred the suspicion of heresy for which a relatively mild punishment was imposed. War-crimes tribunals like the courts of the Holy Office could not believe that a prisoner brought before them could be completely guiltless of any offence.

This case cannot be regarded as a typical Routine War-crimes Trial, since the belated decision to put General Ramcke on trial was reached in order to serve a political purpose. By, for him, a fortunate chance, his name had been put at the end of the long list of prisoners of war in French custody awaiting trial for war crimes. Had his name been put at the beginning of this list his case would have been dealt with as a simple Routine War-crimes Trial and his life would no doubt have come to a violent end without any particular attention being attracted. But although the French tribunals and firing squads worked with untiring zeal, the year 1951 arrived and General Ramcke was still awaiting trial. By then wartime passions had considerably abated: many prisoners were being released without being put on trial. Probably this would have been his fate also but for a stroke of ill-fortune. The Stalin Myth had been exposed as a propaganda fiction; no longer was

Chapter 8 — The Last Phase

it possible even for the most stupid to believe the Communist dictator was a loyal ally after his subjugation of Czechoslovakia and his blockade of West Berlin. To defend Western Europe from the threatened invasion by the Red Army it had become necessary to win the goodwill of the German people and to start re-creating the German Army.

Naturally the prospect of having to deal with a re-armed Germany aroused widespread alarm. Nowhere was this alarm more strongly felt than in France. The French Communists were filled with indignation that the advance of the Red Army to the Atlantic Coast should be obstructed by German troops, and their loud protests were supported by all those in France who regarded Germany as the national enemy. It was decided to compel the rest of the world to understand the gravity of the peril by staging a trial of one of the surviving German prisoners of war in French captivity, so that at this trial the full story of all the cruelties committed during the German occupation of France could be retold and then broadcast to the world.

It happened that the only surviving German prisoner of war in French captivity whose name was at all widely known to the general public was General Ramcke. Not much in fact was known about him except that he had stoutly defended Brest from the Americans and no one knew what offences he was supposed to have committed. The Communist Press, quickly followed by the Left-wing Press, took up the question of his misdeeds with enthusiasm. Very soon all France was ringing with the crimes of "The Butcher of Brest". The French Government acceded reluctantly to the popular demand. The papers relating to General Ramcke were hastily brought from some official pigeon hole where they had been collecting dust for years, charges were framed, and "The Butcher" was brought to a trial without a moment's unavoidable delay in the court room of the Prison Cherche-Midi in Paris on the 19th March, 1951.

An outline of General Ramcke's distinguished career must here be given briefly. Having served in the campaign in France, in 1941 he took a leading part in the conquest of Crete, the most spectacular and, from the losses incurred, the most ruinous exploit by paratroops of the Second World War. He next served as a leader of front-line troops in North Africa, Russia and Italy. He then returned to Germany to supervise the reorganisation of the 2nd Paratroop Division which had been decimated in the recent fighting in Russia. On the 12th June, 1944, he was ordered to take command of this Division which had been sent on ahead of him to France to reinforce the German forces there awaiting the long-expected Anglo-American invasion. He entered France on that date and proceeded to Brittany. On the 20th September he surrendered to the Americans at Brest. The dates are important because all General Ramcke's offences were alleged to have been committed during this short period of three months, during the first part of which until the 31st July he was fully occupied organising the defence of the coast of Brittany and during the second part of which he was engaged in attempting to hold up the American forces after their break-through at Avranches.

Cut off in the Breton Peninsula from the main German forces retreating eastward towards the Rhine, General Ramcke maintained resistance in Brest for thirty-nine days. When at last he was forced to surrender he was treated with every courtesy and honour by the American commander, General Troy H. Middleton. He was first sent to a prisoner-of-war camp near Cherbourg; then transferred to a prisoner-of-war camp in England, and finally flown across the Atlantic to Washington, whence he was taken by train to the great prisoner-of-war camp at Fort Clinton, near Jackson, Mississippi.

Conditions in this camp seem to have been excellent until Germany's unconditional surrender in May 1945, when a campaign was immediately started in the American Press in protest against the "coddling of prisoners, all of whom were undeniably guilty of what Lord Justice Lawrence was later to describe as the supreme international crime, namely of being on the losing side. In order to draw attention to the spiteful deprivations and restrictions imposed on the prisoners in response to this Press campaign, General Ramcke crawled beneath the barbed wire fence surrounding the camp, and posted a letter to army headquarters in Washington. He then returned to the camp. When, however, the camp authorities were ordered by headquarters to investigate General Ramcke's complaints, his escape, of course, came to light and he was put under arrest for a breach of prison discipline.

This incident is important in the light of subsequent events. No doubt the knuckles of a number of prison officials were deservedly rapped and General Ramcke in this way made

Chapter 8 — The Last Phase

a number of vindictive enemies. In accordance with the Moscow Declaration to which the United States was a party, a prisoner of war held by one victorious Power had to be handed over to any other victorious Power which alleged he had committed a war-crime. Down to this time it had occurred to no one that General Ramcke was a war-criminal. It would obviously have been easy for a personal enemy to have conveyed a hint to one of the Allied commissions in Washington that a demand for the surrender of General Ramcke as a war-criminal would be favourably received. At all events, shortly after the above incident he was told that he was being sent back to Europe. Naturally he assumed that he was about to be released in accordance with the requirements of international law. To his surprise the ship stopped at Antwerp in order to put him and one of his comrades ashore. What followed is best described in his own words:

"Hardly had the ship made fast at Antwerp when we were informed by an American officer that we were to be handed over to the British. A British officer of police, a sergeant and six men, took us in charge. Their manners were brutal. With rough cuffs and pushes they fastened Kochy and I together with handcuffs and chains and thrust us with kicks ("mit Fusstritten") into a waiting lorry. We were then driven through Antwerp, under the Scheldt by the celebrated Scheldt Tunnel, via Bruges, to P.O.W. Camp No. 2226 near Ostend."[117]

This deplorable incident took place in March 1946. After spending some time in appalling sanitary conditions in the prison camp near Ostend, General Ramcke was taken for interrogation to the notorious "London District Cage" in Kensington Gardens, London. The British then decided that they had no complaints against him. They did not set him free, however, but sent him over to Paris where, on the 4th December, 1946, he was handed over to the French by whom he was taken in handcuffs and chains, first to the Prison Cherche-Midi, and then to the prison at Rennes in Brittany.

It is only possible to speculate as to the reason for this extraordinary procedure. General Ramcke was unquestionably what prison governors would classify as "a difficult prisoner". He was not only a very brave man — it demands courage to drop with a parachute over enemy territory — but he was remarkably lacking in tact, as several anecdotes which he tells in his autobiography

Advance to Barbarism

show. He was well aware of the rights given him as a prisoner of war by international law and never hesitated to inform his captors when these rights were being infringed. They on their part took the view that the only proper relationship between a prisoner of war guilty of the supreme international crime of being on the losing side was humility and deference on his part and generous magnanimity on theirs. General Ramcke was totally unable to fill the role which his captors, whether American, British or French, expected of him. It seems likely, therefore, that he offended his British captors in the London District Cage in exactly the same way as he had offended his captors in Fort Clinton, Mississippi. Probably personal ill-will towards him accounts for his being handed over by the British to the French in December 1946.

For the next four years General Ramcke was kept in close confinement in the prison at Rennes. The sanitary arrangements of the prison were appalling and discipline was maintained by such penalties as solitary confinement in chains. It was not until 1951 that any charge was brought against him, by which time, as mentioned above, the political situation had been transformed by the outbreak of the "Cold War" between the United States and the Soviet Union.

The French Communists and their leftist allies then decided to re-awaken anti-German feeling by staging a trial of some well-known German prisoner of war. The "Hero of Brest" was the only prisoner still in French hands who fulfilled the necessary requirements. Labelled "The Butcher of Brest" in the French Press, General Ramcke was served with a hastily prepared indictment and for the first time learned what offences he was supposed to have committed. On the 19th March, 1951, over six and a half years after his surrender at Brest on the 20th September, 1944, he was brought before a French military tribunal in the court house of the Prison Cherche-Midi in Paris.

The trial of General Ramcke is only of interest if regarded as an example of the fate to which German prisoners of war were subjected when tried for war-crimes before French military tribunals. It is the only one of these trials which was fully reported at the time in the French Press — it even received some mention in the British Press — and in addition it has been described in detail by General Ramcke himself in his autobiography. The lawyers entrusted with framing the indictment had a difficult task to perform since it was only possible to charge General Ramcke with offences committed between the 12th June, 1944, the date he entered France, and the following 20th September when he surrendered in Brest. Naturally a makeshift document was the result since no one knew why the British had handed him over to French custody. He had only remained in French custody because, long hidden behind the walls of the prison at Rennes, he had become gradually forgotten.

As a makeweight to the main complaint against him, his obstinate resistance in Brest, his accusers brought against him the stock charge brought in most war-crimes trials that before the siege commenced men under his command dealt severely with partisan activity. Hurried investigation disclosed that after General Ramcke had taken command of his division in June 1944 three Breton peasants, all of them members of La Resistance, had been arrested by a patrol of men of a unit of his division for being in possession of weapons, and of being concerned in the murder of three German ambulance-men, whose bodies, horribly mutilated, had been found nearby.

They were subsequently executed by the Security Police. General Ramcke declared that no such incident had ever been reported to him, but if the facts were as stated by the prosecution he would heartily have approved of the execution of the murderers. The charge against him in fact amounted to the charge on which General Yamashita had been convicted at Manila, of failing to control the troops under his command. The prosecution did not press the charge, but went on to deal with General Ramcke's alleged offences during the thirty-nine days during which the siege of Brest lasted.

In a nutshell General Ramcke was charged with causing the death of French citizens and damage to civilian property during the siege.

Unfortunately for the prosecution but most fortunately for the inhabitants of Brest, before the American attack began General Ramcke proposed a truce so that the population of the fortress could be evacuated. The humane and chivalrous General Troy H. Middleton commanding the besieging army readily agreed, and the entire population was allowed to leave Brest with the exception of certain units of Partisans who remained behind in order to harass the Germans from the rear.

Advance to Barbarism

The prosecution called as a witness a Partisan leader named Le Roy who testified that he himself had prudently left Brest before the siege began, but he had left behind four of his men in a secret "hide-out". After the siege no trace of this "hide-out" or of the men he had left in it could be found. It was open therefore to the court to adopt the assumption that it had been discovered and burnt by the Germans who had shot the Partisans found lurking therein.

This indeed might have happened: probably the men were dead and certainly the "hide-out" had ceased to exist. But no evidence of any kind was produced that General Ramcke's troops had been in any way concerned. The siege of Brest was the first example of what may be termed a siege by obliteration. The Americans not only bombarded the besieged city with numerous guns of every calibre but they continuously bombed it from the air. Between August 7th and September 20th there were no fewer than thirty-nine major air attacks by heavy bombers on Brest: in the raid on September 12th no fewer than six hundred bombers took part. Brest was systematically destroyed, district by district; as in the battle for the Monte Cassino in the spring of that year, the defenders found excellent cover in the ruins and long resisted successfully the American infantry attacking behind a screen of phosphoros bombs and liquid fire.

At the end of the siege Brest did not consist of a collection of heavily damaged buildings; it consisted of masses of brickwork and masonry which had been repeatedly churned over by shells and bombs. It was not only impossible to distinguish one building from another but even to guess where the main streets had been. In his memoirs General Ramcke records, "Brest looked like a crater on the moon."

Forming part of this wilderness of debris was no doubt the Partisan "hide-out"; it might indeed have been discovered and destroyed by the garrison, but it was obviously far more likely to have been obliterated by the hurricane of shells and bombs which for the thirty-nine days rained down on Brest.

The prosecution added two supplementary charges. First, that the troops under General Ramcke's command had themselves set fire to Brest during the siege; secondly, they had indulged in plundering the city while the assault was in progress. Why troops should set fire to a city in which they themselves were, the prosecution did not explain. Even more absurd was the charge of plundering, since every member of the garrison knew that surrender was inevitable in either a few days or a few weeks when the survivors would become prisoners of war and of course any loot found on them would be taken from them. In these circumstances a regiment composed of professional burglars might safely be depended on to behave themselves if surrounded in Hatton Garden!

The prosecution finally collapsed when the defence read two affidavits, the one sworn by General Troy H. Middleton himself and the other by his second in command, General Robinson.

General Middleton began by disposing of the charge of plundering by testifying that no articles of plunder had been reported to him as having been found on the captured members of the garrison when they were searched after the surrender.

General Middleton was then asked: "What impression did you form of the methods of conducting war of the German soldiers in Brest and particularly of the 2nd Paratroop Division?" General Middleton replied: "During my entire professional service in two world wars I have never come across better fighting soldiers than the German troops in Brest. This applies particularly to the men of the 2nd Paratroop Division. They impressed me as well disciplined, well trained and remarkably obedient to orders."

In reply to the question: "Have you any knowledge of brutal acts or criminal behaviour on the part of the garrison of Brest?" General Middleton replied: "No acts of brutality or of unlawful methods of warfare were reported to me by my troops. Those of our men who became prisoners of the German troops in Brest were as well treated as one can expect in war. I consider that the measures taken by General Ramcke for the prisoners in his hands were better than I have ever before observed in warfare."

Finally General Middleton was asked: "Have you any observations to make concerning General Ramcke?" To this question he replied: "Of the many German commanders I have met in war and of the round dozen German generals who fell into the hands of my troops, I rank General Ramcke as the most outstanding soldier. I consider that he conducted the defence of Brest in accordance with the best soldierly traditions."

The evidence of General Walter M. Robinson, also taken on commission, was then read to the Court. It confirmed

General Middleton's evidence. In particular General Robinson testified that when the American troops entered Brest, there were numerous fires blazing caused by the phosphoros shells used in the bombardment which, in his opinion, were quite beyond the power of the garrison to master. The Court heard this unwelcome evidence in resentful silence.

This unexpected evidence put the military tribunal trying General Ramcke in an extremely difficult position. Almost the entire French Press had worked itself up into a state of hysteria over the crimes of the "Butcher of Brest". To acquit the accused was therefore impossible. But for the evidence of General Middleton the usual course adopted by war-crimes tribunals might have been adopted, that is to say, the accused might have been convicted and sentenced to death, with no other result than that tension would have been caused between France and Germany, an outcome much desired by Communist and Leftist opinion in France as it could have been used as an argument against the proposed re-arming of Germany.

To hang General Ramcke however in the face of the evidence in his favour given by General Middleton would be resented as an affront in American military circles. Great pride also was felt by the general public in the United States in the story of the capture of Brest, not only as an example of American prowess but of American chivalry; Americans could hardly be expected to welcome the addition of a footnote to that story recording that the gallant defender of Brest was done to death by his French enemies seven years after his surrender to the Americans. But, most important of all, the judicial murder of General Ramcke would have been regarded with the strongest disapproval by the American Government, then striving desperately to enlist German public opinion to the side of the Western Powers. Ever since the end of the War, France had depended on American financial and economic support. If an "agonizing re-appraisal" took place in Washington and the flow of dollars ceased, where could France turn for benevolent support? Would not the loss of the American pension be a high price to pay for the death of one more German general?

There is no reason to think that the French military tribunal trying General Ramcke was any more perceptive of the grave political issues at stake than the average war-crimes tribunal. Fortunately, the tribunal had the guidance of a civil judge, Monsieur Ménéquaux, upon whom, on this occasion at least, the wisdom of Solomon clearly descended. He succeeded in persuading his military colleagues to disregard entirely the evidence given at the trial and to bring in a general verdict of guilty, thus satisfying French public opinion, and then to sentence General Ramcke to five years' imprisonment. As the General had already spent only three months short of five years in rigorous confinement awaiting trial, this sentence entitled the accused to release at the expiration of three months.

Except for the French Communists and their Leftist allies whose stunt had miscarried, and General Ramcke himself, who strongly resented being labelled a criminal for crimes which the court carefully refrained froth specifying, this celebrated war-crimes trial ended to the satisfaction of everyone concerned. On the 23rd June, 1951, General Ramcke was released from the Cherche-Midi Prison and was immediately driven by car to the German frontier. His long ordeal which had begun on the quay at Antwerp in March 1946 was over.

THE TRIAL OF FIELD MARSHAL VON MANSTEIN

This chapter dealing with the final development of the "advance to barbarism", the introduction of war-crimes trials at which the victors tried their own charges against the vanquished, may be fittingly concluded by an examination of what was in many respects the most noteworthy of all the war-crimes trials which followed the Second World War.

This trial was noteworthy for three reasons. Firstly, because the accused, Field Marshal von Manstein, was without question one of the greatest of the military leaders who took part in that struggle; secondly, because the proceedings were not only fully reported in the newspapers at the time, but were afterwards described in detail in a book written by the leading English counsel for the defence, a book which is entitled to rank with Mr. Frank Reel's *The Trial of General Yamashita*; and thirdly, because the fundamental points at issue were fought out by the prosecution and the defence on comparatively equal terms.

It will be remembered that by the time the Nuremberg Trials had at last reached the conclusion preordained at the Yalta

Advance to Barbarism

Conference, the British public had become utterly weary of the subject of the disposal of enemy prisoners of war. An Iron Curtain of Discreet Silence was then drawn over the question. Interest was temporarily revived in 1947 by the sentencing of Field Marshal Kesselring to death, but once his reprieve had been arranged behind the scenes, the British public soon forgot that war-crimes trials were still going on all over Europe. Great care was taken to prevent the British public being reminded of this fact; discussion in print concerning the legality and ethics of these so-called trials was made the subject of a strict taboo. No one, and particularly those who had taken part in them, wanted to hear war-crimes trials mentioned again.

It appears that the British authorities innocently mistook the indifference of the British public to what was taking place for wholehearted approval. In the summer of 1948, it was casually announced that three famous generals, Field Marshal Gerd von Runstedt, Field Marshal Fritz Erich von Manstein, and Colonel-General Strauss, who had spent the previous three years in honourable captivity in England as prisoners of war, were to be sent back to Germany in order to stand their trial as war-criminals.

A storm of protests at once broke forth, far exceeding the outcry which had arisen over the condemnation of Field Marshal Kesselring. What was the reason, it was asked, for bringing these belated charges? "If these men were guilty of war-crimes," wrote Professor Gilbert Murray to *The Times*, "they should have been promptly accused and punished. Nothing can justify keeping these men in prison for three years without a trial."

The Government had no reply to make to this question and the controversy in the columns of the Press and the debates in Parliament were entirely one-sided. In vain the Lord Chancellor, Lord Jowitt, reiterated that he was satisfied in the depths of his heart that the prisoners had a case to answer and that the trials really should take place.

The storm continued. At last, on May 5, 1949, Lord Jowitt announced that the charges against Field Marshal von Runstedt and Colonel-General Strauss were to be dropped. But the case against Field Marshal von Manstein must, he insisted, proceed. "The whole matter for the last six months has been a source of great worry to me," Lord Jowitt declared plaintively. The solution decided on to put an end to Lord Jowitt's six months of worry

Chapter 8 — The Last Phase

can only be regarded as most unfortunate from any point of view. Of the three distinguished soldiers threatened with prosecution as war-criminals, only Field Marshal von Runstedt, the hero of the famous winter-battle of the Ardennes, at the end of 1944, was generally known to the British public. The names of his two comrades, if known at all, were unassociated with any particular event. The reason officially given for the decision not to put him and Colonel-General Strauss on trial was their advanced years and declining health. An excellent reason in both cases, no doubt. But it was a reason that applied equally well in the case of Field Marshal von Manstein who was also elderly and in bad health; he had always been delicate and was now threatened by blindness. The age of all three men was in the neighbourhood of seventy.

So unconvincing an official explanation inevitably invited speculation as to the true reason. Inquiry showed that, although Manstein had spent the last four years of the war on the Eastern Front, he had taken a leading part in the Campaign of France, in 1940, and to his brilliant strategy was generally ascribed the great breakthrough near Sedan on May 13th, which led in a few weeks to the withdrawal of the B.E.F. from Dunkirk and the capitulation of France at Compiègne. In his book, *The Other Side of the Hill*, Captain Liddell Hart writes:

"The ablest of all the German Generals was probably Field Marshal von Manstein. That was the verdict of most of those with whom I discussed the war, from Runstedt downwards. He had a superb strategic sense and a great understanding of mechanized warfare.... From him came the brain-wave that produced the defeat of France — the idea of a tank-thrust through the Ardennes."[118]

A triumph so swift, so complete and, above all, so unexpected must inevitably have produced widespread psychological reactions. When, on May 10th, 1940, two million German troops began the long-awaited attack on the Western Front defended by some three and a quarter million men, confidence reigned supreme that this attack would be victoriously repulsed. No other result indeed seemed possible. On the one side were hurriedly trained German conscripts, many of whom were believed to hope for defeat as the only means of bringing about the downfall of Hitler's regime which they were supposed to hate. Their organisation had been hastily improvised; owing to shortage of raw material their equipment was of poor quality, and they were

Advance to Barbarism

outnumbered by three to two. On the other side were the famous Maginot Line, constructed at such vast cost and considered by the experts as impregnable; the French Army the same instrument which Marshal Foch had led to victory twenty years before, re-equipped and reorganised in accordance with the lessons of the 1914–1918 War; and the B.E.F. made up of 350,000 long-service soldiers, the best trained and equipped army that Great Britain had ever despatched to fight in a European war. Under such circumstances, it is not surprising that few paid attention to the poet Rudyard Kipling's warning against indulging in "frantic boast and foolish word". Thus, on April 5th, 1940, in the apparent security of British G.H.Q., General Sir Edmund Ironside, Chief of the Imperial General Staff, "with the full consent of Mr. Oliver Stanley, the War Minister" gave the following "frank interview on the war," proudly described as being "one of the most outspoken statements ever made by a British military leader in wartime." As reported in the *Daily Mail* the following day, the gallant general said:

"Hitler has 'missed the bus' in not attacking us during the last seven months. We have turned the corner. Having seen the British Army over in France, what we have got in this country, and also the French army, I feel that everything is going on well.

The spirit of the young men is something that has to be seen to be believed. As an actual fact there is no officer in the German Army opposed to us who served in the last war above the rank of captain. We have generals and colonels galore, and so have the French Army — men still in the pink of condition — who commanded in the last war and know what it means.

I know most of the German commanders personally. I should say that most of these men are now feeling very exercised about what they should do if the order was given to 'go'.

In this country today there is no doubt about the reasons for which we are fighting. There is a great silence in Germany. German propaganda is full of lies and this must be bad for morale.

It seems to me that one reason why the German troops are kept in position at the front is that they can be much better controlled there."[119]

Within less than two months of this speech — a verbose and authentic variation of Kaiser Wilhelm's entirely fictional reference, in 1914, to Sir John French's "contemptible little army" — the

Chapter 8 — The Last Phase

B.E.F. was embarking at Dunkirk in order to return to Britain. It was leaving behind it all its guns to the number of 2,300; 120,000 vehicles, including all its tanks, armoured cars and lorries; and all its equipment, ammunition and stores. That the bulk of the troops succeeded in escaping at all was due entirely to Hitler's delusion that the dark menace of Asia overshadowing Europe would induce Great Britain to come to an understanding with Germany in joint self-protection. Few members of the B.E.F. returned to England with more than the clothes which they were wearing.

Anyone but a British Foreign Office official would have foreseen that the decision to single out as a war-criminal the general to whom, it is agreed, was due the credit for this amazing triumph was bound to give rise to regrettable misconstruction. In this speech, General Ironside was only expressing views universally held at the time in the highest military and political circles. We are assured he spoke "with the full consent of Mr. Oliver Stanley, the War Minister." Sudden realisation of the truth must have come as a terrific shock. Resentment at the time must have been widespread in political circles. Inevitably, the trial at Hamburg, in 1949, of Field Marshal von Manstein came to be widely regarded as retribution for his achievements in 1940 which have secured for him a sure place in world history.

It is quite certain that the true explanation of the persistence with which the demand for the trial of Field Marshal von Manstein was pressed is that, if he had been released, it might have been difficult to resist a demand by the Soviet Union for his surrender as a war criminal, in view of the Moscow Declaration of October 1943 and the reciprocal undertakings exchanged in 1945. In accordance with these undertakings, a number of prisoners of war had, in fact, been handed over to the tender mercies of the Poles, Greeks and Serbs. But, in default of a reasonable explanation or, better, of an explanation which could be frankly stated, it was inevitable that untrue and unjust explanations should have been suggested in foreign quarters critical of Great Britain.

Neither the danger of misrepresentation nor any other objection succeeded in shaking for an instant the iron determination of the British Government to proceed unflinchingly with this belated war-crimes trial, an iron determination all the more remarkable since determination of any kind had been conspicuously absent from British foreign policy in regard to every other matter since the War. Hope of appeasing Russian hostility having long since been abandoned, there was no object or advantage to be gained by the trial; public opinion in Great Britain was quite indifferent; a small but influential minority was extremely outspoken in opposition; and those who desired to hear that another German general had been hanged considered it the best policy to remain silent in the hope that the outcry would die down if left unopposed. As a result, the debates in Parliament on the matter were entirely one-sided, but the order to the army authorities to proceed with the trial remained unrevoked.

But, although the opposition aroused by the decision to put Field Marshal von Manstein on trial as a war-criminal failed utterly to shake the resolve of the British Government, it led to other important results. It was strongly urged that, if this war-crimes trial must take place, it should at least be conducted with fairness. The Field Marshal's trial would take place before an English military court and, therefore, he ought to be represented by English counsel. Possibly, because the effects of such an innovation were not at first realised, this proposal was not openly opposed. Probably, reliance was placed on the fact that, the Field Marshal was practically penniless, since all his property being situated in the eastern provinces of Germany annexed by Poland, had been summarily confiscated. In order to deprive him of legal assistance therefore, it only appeared necessary for the British authorities to refuse him adequate funds to pay for his defence. The Bar Council did not even trouble to repeat the ruling, which it had given before the Nuremberg war-crimes trials began that it was "undesirable" that a member of the English Bar should appear for the defence. It remained, therefore, possible to contend that the accused was free to employ any lawyer, English or German, whom he pleased. The fact that he had been robbed of all his money by the allies of Great Britain and, consequently, could not pay for legal aid was plainly no concern of the British Government.

It had, however, been wrongly assumed that the Field Marshal's sympathisers would be content with protesting. The necessary funds to pay for his defence, amounting to some £2,000, were quickly raised by public subscription. The British authorities would, no doubt, have foiled this move by prohibiting the export of British currency for such a purpose but for the fact that one of the subscribers to the fund was no other than Mr. Winston

Chapter 8 — The Last Phase

Churchill. After six months worry, Lord Jowitt was in no mood to bring down on himself the formidable wrath of Mr. Churchill. The opposition ignominiously collapsed. Mr. R. T. Paget, K.C., M.P., generously offered his services without a fee.

Field Marshal von Manstein was formally charged on January 1st, 1949, the farce of confiscating his uniform having been solemnly enacted whereby he was deemed to have become a civilian. The trial commenced in Hamburg on August 22, 1949, and dragged on until December 19 following.

It would be outside the scope of this book to examine the details of the trial of Field Marshal von Manstein. The only real issue in the case is, however, so simple that it can be explained in a few words. The Field Marshal was in command of the army group on the southern wing of the Eastern Front. Facing him were the Russian armies with a numerical superiority of seldom less than four to one. Behind his lines raged a ceaseless and furious struggle between the German security forces and the communist commandos in which the unfortunate civilian population, willingly or unwillingly, joined. This struggle had commenced on the first day that the German armies crossed the Russian frontier when Stalin announced that the war "was not only a war between two armies but at the same time a war of the entire Soviet people against the Fascist German troops". According to Russian official reports, in the Crimea alone, 18,910 German soldiers were killed by the partisan bands, 64 troop trains were blown up, and 1,621 lorries destroyed. Prisoners and wounded were murdered, generally after mutilation; horrifying deeds took place whenever a German hospital was seized by the guerillas.

As has been previously repeatedly stressed, the essential characteristic of civilized warfare is the drawing of a distinction between the enemy combatant forces and the enemy civilian population. But, in the fighting on the Eastern Front, no such distinction could be drawn; any Russian civilian who maintained his civilian status was liable to be executed by his own countrymen as a traitor. The task of combatting this campaign of terror behind the German lines fell mainly on units of the S.D., the intelligence branch of the Geheime Staatspolizei, otherwise known as the Gestapo. These units operated quite independently of the army. They were not subject to military discipline. Their orders came direct from Hitler via Heinrich Himmler, the chief of

Advance to Barbarism

the Schutzstaffel, (the S.S.), the Gestapo and the S.D. There is no question that their orders were to combat terror by terror; there is no reason to think that they did not do their utmost to obey their orders.

In a nutshell, the charge against the Field Marshal was that he knew or should have known what was taking place. There is no question that horrible atrocities were committed by both sides in the struggle. Under the ruling laid down in the London Agreement the atrocities committed by the German security forces counted as "war-crimes", since they were committed "in the interest of the Axis countries".

On the other hand, the atrocities committed by the partisans were not "war-crimes", since the perpetrators ultimately found themselves on the winning side. The Communist atrocities, therefore, were not the concern of the Field Marshal since they were not technically "war-crimes", but he should have been concerned with the atrocities of the German security forces, since these were "war-crimes" committed by the ultimately losing side in an area of which he was in military command although, admittedly, he had no authority or power to prevent them. It was contended, further, that the Field Marshal should have been able to foresee the retrospective law which, some three years later, the victors would become minded to lay down and he should, therefore, have complied strictly with its requirements.

Even since war-crimes trials began in 1945 the British legal Press had been publishing from time to time letters enquiring what exactly was the legal principle or doctrine under which British officers stationed in Germany had acquired the right to sit in judgment on German subjects for offences which they were alleged to have committed when they were subject to the law of their own country. It is a remarkable fact that none of the learned contributors to the legal Press ever wrote supplying the answer to the question, whence these military courts acquired their authority. Yet the answer, first brought clearly to light during the Manstein Trial in 1949, was in fact very simple. At this trial the general public learned that the British officers entrusted with the duty of adjudicating on the charges brought against the Field Marshal for acts committed by him during the War were empowered by a Royal Warrant dated June 18th, 1945, which directed that prisoners of war in British hands charged with war crimes, defined as "violations of the laws and usages of war," should be tried by British military courts.

For four years, every war-crimes trial before a British military court had begun with a formal challenge of the jurisdiction of the court which the prosecution immediately brushed aside by a brief reference to the terms of the Royal Warrant. Rarely, it seems, was the point seriously argued. The lawyers for the defence were foreigners, themselves liable to be sent to a concentration camp if they displayed inconvenient zeal, and the challenge was made by them *pro forma* and generally argued through an interpreter or in halting English. Because, in every case, the trials proceeded, the British public assumed this challenge to the jurisdiction had been adequately refuted.

How baseless was this assumption only became apparent, at least to the British public, at the trial of Field Marshal von Manstein. On the first day of the trial, Mr. Paget challenged the jurisdiction of the court to sit in judgment on his client. The accused, he pointed out, was a prisoner of war. A state of war still existed between Great Britain and Germany. Prisoner of war status is the right of every prisoner taken in war; it does not depend in any way upon the discretion of the captor. The Geneva Convention, to which of course Great Britain and all civilized states were parties, reaffirmed and laid down the long-established principle that a state detaining prisoners of war must deal with them in accordance with its own laws and regulations in respect of its own armed forces. Among the rights of a prisoner of war was the right to a fair trial. A fair trial is what a captor himself considers a fair trial for his own personnel.

The prosecution was relying on the terms of the Royal Warrant of June 18th, 1945. But this document deprived the accused of many important rights which he would have enjoyed under British military law. In particular, he was deprived of the right to be tried by officers of rank equal to his own; the right to demand a precise statement of the offences with which he was charged; and the right to claim the protection of the rules of evidence, that is to say, he was not to be convicted on hearsay evidence. Finally, Mr. Paget appealed to the court not to be overawed by the fact that the document of June 18th, 1945, was labelled a Royal Warrant. In 1916, the House of Lords, in the famous Zamora case, had held that the seizure of a ship under a Royal Warrant was illegal because the seizure in that case was contrary to international law. The Royal Warrant was nothing but a government order. Responsibility for its terms rested on the government; as a constitutional monarch the King signed Royal Warrants on the advice of his Ministers.

Exceptional interest attaches to the reply of Sir Arthur Comyns Carr, K.C., leading Counsel for the prosecution. He began by declaring that he had listened to Mr. Paget's submission "with considerable astonishment". It went, he declared, to the root of this trial, a circumstance which he seemed to think was in itself an objection against it. Rather naively, he pointed out that it had become the practice of war-crimes tribunals to reject this submission; it had, in fact, always been rejected.

He paid a tribute to the majority judgment of the American Supreme Court in the Yamashita case which sent that gallant soldier to his death. He argued that the right to a fair trial given to a prisoner of war by the Geneva Convention only applied to offences committed by the accused after he became a prisoner of war. In any event, the Field Marshal was no longer a prisoner of war since the British Government had seen fit to discharge him from the German army. Perhaps it might seem that much time and trouble had been wasted at Geneva in defining the rights and privileges of a prisoner of war if a prisoner only remained a prisoner of war at the discretion of his captors.

The fact remained that if his captors decided to make a prisoner of war a civilian, they could then do as they pleased with him. Sir Arthur said that he had listened with regret to a King's Counsel speaking slightingly of a Royal Warrant. This document has not been designed to prevent the accused from having a fair trial. It was perfectly right and proper that hearsay evidence should be admissible before a war-crimes trial tribunal because war-crimes are "of such magnitude that it would be impossible to apply to the proof of them the rules by which we are bound in a small case."

It would be interesting to know what impression, if any, the latter argument made on the members of the Court. Even to Sir Arthur himself it must have sounded weak. If sound, it would logically follow "that evidence that would justify a conviction for murder might be insufficient to support a conviction for riding a bicycle at night without a lamp.[120] Mr. Paget admits, however, that he had little hope that the court would uphold his submission.

Chapter 8 — The Last Phase

It was, of course, rejected. To have decided otherwise would have been a reflection on every war-crimes tribunal which had adjudicated on the point during the previous four years. The court would have had no option but to dissolve itself; the prisoner would have left the dock and gone home; and the gallant officers assembled on the Bench would have returned to their military duties. Was it to reach so rapid and lame a conclusion that Lord Chancellor Jowitt had endured six months' worry? It would have needed the combined strength of will of a tribunal composed of supermen to have reached so startling a conclusion. And the Tribunal before which the Field Marshal had been brought was not composed of supermen. It was composed of one Lieutenant-General, one Major-General, two brigadiers and three Colonels.

The composition of the court which decided that it possessed jurisdiction to try him was one of the three main disabilities imposed on the Field Marshal by the terms of the Royal Warrant. Under international law, as confirmed and laid down by the Geneva Convention, he was entitled to be tried by court-martial in accordance with British military law by officers of his own rank. All the officers appointed to try him under the Royal Warrant were of very inferior rank. This was a serious disability, since not one of them had held an independent command of an army or group of armies and, therefore, had had no experience of the difficulties with which he had been compelled to cope.

The second disability deliberately inflicted on the accused was that, in accordance with the Royal Warrant, he was denied any precise statement of the charges he would face when the trial began. The result is described by Mr. Paget as follows:

"When it came to the trial, the charges against von Manstein were 17 in number. They were summarized by a reporter who said that the prosecution had collected everything that occurred in the Eastern war and thrown it at von Manstein's head.

What the prosecution appeared to have done was to list every incident which might contravene any law or usage of war and which had occurred in any area in which von Manstein had served. As this covered huge areas over a period of 4½ years of particularly ruthless war, the prosecution were able to list some hundreds of incidents. These incidents, or particulars as they were called, were then divided into 17 groups, and before each group some order or orders generally issued by the high command were referred to, and the allegation made that the particulars were the result of the orders. Then in front of the orders appeared a statement in varied terms, but to the general effect that von Manstein was responsible for the results of the orders, and finally, at the commencement of each charge appeared the words 'contrary to the laws and usages of war'. What von Manstein was actually supposed to have done and what law or customs were alleged to have been contravened was left quite vague. The result was an enormous document which took well over two hours to read in court.

We asked for detailed explanations of what the charges meant, and submitted to the prosecution some 20 foolscap pages of questions. These questions the prosecution refused to answer. When we objected to the charges in court, the reply of the prosecution was that at Nuremberg and Tokyo the charges had been vaguer still! The real answer was that the Royal Warrant gave to the accused no right to know what charges were brought against him, and we had to be content with whatever the prosecution gave us."[121]

The third disability was even more grave. By the express terms of the Royal Warrant, the accused was deprived of the protection of the rules of evidence. At a more famous and equally unsatisfactory trial, two thousand years ago, the high priest, Caiaphas, was in a position to exclaim, "Answerest thou nothing? What is it which these witnesses witness against thee?" But, apart from one witness so unsatisfactory that his evidence was withdrawn by the prosecution with the consent of the court, not a single witness testified anything against Field Marshal von Manstein. So far as the prosecution was concerned, the court house need not have been provided with a witness box. Reliance was placed entirely upon some 800 documents which took twenty days to read to the court. They were accepted *en bloc* by the court at their face value without proof of authenticity, authorship, or issue.

The defence strove vainly to insist that, when oral evidence was readily available to support a charge, an affidavit should not be accepted. In particular, Comyns Carr blandly produced three statements incriminating the Field Marshal, purporting to have been made by three S.S. officers who had been sentenced to death by the American authorities. These three men were still alive, but

Chapter 8 — The Last Phase

the American authorities refused to allow them on any account to go into the witness box to give sworn evidence in support of their alleged statements.

Mr. Comyns Carr professed indignation at the suggestion that the refusal of the American authorities was due to fear that the condemned men might disclose what means had been employed to induce them to sign these statements, or that they might seize the opportunity to describe publicly the treatment which they, themselves, had received from their American captors.

There could be no dispute as to the methods commonly employed by the American authorities to obtain confessions, since a report of a special commission appointed by the Secretary of the U.S. Army, Mr. Kenneth C. Royall, had just been published, which described and denounced these methods. From this report, it appeared that, apart from unrestricted physical violence — most of the German victims of the Malmedy war-crimes trials at Dachau were found to be rendered impotent from blows or kicks — the commission found that confessions had frequently been obtained by staging mock-trials.

This procedure was adopted in cases where there was no evidence at all against the prisoner, so that even a military tribunal might hesitate to convict. Such an unsatisfactory state of affairs was remedied by bringing the prisoner before a court composed of investigators dressed as judges, who pretended to sentence him to death. He was then informed that, if he would confess, he would be reprieved. If he then signed the confession placed before him, he was immediately brought before the real military tribunal authorised to try his case which, relying on his confession, would sentence him to death. The commission reported that this trick had been successful in many cases.

Nevertheless Comyns Carr argued that the court might safely accept the statements of the S.S. officers and their presence in the witness box was quite unnecessary. Readers of Charles Dickens will remember that at the trial of Bardell v. Pickwick, Sam Weller was told by the judge that what the soldier said was not evidence. At Hamburg, it was maintained that although what the soldier said might not be evidence, what the S.S. man said was evidence which could be accepted without hesitation. The fact was apparently overlooked that Lord Jowitt, in his memorable speech on May 4th, 1949, had given the House of Lords a solemn assurance that the trial of the Field Marshal "would be conducted in accordance with our great traditions."

For hundreds of years it has been a tradition of English criminal law that hearsay evidence is inadmissible. It is unthinkable that, when he gave this assurance, the Lord Chancellor did not know what were "our great traditions." We are bound to accept the alternative assumption that he was unfamiliar with the terms of the Royal Warrant under the provisions of which the Field Marshal's trial would take place.

It is a relief to turn from such speculations in order to justify the claim made above that the trial of Field Marshal von Manstein must be regarded as a model war-crimes trial. During the four years which had passed since the introduction of war-crimes trials, several noteworthy reforms had been effected. For example, the accused was no longer referred to in the Press as a war-criminal even before the charges were read, as had previously been the custom, and he was no longer subjected to flagrant bad manners by the court. Although, in the indictment, he was simply described as Erich von Manstein, this was treated throughout merely as a convenient legal fiction in pursuance of the principle laid down at Nuremberg that the rights of a prisoner of war are lost if, somehow, he is deprived of his rank by his captors.

Throughout the trial, Field Marshal von Manstein was treated with the respect and consideration due to his rank and brilliant military achievements, When he entered the witness box, the members of the Court quickly forgot that they were supposed to by trying a war-criminal and settled down to hear, understand and profit by a five-hour lecture on strategy which they were privileged to receive from one of the greatest soldiers of his generation.

No doubt, at the back of their minds was the thought that, one day, they themselves might be called upon to cope with similar difficulties in a campaign against the same foe with whom "this benign, white-haired, half-blind old man had fought." To quote the correspondent of the *Daily Mail*, when Manstein entered the witness box, "the court room was immediately changed into a lecture hall of a staff college. Leaning forward to catch every word, the red-tabbed British officers heard him give a five-hour lecture on military strategy and full details of his Russian campaigns without reference to a note."[122]

Chapter 8 — The Last Phase

If, as is to be hoped, these British staff officers benefited by the instruction given to them, this part of the trial, at any rate, was not an entire waste of time.

There is no interest whatever in the last phase of the average war-crimes trial. All accounts agree that, after weeks and perhaps months of indescribable tedium, the only emotion felt by anyone at the end, including probably the accused, is profound relief. Some have compared a war-crimes trial with a bull-fight. Others consider the comparison unfair, to which subject of the comparison there is a difference of opinion. But the Manstein trial was not a typical war-crimes trial. Mr. Paget's final speech for the defence made a deep impression on the Court. It ended with the solemn warning, "It is not within your power to injure the reputation of Manstein, you can but injure your own."

Mr. Paget admits that, at the conclusion of the case, he had become confident of an acquittal. One of the prosecuting team was heard offering odds of two to one on a clear acquittal but found no takers. In the usual war-crimes trial, the odds in favour of a conviction could only be expressed by some astronomical figure. The Manstein trial was a model war-crimes trial. The reply of the prosecution was long but, compared with the opening, moderate and subdued. The most effective argument employed was the undeniable assertion that "acquittal of von Manstein would make nonsense of all other trials."[123]

Every possible allowance should be made for the difficulties which faced the members of the tribunal. They were officers of very inferior rank to the accused, and not one of them had had any experience with primary warfare. They possessed no personal knowledge of the difficulties of a commander-in-chief engaged in a campaign against a powerful enemy, in numbers greatly superior to his own, who finds his long lines of communication attacked by the civilian population.

They were in the position of a committee of the boxing board of control called upon to enquire whether an all-in wrestling champion had infringed certain of the Queensbury Rules. Their only desire was to do their duty. The charges were based on a haphazard collection of some 800 disconnected documents in a foreign language which it had taken twenty days to read. What facts could be deduced from this wild chaos? Mr. Paget's arguments appeared conclusive and were supported by common sense. But Mr. Comyns Carr could point to the undoubted fact that every war-crimes trial tribunal, British and foreign, had, to date, accepted his contentions without hesitation. The complete lack of any admissible evidence such as would justify a conviction for petty larceny would appear to have made their task easy. But could it be believed that the Lord Chancellor would have worried for six months about a case which could only end in an outright acquittal? Concerning the law governing the subject, the only thing certain about it seemed to be that the authorities contradicted each other on every point at issue.

For guidance on the difficult points of international law which were bound to arise during the trial, the tribunal had been provided with the judge of the Surrey County Court acting as Judge Advocate General. The task of this functionary, Judge Collingwood, could hardly have been more onerous. With no staff to assist him, he had to marshal some 800 documents and to prepare a summing-up which would cover all the points at issue raised in the seventeen charges. It is agreed that he performed this task admirably; nothing could have been fairer than his handling of the facts.

But questions of international law rarely, if ever, arise in county courts, the jurisdiction of which is limited to claims in which the amount in dispute does not exceed £400. Judge Collingwood had made no special study of international law. Further, in the Surrey County Court, litigants dissatisfied with his rulings on breach of contract, running-down actions, the provisions of the Rent Restriction Acts, and other subjects on which he had wide experience, had a right of appeal to the High Court. But, at this war-crimes trial at Hamburg, the mantle of infallibility which the Nuremberg Tribunal had assumed had been draped round Judge Collingwood's shoulders. From his rulings on international law the accused had no appeal.

Suffice it to say, Judge Collingwood rejected every important contention of the defence. He advised the tribunal that neither superior orders nor acts of state were any reply to the charges and that the accused was responsible for the full exercise of executive power within the area of his command, whether this power had been given solely to him or whether he had shared it with others. He laid down that the accused was bound to comply with the rules of civilized warfare whether his opponents

Chapter 8 — The Last Phase

complied with these rules or not. This latter ruling was particularly remarkable as the *British Manual of Military Law* declares just the opposite, as follows:

"The rules of international law apply only to warfare between civilized nations where both parties understand them and are prepared to carry them out."

Most remarkable of all, however, was Judge Collingwood's ruling that the execution of prisoners as a reprisal was illegal, under all circumstances. On this point the *British Military Manual* is most explicit. Article 453 lays down:

"Reprisals between belligerents are retaliation for illegitimate acts of warfare for the purpose of making the enemy comply in future with the recognized laws of war. They are not a means of punishment, or arbitrary vengeance, but of coercion."

To remove any possible doubts on the matter, Article 454 adds:

"Reprisals are an extreme measure because in most cases they inflict suffering upon innocent individuals. In this, however, their coercive force exists and they are indispensable as a last resource."

It is not clear whether Judge Collingwood thought that the authors of the *British Military Manual* went astray in this exposition of international law or whether he considered that reprisals were permissible to British generals but illegal in all circumstances to foreign generals or, at any rate, to German generals. It is certain, at least, that a British general who acted strictly in accordance with the directions of the *British Military Manual* would have no reason to fear a British court-martial. It is, no doubt, equally certain that he would now find this little protection in the event of his discovering himself on the losing side and being subjected by his captors to a war-crimes trial. In a letter to *The Times*, written immediately after the trial, Captain Liddell Hart concludes:

"I have studied the records of warfare long enough to realise how few men who have commanded armies in a hard struggle could have come through such a searching examination, of their deeds and words, as well as Manstein did. His condemnation appears a glaring example of either gross ignorance or gross hypocrisy."[124]

Some may think that this opinion makes insufficient allowance for the enormous difficulties of the task which the

Advance to Barbarism

tribunal had had to face. They had nothing to do with the decision to charge the Field Marshal as a war-criminal: this decision was entirely the responsibility of the British Government. They had nothing to do with the framing of the seventeen charges: two of the charges had been brought by the Communist Polish Government, and fifteen by the Communist Russian Government. The purpose of the trial must have been as obscure to them as to everyone else. They were asked to find as proved facts which the prosecution admitted could not be proved in accordance with the recognised rules of evidence. On difficult points of international law, upon which even the experts disagreed, they were under the guidance of a county court judge. Thoroughly fuddled and confused, who can doubt that they did their best?

Everyone knows the story of how, during the Crimean War, an aide-de-camp galloped up to the Light Brigade with the order to charge the enemy's guns. "What enemy, Sir, what guns?" enquired Lord Lucan testily. "There are the enemy, my Lord, there are the guns!" replied the aide-de-camp, slightly scandalised by the question, with an airy wave of his hand towards the enemy's positions. Lord Lucan did not condescend to ask further questions: his duty was to command the British Cavalry Division in the Crimea and not to try to make sense of the commander-in-chief's orders. Clearly, the commander-in-chief wanted the Light Brigade to charge the enemy's guns. So, he communicated the order personally to the commander of the Brigade, Lord Cardigan. The latter was equally bewildered. Still, his duty as a soldier was to carry out orders, not to try to interpret them. He was bound to assume that his superiors knew what they were doing. Drawing his sabre, he led his squadron in a charge in what proved to be the wrong direction down a valley destined to become immortal as the Valley of Death.

Neither at Balaclava, in 1854, nor at Hamburg, in 1949, it a soldier's duty to ask questions about orders. "Theirs not to reason why " — particularly on subjects about which the experts contradicted each other. The gallant band composed of one Lt. General, a Major-General, two Brigadiers, and three Colonels figuratively straightened their shakos, drew their sabres, exclaimed "Hurrah!" in unison and led each other to the charge. That "someone had blundered" was obvious in both cases, but in neither did this affect the simple duty of a soldier. At Balaclava

Chapter 8 — The Last Phase

the result was dismissed as magnificent but not war; at Hamburg, the result may be dismissed as far from magnificent and certainly not law.

The findings of the tribunal can be briefly summarised. There were seventeen charges in all, two from Polish sources and fifteen from Russian. Field Marshal von Manstein was acquitted outright on eight charges, including the two Polish charges which, as Mr. Paget says, "were so flagrantly bogus that one was left wondering why they had been presented at all." He was held accountable on seven charges, after the prosecution had been permitted by the court to modify them after the close of the case for the defence — a very questionable procedure. So modified, the upshot may be regarded as equivalent to an acquittal. On two charges, only, was the Field Marshal held to be guilty.

The two charges upon which he was held guilty were, first, that he had permitted Russian prisoners to be used in clearing mine-fields; the Allies after the war made it a common practice to use German prisoners of war for mine-clearing. Secondly, that he permitted Russian civilians to be deported from his area for work in Germany; at the time the tribunal was deliberating on this charge, it was common knowledge that in Russia and Siberia there were tens of thousands of civilians deported for forced labour, not only from Eastern Germany but also from the Baltic countries overrun and annexed by Russia in 1939, and from Hungary, Finland and Roumania.

The Field Marshal's conviction on the charge that he had permitted Russian civilians to be deported from his area for work in Germany is particularly remarkable because, at the time it was alleged he committed this offence, the Allied leaders were formulating and approving the Morgenthau Plan which specifically approved the use of "forced German labour outside Germany" as a form of reparations.[125]

It should also be observed that, at the time of von Manstein's trial, it was very widely known that several millions of prisoners of war were being detained by the Soviet Government for forced labour in Russia.

According to estimates prepared by the information section of NATO, these prisoners included 2,000,000 Germans, 370,000 Japanese, 180,000 Roumanians, 200,000 Hungarians, and 63,520 Italians. According to the NATO estimates, 40 per cent of these could in 1952 be reckoned as dead. The surviving 60 per cent were still working as forced labour.[126]

Compared with the gravity of the original charges, as outlined in Comyns Carr's opening speech, the offences of which the Field Marshal was found guilty may be dismissed as trivial. Nevertheless, the "sixty-two year old, white-haired, half-blind soldier" was solemnly informed that he "must serve eighteen years in prison to start from today: the period of four years which you have already spent in custody has been taken into consideration."

Having regard to the tributes paid by the defence to the courtesy and humanity of the tribunal, it is regrettable that the phrasing of the judgment gives so unpleasant an impression. Obviously, it could make no difference to an elderly invalid whether the four years he had spent as a prisoner of war were taken into account or not.

Assuming that it was really intended that he should serve his sentence, his chances of emerging a free man amounted to nil, whether his sentence was eighteen years or eighty. Equally unpleasant is the impression made by the subsequent reduction of the sentence from eighteen to twelve years.

This ostentatious display of anxiety that the length of the sentence should exactly fit the crime appears such transparent humbug that it is difficult to consider it with patience. It must be left for persons with a mathematical turn of mind to work out what would have been a suitable penalty to inflict, had the accused been found guilty on all seventeen charges, assuming that a sentence equivalent to a life sentence was a fitting penalty for two of the least serious of these charges—charges of which the accusers themselves were notoriously guilty.

The court gave no indication of the grounds upon which they had accepted certain charges and rejected the others; whether they had accepted the principles of international law as laid down in the *British Military Manual* or whether they had preferred to be guided by the views on international law accepted in the Surrey County Court; or to which charge they attached particular gravity, or by what calculation they had arrived at the penalty of eighteen years. There was, in fact, no apparent connection between the findings and the sentence.

The most charitable view is that the tribunal was, at the conclusion of the case, so completely befuddled by the ordeal through which they had passed that they overlooked the fact that their verdict amounted to an acquittal, and proceeded to pass a sentence of life imprisonment as the obvious alternative to the death penalty. Having decided not to acquit, they probably imagined that they were being lenient. A complete disappearance of all sense of proportion is commonly a symptom of a general paralysis of the reasoning powers resulting from prolonged mental exertion along unfamiliar paths.

British foreign policy has often greatly puzzled foreigners. Frequently it has appeared an insane compromise designed to serve conflicting aims; not seldom, it has appeared to be directed to no apparent aim of any kind. But the gradual acquisition of an Empire which, by 1919, had come to include more than 11,500,000 square miles, that is to say, about a fifth of the land surface of the globe, with a population of over 400,000,000, about a fourth of the world's inhabitants, appeared to establish that "Though this be madness, yet there is method in't." Hence rose the legend of perfidious Albion.

Mr. Paget expresses the opinion that the Manstein trial "was a political as opposed to a judicial process." It was, in fact, an act of policy by the British Government, decided upon deliberately, according to Lord Jowitt, after he had been given six months worry. The question, therefore, naturally arises as to what was the precise political object which this act of policy was intended to serve. In spite of ingenious and widespread speculation outside Great Britain, this question has remained unanswered to this day.

In order to solve this mystery two very material facts must be taken into consideration; first the obligations into which the British Government had entered to hand over any prisoner of war in British custody accused by an ally of Britain of a war-crime, and secondly the indignant opposition aroused in British military circles at the prospect of a distinguished European soldier being handed over to his communist enemies to be slaughtered in accordance with the ancient traditions of primary warfare. In the British Army, at least, the traditions of civilized warfare survived.

The real struggle concerning Manstein's fate took place behind the scenes before his trial began. On the one side were his military opponents in the great campaign in France in 1940, all the more determined by their defeat in that year to vindicate the traditions of European civil warfare.

Advance to Barbarism

On the other side were the politicians, fearful of giving the Communist tyrant Joseph Stalin technical ground for complaint. The struggle ended with a characteristically British compromise. It was decided that a British military tribunal should be assigned the fantastic task of deciding whether certain alleged acts committed in ferocious primary warfare were reprehensible if judged by the standards of civilized warfare. Foreign critics should note that the outcome of this irrational compromise ultimately achieved the two-fold purpose intended: the British traditions of civilized warfare were outwardly maintained; Stalin was given no pretext for repudiating his treaty obligations with his allies; and Field Marshal von Manstein's life was saved from his vindictive Russian and Polish enemies.

Postscript

Now that the truth is no longer obscured by the myths of propaganda, only one question of universal interest remains concerning that unique period of history labelled in this book "the advance to barbarism". There can be no question that this retrograde movement of civilization began in 1914. Historians will long find in the distinctive characteristics of this period, genocide, terror bombing, mass-deportations of populations and war-crimes trials, numberless problems for investigation and dispute. But only one problem remains of personal interest to everyone.

Has the series of chain reactions which began with the outbreak of the European civil war in 1914 come to an end?

No one dreamed in 1914 that the war which had just broken out would cause any more lengthy and violent reaction than any previous civil war, although the furious passions which it generated from the start puzzled many observers. Within a year of the outbreak of hostilities, in explanation of the boundless enthusiasm which inspired his troops, mostly volunteers, setting forth on the Dardanelles expedition, General Sir Ian Hamilton wrote in his diary, "Once in a generation a mysterious wish for war passes through the people." He offered no diagnosis of this mysterious wish. No doubt the subject will be cleared up one day in the usual way by giving it a Latin name. Looking back after nearly twenty years at a time when the Wicked Kaiser Myth was still accepted by most professional historians, Field Marshal Lord Allenby declared, "The great War was a period of lengthy insanity." Looking back after the passage of another thirty years it is clear that the so-called Great War was a relatively mild preliminary symptom.

The mysterious periodic wish which found expression in 1914 had been generated among the leading members of the White Race during the latter end of the 19th century, a period to them of such absolute security and boundless prosperity that war had come to seem a relief from boredom. For a decade an explosion had been inevitable. The fatal spark was provided on the 28th June, 1914, by a moronic student named Gavril Princep successfully carrying out the mission entrusted him by certain leading members of the Serbian Government to murder at Serajevo the Austrian Archduke Francis Ferdinand.

Are there reasonable grounds for thinking that the chain reaction set in motion by the murder of the heir to the Austrian throne has at last come to an end?

It is difficult to keep this question distinct from the question so often asked, what will be the consequences to the human race of the invention of the atomic bomb?

In origin the discovery of the secrets of nuclear fission and of the retrograde movement in human affairs which began in 1914 are quite unconnected.

The atomic bomb was the practical application for the purpose of destruction of the discoveries by the physicists in the mid-19th century of the nature of the atom. By the end of the century it had become established that enormous forces were locked up in the atom and the possibility was dimly realised that it might be possible to use these forces to cause an explosion of unprecedented violence. By the commencement of the Second World War, the means by which this aim might be achieved had been realised and Albert Einstein appealed to President Roosevelt to spare no pains or expense to test whether the theoretical knowledge obtained by laboratory experiments could be used for constructing a contraption which would be able to blot out human life on a gigantic scale.

It was an unhappy chance that the secrets of atomic structure should have been finally mastered in 1945. It is without question the greatest tragedy in human history that mankind should have become possessed of unique powers of self-destruction just at a time when mankind had never before been less fitted to use these powers sanely.

It is certainly arguable that the atomic bomb would never have been constructed except during a ferocious war when nothing seemed to matter but the attainment of victory. Laboratory experiments in peacetime could only have confirmed a theoretical possibility of making an atomic bomb: in peacetime no government could have undertaken the fabulously costly tests which were necessary to establish this theoretical possibility was practical. Also in peacetime no government could have faced the general opprobrium which it would have incurred from an attempt, on too gigantic a scale to be kept secret, to construct a contraption designed not for use on the battlefield but to blot out civilian populations.

It is arguable also that the atomic bomb when constructed would not have been tested by dropping it on a defenceless city had not the conscience of mankind been previously paralysed by a long series of crimes against humanity.

Certainly the dropping of the first atomic bomb on Hiroshima may be regarded as a natural sequel to the adoption three years before of the Lindemann Plan to initiate a terror bombing campaign against Germany. It was inspired by the same spirit and it may fairly be regarded as the final and supreme example of terror bombing without disguise and excuse.

There is a remarkable similarity between the mass air raid on Dresden and the attack on Hiroshima six months later. No one protested when in 1967 Lord Boothby described the air raid on Dresden as "a dastardly act", not because of the number of victims but because it served no military purpose.[127] The dropping of the first atomic bomb was also an act of pure terrorism. It fulfilled no military purpose of any kind. Belatedly it has been disclosed that seven months before it was dropped, in January 1945, President Roosevelt received via General MacArthur's headquarters an offer by the Japanese Government to surrender on terms virtually identical to those accepted by the United States after the dropping of the bomb: in July 1945, as we now know, Roosevelt's successor, President Truman, discussed with Stalin at Bébelsberg the Japanese offer to surrender.

The motivation behind the dropping of the atomic bomb on Hiroshima may be said to be still a subject of dispute. It is certain that Truman did not give the order for it to be dropped on the insistence of his military advisers. Some of the scientists concerned in its construction opposed this step on humanitarian grounds: others including the famous Jewish physicist Dr. Robert Oppenheimer were in favour because, they urged, only by a test in war conditions could it be demonstrated that their long and costly efforts had succeeded in creating a weapon of unique power for taking human life.[128] In short the Japanese people were to be enlisted as human guinea-pigs for a scientific experiment.

Although no military or political purpose existed to be served, President Truman gave the necessary order to drop the bomb: some seventy thousand men, women and children were killed in a fraction of a second.

Reverting to the question, "Are there reasonable grounds for thinking that the chain reaction triggered off in 1914 by Princep's crime has at last petered out?", the invention of the atomic bomb has made it possible to give an optimistic reply.

Each stage of this chain reaction was the natural consequence of the one which preceded it. Throughout the process the next stage was long beforehand plainly discernible. The furious passions aroused by the First World War led inevitably to the Versailles Diktat which in turn led inevitably to the Second World War during which all restraint was in the end abandoned. When hostilities ceased in 1945 the next stage of the chain reaction seemed obvious. Roosevelt's blind subservience to Stalin at die Teheran Conference in 1943 foreshadowed the subjection of Western Europe by force to Communism. It appeared only a matter of time before Stalin would feel himself strong enough to abandon the pretence of being a loyal ally in a crusade for democracy when he would of course order the Red Army to advance. This time seemed to have arrived when Stalin in 1948 threw off the mask of friendship and ordered West Berlin to be blockaded. But the crisis passed and what seemed inevitable did not take place. The only reason was Stalin belatedly realised that the United States alone possessed a stock pile of atomic weapons and prudently decided to postpone the use of force. As a consequence the Morgenthau Plan, the projected next step along the road to barbarism, was cancelled in order to enlist the aid of the German people for the defence of Europe.

Thus occurred the first break in the chain reaction which had been proceeding without interruption for over three decades.

Another reason for optimism is that the invention of the atomic bomb has entirely transformed the conditions and prospects of warfare. The poet Rupert Brooke expressed the outlook to war of a generation bored by uneventful years of peace and prosperity when he wrote in 1914, "Now God be thanked who has matched us with His hour!" The mere existence of atomic weapons makes it impossible for anyone now to feel as Rupert Brooke felt when in a letter he wrote before setting out on the Dardanelles expedition,

Postscript

"It is too wonderful for belief: I had never imagined Fate could be so kind. I have never been so happy in my life, so pervasively happy! I suddenly realise that the ambition of my life has been — since I was two — to go on an expedition against Constantinople!"

The prospect of strutting in a victory parade through Constantinople or some other capital has ceased to be alluring now that it must be clouded with the knowledge that concurrently one's own homeland might be being turned into a radio-active rubbish heap.

Finally, leaving out of account the changes brought about by the invention of nuclear weapons, the conditions of warfare with conventional weapons have reverted to conditions similar to those which existed in the 18th century. A modern army no longer consists of hordes of hastily-trained conscripts. The military strength of a country now consists of long-service soldiers trained in the use of complicated weapons, transport and equipment. Such troops will fight in accordance with the orders of their executive government: they do not need to be inflamed by mendacious hate-propaganda.

To intensive hate-propaganda can be traced all the unique features of the period labelled in this book "the advance to barbarism" — genocide, terror bombing, mass-deportations and war-crimes trials.

Now that the necessity no longer exists for rulers to employ hate-propaganda as a stimulus to sustain the martial spirit of their subjects, it appears reasonable to hope that the chain reaction which began in 1914 has come to an end and that a new period of history has commenced in which will be absent the characteristics which are the products of hate-propaganda.

BIBLIOGRAPHY

C. R. Ballard, *The Military Genius of Abraham Lincoln*, Cleveland: World Publishing Co., 1952.
Maurice Bardèche, *Nuremberg*, Les Sept Coleurs, 1948.
Harry Elmer Barnes, *In Quest of Truth and Justice*, National Historical Society, 1928. *The Genesis of the World War*, Knopf, 3rd Ed., New York, 1929. *Blasting the Historical Blackout*, Privately printed, 1961.
F. Beck and W. Godin, *Russian Purge*, Hurst & Blackett London, 1951.
Montgomery Belgion, *Epitaph on Nuremberg*, Falcon Press, London, 1946. *Victors' Justice*, Regnery, Chicago, 1949.
Charles Bewley, *Hermann Göring and the Third Reich*, Devin Adair, New York, 1962.
James F. Byrnes, *Speaking Frankly*, Harper, New York, 1947.
Lord Casey, *Personal Experiences*, Constable, London, 1962.
William Henry Chamberlin, *America's Second Crusade*, Regnery, Chicago, 1950.
Sir Winston Churchill, *Closing the Ring* (Vol. 5 of *The Second World War*), Cassel, London, 1952.
Triumph and Tragedy (Vol. 6 of *The Second World War*), Cassel, London, 1954.
Michael F. Connors, *Dealing in Hate*, Britons Publishing Co., London, 1966.
Maximilian Czesany, *Nie wieder Krieg gegen die Zivilbevölkerung*, Selbstverlag des Verfassers, Graz, 1961.
T. K. Derry, *The Campaign in Norway*, H.M. Stationery Office, London, 1952.
Charles Foley, *Commando Extraordinary: The Exploits of Otto Skorzeny*, Longman, Green & Co., London, 1956.
General J. F. C. Fuller, *Armament and History*, Eyre & Spottiswoode, London, 1946.

The Second World War, Eyre & Spotiswoode, London, 1948.
David Maxwell Fyfe (Lord Kilmuir), *Political Adventure*, Weidenfeld & Nicholson, London, 1964.
Victor Gollancz, *The Case of Adolf Eichmann*, Gollancz, London, 1961.
Colonel A. Goutard, *The Battle of France, 1940*, Frederick Muller, London, 1958.
Stephen Graham, Stalin, Hutchinson, London, 1939.
Lord Hankey, *Politics: Trials and Errors*, Pen-in-Hand, Oxford, 1950 and Regnery, Chicago, 1950.
Sir Arthur Harris, *Bomber Offensive*, Collins, London, 1947.
Capt. B. H. Liddell Hart, *The Revolution In Warfare*, Faber & Faber, London, 1946.
The Other Side of the Hill, Cassell, London, 1948.
Sisley Huddleston, *Pétain: Traitor or Patriot*, Andrew Dakers, London, 1951.
France: *The Tragic Years, 1939-47*, Devin-Adair, New York, 1955.
David Hoggan, *Der erzwungene Krieg*, Tübingen, 1961.
Ernrys Hughes, *Winston Churchill in War and Peace*, Unity Publishing Co., Glasgow, 1950.
David Irving, *The Destruction of Dresden*, Kimber, London, 1963.
Harold Lamb, *The March of the Barbarians*, Hale, London, 1941.
Dr. Paul Leverkühn, *Verteidigung Manstein*, Nölke Verlag, Hamburg, 1950.
Joseph Mackiewicz, *The Katyn Wood Murders*, Hollis & Carter, London, 1951.
Philip Magnus, *Kitchener*, John Murray, London, 1958.
Viscount Maugham, *U.N.O. and War Crimes*, John Murray, London, 1951.
R. T. Paget, *Manstein*, Collins, London, 1951.
Arthur Ponsonby, *Falsehood in War-time*, Allen & Unwin, London, 1928.
General H. B. Ramcke, *Fallschirmjäger*, Lorch-Verlag, Frankfurt am Main, 1951.
A. F. Reel, *The Case of General Yamashita*, University of Chicago Press, 1949.
Dennis Richards, *The Fight at Odds* (Vol. 1 of *The Royal Air Force 1939-45*), H.M. Stationery Office, London, 1953.
Axel Rodenberger, *Der Tod von Dresden*, Das Grüne Blatt, Dortmund, 1951.

Elliott Roosevelt, *As He Saw It*, Duell, Sloan & Pearce, New York, 1946.
Hans Rumpf, *Das war der Bombenkrieg*, Gerhard Stalling Verlag, Oldenburg, 196L
Hermann Salingré, *Im Grossen Hauptquartier*, Hoffmann, Berlin, 1910.
J. M. Spaight, *Bombing Vindicated*, Bles, London, 1944.
Sir Charles Snow, *Science and Government*, Oxford University Press, London, 1961.
C. C. Tansell, *Back Door to War*, Regnery, Chicago, 1952.
A. J. P. Taylor, *The Origins of the Second World War*, Hamilton, London, 1961.
Freda Utley, *The High Cost of Vengeance*, Regnery, Chicago, 1949.
F. J. P. Veale, *Crimes Discreetly Veiled*, Cooper Book Co., London and Devin-Adair, New York, 1958.
Sir Charles Webster and Dr. Noble Frankland, *The Strategic Air Offensive against Germany, 1939-45*, H.M. Stationery Office, London, 1961.
E. Wingfield Stratford,
The Victorian Sunset, Routledge, London, 1932.
The Victorian Aftermath, Routledge, London, 1933.

Footnotes

[1] Contributed to the American version of this book published by the Nelson Publishing Company, Appleton, Wisconsin, U.S.A., 1953.

[2] Contributed to the second edition of the German translation of this book entitled *Der Barbarei entgegen*, published by Verlag Karl Heinz Priester. Wiesbaden, 1962.

[3] See Lord Allenby's Rectorial Address to Edinburgh University on the 28th April, 1936, three weeks before his death.

[4] "Sir Hugh Trenchard, Chief of the Air Staff from 1919 to 1929, had a decisive influence on the future of the R.A.F." write Sir Charles Webster and Dr. Noble Frankland, the joint authors of The Strategic Air Offensive against Germany (H.M. Stationery Office, London, 1961, Vol. 1, p. 42).
They explain that the essence of his policy was that "future wars would be won by producing such moral effect on the enemy civilian population that its government would have to sue for peace. The advantage of destroying military installations and factories was recognised but he maintained that it was easier to overcome the will to resist among the workers than to destroy the means to resist" (p. 86).

[5] *The Destruction of Dresden* by David Irving, London, Kimber, 1963.

[6] *The Strategic Air Offensive*, H.M. Stationery Office, London, 1961.

[7] *The Evolution of Warfare*, by B. H. Liddell Hart, London, Faber & Faber, 1946, Page 75.

[8] *Advance to Barbarism*, by A. Jurist, London, Thompson & Smith, 1948. Another noteworthy book written from the same standpoint is *The Law and Custom of the Sea*, by Dr. Herbert Arthur Smith (London, Stevens, 1948) which condemns the conviction of Admiral Dönitz by the Nuremburg Tribunal as a gross miscarriage of justice.

[9] *Epitaph on Nuremberg* by Montgomery Belgion, London, The Falcon Press, 1946. Three years later a revised and amplified

version of this book was published in the United States under the title *Victors Justice* (Chicago, Regnery, 1949).

[10] See the Report of the International Conference on Military Trials, London, 1945, published in 1949 by the Washington State Department, Pages 104-106 and Page 303.

[11] Emphatic disapproval was however expressed by no less weighty a legal authority than Viscount Maugham, formerly Lord Chancellor of England. See his book with a postscript by Lord Hankey, U.N.O. and War Crimes, London, John Murray, 1951.

[12] *The Trial of Adolf Eichmann*, by Victor Gollancz, London, Gollancz, 1961. p. 21.

[13] *Science and Government* by C. P. Snow, Oxford University Press, London, 1961, pages 47-51.

[14] *Bombing Vindicated*, by J. M. Spaight, London, Bles, 1944.

[15] *Bomber Offensive*, by Sir Arthur Harris, London, Collins, 1947.

[16] *Politics: Trials and Errors*, by Lord Hankey (Oxford, Pen-in-Hand, 1950).

[17] A German translation of this American Edition was published in 1954 and a revised version in 1962. A Spanish translation was published in 1954.

[18] *Dean Inge*, by Canon Adam Fox, London, Murray, 1960.

[19] *Selected Essays* by Havelock Ellis, London, Dent & Sons, 1936, p. 195.

[20] *Footsteps of Warfare*, by R. L. Worrall, London, Davies, 1936, p. 2.

[21] Sir Arthur Keith, *The Antiquity of Man*, London, Williams & Norgate, 1925, Vol. 1, p. 175. It is recognised, of course, that the intellectual faculties of Neanderthal man were less developed than those of modern man.

[22] *Ibid.*, p.136.

[23] H.F. Osborn, *Men of the Old Stone Age*, London, Bell & Son, 1926, p. 258.

[24] Ibid., p. 272.

[25] J.M. Spaight, *Bombing Vindicated*, London, Bles, 1944.

[26] George Orwell, *Nineteen Eighty-four*, New York, Harcourt, Brace, 1949.

[27] See *America's Second Crusade* by William Henry Chamberlin, Chicago, Regnery, 1950, pp. 303 to 310 and *Roosevelt's Road to Russia* by George N. Crocker, Chicago, Regnery, 1959, pp. 229 to 240.

[28] The ancient attitude toward a prisoner taken in war was well expressed in the definition recently given by Mr. Winston Churchill in the debate on the Korean War on July 1, 1952. "What is a prisoner of war? A prisoner of war is a man who has tried to kill you and, having failed, asks you not to kill him."

[29] M. R. Davie, *The Evolution of War*, New Haven, Yale University Press, 1929, p. 194.

[30] Captain Liddell Hart, *The Revolution in Warfare*, London, Faber, 1946, p. 81.

[31] For a revision of the earlier view that the Assyrians had no interests, or made no achievements, outside the field of warfare, see A. T. Olmstead, *History of Assyria*, Scribner, 1923, Chap. XLIX.

[32] Champlain, writing in 1613, accepts the latter explanation of this practice in the case of the Hurons and Algonquins of the St. Lawrence.

He writes, "The rest of the prisoners were kept to be put to death by the women and girls who by their subtlety invent more cruel tortures than the men and take pleasure in it." The opinion of this eye-witness, considered in relation to the proposal put forward in the *Daily Mail* of the 29th November, 1945 (see p. 15), raises the possibility of sensational developments in the mock-trials which will inevitably follow the next war.

[33] There is recent evidence that this primitive female characteristic has survived to the present day among backward peoples even of modern Europe. Thus *Island of Terrible Friends* by B; Strutton (Hodder, London 1961), is based on the experiences of Major James Rickett, a British army doctor who served with Tito's Communist Partisans. He declares that the female Partisans took the lead in torturing and murdering German wounded and prisoners.

[34] Some 25,000 people were butchered in this massacre, "not one in fifty of whom was armed," Francis Watson, *Wallenstein*, London, Chatto & Windus, 1939, p. 326. Nearly ten times this number of victims are believed to have perished in the bombing of Dresden three centuries later on February 13, 1945. Certainly not one in fifty of the women and children refugees killed on this occasion was armed.

[35] Harold Lamb, *The March of the Barbarians*, London, Hale, 1941, p. 162.

[36] It is interesting to note that Henry took part in 1390 in the first recorded siege of Vilna, the scene of so much subsequent fighting

Advance to Barbarism

between the peoples of Europe and the inhabitants of the Eurasian hinterland. The same issues were at stake when Charles X of Sweden captured the city in 1702, when Napoleon fought near here in 1812, when Hindenburg won his great victory of Vilna in 1915, and when Manstein made his famous tank thrust though the city in 1941.

[37] The celebrated recruiting poster would have been more aptly worded, "What did you do in E.C.W. 8a, Daddy?"

[38] *The Revolution in Warfare*, by F. H. Liddell Hart, London, Faber, 1946. When this book appeared many people thought this passage unreasonably harsh. We of course know that Liddell Hart was referring to terror bombing carried out in accordance with the Lindemann Plan which in 1946 and for nearly twenty years afterwards was a jealously guarded state secret.

This opinion could not however even then be dismissed out of hand. The author was a recognised authority on military matters. Lloyd George described Liddell Hart as "the highest and soundest authority on modern warfare." Similar tributes have been paid him by Field Marshal Wavell, by Sir Winston Churchill and by Field Marshal Montgomery.

[39] See comment in J. U. Nef, *War and Human Progress*, Cambridge, Harvard University Press, 1950, pp. 139-140.

[40] See the *Weekend Telegraph* of the 2nd July, 1965, in which Major General Jack Churcher tells an anecdote which he evidently regards as amusing concerning the "arrest" of Admiral Dönitz at Flensburg in May 1945. The distinguished prisoner, he tells us, was told "to collect the minimum of luggage to take to his confinement quarters. When Dönitz's batman appeared with the luggage packed, the arresting officer said, 'You are not going on holiday but going to prison: you have the choice of one suitcase.' The Admiral was quite upset but had to choose one. He chose badly: when his luggage was examined at Luxembourg, it contained nothing but pants and vests."

[41] As a result of the introduction of plate armour in the 15th century the combatants suffered little danger in the actual fighting. As King James I once observed with his pawky Scotch humour armour conferred two great benefits on those wearing it—"It preserves one from injury and prevents one from injuring other people."

[42] In a church at Edgware, Middlesex, is a memorial tablet to a lady

who died in 1705. Among the many virtues ascribed to her is, "She was religious without Enthusiasm."

[43] Sir Charles Napier was under no illusion as to this war. Previously he had recorded in his diary, "We have no right to seize Scinde, yet we shall do so, and a very advantageous, useful, humane piece of rascality it will be." See B. Thompson and B. T. Garratt, *British Rule in India*, London, Macmillan, 1934, p. 356.

[44] *The Revolution in Warfare*, p. 44.

[45] New York, Putman, 1940.

[46] See Freda Utley, *The High Cost of Vengeance*, Chicago, Regnery, 1949.

[47] In Montgomery Belgion's *Victors' Justice*, Chicago, Regnery, 1949, will be found a collection of the facts relating to this subject disclosed down to the date of its publication. See also, Freda Utley, *op. cit.*

[48] Yet it must be confessed that much more has been said. See for example A. G. Macdonell, *Napoleon and His Marshals*, London, Macmillan, 1934, pp. 327-330.

[49] C. E. Vulliarmy, *Crimea*, London, Cape, 1939, p. 349.

[50] See Hesketh Pearson, *The Hero of Delhi*, London, Collins, 1939, p. 211.

[51] It is, perhaps, noteworthy that in place of paying a tribute to Alexander for proving himself two thousand years in advance of his time, his recent biographer, Arthur Weigall, comments on the trial of Bessos: "The fact that Alexander did not pause to consider what cultured Athens would think of his action is sufficient evidence of his unbalanced state of mind at this time." — Arthur Weigall, *Alexander the Great*, London, Butterworth, 1933, p. 262.

[52] Hart, *The Revolution in Warfare*, p. 60.

[53] Contemporary public opinion in Britain regarding this exploit was divided. *The Annual Register* condemned it roundly as "a return to the times of barbarism." *The Times*, on the other hand, commented complacently, "That ill-organized association (i.e. the United States) is on the eve of dissolution, and the world is speedily to be delivered of the mischievous example of the existence of a government founded on democratic rebellion." Few predictions, even of *The Times*, have remained more signally unfulfilled!

[54] On the contrary the Air Marshal informed the German people — "I will speak frankly to you about whether we bomb single military

targets or whole cities. Obviously we prefer to hit factories, shipyards and railways. But those people who work these plants live close to them. Therefore we hit your homes and you." This was certainly frank although as we now know it was untrue.

Four months before, in March 1942, the Lindemann Plan had been adopted by the British Government by which working-class houses had been given priority over factories, shipyards and railways as objectives for air attack.

[55] The worthy Salingré's description of this memorable incident deserves record in his own words: "Napoleon III. sah verhältnismässig gut aus, nur die Situation, in der er sich befand, machte einen traurigen, herzbeklemmenden Eindruck, und man mag es mir verzeihen, wenn ich gestehe, dass er mir in diesem Augenblicke leid tat. Ich fühlte in diesem Moment so etwas, als dürfe man diesen unglücklichen Mann nicht noch tiefer in den Kot treten, ich zog respektvoll den Hut, da er gerade auf mich blickte und empfand eine Art Befriedigung, als ich sah, dass er meinen Gruss bemerkt hatte und dankte." (*Im Grossen Hauptquartier*, p. 68).

[56] E. C. Wingfield-Stratford, *The Victorian Sunset*, London, Routledge, 1932, p. 164.

[57] Wingfield-Stratford, *op. cit.*, p. 268. On the manner in which the press stimulated diplomatic tension, see O. J. Hale, *Publicity and Diplomacy*, New York, Appleton-Century, 1940.

[58] *The Victorian Aftermath*, by E. C. Wingfield-Stratford, London, Routledge, 1933, page XIX. Field Marshal Lord Allenby neatly expressed this view of the subject when he declared, "The Great War was a lengthy period of general insanity."

[59] In 1914 British professional historians and gutter journalists combined together in an unholy alliance to represent Kaiser Wilhelm II as a man of unparalleled wickedness, unspeakable cruelty, boundless ambition and conscienceless perfidy who had spent his life plotting the conquest of his peace-loving neighbours. This propaganda fiction won worldwide acceptance. It was not until the centenary of the year of his birth, on the 15th July 1959, that the "Wicked Kaiser Myth" was formally repudiated by a semi-official broadcast by the B.B.C.

Many leading men who had known Kaiser Wilhelm took part and paid tributes to his memory. With regard to war-guilt, it was admitted that "Wilhelm's responsibility was unquestionably small in comparison with that of Isvolski and of Count Berchtold." Wilhelm was, in fact, "a clever man who thought he understood the vulgar, bustling, aggressive, competitive age in which he lived and who utterly misjudged it." (See the article by the present author entitled "The Wicked Kaiser Myth" in the American quarterly SOCIAL JUSTICE REVIEW, St. Louis, April 1960.)

[60] *Lord Kitchener: Portrait of an Imperialist* by Sir Charles Magnus, Murray, London, 1958, at page 122.

[61] See *An Intimate Diary of the Peace Conference and After* by Lord Riddell, Gollancz, London, 1933.

[62] Both these celebrated legal actions concerned great fortunes which were claimed by impudent impostors. In both the claims were supported by reckless perjury. With enormous expense and trouble both claims were finally conclusively disproved. Nevertheless, in both cases a numerous section of the British public remained unshakably convinced that the impostors had been unjustly treated.

[63] See Sisley Huddleston *Pétain: Traitor or Patriot*, London, Andrew Dakers, Ltd. 1951.

[64] General J. F. C. Fuller, *Armament and History*, London, Eyre and Spottiswoode, 1946, p. 182

[65] In the opinion of Mr. James F. Byrnes, "Molotov's two conferences with Hitler on the 12th and 13th November, 1940, marked the turning point of the war." As the price of a pledge by the Soviet Union to honour the pledge given the previous year by the Soviet Union not to attack Germany, Molotov demanded a protectorate over the whole of the Balkans, and the right to establish a military, naval and air base on the Dardanelles, which would dominate the Mediterranean and turn the Black Sea into a Russian lake. "Molotov's demand for a definite and immediate answer on November 13th was his worst blunder," writes Mr. Byrnes. (See James P. Byrnes, *Speaking Frankly*, New York, Harper, 1947, p. 288.) Convinced that the pledge which had been obtained from the Soviet Union the previous year was worth nothing, and unwilling to pay such a price for another pledge of equal value, Hitler rejected Molotov's demand. Thenceforth, he regarded a Soviet attack on Germany as merely a question of time and, nine months later, wisely or unwisely, decided to forestall this attack before the United States was ready to take an active part in the war.

[66] J. M. Spaight, *Bombing Vindicated*, London, Bles, 1944, p. 74.
[67] J. M. Spaight, *op. cit.*, p. 43.
[68] Hart, *The Revolution in Warfare*, p.72.
[69] Yet this book attracted amazingly little attention. As we have seen, in November, 1945, eighteen months after the truth had been disclosed in this book, the *Daily Mail* could refer casually to "Goering and Co." as the parties responsible for the sufferings of British housewives in the Blitz. See page 44.
[70] Article in *The Star*, December 12, 1946, by Air Marshal Harris.
[71] *Science and Government* by Sir Charles Snow, London, Oxford University Press, 1961.
[72] *Advance to Barbarism* by F. J. P. Veale, Appleton, U.S.A., Nelson Publishing Company, 1953.
[73] Air Marshal Sir Arthur Harris, *Bomber Offensive*, London, Collins, 1947, p. 242.
[74] *The Times*, February 16, 1945.
[75] It has now been established beyond question that the British air chiefs knew before the raid that Dresden was full of refugees. As part of the so-called Air Offensive on Germany the R.A.F. dropped not only bombs but propaganda leaflets entitled "Nachrichten für die Truppen". The issue of February 13th, 1945, the date of the raid, contained an article entitled "Partei flieht aus Dresden" in which it was alleged that all the schools in the city had been closed to provide shelter for "an army of refugees" arriving from the east. David Irving comments, "Having dropped this leaflet on the burning city, it ill becomes the R.A.F. to claim afterwards to have known nothing of the refugees."
[76] Graphic accounts of this great mass air raid are given by survivors in *Der Tod von Dresden* by Axel Rodenberger, published by instalments in the weekly paper, *Das grüne Blatt*, beginning February 25, 1951.
[77] *The Strategic Air Offensive against Germany, 1939–45*, by Sir Charles Webster and Dr. Noble Frankland, H.M. Stationery Office, London, 1961, p. 115.
[78] See the Introduction of this book, page 20.
[79] *The Destruction of Dresden* by David Irving, London, Kimber, 1963.
[80] *Sunday Telegraph*, October 1st, 1961. See also the quotations from *Hansard* cited on pages 19–22 of this book.

[81] Until the secret correspondence in code between Churchill and Roosevelt, which was revealed by Tyler Kent and which remains a closely guarded state secret, has been published and proved the contrary, it is reasonable to assume that in it Roosevelt pledged himself to involve the United States in the war provided he was given time to do so. See *Back Door to War* by Dr. C.C. Tansill, Regnery, Chicago, 1952, pages 5878.

[82] See *The Battle of France* by Colonel A. Goutard (Miller, London, 1948, page 145).

[83] For example, *The Case of General Yamashita* by Frank Reel (University of Chicago Press, 1949) and *Manstein* by R. T. Paget (Collins, London, 1951). The details of the trial of Field Marshal Kesselring remain, after twenty years, safely buried in an official record.

[84] Elliott Roosevelt, *As He Saw it*, New York, Duell, Sloan and Pearce, 1946, pp.188-191, previously published in *Look* (see issue of October 1, 1946). Mrs. Eleanor Roosevelt, the widow of the President, supplied the foreword to her son's book, so that his account of what took place at Teheran must be regarded as the authorised version of the Roosevelt clan, whatever versions others may later see fit to give us.

[85] Eden's unruffled demeanour certainly contrasts strongly with Mr. Churchill's uncontrollable indignation. Their attitude to terror bombing was similarly different. Churchill never quite overcame his misgivings—see page 194: Eden's only criticism of the Lindemann Plan was that it excluded from attack working-class houses in cities with less than 50,000 inhabitants—see his letter to Sir Archibald Sinclair quoted on page 195.

[86] Not until the Iron Curtain is lifted shall we know how many Germans captured on the field of battle or arrested after the termination of hostilities by the G.P.U. were done to death either summarily or after some form of trial. Including those liquidated in Prague and Warsaw, and those lynched in remote districts, the total probably vastly exceeded Mr. Stalin's stipulated figure of 50,000.

[87] In a nutshell the Morgenthau Plan was designed to bring about, artificially, in Germany the conditions of poverty, distress, and degeneration existing at that time in parts of the American South as a result of natural economic causes, which have been

so graphically described by Erskine Caldwell in *Tobacco Road*. Mr. William Henry Chamberlain, in his book *America's Second Crusade* (Chicago, Regnery, 1950, p.306) writes as follows: "It is no exaggeration to say that the Morgenthau Plan, accepted by Mr. Roosevelt and Mr. Churchill at the Quebec Conference in September 1944, if applied would have been an indiscriminating sentence of death for millions of Germans. The area in which it was proposed to forbid all heavy industries and mining is one of the most urbanized and thickly populated in Europe."

[88] See Article 19 of the Charter attached to the London Agreement.

[89] Mr. Montgomery Belgion points out, in his *Victors' Justice*, p. 76, that at Nuremberg "the chief Russian prosecutor was a lieutenant-general but the senior of the two Russian judges was only a major-general." The former was the spokesman of the Soviet Government; the latter had a no more active role to play than Henry VIII's judges at Glastonbury.

[90] *Stalin*, by Stephen Graham, Hutchinson, London, 1939, p. 37.

[91] *Russian Purge*, by F. Beck and W. Godin, Hurst and Blackett, London, 1951, p. 87.

[92] See the article, *The Wrong Road to Peace*, in the *New Republic*, June 28, 1933, pp. 171-174.

[93] [Philately is the study of postage stamps. — Ed.]

[94] Even the great Lord Mansfield spoke with approval of "the trite maxim of the constitutional law of England that private mischief had better be submitted to than that public detriment should ensue."

[95] See Dr. Taylor's review of *Rudolf Hess: The Uninvited Envoy* by James Leasor (Allen and Unwin, London, 1962) in the *Observer* of May 6th, 1962.

[96] Not only beneath the dreaming spires of Oxford but among the untutored savages of Africa the proceedings at Nuremberg have soon become a byword of disrepute. This was shown in 1967 when Moise Tshombe was kidnapped by his enemies when travelling on a British plane and taken a prisoner to Algeria: reports from the Congo, published in the British and American newspapers explained that his political rivals in the Congo intended to demand his extradition from Algeria in order that he might be executed for treason *"after a Nuremberg trial."* For example, see the report of the correspondent of the *Sunday Express*, July 9, 1967.

[97] This ruling of the Nuremberg Tribunal was dutifully followed subsequently by lesser war-crimes tribunals. For example in August 1947 at Dachau before an American military tribunal this ruling saved the life of Otto Skorzany, the most famous commando leader of the Second World War, known in the popular press as "the most dangerous man in Europe" on account of his daring rescue of Benito Mussolini and his kidnapping of the Hungarian Regent, Admiral Horthy. For want of any more plausible charge, Skorzany was accused of conducting warfare with troops wearing captured enemy uniforms contrary to the code of civilized warfare. Everyone knew of course that this had long been routine practice of commando leaders on both sides. But Skorzany was being kept in strict confinement and was thus unable to call evidence to establish this fact, well known to the members of the court who exercised their legal right to profess judicial ignorance of what could not be proved by sworn evidence laid before them. Skorzany's fate appeared sealed.

It happened however that the news of this prosecution came to the ears of the most celebrated British leader of the resistance movement in France, Wing Commander Yeo-Thomas, whose *nom de guerre* was the White Rabbit. To him judicial ignorance in the circumstances seemed blatant hypocrisy, and he volunteered to give evidence for the defence. He told the tribunal that it had been his frequent practice to lead resistance units dressed in captured German uniforms on sabotage raids against the occupying forces. In these raids, he said, enemy uniforms were in the first place obtained by French civilians, secret members of the resistance movement, catching German soldiers off-duty unawares, killing them and appropriating their uniforms and papers.

In view of this unwelcome evidence, judicial ignorance became impossible and the court followed the ruling of the Nuremberg Tribunal in the Donitz case and granted the practice of conducting warfare in enemy uniforms a certificate of innocence. Skorzany was acquitted without further argument.

See *Commando Extraordinary* by Charles Foley, London, Longmans, 1954, pages 161-177.

[98] *Politics: Trials and Errors* by Lord Hankey, Pen-in-Hand, Oxford, 1950, page 78.

[99] *The Campaign in Norway* by Dr. T.K. Derry, H.M. Stationary Office, 1952.

[100] *Political Adventure,* Weidenfeld and Nicholson, London, 1964.

[101] *Hermann Göring and the Third Reich* by Charles Bewley, Devin-Adair, New York, 1962.

[102] See the articles by the present writer, *The Great Krupp Myth* in Social Justice, June 1963, and *A War Myth on Trial* in Social Justice, January 1964.

[103] See the article *The Tokyo War Crimes Trials* by George F. Blewitt in *American Perspective,* Summer 1950.

[104] See *Politics: Trials and Errors* by Lord Hankey, Pen-in-Hand, Oxford 1950, page 80.

[105] ["My object all sublime / I shall achieve in time / To let the punishment fit the crime / And make each prisoner pent / Unwillingly represent / A source of innocent merriment!" — Chorus to the song "A more humane Mikado"–Ed.].

[106] In a photograph described as "the last of the Nuremberg trials" which opened on February 5th 1948, published in the *Illustrated London News* of March 6th 1948, it was noted with surprise that all the thirteen occupants of the dock, three Field Marshals, nine Generals and one Admiral, were attired in civilian clothes. This was an essential feature of the proceedings in accordance with the theory that a soldier ceases to be a soldier and loses all his rights as a soldier if he be stripped of his uniform. By the same reasoning, of course, a king must be deemed to abdicate every time he retires for the night unless he takes the precaution of wearing his crown in bed as a nightcap.

[107] See the interview with General Lesse, reported by Major Redman in the *Sunday Pictorial,* May 11, 1947.

[108] See the speech of Lord Justice Lawrence (then recently created Lord Oaksey) in the House of Lords on the 27th April 1948, in which he said, referring to the Nuremburg Trials, "We have just been joining with other countries in putting to death our enemies in Germany."

[109] See the articles "Nicht Gnade sondern Recht" published by *Der Stern*. The issue of August 5, 1951 contains a photostatic copy of Viscount Alexander's letter, dated July 26th, 1951, reproduced in the *Daily Express* of August 9, 1951.

[110] It was no doubt in contemplation of further "tragic mistakes" being perpetrated that the Bishop of Monmouth justified the destruction of the Monte Cassino on the ground that "Jesus Christ came to save souls and not to preserve the Temple of Jerusalem."

Footnotes

This is, perhaps, the most perfect example of a non sequitur in the English language!

[111] A. Frank Reel, *The Case of General Yamashita*, Chicago, University of Chicago Press, 1949.

[112] R. T. Paget, *Manstein*, London, Collins, 1951.

[113] *The Peninsular War*, Oxford, Oxford University Press, 1902-1922, Volume I, p. XI.

[114] The soldier, Sir William Napier, refers to Suchet's methods as "vigorous and prudent measures" while the civilian, Professor Oman, refers to them as "a series of atrocities". Quat homines, tot senteniae! ["There are as many opinions as there are men."–Ed.]

[115] In *Crimes Discreetly Veiled*, published by Cooper Book Coy, London, and Devin-Adair, New York, in 1958. A German translation entitled *Verschleierte Kriegsverbrechen* was published by Priester Verlag, Weisbaden, in 1959 and a Spanish translation entitled *Crimenes Discretamente Ocultados* by Editorial Nos, Madrid, in 1961.

[116] So described in an official reply dated the 26th June, 1953, by Senor Scelba, Italian Minister of the Interior, to an appeal for clemency for Major Reder by the Austrian State Secretary, Graf.

[117] *The Case of General Yamashita* by A. Frank Reel, University of Chicago Press, Chicago, 1949.

[118] The annexation of the Philippines from Spain in 1899 inspired Rudyard Kipling to write his famous poem, "Take up the White Man's burden" in which is enshrined the very spirit of what is now called "Colonialism".

[119] Article 19 of the Charter (See page 240 of this book) should be compared with Section 16 of MacArthur's regulations, which reads: "The Commission shall admit such evidence as in its opinion would be of assistance in proving or disproving the charge, or such as in the Commission's opinion would have probative value in the mind of a reasonable man." In particular the court was authorised to accept (1) any document which appears to have been issued or signed without proof of the signature or the issuance of the document; (2) all affidavits, depositions or other statements and any diary, letter or other document appearing to the Commission to contain information relating to the charge; (3) a copy of any document or other secondary evidence of its contents, if the Commission believes that the original is not available or cannot be

produced without undue delay.

[120] *Fallschirmjäger* by General H. B. Ramcke, Lorch-Verlag, Frankfurt am Main, 1951, page 101.

[121] R. T. Paget, *Manstein* p. 72-73.

[122] *The Daily Mail*, October 22, 1949.

[123] R. T. Paget, *Manstein* p. 81.

[124] Capt. Liddell Hart, *The Other Side of the Hill*, London, Cassell, 1948, pp. 70-71.

[125] See William Henry Chamberlin, *America's Second Crusade*, Chicago, Regnery, 1950, pp. 210, 307.

[126] See *Time*, July 7, 1952.

[127] See Lord Boothby's letter to the *Sunday Express* published on the 15th January 1967.

[128] At the enquiry before the U.S. Atomic Energy Commission in the Spring of 1954 to investigate his alleged communist associations, Dr. Oppenheimer explained, "When you see something which is technically sweet, you go ahead and do it.... We always assumed that if the bombs were needed, they would be used.... We wanted to have it done before the war was over and nothing more could be done."

His colleague Dr. Alvarez testified more tersely. "We wanted some method of testing the effectiveness of the bomb over enemy territory."

See the article *The Oracles are Dumb* by Isabel Paterson in the *National Review* of May 23, 1956, page 12.

Index

A

Air Marshal Harris 21, 25, 164, 165, 169, 170, 177, 178, 191, 192, 354
Air Marshal Trenchard 23, 193, 195, 197
A. J. P. Taylor 241, 255, 346
Albigensian Crusade 65, 73, 74
Alexander the Great 111, 221, 222, 351
Alsace Lorraine 127
Ambrose Spinola 84, 85
Archibald Sinclair 12, 14, 20, 186, 187, 190, 355
Arthur Keith 33, 34, 348
Asshurnazirpal 53, 54, 55, 162
Assyrians 51, 52, 54–60, 62, 63, 66, 131, 184, 349
Atlanta 114–116
Aurignacian 32–34
Australian aborigines 31, 32
Austro-Hungarian Empire 133, 287
Aztecs 58

B

Babylon 51, 52
Basil the Bulgar-Slayer 65
Bismarck 61, 118–120, 122–124, 126, 128, 148
Blitz 37–39, 159, 160, 164, 165, 354
Boer Republics 98
Bolshevik Revolution 222
Borodino 106
Breslau 71, 179
British Empire 22, 79, 111, 131, 134, 136, 138–140, 145, 198, 215, 216
Brussels Declaration of 1865 90
Byzantine Empire 65, 73

C

Catherine the Great 102
Charles Martel 70
Charles Portal 20, 185
Charles Snow 11, 20, 28, 173, 188, 346, 354

Advance to Barbarism

China 36, 61, 67, 68, 69, 70, 206, 269, 300
Chivalry 82, 84, 86
Christianity 64, 66, 82, 134
Churchill 11, 16, 17, 20, 23, 25, 37, 38–40, 43, 130, 158, 159, 171, 172, 178, 184–186, 191, 197, 199, 200, 202, 206, 207–212, 214–216, 227, 231, 247–250, 270, 278, 323, 344, 345, 349, 350, 355, 356
Clausewitz 98, 194
Clement Attlee 191, 192
Cold War 44, 312
Compiègne 146, 155, 157, 319
Council of Nicaea 19
Crimean War 77, 92, 109, 334
Cro-Magnon 32, 33
Cromwell 3, 218, 251

D

Dahomey 56, 57
Daily Mail 37, 39, 40, 320, 330, 349, 354, 360
Danzig 150, 151, 253
Dark Ages 7, 64, 70, 74, 77
David Maxwell Fyfe 253, 254, 257, 345
De la Rey 112
Dönitz 10, 205, 242, 246, 347, 350
Douglas Haig 141, 155, 192, 193
Dresden 2, 13–15, 20, 54, 78, 103, 107, 166, 177–186, 189, 341, 345, 347, 349, 354
Duke of Wellington 103, 109, 283

E

Easter Rebellion 138
East Prussia 78, 179
Edward VIII 21, 22
Egypt 46, 47, 61, 226, 251, 256
Eisenhower 118, 179
Emeric de Vattel 100, 102, 112, 121, 143

F

Field Marshal Montgomery 73, 107, 270, 284, 350
Fleet Street 22, 121
Fourteen Points 142, 147, 264
Francis of Assisi 71
Franco-Prussian War 119
Frederick the Great 76, 93, 95, 96, 179

Index

G

Gaul 49
General MacArthur 26, 267, 301—307, 341
General Ramcke 274, 308—317
Genghis Khan 70, 79, 102, 145, 162, 206, 213
Goebbels 19, 252
Great Council of England 223

H

Hague Convention 272
Han Dynasty 67
Harry Dexter White 43, 44
Havelock Ellis 30, 34, 348
Henry Morgenthau 43
Himmler 8, 252, 257, 323
Hiroshima 2, 54, 78, 183, 188, 189, 341
Hitler 10, 13, 21, 24, 61, 67, 129, 140, 142, 143, 147, 149—153, 155, 157, 159, 161, 163, 164, 174, 176, 177, 194, 198, 199, 205, 210, 215, 221, 227, 240, 249, 252, 255, 258, 278, 280, 319, 320, 321, 323, 353
H.M. Stationery Office 5, 16, 20, 170, 173, 175, 344, 345—347, 354
Holy Roman Empire 75
Hundred Years War 74, 77

I

India 66—68, 70, 102, 150, 267, 298, 307, 351
International Military Tribunal 228, 230, 236, 237—239, 241, 244, 250, 255, 256, 264, 271, 307
Iron Curtain 71, 72, 80, 271, 275, 276, 277, 318, 355

J

James Wolfe 97, 98
Jews 198, 255, 257, 267
Joan of Arc 222—224
Jodl 282
Justice Birkett 233, 239, 241, 245, 250, 253
Justice Frankfurter 304
Justice Jackson 24, 253, 304

K

Kaiser Wilhelm 122, 126, 127, 129, 152, 320, 352
Katyn 23, 150, 209, 211, 212, 238, 239, 243, 254, 345
Keitel 78, 96, 121, 156, 157, 168, 250, 282
Kesselring 111, 263, 272, 274—285, 289, 296, 297, 318, 355

Khrushchev 139, 189, 227
King Eannatum 48, 51
Kipling 130, 134, 137, 138, 320, 359
Kitchener 111, 130, 131, 140, 345, 353
Knights Templars 71
Königsberg 78

L

l'affaire Simpson 22
League of Nations 8
Lenin 79, 139, 145, 149, 213, 224, 227, 234, 235
Liddell Hart 16, 50, 81, 99, 111, 163, 164, 319, 333, 345, 347, 349, 350, 360
Lincoln 114, 115, 117, 344
Lindemann 11, 12, 15–17, 19, 25, 28, 54, 105, 130, 170, 173, 176, 177, 184–186, 189, 191, 193, 202, 204, 238, 242, 254, 257, 263, 295, 341, 350, 352, 355
Lindemann Plan 11, 12, 15–17, 19, 25, 28, 54, 105, 170, 173, 176, 177, 184, 185, 189, 191, 193, 204, 238, 242, 254, 257, 263, 295, 341, 350, 352, 355
Lloyd George 138, 139, 185, 350
London Agreement of 1945 130
Lord Hankey 4, 5, 26, 232–234, 248, 249, 265–267, 291, 345, 348, 357, 358
Lord Justice Lawrence 38, 233–241, 254, 279, 310, 358
Lord Methuen 112

M

Macaulay 86, 87, 95, 98
Marshal Blücher 225
Mesopotamia 46, 48, 51
Mexican War 113
Mexico 57, 58
Monte Cassino 275, 278, 314, 358
Morgenthau Plan 43, 44, 179, 335, 342, 355, 356
Mussolini 57, 270, 357

N

Napoleonic Wars 2, 77, 128
Neanderthal 33, 34, 35, 348
Nikitchenko 18, 24, 203, 228, 252, 269, 304
Normans 51

O

Ottoman Turks 73

Index

P

Palatinate 88, 94
Palestine 33, 110
Pétain 156, 345, 353
Polish Corridor 150, 152, 153
Pomerania 60, 131, 183
Potsdam 108, 109, 118, 148

Q

Quebec Conference 43, 44, 356
Queen Victoria 92, 123, 128, 131, 226

R

Raeder 98, 205, 230, 241, 245–251, 256, 265, 282
Rahabinode Pal 243, 244, 305
Red Indians 55, 60, 113, 114, 118, 119
Red Star Brigade 286–289, 292–294
Ribbentrop 252
Richelieu 75
Robert H. Jackson 242, 253, 257
Roman Empire 64, 67, 68, 70, 75
Romans 49, 51
Roosevelt 23, 43, 122, 128, 129, 185, 194, 202, 206–210, 214, 215, 227, 303, 340–342, 346, 348, 355, 356
Rousseau 31

S

Samuel de Champlain 55
Saracens 70, 80, 82
Sargon of Akkad 51
Seven Years War 77, 93, 113
Silesia 60, 71, 76, 131, 179–183
Sobieski 74
Soviet Criminal Code 220
Spandau 241, 248–250
Sparta 53
Speer 191
S.S. 8, 257, 262, 324, 328, 329
Stalin 8, 23, 129, 131, 139, 188, 202, 205–215, 220, 227, 228, 234–236, 238–240, 251, 265, 270, 285, 288, 298, 304, 305, 308, 323, 338, 341, 342, 345, 355, 356
Stone Age 31, 33–36, 348
Streicher 245, 259

Sudetenland 60
Sven Hedin 36

T

Tamerlane 57, 163, 213
Tannenberg 135
Teheran Conference 23, 206, 208–212, 216, 235, 342
Ten Commandments 45
Teutonic Knights 71, 74, 78
The Times 27, 144, 145, 180, 181, 249, 295, 318, 333, 351, 354
Thirty Years War 7, 65, 74, 75, 77, 88, 89, 94, 97, 101, 102, 108
Tiglath Pileser I 53
Treaty of Versailles 18, 24, 147, 149, 151, 152, 198, 253
Trenchard 8, 23, 164, 184, 193, 195, 197, 199, 347
Trevor Roper 255

U

Ulysses S. Grant 114
United Nations 62
United States 1, 4, 9, 27, 44, 61, 79, 90, 112–115, 129, 149, 168, 180, 188, 189, 194, 198, 220, 227, 229, 233, 242, 265, 273, 281, 287, 291, 298, 301, 302, 307, 311, 312, 316, 341, 342, 348, 351, 353, 355
U.S. State Department 18

V

Valerian 84
Vienna 73, 74, 80
Vietnam 15, 26, 298
Vikings 82
von Manstein 157, 267, 271–273, 281, 292, 317–319, 321–323, 325, 327, 328, 330, 331, 335, 338
von Runstedt 157, 318, 319

W

Walter Bagehot 30
Walter Reder 262, 274, 285
War Crimes Commission 224, 231
War of the Austrian Succession 77
White Supremacy 30, 188, 307
Wicked Kaiser Myth 6, 135, 339, 352, 353
William Tecumseh Sherman 114

Y

Yagoda 8, 220, 235
Yalta Conference 17, 23, 24, 128, 157, 205, 222, 224, 229, 240, 269, 270, 304, 317
Yamashita 78, 157, 273, 281, 296–307, 313, 317, 326, 345, 355, 359
Yellow Peril 127

Printed in Germany
by Amazon Distribution
GmbH, Leipzig